Comparing Broadcast Systems

Comparing Broadcast Systems

The Experiences of Six Industrialized Nations

DONALD R. BROWNE

Professor of Speech-Communication
University of Minnesota

 IOWA STATE UNIVERSITY PRESS / AMES

To the memory of Kathy

© 1989 Iowa State University Press, Ames, Iowa 50010

Manufactured in the United States of America

First edition, 1989

Library of Congress Cataloging-in-Publication Data

Browne, Donald R.
   Comparing broadcast systems : the experiences of six industrialized nations / Donald R. Browne.
      p. cm.
   Bibliography: p.
   Includes index.
   ISBN 0-8138-0113-3
   1. Radio broadcasting. 2. Television broadcasting.   I. Title.
HE8689.4.B76 1989
384.54 – dc19   88–34693
                                                                                            CIP

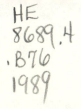

Contents

6. Japan: *From Kabuki to Crime Drama*   303

7. What's Comparable, What Isn't, and What It Means   357

Preface

A S more and more U.S. colleges and universities offer courses on the mass media as social institutions, many of them have elected to include courses in comparative media studies in which the U.S. experience is considered with reference to the experiences of other nations. Such courses allow students to see that there are many different ways to finance, supervise, and program the media; they also may demonstrate that there is very little that is inevitable about media history and structure. Such discoveries, at their best, will lead students to reconsider the functions of the mass media in the United States and elsewhere. That reconsideration should lead to a realization that national characteristics help to determine only a part of any one nation's experience with the media, and that nations increasingly are influenced by one another's experiences, sometimes for good, sometimes for ill.

In this book I limit my coverage to the broadcast media, and chiefly to the experiences of six industrially developed nations, with scattered references to other nations. While many of the developing, or Third World, nations have erected novel structures and have made innovative uses of radio and television, most of them have been influenced heavily by the experiences of the industrially developed nations, several of which were their colonial rulers when broadcasting began.

The six nations that I have selected for case study treatment — France, the Netherlands, the two Germanies, the Soviet Union, and Japan — have been chosen on the basis of three characteristics: their influence on other broadcast systems, their adoption of unusual approaches to the structure and use of the broadcast media, and the relative scarcity of material on them in English. Great Britain, Canada, and Australia present many interesting examples of uses and structures, and I make many references to them in the opening and closing chapters. They have also been influential in other parts of the world. But all three have already been covered in many books, monographs, and articles in English.

It will quickly become evident that I have a strong historical orientation. That is because of my conviction that, to borrow the old adage, those who refuse to learn from history are bound to repeat its mistakes. Also, I feel that a historically based account of a broadcast system throws into sharper relief just how dynamic an institution broadcasting is, and how political, cultural, and economic forces, singly and in combination, affect its development over time. Such an account also underscores one of my long-held beliefs: that there is nothing inevitable about the form that broadcasting takes in any nation. History, especially when we see it at work in a number of broadcast systems, shows us that external as well as internal developments shape systems over time, often for different reasons and with varying degrees of power and duration.

While I cannot claim to have experienced as a citizen the effects of the broadcast media in the six nations covered here, my outsider's acquaintance is quite thorough: two periods in the Soviet Union (1970, 1985), three in Japan (1970, 1976, 1985), and four or more in each of the two Germanies, the Netherlands, and France, from 1956 through 1986. I completed work on the manuscript in April 1988.

I have received much encouragement, assistance, and cooperation from hundreds of individuals but wish to give particular thanks to the following: Harrie Bos, Kees van der Haak, and Bert Steinkamp (the Netherlands); Antoine de Tarlé, Claude-Jean Bértrand, and Rouget L'Estaire (France); Manfred Jahnke, Hans Bausch, and David Rummelsberg (West and East Germany); Joe Adamov, Gene Parta, Henrikas Yushkiavitshus, and Burton Paulu (the Soviet Union); Tadao Nomura, Chosei Kabira, and Hiroko Nishida (Japan); Chris Sterling (bibliography); and Douglas Boyd (general). I am also grateful to the Department of Speech-Communication, the Office of International Programs, the McMillan Fund, and the Graduate School, all of the University of Minnesota, and to the Fulbright-Hays Program and the North Atlantic Treaty Organization for various forms and amounts of financial assistance over the years, making sixteen overseas trips possible.

The organization of the chapters that follow coincides with the organization of my course on comparative broadcast systems at the University of Minnesota: I begin with a consideration of elements that will serve as the structural backbone of a comparative consideration, follow that with the British system (not treated separately in this book), the French system (reasonably clear-cut), the Dutch system (quite complex), the systems of the two Germanies (a good contrast between noncommunist and communist approaches), the Soviet system (communist, and thus related to the East German system), and the Japanese system (a nonwestern approach with a western structure). I conclude with a summation and speculation on what an ideal system of broadcasting might look like. I could create (and have created) other orders of consideration that would be equally logical.

I do hope that this book will start readers really thinking about what broadcasting was, is, and could be. It is easy to lapse into a chronicle approach, but I want to show not just the whats of broadcasting, but the whys and hows. *The Underground Grammarian* of November 1987 contained a fascinating article entitled "The Age of Outformation." After presenting the need for the establishment of an ordering principle, the (anonymous) author decried the mindless devotion to facts and observed that "Cluttered will better describe the mind that is full of bits of news of this and that, a junkyard in which everything lies where it fell." If I have avoided the junkyard syndrome, I shall be content.

Acronyms

ABC (United States) – American Broadcasting Company
ABC (Japan) – Asahi Broadcasting Company
ABC (Australia) – Australian Broadcasting Commission (after 1982, Corporation)
ABCB – Australian Broadcasting Control Board
ABT – Australian Broadcasting Tribunal
ABU – Asian Broadcasting Union
ACT – Action for Children's Television
ACTF – Australian Children's Television Foundation
AFN – American Forces Network
AIM – Accuracy in Media
ARD – Arbeitsgemeinschaft der öffentlich-rechtlichen Rundfunkanstalten der Bundesrepublik Deutschland
A2 – Antenne 2
AVRO – Algemeene Vereeniging Radio Omroep
BBC – British Broadcasting Corporation
BR – Bayerischer Rundfunk
BRT – Belgian Radio and Television
BSB – British Satellite Broadcasting
CATV – Community Antenna Television
CBC – Canadian Broadcasting Corporation
CDU – Christlich-Demokratische Union
CEO – Centre d'Études d'Opinion
CESP – Centre d'Études des Supports de Publicité
CFR – Companie Française de Radio
CLT – Companie Luxembourgeoise de Télédiffusion
CNCL – Commission Nationale de Communications et de Libertés
CNN – Cable News Network
COMECON – Council for Mutual Economic Assistance
CRTC – Canadian Radio-Television and Telecommunications Commission
CSU – Christlich-Soziale Union
DBS – Direct Broadcast Satellite
DLF – Deutschlandfunk
DRADAG – Drahtlose Dienst A.G.
EBU – European Broadcasting Union
EEC – European Economic Community
EO – Evangelische Omroep
FCC – Federal Communications Commission
FFA – Filmforderunganstalt

FIR – France Inter Regions
FRC – Federal Radio Commission
FR3 – France Regions 3
GEZ – Gebuhreneinzugscentrale
GHQ – General Headquarters for the Allied Powers
HA – Haute Autorité
HBO – Home Box Office
HI-OVIS – Highly Interactive Optical-Visual Information System
HR – Hessicher Rundfunk
IBA – Independent Broadcasting Authority
ICN – International Cable Network
IFOP – Institut Français d'Opinion Publique
ITA – Independent Television Authority
ITU – International Telecommunications Union
KRO – Katholieke Radio Omroep
KTA – Kabeltelevisie Amsterdam
KtK – Commission for the Construction of a Technical Communications System
LR – Linksrheinische Rundfunkunion
MATV – Master Antenna Television
NAB (United States) – National Association of Broadcasters
NAB (Japan) – National Association of Commercial Broadcasters
NCCB – National Citizens Committee on Broadcasting
NCRV – Nederlandse Christelijke Radio Vereeniging
NDP – Netherlands Daily Press
NDR – Norddeutscher Rundfunk
NHK – Nippon Hoso Kyokai
NOB – Nederlandse Omroep Bedrijf
NOS – Nederlandse Omroep Stichting
NOZEMA – Nederlandse Omroep Zender Maatschappij
NRU – Netherlands Radio Union
NTS – Netherlands Television Foundation
NTV – Nippon Television
OAS – Organisation de l'Armée Secrète
ORF – Österreiches Rundfund und Fernsehen
ORTF – Office de Radiodiffusion-Télévision Française
OTS – Optical Technology Satellite
PTT – Post, Telegraph and Telephone administrations
RAI – Radio Audizione Italiana
RB – Radio Bremen
RFP – Régie Française de Publicité
RIAS – Rundfunk im Amerikanischen Sektor (Berlin)
RMC – Radio Monte Carlo
RRC – Radio Regulatory Commission
RSFSR – Russian Soviet Federated Socialist Republic
RTF – Radiodiffusion-Télévision Française

RTL – Radiodiffusuion-Télévision Luxembourgeoise
SDR – Suddeutscher Rundfunk
SFB – Sender Freies Berlin
SFP – Société Française de Production
SLII – Interministerial Information Liaison Service
SOFIRAD – Société Financiére de Radiodiffusion
SPD – Socialist Party of Germany
SR (West Germany) – Saarländischer Rundfunk
SR (Sweden) – Sveriges Radio
STER – Stichting Ether Reklame
SWF – Sudwestfunk
TASS – Telegraph Agency of the Soviet Union (*Soyuz*)
TBS – Turner Broadcasting System
TDF – Télédiffusion Française
TF1 – Télévision Française 1
TROS – Televisie Radio Omroep Stichting
UNESCO – United Nations Educational, Scientific and Cultural Organization
UPITN – United Press/Independent Television News
VALA – Viewers and Listeners Association
VARA – Vereeniging van Arbeiders Radio-Amateurs
VAT – Value Added Tax
VCR – Videocassette Recorder
VOA – Voice of America
VOO – Veronica Omroep Organisatie
VPRO – Vrijzinnig Protestantsch Radio Omroep
WDR – Westdeutscher Rundfunk
YLE – Yleisradio O.Y.
ZDF – Zweiten Deutschen Fernsehen

Comparing Broadcast Systems

1

Comparing Broadcast Systems

W E may assume from the start that no two broadcast systems are absolutely alike. All have been influenced to greater or lesser degrees by other broadcast systems, and all have been influenced by geographic, demographic, linguistic, economic, cultural, and political forces in their own and neighboring countries. There is no full, perfect, and sufficient model for an ideal broadcast system. Even if there were, changing circumstances probably soon would render it invalid. Broadcasting is as dynamic as society itself, although it may not change at the same pace. It may lead or be accused of leading or following public taste, or it may be "just about right." But for which publics?

Broadcasting is shaped by more forces than are most other institutions, and because it is so patently a *social* institution, that shaping may be even less predictable than it would be for an institution more removed from such daily and highly visible (and audible) contact with the public. The present chapter and the studies that follow are not offered with the idea that they will lead to models or predictive formulas. Instead, they are intended to aid in understanding broadcasting more clearly by considering the factors that influence it, and then presenting, through the experiences of six nations, the manner in which those factors have affected specific broadcast systems. I draw those experiences together in the final chapter, but in the spirit of offering points that may be worth considering whenever there is discussion of the possible "reform" of broadcasting. That same spirit leads me to conclude with thoughts on the "ideal" broadcast system, if it could in fact exist.

I begin with a consideration of five fundamental factors in broadcasting. Geography, demography/linguistics, economy, culture, and politics cannot fully explain the development of broadcast systems, but they do serve as common denominators and help to establish parameters for further comparisons. Although they are treated as distinct entities, you should be aware, as the chapters on specific nations soon will illustrate, that they interact to varying degrees, and that the nature and extent of interaction varies over time, some elements waxing and waning in influence, others remaining quite stable.

Basic Factors

GEOGRAPHIC   The physical disposition of a nation has a major effect upon the development of its broadcasting system. The ideal nation, from a geographic point of view, would be one that is circular in shape and either without mountains (if the country is small) or with a small core of mountains in the very center (if the country is of medium size). With transmitters placed in the center of either country, it should be possible to reach all parts of the small nation, while the mountainous core of a medium-sized country could serve as a transmitter tower and help extend the signal to its borders.

Few nations have such geographic characteristics. The Netherlands is small, comes reasonably close to being circular, and certainly is flat. Sri Lanka is oval shaped, not much bigger than the Netherlands, and has a central core of mountains; the Republic of China-Taiwan closely resembles it. Some Caribbean and Pacific island nations are similarly shaped, and even smaller than Sri Lanka or Taiwan. France has a mountainous core that is reasonably central, and the other French mountain ranges are at the borders. However, most small and medium-sized nations have hilly or mountainous terrain that runs across the landscape at various angles, leaving some viewers and listeners in hard-to-reach valleys, where it will be extremely expensive to bring signals to them. Often nations will be long and fairly narrow, as well, which means that circular broadcast signals will spill into the sea or into neighboring countries unless elaborate and costly precautions are taken to shape the signal to a noncircular pattern. Nations such as Japan, Great Britain, Norway, Sweden, and Finland, which face both problems, have to invest tremendous amounts of money in reaching all of their viewers and listeners, and even then coverage is not 100 percent for each and every broadcast service.

Size is an important variable here. On the whole, it would seem more feasible for a small to medium-sized nation to consider developing a national broadcasting system rather than a set of regional or local services; there is a certain economy of scale involved in the former. Of course, not all such nations have developed national systems, but many European countries have, and two of the major colonizers among them — France and Great Britain — have left the same legacy with their former colonies in Africa and Asia.

Large nations might be expected to favor the development of regional and/or local services, particularly if, as is usually the case with such nations, there is an uneven distribution of the population to go along with the vast spaces and great topographical variety. Several of the world's largest nations display those characteristics and have at least partially adopted that solution. The United States, Canada, China (before the communists assumed political power in 1949), Australia, and Brazil all seemed fairly indifferent to the development of national systems during the early years of broadcasting in their countries, although by the late 1920s Australia and Canada had begun to give national services more serious attention, and the United States had developed a clear channel system of frequency allocation that would bring at least a few stations to even the most geographically isolated listeners during the nighttime.

Not that most broadcasting systems started life at the national level. Up until the mid-1920s, broadcasting generally was considered more of an amusement than anything else, and there was little interest on the part of governments in seeing it develop to serve the entire nation. The postmaster general's insistence that British companies wishing to broadcast band themselves together to provide a national service was a rarity in its time (1922), although it had a counterpart in the USSR, where Lenin encouraged the development of a national service.

Geographical neighbors also play a role in the development of domestic broadcasting systems. An isolated island can broadcast slightly beyond its national borders without disturbing its neighbors; a nation such as Switzerland, if it were to do the same, would reach West Germany, France, Italy, and Austria. Even at that, Switzerland has the advantage of being fairly circular, whereas Austria, which is long and narrow, could not broadcast from a single central location without major spillover into five or six neighboring nations and minor spillover into two or three more. That can be turned into a virtue of sorts, as Luxembourg proves: Its radio service (in private hands, but with the government as a major controller) spilled over into many surrounding countries and in the early 1930s began to broadcast in the languages of those countries and to carry ads directed at their listeners.

DEMOGRAPHIC/LINGUISTICS   Anyone who has traveled across the United States is well aware of its uneven distribution of population. The extremes are probably most vivid when approaching or leaving Phoenix, Salt Lake City, or Denver, where population density changes dramatically within a range of fifteen to twenty miles. The more uneven the distribution, the more difficult it becomes for most medium-sized to large countries to furnish a broadcast service for everyone *unless* there is a commitment to some form of national service, as the United States, Canada, Australia, and, much later, Brazil, all eventually realized. Such a national service is far more costly per inhabitant than in a small, densely populated nation such as Belgium, the Netherlands, Kuwait, Hong Kong, or Singapore. The existence of a highly urbanized population often has favored the development of local services, as in the 1920s in the United States, Canada, Australia, and Brazil, but also in several European nations, among them France, Germany, Norway, and Spain.

It is not just a matter of how the population is distributed across the country; it is also a matter of just *where* it is distributed. For example, major cities are found all across the United States. In Canada, most of them are within fifty miles of the U.S. border and thus are within easy reach of U.S. broadcasts, which have had major influences on the development of Canadian broadcasting. Most of the major cities in the Netherlands lie on a strip of land that is thirty miles wide and ninety miles deep, which made them easy targets for "pirate" (unauthorized) radio and TV broadcasts in the late 1950s to early 1970s. Most of the heavier concentrations of British listeners are on or close to the sea, which made them easily reachable by marine pirate radio broadcasts in the 1960s and again in the 1980s. In both cases, the pirates affected the development of the domestic broadcast systems. Radio and TV broadcasts in West Berlin carry far into the German Democratic Republic and vice versa: The city is a densely populated "island," or enclave, in the middle of the GDR. West Berlin broadcasts have caused the GDR to place special effort on producing entertainment so as to compete more effectively for listeners and viewers in their own country, and to a lesser extent in West Berlin.

In all of those cases, influences from abroad would have been minimized if it had not been for the existence of a common language. French-language broadcasting in Canada is not all that heavily influenced by U.S. broadcasts, even though Montreal and many other cities and towns in Quebec are near the U.S. border. That is because many Quebec viewers and listeners prefer French-language broadcasts, and few U.S. stations broadcast in French. But the German spoken in the GDR is pretty much the same as that spoken in West Berlin. The pirates off Great Britain have been operated for the most part by Britons, Canadians, Irish, and Americans.

Most of the industrially developed nations have the advantage (for the development of broadcasting, at any rate) of a single, common language. That is true of most of the nations of Europe (Switzerland, Yugoslavia, the USSR, and Czechoslovakia are exceptions), for the Arab world, for Latin America, and for Japan and Australia. The situation is far worse for the nations of sub-Saharan Africa and for South Asia, where there may be a dozen or more languages spoken by sizable segments of the population. If a country is large, it may be possible to regionalize the broadcast service to some extent, as the USSR and India have done: There, most of the major linguistic groups fall into fairly neat geographical divisions. But if a country is small, as is the West African nation of Guinea, and has Guinea's dozen or more tribal languages, all of roughly equal status, regionalization can be pretty expensive.

There is another consideration, as well: national unity versus regional or local identity. Most Americans have little trouble thinking of themselves as, say, Saint Paulites, Minnesotans, and Americans simultaneously. It isn't always that easy for people in other countries, and they may have particular difficulty with the notion that the country as a whole has any meaning for them. The troubled situation in Lebanon probably stems in part from lack of any sense of national identity on the part of most Lebanese, and disturbances in India, Pakistan, Zaire, and many other countries show that national unity often is very fragile. Should a broadcast system particularly encourage national identity as opposed to regional or local identity, or vice versa? Or should it seek some sort of balance, which often is more expensive than favoring either of the first two options? Guinea provides both a national service (in French, which few Guineans speak, but it was the language of Guinea's colonial ruler) and a tribal language service. The latter features such short blocks of airtime per language that a listener has to know exactly which half hour or so of the day her or his language will be on the air or miss out. The compromise is expensive and not particularly efficient, but the number of languages to be covered and the relative poverty of the country mean that there are few alternatives.

Even the industrially developed countries over the past two decades have become more aware of linguistic (often ethnic) minorities. The migration of "guest workers" within Western Europe, where Turks, Greeks, Portuguese, Spaniards, Italians, and North Africans have entered the work forces of West Germany, France, the Netherlands, and so on in considerable numbers, has raised such awareness. There have been indigenous movements, as well: The Welsh in Great Britain made a major case of their demands for a separate Welsh-language television service and finally achieved their goal in the late 1970s. Services in Lapp have spread across northern Scandinavia. Some of the French regional stations formed in the early 1980s began to broadcast in regional languages such as Breton. There is a Basque language TV station in Spain. There is even agitation for broadcasts in Cornish over the British Broadcasting Corporation (BBC) Radio Cornwall, although probably no more than two hundred to three hundred people living there can speak it. Most of those linguistic pressures do not threaten national unity, although Basque and Corsican nationalist movements sometimes have become violent, and the Breton separatist movement seems a bit feistier these days.

ECONOMIC   Throughout most of its existence, broadcasting has been a fairly expensive venture. By that token, it stands to reason that wealthier nations would find it easier to support than would poorer nations. However, poverty does not seem to have deterred any nation from establishing a broadcast service—even the tiniest, poorest Caribbean island nations all have their own radio stations—although it may have kept those services modest. The economy and broadcasting are directly related in other ways. Every major method of financing broadcasting (See "Financing" in this chapter) is dependent to some extent on the short-term and long-term economic health of the country. A recession generally means that there will be a tightening of the national budget, of individual and corporate donations, of advertising, and of the purchase of radio and television receivers. Annual license fees probably will not be lowered, but they will not increase, either, despite increased costs for broadcasting, which must be met by revenues from somewhere if cuts in service are to be avoided.

The overall economic philosophy of a nation also may influence modes of financing the broadcast system. A communist economy ordinarily does not consider advertising to be a particularly desirable way to finance broadcasting, although many communist nations do advertise over radio and television (the money goes to the state). A capitalist economy sees advertising as normal business practice, and, where broadcast advertising is concerned, as a further stimulus to the economy, since ads induce people to spend more on goods and services. A socialist economy may take a middle road, although it seems far more likely to generate money through an annual license fee assessed against households with radio and TV sets than do the communist or capitalist economies. It also is somewhat more tolerant of advertising than the former, but less likely to leave it uncontrolled than the latter.

The ways in which the population earns its money also affect broadcasting, in that certain sectors of the economy need, or are thought to need, the up-to-the-minute information that broadcasting can provide. Any economic activity directly affected by the weather — fishing, farming, recreational sports — will need timely weather forecasts. Livestock and grain farmers and dealers will want livestock and grain market reports. A free enterprise economy often demands regular stock market reports. Local or regional broadcast services may be more efficient in providing such specialized information than are national services — of what interest are hog market reports to most Londoners or New Yorkers? — but national services usually feel obligated to carry them if there is no alternative broadcast service to do so.

There is also the nebulous matter of how a broadcast service may promote or discourage various economic philosophies by its broadcasts. Books written by communists about capitalist broadcast systems often conclude that those systems support the capitalist economic philosophy by various means: by giving little if any attention to the worker's point of view,[1] by giving prominence to statements made by the country's economic leaders in management and government, and even by carrying ads, which themselves seem to indicate that the economy makes plenty of goods and services available to everyone. Critics of communist broadcast systems have noted their frequent use of individuals as economic models: farmers, factory workers, and so on, who overfulfill work quotas, introduce more labor-efficient methods, overcome skepticism among fellow workers, and encourage group participation.

Finally, since most broadcast equipment is manufactured in the industrially developed nations, the developing, or Third World, nations must dig into their limited, precious reserves of "hard" (internationally convertible) currency to pay for its acquisition and maintenance. That condition can limit the expansion of broadcasting; in extreme circumstances, it can even bring broadcasting to a halt until money can be found for imported replacement parts and/or imported technicians to install them. The same applies to the purchase of energy for power transmitters: Many developing nations have little or no domestic energy-generating capacity and must import oil for the purpose — again, usually having to pay for it in hard currency.

CULTURAL   Cultural subdivisions are a part of every nation. Whether
        based on language, economic class, religious or political affiliation, education, or a host of other elements, and whether existing singly or in

various combinations, they are what give nations their "national character." They can serve as elements of national unity or division. Their
strength may come from historical tradition, economic or political power,
a sudden catastrophic event (e.g., assassination of a prominent figure), or
sheer force of numbers. The mass media may help bring them to the
attention of the general public, but they themselves may bring pressure on
the media to devote more attention to their causes.

Most broadcast systems have at least some provision for mirroring
the interests of at least a few cultural groups. In some cases, there are
designated language services; special programs or even entire stations to
serve ethnic minorities; popular music stations; "high culture" stations;
stations promoting educational development; and stations operated by
political parties, the military, religious organizations, or labor unions.
However, with the exception of religious stations, most of the last-named
group of stations carry broadcasts for more than just their own members.

Some of those groups will have sufficient economic strength that
stations in advertiser-supported broadcast systems can make a profit while
serving them, as many Spanish-language, black-oriented, and (more
rarely) classical-music stations do in the United States. More often, however, it will be necessary for the nation's legislative body, the broadcast
system itself, or some governmental agency charged with the administration or regulation of broadcasting to encourage or require some forms of
service to cultural groups. That could be done by reserving broadcast time
for them on national, regional, and/or local services, by granting them the
use of entire stations (e.g., Channel Four's Welsh-language service in
Great Britain), by making it possible for them to acquire their own stations through the help of government grants and low-interest loans, or by
providing them with access to transmitter facilities at low cost, but having
them be responsible for financing their own program and administrative
activities (e.g., the *närradio,* or neighborhood radio, services of Norway,
Sweden, and Denmark).[2]

The granting of special broadcast rights to various cultural groups
can open Pandora's box in some cases. The creation of a popular-music
radio station by the Dutch broadcasting system in the late 1960s — itself an
attempt to win back listeners from broadcast pirates beaming "nonstop
pop" to Dutch audiences — resulted in the claim by high culture advocates
that their interests were being neglected and led to the creation of a high
culture radio service in the mid-1970s. United States educators staked their
claim to reserved frequencies for FM broadcasting before World War II
and for television just after the war; their argument was that commercial
broadcasters never would find it in their own interests to allow the educa-

tors much airtime over commercial stations. But the educators eventually ended up competing with other nonprofit groups for the use of those reserved frequencies, since those other groups could make the same argument for themselves.

The question of where the cultural subdivision of broadcasting should start or stop is a very difficult one to answer. It is more difficult for broadcast systems in countries where there is but one national service, little or no time or facilities available for regional or local broadcasting, and a society resembling a cultural crazy quilt tacked together by outsiders — in other words, the sort of situation that exists in so much of sub-Saharan Africa and south Asia. And even if time and facilities are available, is it conducive to national unity to mirror the many, diverse, and often conflicting interests of the various groups?

Furthermore, cultural groups themselves seldom are monolithic entities. Most contain factions, and often the factions do not see eye to eye. If the administrators of the broadcast system are in charge of deciding who gets to use what amounts of airtime and when, which criteria will they employ in making those decisions? If the groups have to do it themselves, will this encourage a sort of gang warfare, as appears to have happened at times within the major political parties of West Germany, where radical groups within the parties have fought for airtime to present their particular points of view? And if some governmental authority, whether legislature or regulatory agency, has to make such decisions, will party politics ultimately determine who gets what?

No broadcast system anywhere in the world yet has found a formula for satisfying all of the people all of the time. Some have left it to economics — if the group has the money, it can develop a broadcast service. Some have imposed a few overall criteria for satisfying the largest or most vocal or most politically powerful groups and have left the rest up to fate or circumstance. (The development of the Channel Four Welsh Service is an interesting illustration of how circumstances can change.)[3] A few, as in the Netherlands, have established systems where it is reasonably easy for groups to gain access to the airwaves so long as all but the major groups don't ask for it very often. Cable television, with its multiple-channel capacity, has been hailed by some as the answer to the problem of limited airtime for cultural groups. It may be a technical answer, but who will pay for the productions, and if there are, as Mao Tse-Tung put it, "a hundred flowers blooming, a hundred schools of thought contending," how many of them will listeners and viewers make the effort to seek out? And will societal cohesion increase or diminish?

POLITICAL   Just as economic philosophies can influence the nature of
broadcast systems, so can political philosophies make their mark. All
broadcasting systems fall under governmental jurisdiction in at least one
sense: Any authorized use of the frequency spectrum for broadcasting
must be licensed by the government as a condition of belonging to the
International Telecommunications Union (ITU), a United Nations body
that attempts to keep users of the spectrum from interfering with one
another. All sovereign nations of the world belong to the ITU, although
not all cooperate fully with it.[4]

Membership in ITU requires only that governments license use of the
spectrum on a technical basis: broadcast frequency, time of day, power,
and direction of signal. It does not involve control of program content.
However, very few governments have refrained from controlling program
content to some degree, and since governments generally are made up of
political parties (there are few absolute monarchies left in the world!),
politics and broadcasting interact.

The political spectrum runs as broad a gamut as does the frequency
spectrum but does not enjoy anywhere near as clear a set of definitions.
The categories I use are inspired by the Siebert et al. four theories of the
press but depart from them in several respects.[5] Those theories are useful,
however, because they posit numerous links between political philosophies
and media systems.

Libertarian (and Possibly Laissez-faire)   The libertarian government is often associated with capitalist nations, and more particularly with
"conservative" governments (here meaning those more favorable toward
private enterprise and less favorable toward government regulation of its
practices). This philosophy holds that interests (whether economic, philosophical, or whatever) should be allowed to "fight it out" among themselves, and the public will decide which ones it favors. Laissez-faire governments generally are regarded as being even more permissive in these
respects than are libertarian governments, especially in promoting economic competition.

It follows, then, that libertarian governments should be willing to
license as many users of broadcast frequency spectrum space as the spectrum will hold and to impose very few criteria for deciding who shall
receive frequencies. Few governments are in fact that open-handed or
nonjudgmental in practice, but many are pretty liberal, as witness the
thirty-five mediumwave (AM) stations licensed in Quito, Ecuador, or the
eighteen FM stations in Manila, the Philippines. If stations in such countries feel that they must alter their program mix in order to remain competitive, it is generally easy for them to do so. The attempt in the United

States during the 1970s to give audiences some say in whether changes in broadcast formats were in *their* best interests seems to have been the exception that proves the rule, and that movement itself was short-lived.[6]

Libertarian governments also are apt to take a dim view of governmental financial support for broadcasting, or indeed of any form of financial support other than advertising. The governments of Latin America, most of which historically have been laissez-faire, have done little to promote the development of public broadcasting; even the educational services generally are financed by the Roman Catholic Church or some other institution that raises its own funds. United States government support for public broadcasting was almost nonexistent until passage of the Public Broadcasting Act of 1967, and the Reagan administration, notably more laissez-faire than its immediate predecessors, sought to cut back sharply on the annual congressional appropriation for public broadcasting.

Libertarian or laissez-faire governments are not indifferent to the nature of broadcast programming, however. Most of them issue few if any formal rules or even guidelines on program content, but they feel perfectly free to step in when the occasion seems, in their view, to demand it. Many of the civilian and military governments of Latin America even have suspended or removed stations from the airwaves for being "overcritical" of the government. However, the many stations that stick to entertainment and to news from officially approved sources have little to fear from such governments.

Social Responsibility Mixed capitalist-socialist political/economic systems often are thought of as promoters of "socially responsible" broadcasting, regulating not only physical access to the airwaves but also the nature of programming. Social responsibility embodies the concept that, while the media may possess and exercise some degree of responsibility toward society on their own, nevertheless they need occasional or even more than occasional reminders of that responsibility, and possibly a set of requirements to encourage them to carry it out. Regulation by broadcast law, administered by a designated unit of government, is not a common practice in social responsibility systems, however. Instead, the broadcast organizations themselves are expected to evolve their own written and/or unwritten codes of practice and to be under the scrutiny, if not the supervision, of a public body. This may be a board of governors and/or a broadcasting council, with members appointed by the government and/or public organizations (churches, labor unions, etc.) and/or the broadcasters themselves. The board or council may or may not report to the public and the government. Whether it does or not, the national legislative body probably will discuss the performance of broadcasting each year when budgets are approved: Even though broadcasting under a social-responsibility government usually is financed in large part by annual license fees assessed on viewing and listening households, the legislative body generally must approve its annual budget.

A social-responsibility government generally restricts the licensing of broadcasting to one or two organizations. If there is more than one, usually it is because a "conservative" (pro–private industry) government has permitted or encouraged the development of a second, commercially supported organization, as has occurred in Japan and in Great Britain. Monopolistic services generally are thought to better serve the needs of a wide spectrum of society: If there is only one service available, and if all listeners and viewers pay for it, that service *should* attempt to cater to as many needs and tastes as possible. Also, a monopoly makes it easy to pinpoint responsibility.

Advertising does occur over most social-responsibility broadcast systems, but usually in restricted amounts, and often under the supervision of an autonomous or semiautonomous organization (e.g., the Netherlands' Stichting Ether Reklame [STER]), so as to emphasize the separation between advertising and program content. Social-responsibility governments also may approve special financial appropriations for specific needs, for example, the introduction of color television, if those needs far exceed the existing budgetary resources of the broadcasters. Such appropriations, however, are not a regular practice of these kinds of governments.

Most social-responsibility governments reserve for themselves the right to have access to the airwaves, and broadcast laws, when they exist, usually contain provisions for this. However, the broadcasters generally are free to make announcements stating that the government has requested airtime, which might reassure the listener or viewer that the broadcaster is not playing political favorites by allowing such access.

Communist While social-responsibility governments have some general notion of the roles that broadcasting can and should play in serving society, specific elements of that role generally go undefined. Communist governments, however, have a more specific notion of that role and of the ways in which broadcasting can and should fulfill it. To some degree, then, the communist and social-responsibility philosophies have common roots.

According to the communist philosophy, broadcasting should promote certain behaviors and discourage others. Encouraged behaviors would include working for the common good, being ready to defend and extend the gains made under communism, having an appreciation of cultures (especially domestic) other than one's own, participating to varying degrees in the political process, and supporting the cause of the working classes in other countries. Types of behavior commonly discouraged would include criminal behavior, participation in organized religious activities, self-centeredness, and any tendencies to place trust in the motives of noncommunist (but especially capitalist) governments. While programming does not deal exclusively with these types of behaviors, they *are* frequent themes and subthemes of everything from newscast items to quiz shows.

Communist governments usually prefer to finance broadcasting from annual government appropriation, although at one time annual license fees were quite common. Apparently they prefer to spread the cost of broadcasting to all who contribute to the national budget, whether those people can receive the broadcasts or not. Such a policy may help encourage people to buy receivers, as they are already paying for the service, and it certainly gets across the point that broadcasting is for all the people, in theory if not in practice. Such governments also permit advertising in limited amounts, not so much as a source of revenue (the money goes to the national budget and not to the broadcasters), but as a way of promoting new products and encouraging the sale of those that are a glut on the market.

Broadcast laws in communist countries usually are not very specific on program content and are not really necessary anyway, as there is only one broadcasting organization and decision-making positions are occupied by communist party members who are well aware of what the party expects from the broadcast system. The public may be encouraged to write to or visit the broadcast organization in order to voice complaints, but the legislative bodies (e.g., the Supreme Soviet) as a rule do not debate broadcast policy or review broadcast performance, and boards of governors and broadcasting councils drawn from the pubic are rare.

Authoritarian   Whereas the three previous philosophies generally involve elected governments, authoritarian governments usually exist where there has been a seizure or consolidation of power, often in the form of a military coup, but sometimes in the form of an elected government that subsequently has outlawed other political parties, perhaps suspended parts or all of the constitution, and occasionally has abolished elections altogether. The National Socialist (Nazi) government, which ruled Germany from 1933 to 1945, is a classic example of this form of government.

Authoritarian governments generally are very interested in broadcasting. While they don't always operate broadcasting systems themselves, they let it be known that stations are expected to refrain from criticism of the government, and that the government will use stations to broadcast whenever and whatever it deems necessary. Broadcasters may or may not be expected to provide "socially responsible" programming, although it isn't unusual for an authoritarian government to ban certain types of entertainment that it considers "decadent influences," as the Nazis did when they banned the broadcasting of jazz in 1935.

The financing of broadcasting probably will continue in the same form under an authoritarian government as under the previous government, with one exception: Annual license fees are likely to be abolished or reduced due to a desire on the part of most authoritarian governments to increase listening and viewing and even to curry favor with society (although it is doubtful that the existence of a license fee, at least in the last few decades, has kept many people from purchasing radio or TV sets). The Nazis, for example, exempted numerous groups, including World War I veterans and old-age pensioners, from paying license fees. Likewise, the administrative structures of broadcast organizations probably will not change, although the Nazis eventually did incorporate all broadcast activities into the governmental structure.

If there is any one thing that characterizes broadcasting under an authoritarian government, it is the randomness, the unpredictability of governmental involvement. This seems particularly true when the previous government's philosophy had been laissez-faire and many competing stations were in operation. In Chile, which went from a laissez-faire, to a mild social-responsibility, to a mild communist, to an authoritarian government over the period 1965–73, most of the stations underwent few changes in programming policies, perhaps because the two middle governments were in power for too brief a period to effect widespread changes. But the authoritarian regime there has been in power for about fifteen years—ample time for changes—and yet there have been very few, probably because the programming broadcast by the vast majority of stations (mostly light entertainment) represents no particular threat or challenge and might even serve to keep the population pacified. Instead, governmental involvement has taken the form of occasional disciplinary measures against individual stations, often for vaguely defined offenses and seemingly as a way of reminding broadcasters that the government is ready to use its power when and where it chooses.[7]

I devote the rest of this chapter to discussion of several questions more specific to broadcast systems than those just covered: Where does the money come from? How is broadcasting administered and influenced both internally and externally? What does it produce? Can its usage be planned more methodically?

Financing

The old adage "whoever pays the piper calls the tunes" may or may not apply to broadcasting. It seems to depend a great deal upon whether there is more than one source of financial support and more than one broadcasting organization in a country. If there is only one of each, financial support can usually be used to control broadcasting with relative ease. Similarly, if the government is willing to be dictatorial enough, it really does not matter where the money comes from or how many broadcasting organizations receive it.

No system of financing can insure freedom from outside interference, either, nor can any guarantee a steady supply of all the money a broadcaster might wish or need. There are advantages and disadvantages to each system, and some appear to complement each other better than do others. Briefly, the following are the major and minor modes of financing broadcasting.

ADVERTISING   Advertising is used as the chief means of financing broadcasting in North, Central, and South America and the Caribbean and in the "nonpublic systems" of Great Britain, Japan, and Australia. It has been a minor but increasingly important source of support in most of Western Europe and in parts of Africa and Asia since the early 1920s. Broadcast advertising is one of the most controversial forms of financial support; many critics have linked it with catering to mass tastes, ignoring minority audiences, and promoting a capitalist outlook on life by emphasizing competition, individualism, and material gain.

It also is one of the more undependable forms of support, in that economic slumps may reduce ad revenues considerably. (This isn't inevitable, however; broadcast advertising actually increased markedly during the U.S. depression of the early 1930s). Also, in a competitive market — and heavy reliance on advertising generally is associated with systems in which a large number of stations are licensed to broadcast — competition itself will cause unpredictable rises and falls in revenues for individual stations. In attempting to recover from such losses, stations may lower the quality of their services in order to cut costs and may drop programs that attract small audiences, no matter how devoted those audiences may be.

Nations differ in their approaches to regulating the amount and nature of advertising. Laissez-faire governments tend to leave regulation to "marketplace forces," and if a station can contract and carry, say, thirty or forty minutes of ads per hour, as some Latin American stations do on occasion, that is perfectly all right. Nor does it seem to make much difference what the ads promote, whether smoking, astrology, patent medicines, or dating services, so long as the product is not illegal. Other governments may encourage broadcasters to regulate themselves in these respects, as the United States, Canada, Japan, and Australia do with regard to their private broadcasting sectors; however, those governments also may establish guidelines and even a few prohibitions (e.g., no tobacco-product ads, no political advertising) and may charge government commissions or agencies with the responsibility of administering them.

Nations with only one or two broadcasting organizations generally do not expect or even desire advertising to furnish the major share of financial support. In such cases, the organizations generally establish their own bodies for the regulation of advertising, for example, the Advertising Control Division of Great Britain's Independent Broadcasting Authority, although separate bodies may be created, too, as with the Netherlands' STER. In both cases, the government, usually through the legislative body or the minister responsible for broadcasting, generally establishes overall limits on amounts of advertising (usually ten to thirty minutes a day for TV, sometimes slightly more for radio, and very often during designated time periods only, with no interruption of programs).

Very few systems allowing advertising will permit sponsorship—the assumption of the costs of making a program and of its total airtime in return for named identification with the program, for example, the *Chevrolet Hour.* Full sponsorship was linked with deceptive practices in U.S. quiz show scandals of the late 1950s,[8] and most sponsorship in the United States now involves several different sponsors per show, with the various sponsors exercising some influence and control over one another. But other countries seem either wary of the practice because of the influence sponsors might have over program policies or unconvinced that it is worth the extra investment; only in Canada, Japan, Australia, and Latin America does sponsorship appear to any extent, while it is beginning to appear in Great Britain as of the late 1980s.

There is also the question of whether advertising is more or less of a financial burden for listeners and viewers than are other means of support. As advertising costs are passed along to the consumer in the price of the product or service, obviously the audience *does* pay. But presumably not all of the audience pays equally: People's consumption habits differ, and big-ticket items such as real estate and higher education rarely are advertised over radio and TV. Certainly the audience is less aware of paying for broadcasting in this way than it is with annual license fees or individual contributions.

Finally, advertiser support does have the possible advantage of making the broadcaster very much aware of the size and composition of the audience, since both elements have great bearing on the rates to be charged for advertising time. That means that an ad-supported service is not likely to become the exclusive province of the intelligentsia or of a political or religious group, but instead will seek to reach the mass public at least some of the time. Also, many broadcasters, including those in systems where ad support is minimal or nonexistent, believe that a commercial system will operate more efficiently and more cost-effectively than will systems supported principally by license fees or by the government. However, it is quite possible that cost efficiency comes as much from widespread competition as it does from reliance on ads; if there is a system in which a large number of stations compete for license fee money or government support, that might induce more efficiency!

ANNUAL LICENSE FEES   Based on a concept of broadcasting as a "luxury" service to society, the annual license fee really is a user fee. Some countries assessed it from the earliest days of broadcasting, while others introduced it later in the 1920s or during the 1930s. It made particularly good sense when radio, and later television, did not reach that many people (lack of sets, inadequacy of transmissions). Those who could hear and see paid; those who couldn't, didn't.

As ownership of radio and TV sets and extent of signal coverage approaches 100 percent of the population, which it does in the United States, Canada, Japan, Australia, and much of Western Europe, a user fee no longer makes quite so much sense in some respects, especially in efficiency of collection: Roughly 5–10 percent of the proceeds from license fees go to cover the costs of collection, which usually is done by the national postal telephone and telegraph service (PTT). Furthermore, license fee money rarely goes directly to the broadcast organization; it first passes through the hands of the national legislative body, which sometimes sets aside a portion of it to cover transmission costs (some countries have transmitter systems operated by PTTs rather than by broadcasters) and possibly a portion to help reduce governmental deficits having nothing to do with broadcasting. In view of this, it would seem to make more sense to abolish the license fee and simply give the broadcast organization an annual governmental appropriation, which many countries do.

Defenders of the license fee have answers to that argument. For one thing, they claim, the fee is at least a rough indication of the amount of money that should be going into broadcasting and gives broadcasters some notion of what their budgets will be for the next fiscal year. Governments may be far more capricious with appropriations, especially during economic downturns, and besides, license fees rarely are reduced. For another, the license fee can act as a buffer between government and broadcaster: If the government does not appropriate the money as part of the national budget, it may have less say in how the money is spent (which doesn't prevent a determined government, as some in France have been, from telling broadcasters exactly what it expects, notwithstanding a license fee). For a third, the public may feel a greater sense of involvement with broadcasting, and vice versa, if both realize that the public is making specific payment for the service. License-fee-based broadcasting systems do seem more likely to establish and work through councils and committees drawn from among the audience and to conduct more frequent and thorough qualitative studies of audience reactions to program content, than do systems based on other forms of support. They also offer a wider variety of programming for more subgroups of the population than do ad-supported broadcast systems.

But the license fee does not allow broadcasters much control over increasing their revenues. Unlike ad-supported systems, they cannot use sheer audience size per program or per week to justify higher rates. The size of license fees is proposed by broadcast organizations but almost always established by legislative bodies. Raising license fees, so most legislators reason, is almost certain to raise citizen ire, as there is such a visible increase in what citizens have to spend. Broadcast organizations attempt to justify increases in several ways — through their own broadcasts, in press interviews, in public meetings held by them, and by legislative testimony — but they rarely receive the full increase they request. Furthermore, any increase they do receive is likely to have to remain at that level for a three- to five-year period, regardless of the rate of inflation during that time.

There also are four problems of fairness associated with the license fee. First, not every viewer or listener pays it: Most license-fee-based systems have 5–15 percent noncompliance rates, although Japan claims something closer to 3 percent. (Perhaps the Japanese are more law-abiding, or perhaps they are readier to pay because the Japan Broadcasting Corporation (the NHK) collects the fees itself and at the same time asks people to comment on the quality of the broadcast service.) It is very expensive to search out noncomplying households, although electronic set-detection equipment — virtually useless for tall apartment buildings — and payment of "fink fees" to people who disclose noncomplying neighbors sometimes have been used to ferret out cheaters.

Second, some license-fee-supported organizations operate alongside ad-supported organizations. Great Britain, Japan, and Italy all are set up this way. Can a listener or viewer claim to listen to or watch only the ad-supported service, thus exempting themselves from paying the license fee? A few people have advanced such claims in British courts, and the courts have dismissed them on the grounds that the license-fee-supported service is available to anyone in the household, and no member of that household can truly guarantee that no other member ever watches or listens to it. Furthermore, authorities can never really be certain that no one views or listens to it short of invading the privacy of the home.

Third, there are some areas in some countries so physically remote or isolated that broadcast service for them is poor to nonexistent, yet because many people living there do possess sets (they may be able to receive signals from neighboring countries), they are required to pay license fees. Some people count on their physical remoteness to keep fee collectors away; others criticize what they see as a form of taxation without representation. In turn, however, license-fee-supported systems generally have gone to great expense to insure that all households have access to at least some of their broadcast services, and broadcast signal coverage in such systems is likely to be more complete than it is with other systems.

And fourth, there is the problem of equitability of services. As license fees are assessed and collected on a national basis, it can be extremely difficult to justify establishment of geographically specialized services, unless those services are for linguistic or ethnic minorities. One reason for the relative lack of development of local radio and TV services for major urban centers in Europe until fairly recently appears to have been the political problem of justifying the creation of an additional service for a portion of the national population — and a portion that often is viewed by small-town and rural dwellers as already privileged enough.

ANNUAL GOVERNMENT APPROPRIATIONS   Treating broadcasting as a public service to be made available to the general public, the annual appropriation spreads the cost of furnishing the service over all members of society who contribute to the nation's annual budget, whether or not they choose to view or listen, or are even capable of viewing or listening. The annual appropriation may be the only practicable way to develop a broadcast service in a country where there are too few viewers or listeners to permit raising much money through advertising or through annual license fees, and many developing nations have relied upon this means of financing their new or rapidly expanding services.

However, very few nations with annual government appropriations ever have dropped that system of financing in favor of an alternative system once the audience has grown to a respectable size. The difficulty and expense of collecting license fees and the lack of strongly consumer-based economies that advertising requires may help to explain this seeming devotion to annual appropriations, but part of their attractiveness may lie in the degree of control that the government itself can exercise through them. Both the Canadian Broadcasting Corporation (CBC) and the Australian Broadcasting Corporation (ABC) at one time were supported by license fees, but that support was replaced by annual appropriations. Both countries are vast and unevenly populated, which meant that license-fee collection was particularly expensive, as was the large transmission system needed to carry signals (especially television signals) to audiences throughout the land. However, politicians from the major political parties also seemed to favor the switch because it would remove the politically unpopular necessity of raising license fees, and because annual appropriations would make it easier to influence broadcast policies at the CBC and the ABC.[9]

Certainly the annual appropriation avoids the cost of license-fee collection, and it also may allow the government to expand and improve broadcast facilities more quickly and thoroughly than would license fees or ad revenues. One also might expect that there would be a greater likelihood of an annual public (legislative and/or administrative) review of broadcast performance when the government must decide how much to spend on it. However, this is not true of the East European or developing nation systems, where annual appropriations are most common. (It *is* the practice in Canada and Australia, however.) If the political system of the country is multiparty, the broadcast organizations may be able to get the major parties to outbid one another in appropriating money for a strong public broadcast service, while at the same time using interparty rivalry to help insure that no one party becomes too influential where program policy is concerned.

But most East European and developing nations do not have strong multiparty systems, and most are careful to place the administration of broadcasting in the hands of people who belong to or are sympathetic toward the ruling political party. Top-level broadcast administrators generally are replaced when a new party gains power in a system based upon annual appropriations, while license-fee-based systems usually are far more stable in that respect. (France is a notable exception to the latter, and Canada and Australia to the former.) In fact, it is quite common for political leaders in appropriations-based systems to make "recommendations" (often tantamount to edicts) on broadcast policy through the ruling political party rather than through a government ministry in charge of broadcasting. There is every expectation that broadcasters will attempt to comply with those "recommendations," since the ruling political party usually will have great influence over the size of the appropriation, whatever the other parties (if there are any) may say or think.

As I mentioned earlier, annual government appropriations are subject to fluctuations in the national economy. If broadcasting is not a terribly important part of national life, the government may feel little compunction in cutting back on the appropriation. Even if it *is* important, the government may urge broadcasters to increase other sources of revenue, especially sales of programs abroad and advertising (if there is any). Such urging takes place almost every year when the Canadian Parliament discusses next year's appropriation for the CBC. And with such budgetary unpredictability, it becomes very difficult to engage in long-term planning. All in all, broadcasters who work in such systems treat the annual appropriation as a necessary evil, and some feel that it reduces creativity and investigative reporting while it increases inefficiency: If political influence is used to create and fill positions, those filling them often don't feel disposed to overwork themselves or to go out on any creative or investigative limbs.

A final note: Most annual appropriations are made at the national level, but there are a few instances of state (or province or district) and local government appropriations, especially in Canada and the United States. School districts in some parts of the United States also appropriate money for educational broadcasting. There even have been a few instances of city government financed and administered broadcasting stations in the United States.

INSTITUTIONAL SUPPORT   Stemming from the democratic notion that if you want something done you should do it and pay for it yourself, institutional support is a mode of financing that had its heyday early in broadcast history but that still appears in limited ways in certain countries, and in a major (but modified) form in the Netherlands. Most institutional support for broadcasting has come from educational and religious organizations, although there have been cases of stations and services supported by department stores, newspapers, labor unions, political parties, and the military. (A military coup in a country does not necessarily mean that the military will run the broadcast services, and if it does, it won't run the service for the particular benefit of military audiences.)

Institutionally supported stations usually are found in countries with laissez-faire or libertarian governments, as in North, Central, and South America, where a multitude of stations broadcast in almost every country of any size. They are few in number in Canada (which had problems with a religious station in the 1920s, but which has permitted educational stations) and in Australia (which has a few university student-run stations) and generally absent in license-fee and annual appropriations systems elsewhere. The Swedish, Norwegian, and Danish *närradio* services require that organizations using airtime pay their own programming costs, but a government-appointed board decides who will have access to airtime, and the airtime itself is quite limited for each group, since there are only a few public-authority-operated transmitters for *närradio* to use.

While institutionally supported stations do spare the government and the public a certain amount of expense, they also constitute a form of broadcasting that depends upon the organization's ability to continue to afford the cost. This has two implications: First, only the wealthier organizations can afford such an expensive activity and probably won't be tolerant enough to share their airtime with those less able to pay; and second, the organizations themselves may constitute an uncertain funding base, so that organizationally supported stations might decline in quality or even go off the air altogether in times of economic stress, as happened with many U.S. educational broadcasters during the depression of the early 1930s.

One other form of institutional support was used quite widely in the 1920s. Manufacturers and dealers in radio sets and parts, and sometimes phonograph record companies, developed stations to stimulate public purchase of their goods. The United States, Canada, Australia, Great Britain, France, Germany, the Netherlands, and several other countries saw broadcasting develop largely or in part because the manufacturers and dealers set up stations. But most of them did not see this line of work as an integral part of their business, and once the public had become numerous and steady consumers of radio, they were ready enough to get out of the programming business, so long as someone else would be sure to provide it.

Educational and religious organizations have been interested in operating their own stations because they wish to reach audiences whom they consider ill served, underserved, or not at all served by other stations. (There are exceptions: Some U.S. educational institutions operate commercial stations as revenue-generating enterprises.) Most other organizations operate stations either to produce revenue for the organization or as a public relations tool. Many U.S. newspapers and department stores that operated their own stations in the 1920s did so to remind people of their existence and to engender goodwill, which might translate into purchase of the newspaper or patronage of the department store; they did not advertise their own goods and services in any specific way. As broadcast advertising became more common, such stations either began to accept advertising from a wide assortment of customers or went out of existence as the stores and newspapers found it cheaper to place ads about themselves on other stations rather than bear the costs of operating their own. Newspapers continue to be major investors in or even operators of stations in Japan, Australia, Canada, and Great Britain, and many of them are attempting to gain a foothold in the licensing of cable and pay-cable operations, as well as direct broadcast satellite (DBS) services, throughout Western Europe.

Finally, there are limited numbers of "community-operated" stations (mostly radio) in the United States, Australia, France, Canada, and a few other nations. These really are "community of cultural or social interest" stations. Funding usually comes from corporate or individual contributions, and costs are kept low through the use of volunteer or low-wage labor: Everyone from janitor to station manager works for little or no money. Programming usually is a mix of locally produced material (even the music often is locally produced) designed to cater to a wide range of needs and tastes within the community. Some of the Scandinavian *närradio* services are of the same nature.

CORPORATE AND INDIVIDUAL CONTRIBUTIONS Treating broadcasting as a sort of charitable institution (in a few countries, such as the United States, contributions to certain types of public stations qualify as tax deductions), contribution-based broadcasting almost never occurs in isolation. Few stations would care to risk their existences on the possibility of receiving such funds, partly because they fluctuate so much due to changing tax laws and the state of the economy. There were stations that attempted to survive largely through listener contributions in the Netherlands and the United States during the early 1920s, but they didn't last.

In more recent times, corporate and individual contributions have become an important and even major source of income for public radio and television in the United States, as anyone who has had to sit through another "pledge week" (semiannual, or more frequent, broadcast campaign for contributions) can testify. Some U.S. stations even hold auctions of donated goods in order to raise money. Corporate givers receive a certain amount of mention (corporate name, brief description of nature of goods and services) on the air in return for their contributions. Very few other countries encourage or even permit corporate contributions, and very few allow solicitation of individual contributions, although the broadcast organizations in the Netherlands recruit paying members, and the radio clubs in Portugal and Spain and in their one-time colonies have or have had paying supporters.

Aside from the uncertainty of contributions, there is another problem. Corporate donors are very likely to want to support stations and programs that complement their own cultural and sometimes political perspectives. United States corporate donors such as Mobil Oil often have been criticized for supporting little besides high culture programs that would appeal to an affluent white viewership and even for pressuring public broadcasting to carry certain programs that the broadcasters themselves might not have chosen (sports, certain British-produced TV drama).[10]

SALES OF GOODS AND SERVICES   Taking the approach that broadcasting can generate some of its own revenue, this form of support appears in many systems but is a major contributor in none. Its most common manifestation is the sale of programs, domestically and abroad. The United States, Great Britain, Mexico, Brazil, Japan, West Germany, and until the Arab Boycott of 1979, Egypt, all are major program exporters. Most U.S. programs are sold overseas by businesses organized for the purpose, and the stations and networks earn very little this way, but broadcast systems in the other countries generally sell their own programs and may earn as much as 5 percent of their annual budgets through such sales. Many other countries have tried to break into the overseas sales market, and Canada and Australia have had some success in selling their material to U.S. cable TV, but as in so much else, it takes money to make money, and few broadcasters are willing to invest the substantial sums needed for successful overseas sales efforts. Some broadcasters, especially in Canada, Great Britain, and the United States, see some commercial possibilities in selling original (made by the system, but not shown by it) programs to pay-cable systems in their own countries, which often are run as private businesses.

A number of broadcast systems sell weekly program guides, and in a few countries (Great Britain and the Netherlands), only the broadcasters are allowed to sell them. In addition to generating income from newsstand and subscription sales, there is also income from the sale of advertising space in the guides. A few broadcasters publish other periodicals: The BBC's *The Listener* is a very prestigious literary weekly. A number of broadcasters publish books and pamphlets to go along with their broadcasts, especially educational programs, but few of these more than break even. And, since publishing anything costs a fair amount of money, publishing ventures run by broadcasters seldom earn more than 1 or 2 percent of the annual budget, over and above publishing costs themselves (editorial staff, printing, and distribution).

As the "new media" (cable, videotext, teletext, pay cable, DBS) develop, many broadcast systems are attempting to insure that they get a share of the action, or even all of it, although private industry seems to have gotten a foothold even in countries where only a single public broadcast system exists (e.g., the Netherlands). Since those services already are or will be paid for by individual users, they represent a potential revenue-generating source for broadcasters. The BBC and the Independent Broadcasting Authority (IBA) both have teletext services for those British viewers who wish to pay for them, although neither as yet operates at a profit. Some national broadcast systems may enter the pay-channel business, and France introduced an independent pay TV service in 1984. However, some nations (e.g., the Netherlands) have decided to allow private industry to operate such services, either alongside the existing broadcast system or exclusively. Most of the new media will require massive infusions of capital, and many national broadcast systems do not have sufficient financial reserves to begin to cover the costs. Government loans would be a possibility (several countries issued them in the 1960s to help cover the conversion to color TV), but much of Western Europe, and indeed the rest of the world, is feeling the economic pinch as of the mid-1980s, and a number of the more conservative governments would rather see such services developed by private industry. Also, conventional cable systems in many Western European countries and in North America already are operated by private businesses and under local franchise agreements, although often there are national laws that apply to them, too.

ODDS AND ENDS   Having no convenient title to describe some of the
    more exotic revenue-generating mechanisms, "odds and ends" will
have to cover the lot! A few nations (e.g., Tunisia) have placed a special
broadcast tax on electricity bills, reasoning that consumers of electricity
probably are using some of it to run radio and TV sets. A few nations
(e.g., Canada, the Soviet Union) at one time imposed special purchase
taxes on receivers, with the money generated going to help support

broadcasting. The problem with such a tax was that there were boom and bust years for set sales, while broadcasting needed a steady, reasonably predictable flow of income. Very few nations today have such a tax, which also encourages smuggling in sets from outside the country.

In the early years of broadcasting, when equipment was primitive and inexpensive (many people made their own), and when some countries did very little to regulate broadcasting, it was possible for individuals to operate their own stations, often as a hobby and usually financed out of their own pockets. As broadcasting became more sophisticated, more expensive, and more heavily regulated, personal ownership for the most part disappeared and is now found only in the form of very low-power, land-based, and generally urban pirate (unauthorized) radio stations. These stations number in the hundreds and possibly thousands in the United States, Canada, and some Western European countries, and are even present in Eastern Europe and the Soviet Union. Few of them last very long; either the operator tires of the hobby or is detected by authorities and put off the air. Some of them, especially in France, Great Britain, and the Netherlands, have managed to keep alive by selling small amounts of airtime to advertisers.

Because of the growing costs of broadcasting (especially color TV), many broadcast systems use a combination of sources of support to finance themselves. License fees and advertising often are found together, annual government appropriations and advertising less often, and license fees and annual appropriations almost never (that might amount to double taxation of a listener or viewer). Individual and corporate contributions usually come in combination with institutional support and government appropriations. And irrespective of the major form of support, most broadcast systems would like to generate extra revenue by selling some of their services.

Whatever the financial sources, there is a set of questions that should be applied to them. Is financing continuous, or is it sporadic? is it predictable in amount, or does it fluctuate? Is it easy or difficult to increase? Obviously, the more continuous, predictable, and increasable, the better, but there remains a more fundamental question: What sorts of controls and influences does each bring from outside the broadcast system itself? How will they affect program decisions? Since many controls and influences are quite sporadic, subtle, undocumented, and even sometimes unintentional (or not perceived as intentional), they are often difficult to detect. Still, every system has them, and you will have a better idea of how they manifest themselves after reading about the various national systems covered in this book.

Supervision, Control, and Influence

With the possible exception of the low-power, land-based pirate radio operations, all broadcast stations and systems are subject to supervision, control, and influence, sometimes from within the station and sometimes from without. Broadcasters sometimes claim that they and they alone should make final decisions on what is to be broadcast, when, and how. They base this claim on the need for professional judgment: Hire the best person for the job, then invest her or him with the responsibility to carry it out. If she or he fails to do so, the administrative staff of the station or system should impose any disciplinary measures — not the Parliament, not a panel of listeners and viewers, not the courts.

If administrators always were professional broadcasters themselves, and if they were 100 percent honest, thorough, and omniscient, there might be more to that argument. After all, doctors and lawyers police themselves to a great extent. But there is some question as to whether broadcasting *is* a profession, with an agreed-upon set of professional standards. Furthermore, the money needed to keep it operating often comes from public funds. And because broadcasting must be licensed by the government in order to conform to ITU standards, it is a relatively small step for many governments to place program supervision, control, or influence alongside technical control. For those and other reasons, it is well-nigh impossible to find a station or system that does not have some outside forces that involve themselves in the program decision-making process. Some will be major forces, some minor; few will operate all of the time or seek to influence all forms of programming. Some will be more effective at certain times than at others; some will try to enhance their effectiveness by combining forces with others. Some will come from within the broadcasting organizations, others will come from outside, and particularly from the government and the public. Those presented here have one thing in common: All are carried out through established organizations and have a continuing existence (which means only that they aren't temporary or *ad hoc).*

INTERNAL CONTROLS   There are several possible levels and forms of
      internal control. In countries where there are large numbers of individually owned and operated stations, as there are in the United States, Canada, most of Latin America, Japan, Great Britain, and Australia, there are likely to be networks and associations of broadcasters, and all levels will have controls of various sorts. In countries with one or two

centralized broadcasting organizations, there is no need for associations and little need for separate control at the local level, since most such countries either do not have local broadcasting or place it firmly under the control of the national organization.

Individual Stations   Very few individual stations have formal codes of conduct that guide their programming policies. Instead, the tendency is to leave program regulation to the network or national organization, since it is from those sources that much if not most of the individual station's programs come. However, individual stations sometimes do have advisory committees composed of people living within the station's coverage area. usually station administrators appoint advisory committee members, and while there may be an attempt at "representativeness" by choosing members who are young, old, rich, poor, and so on, the usual tendency is to choose people the administrators know to be interested in broadcasting but not severely critical of it. As the committees *are* advisory, their only power is that of moral force and of the presumed need for the administration to heed what they say at least some of the time, lest the members see the process as a waste of their time. The committees may or may not be required by law (they are for certain categories of public broadcasting stations in the United States, but in most countries they are not), but few broadcasters would want to risk offending their members to the point of mass resignations and the attendant bad publicity.

Station administrators must take responsibility for their broadcasts, whether locally originated or coming from outside. There may be a certain amount of "buck-passing" if the offending broadcast comes from the network or national organization, but it is expected that local administrators listen to and watch program material coming from the outside and make their own decisions as to whether anything in it is not suitable for local tastes. There are no precise laws or even guidelines to assist local administrators in making such decisions, however, aside from right of reply issues, which in some countries are governed by laws (e.g., the Netherlands) and doctrines (e.g., the United States). If there is a local advisory committee, it might be of some help, but usually such decisions have to be made on the spur of the moment.

Network or National Organization   Networks and national organizations are quite likely to have codes of conduct that influence their programming. If programs come to the network or organization from a variety of domestic sources, as is true in the United States and increasingly of Western European systems (which sometimes are encouraged by their governments to have at least some productions made outside the system because that often ends up being less costly), such codes are necessary to insure that outside productions are in line with network or organization program policy. Even if most productions are made within the network or organization, there will be a need for an overall set of standards, since the numbers of programming departments (drama, quiz shows, call-ins, etc.) and personnel involved are considerable. Standards usually deal with treatment of sexually explicit material, violence, ethnic minorities, religious and political groups, children, and possibly the handicapped. Terms of reference often are not very specific, and the need for artistic integrity often can allow a producer to ignore certain aspects of the standards. Time of broadcast may be another mitigating circumstance, and a number of countries (e.g., Great Britain and West Germany) are looser with standards after 9:00 P.M. or so than they are before that hour, especially where sex and violence are concerned.

The program standards and practices departments that preview scripts, rehearsals, and tapings of entertainment programming in the U.S. commercial TV networks are a rarity; most systems around the world are far more informal in their previewing practices, and many have no systematic approaches. Instead, it is left up to the discretion of the head of the particular program service and to the central administrative staff to look in on productions if they wish. The U.S. commercial system features far more production of entertainment shows outside the network (almost 100 percent) than do systems in other industrialized nations, many of which produce well over half of their own entertainment in the system's own studios. That may help to explain why pre-broadcast supervision is more informal in other countries. Administrators *may* discuss programs once they have been aired, although that usually occurs only if there has been a highly publicized problem with a show or a major research report on audience reactions to it.

Many networks and national organizations, especially in smaller and/or poorer nations, rely heavily upon imported programming to fill sizable portions of their broadcast schedules. In some of these, there are various categories of forbidden material (sexual display and violence, or at least certain treatments of them, are most often taboo, but religion in some forms may be included, as well), and "censors" working at the central station or from within the Ministry of Information audition incoming material. Entire shows may be rejected, although it is more common to select offending material and edit it out. Many U.S. and other foreign TV series emerge from the process in a barely recognizable state in such countries as India and Saudi Arabia, where "sexually suggestive" dress can cover a wide area.

Broadcaster-appointed advisory councils are fairly common in license-fee-supported broadcast systems. Most Western European national broadcasting organizations have such councils, which may have very general or very specific mandates. Great Britain's BBC and IBA have both forms: general advisory councils to advise in theory on anything pertaining to broadcasting, and specialized advisory councils to deal with programming for such subject areas as education, religion, and charities. The broadcasters do not have to heed the advice given by the councils, and the general bodies often have little to give on their own, preferring to respond to specific questions and issues put to them by the broadcasters. The specialized councils are more apt to expect to have some meaningful influence upon the decision-making process, however: Most of their members are experts (or at least persons of note) in the field covered by the particular council and are accustomed to being listened to.

Advisory council activities rarely receive much publicity, and it is doubtful that the general public knows much about their existence or their impact on the system. As with local advisory councils, members of the national councils often are chosen because they have shown some interest in broadcasting. They are not encouraged to think of themselves as representatives of the general public or of any particular interest group or profession. Most broadcast organization protect their council members from becoming widely known to the public (unless of course a member wishes to become widely known) by revealing their identities only in annual reports and other less-than-widely-distributed documents. Council meetings and recommendations similarly receive little publicity in most broadcast systems, either through the printed press or through broadcasting itself.

A few broadcast systems have appointed review boards through which the public may register complaints about programming, usually having to do with incorrect, misleading, or incomplete information contained in a broadcast. Both the BBC and the IBA developed such bodies in the early 1970s, partly as a response to some public criticism alleging unfair broadcast treatment of people and institutions. The BBC review board was staffed by reputable individuals (e.g., a retired chief justice), while the IBA review board drew its members from its own administrative staff and the IBA General Advisory Council. Neither board meted out penalties, although both on occasion reached judgments critical of producers, directors, or others involved in production. Those judgments were made available to the press, which sometimes printed them, and the BBC regularly printed its board's judgments in a BBC weekly magazine, *The Listener.*

The major problem with such boards is that the public, if it knows anything about them, may be inclined to doubt that the broadcasters would appoint members who might be very critical of broadcasting. Furthermore, if there is no specific evidence of disciplinary action taken against broadcast staff who are found "guilty," that cynicism may increase. It is partly for those reasons that the BBC and IBA boards were merged into one body with government-appointed members in 1982. (The IBA has continued to operate an internally appointed Complaints Review Committee.) However, it remains the case that the broadcasters themselves decide what to do with the judgments rendered by the new Broadcasting Complaints Commission; there are no specific legal penalties attached to those judgments.

Broadcaster Associations In most countries where there are national associations of broadcasters, there will be some sort of voluntary code of broadcast practices. Sometimes this is a brief, vaguely worded document speaking to the need for all broadcasters to remember their responsibilities to their audiences, but with no specification of how a broadcaster who fails to remember those responsibilities might be penalized. A few nations (e.g., the United States, Japan, and Canada) have more elaborate codes of practice, although the wording often may be just as vague and the penalties just as unspecified. The United States National Association of Broadcasters Television Code (suspended as of 1982 following a negative legal decision on one aspect of the code) contained various prohibitions against sexual display but added the statement "unless its portrayal is essential to the plot." The Japanese National Association of Commercial Broadcasters Television Code contains similar statements. Both countries feature a great deal of violent fare during prime-time hours, and there is little evidence that the codes have had much influence over the nature or amount of such programming.

Part of the reason may be lack of penalties, although codes can bring peer-group pressure to bear on an individual broadcaster who appears to be stepping out of line. Self-regulation, after all, is based at least in part on the idea that, if the industry regulates itself, the government will not have to regulate it, or at least not as much. But if excesses in programming, however a code may define these, are committed by the largest and most powerful members of the broadcasting association, will the association itself have much force of moral suasion? And are broadcasters necessarily well equipped to judge what might be excessive? Some national associations have appointed advisory panels for certain activities (children's advertising, medical products), but that is not a general practice. Still, national associations and their codes can have an impact on programming, as the U.S. National Association of Broadcasters (NAB) showed by keeping hard-liquor advertising off radio and television for over five decades.

Associations exist within the broadcasting organizations, as well. Several countries have associations of broadcast journalists, such as the United States Radio-TV News Directors Association and the British National Union of Journalists. They work for the improvement of professional standards and defend the integrity of their work when it is questioned through the country's political or legal systems. They also may campaign for higher wages or better working conditions.

There also are associations of broadcast-related organizations. Perhaps the best known of these, at least in countries where advertising is common, is the association of advertising agencies. Those in Great Britain, Canada, Australia, and the United States have attempted to set general standards for advertising, including broadcast advertising. Occasionally such associations have allied themselves with associations of broadcasters by endorsing the broadcasters' codes and refusing to deal with stations that do not subscribe to those codes. For the most part, however, associations of advertisers face the same limitations as do their broadcasting counterparts.

EXTERNAL CONTROLS

National Governments   The traditional division of government into legislative, executive, and judicial branches works well for an examination of government's role in controlling, supervising, and influencing broadcasting. Most countries have legislative, executive, and judicial bodies, and most of those bodies become involved with broadcasting in one way or another. Relatively few countries have administrative agencies, but I have included them here because of their considerable importance in U.S., Canadian, Australian, and a few other broadcast systems.

Legislative bodies in most countries have three major methods for dealing with broadcasting: appropriation of the annual budget, development and amendment of laws governing broadcasting, and appointment of committees to review the performance of the broadcast system. Where the budget is concerned, even countries with license-fee-based systems usually give the legislature responsibility for approving the annual budget, although rarely does that power extend to blocking or increasing expenditures on specific programs. Lawmaking and amending probably will not be as frequent an activity, and the tendency in most countries is to formulate laws that are quite general, rather than being

loaded down with specifics that seek to regulate every possible programming contingency. Review committees may come from within or from
outside the legislature; while there is a tendency for the former to be
more political than the latter, most countries with such committees
(Canada and many Western European countries) attempt to create bipartisan or nonpartisan bodies. Only one country, Great Britain, has a
systematic approach to the formation of such committees: Originally
they were to be appointed every ten years, but the intervals have grown
longer in the past few decades, notwithstanding which there is a commitment to their appointment at regular intervals. Most countries appoint
them on a perceived need basis: Whenever a major problem or technical
development appears (or looks as if it is about to appear) on the scene, a
committee is appointed. Both approaches have points in their favor, but
periodic review does have the advantage of permitting the assessment of
broadcasting in a noncrisis atmosphere.

Because review committees generally are expected to report on
public satisfaction with broadcasting, they usually take public testimony,
whether in hearings conducted around the country or in invited written
appraisals or both. That approach usually means that the work of the
committee itself will receive considerable public attention, especially in
the press, which loves to cover the trials and tribulations of a rival
medium. In turn, there is a climate of expectation regarding the possible
outcomes of a committee report, so that, even though the legislative
body is free to ignore the report completely if it wishes, it is not very
likely to do so. If the political balance of power shifts between the time
the committee is appointed and the time it reports, there may be some
effect on what gets enacted, as there was in Great Britain in the late
1970s, but even there the bipartisan or nonpartisan nature of the committee probably will mean that at least some of its recommendations will
be heeded.

Legislative bodies also may conduct specific investigations of specific broadcasts, as the United States Congress has done on occasion, but
that practice is uncommon in the United States and almost unheard of
elsewhere. It may be that legislatures simply are too unwieldy and too
slow to respond to be able to exercise much control or influence over
specific program decision making.

Executive bodies (I include various types of chiefs of state and their
cabinets) generally have three major means of exercising control and
influence, as well: the proposal of budgets (in systems where there are
annual government appropriations), the appointment of members to supervisory bodies (and even in some cases of top administrative officials
in the broadcast system), and the systematic involvement of the ruling

political party in the staffing of the broadcast service. Budgets may be passed by legislatures, but the executive branch often prepares them, and failure on the broadcaster's part to convince the executive body that more money is needed can make it awfully difficult to convince the legislature to approve any increase. The power of appointment likewise can give the executive body considerable access to decision-making bodies: An individual who is beholden to the executive branch for her or his prestigious position on the broadcasting system's board of governors is likely to listen when that body talks.

Some countries make such appointments a bipartisan matter (e.g., through a bipartisan committee or with the advice and consent of the legislature), while others have laws limiting membership on such supervisory bodies to certain numbers of individuals from the political parties, staggering terms of appointment so that they will not necessarily coincide with changes in political leadership, and so on. And in countries with one-party systems, membership in that party, and the endorsement of the party's leaders (who usually hold executive positions in government), may be necessary to win appointment to any position of responsibility in broadcasting. (That also may be true in multiparty systems, as it usually has been in France.)

Judicial involvement in broadcasting usually is limited to judging cases in which there are allegations of illegality in broadcast practices. Some of those cases may arise under specific laws governing broadcasting, while others may come from more general bodies of law, such as laws governing libel, slander, misrepresentation, and so on. The courts also may be called upon by various parties — the public, the government, broadcasters themselves — to review decisions made by administrative bodies or lower courts. Although courts make judgments on individual cases, these can influence the overall development of broadcasting, as have United States Supreme Court decisions on network-affiliate station relations and on the legal validity of the Federal Communications Commission's Fairness Doctrine.

Regulatory agencies may be relative rarities in broadcast regulation, but those that do exist generally are quite influential. The Canadian Radio-Television and Telecommunications Commission, the Australian Broadcasting Tribunal, and the United States Federal Communications Commission all are active in the control and supervision of broadcasting. Regulatory agencies generally are developed by legislatures, which also finance them, so that they are open to a certain amount of legislative influence. Their top officials often are appointed by the executive branch, which presents the opportunity for influence from that quarter. and the courts usually are empowered to review their decisions, so that the agencies must be sensitive to the legality of their actions. Yet they are a means of insuring that a specialized and potentially influential public activity will be supervised on a continuing basis, which the legislative, executive, and judicial branches themselves never could find the time to do.

Such agencies makes sense only in countries where there are relatively large numbers of individual broadcast stations, as is true of Australia, New Zealand, Canada, France, the United States, and, to a lesser degree, Great Britain. All of them have regulatory agencies. Yet Japan, which also has many stations, has no regulatory agency with any real power (the U.S. occupation government tried to impose one after World War II, but it never took root). Most of the Latin American countries and Italy have many stations, as well, but not regulatory agencies. (Perhaps regulatory agencies are largely Anglo-Saxon concepts!)

Regulatory agencies have various ways of dealing with broadcasting. There are periodic renewals of licenses to broadcast in Canada, Australia, and the United States. The public generally is invited to comment on station performance at license-renewal time, and in Australia and Canada the agencies hold their hearings in the communities served by the stations. However, the broadcast laws administered by the agencies often are complex, and in all three countries there are frequent criticisms of the way in which the system puts the public at a disadvantage, especially in terms of understanding the laws and the legal procedures accompanying them. Sometimes the agencies have attempted to educate the public, and in the United States specialized organizations have arisen to help citizen groups to hold their own before the Federal Communications Commission (FCC), but such organizations usually have been dependent upon the monetary support of foundations, and that support has been uncertain in recent years. There also have been accusations in Australia and in the United States that the regulatory agencies are more sympathetic to the broadcasters than they are to the public because agencies and broadcasters "understand one another," "talk the same language," and so on. Since the important positions in the agencies often are held by former broadcasters and communications lawyers, there may be some truth to that accusation. Certainly the agencies are not representative of the general public.

Another sort of agency—sometimes a full-blown ministry or government department—is the aforementioned postal, telephone, and telegraph service, or PTT. This agency often has tremendous power to set rates for uses of a wide variety of communication services and even to determine whether further communication services (e.g., cable, DBS) should be allowed, and if so, under what conditions.[11] It also may be the agency through which the national broadcast system reports to the government.

Municipal and State Governments   Most countries either do not have
states or vest no political power in them, and their regulatory force
in broadcasting generally is minimal or nonexistent. However, West Germany's broadcast system is state, rather than federally, operated, provinces in Canada have established educational broadcast services, and
some states in the U.S. regulate cable TV and provide public radio and
television services.

Municipalities generally have been just as uninvolved in the regulatory process, although city governments occasionally finance their own
radio stations. But cable television when it appeared in the 1950s in the
United States and Canada and more recently in Western Europe often
came under the partial control of city governments, perhaps because it
was regarded as a utility, like telephone or mass transit service. City
governments usually confine themselves to insuring a certain standard of
technical quality and specified numbers and types of channels of service,
in addition to regulating the rates charged for service (a power that U.S.
cities lost in January 1987). Rarely do they concern themselves with
program content, although the provision of "soft-porn" channels on
some cable systems has aroused the attention of city administrators.

Educational systems, which sometimes receive their financial support from municipal- and/or state-levied taxes, also may establish
broadcast services and are responsible for controlling their output. Since
such systems usually are operated by the system's own staff members,
that control is easy to exercise.

Trade Unions   While trade unions may and often do act as an outside
pressure group on broadcast systems, they also function in many
countries as "insiders." Most of the industrialized nations of Western
Europe and North America have broadcast systems with some union
membership. That is especially true of the highly centralized systems and
of broadcast networks, where union membership may well extend from
one end of the production process to the other, with higher administrative staff the only really significant nonunion group.

Broadcast unions have several ways of bringing pressure to bear on
broadcast systems, including soliciting the support of the larger union
structures to which some of them belong and of other, nonbroadcast
unions. They may have access to the press (union-owned papers and
periodicals still flourish in some countries), they may engage in work

slowdowns, and of course they may strike. Broadcast unions in the United States generally have gone on strike for higher wages and improved physical working conditions; rarely do they strike to protest the content of broadcasts. However, TV directors, producers, and writers did bring a "denial of First Amendment (freedom of speech) rights" case to court in the family viewing time controversy[12] and went to Congress to testify against heavy network use of reruns.

Western European unions generally have been more willing to threaten to strike over issues involving broadcast content and at times actually have gone out on strike for those issues. Perhaps the most famous example of that was the strike by French broadcast news personnel during the 1968 general strike in Paris and other parts of the country. They were protesting the government's refusal to allow them to report the strike in what they considered an unbiased manner; the government wanted coverage entirely favorable to itself and unfavorable to the general strikers. As a result, French TV screens were dark for some of the newscasts and carried government statements at other times. Most of the strikers never did get their jobs back following the strike.

There also has been an interesting movement in a few countries toward "editorial codetermination." Some broadcast journalists, frustrated with what they see as bias among their editors or higher administrators, have requested or demanded a voice in the editorial decision-making process. That movement appears to have been most powerful in West Germany, where certain journalists have been disturbed at what they perceive as political bias among "higher-ups" and have sought to offset it (perhaps with their own biases) through codetermination. No West German station has a policy allowing for this, but it has been the subject of occasional experiments, and a member of the news staff sits with the Broadcasting Council in Radio Bremen.

There have been a few instances where printers have refused to print issues of newspapers that they felt misrepresented union positions (that happened in Great Britain in the 1970s). So far, there has been no similar occurrence in broadcasting, but certainly it could happen, if technicians operating transmitters were to react negatively to a certain broadcast policy, or even to individual broadcasts. The transmitting equipment is in the hands of the post office in many countries, but technical personnel usually belong to unions, too.

Unions have one other possible effect upon programming. Usually they are zealous in the protection of job security for their members. In some Western European countries, stringers and other part-time, occasional staff may receive full job security if they have been employed by the broadcast system for a certain period of time (usually over a number of years). That has made some broadcasters reluctant to use part-timers; however beneficial they might be in covering events that otherwise might not get covered, those broadcasters do not feel that it is worth the eventual cost of restricting the broadcaster's freedom of movement. Broadcast administrators also often are critical of the need to send four- or five-person crews out to cover events when experience (usually that of U.S. stations) has shown that two could do the job. Union rules often call for such crews, but the unions would argue that the end result is a higher quality product.

The Public As previously noted, the public may be involved in the supervision and control of broadcasting through advisory committees and through governmentally appointed bodies. In both cases, however, the initiative is not the public's: Broadcasters usually appoint advisory committees, and legislators or the executive branch usually choose the members or at least designate the categories for public participation. Broadcast systems in all countries have various devices for eliciting feedback from the public. Surveys, letter writing, telephone calling, public meetings, all may serve as bridges between broadcaster and public. Telephone calls and mail may or may not be solicited by the broadcaster, but surveys and public meetings are the broadcaster's choice. Likewise, governmental bodies develop their own rules for dealing with the public.

Still, there are some examples of continuing activities aimed at controlling or influencing broadcast systems that are developed and operated by the public, or, more often, a specific public-interest group. The United States has had public-interest groups active in this field since the 1930s, and several of the groups have been able to achieve at least some of their aims, particularly during the heyday of citizen activism in the late 1960s to late 1970s. Action for Children's Television (ACT) perhaps is the most famous, but the National Citizen's Committee on Broadcasting (NCCB), Accuracy in Media (AIM), and several others also have had an impact on broadcast legislation and broadcast programming.

Such groups generally have been less numerous in other parts of the world, although Canada had a very active Canadian Radio League from the late 1920s to the late 1930s, and it continued to function until the 1960s.[13] Australia also has had an active citizen's committee on children's broadcasting, generally acknowledged to have helped lead to the development of the Australian Children's Television Foundation. The ACTF, a federal and state government financed body, in turn has been given credit for developing and lobbying for an amendment to the Australian Broadcasting Act that set a minimum requirement for TV programming made specifically for children.[14]

Great Britain's National Viewer's and Listener's Association (VALA) has been in existence since the early 1960s. Led by a former girls' school headmistress, Mary Whitehouse, VALA has attempted to achieve a reduction in the amount and explicit nature of sex and violence in television entertainment. In more recent years, ethnic minorities in Great Britain have sought a more balanced portrayal of their members, and some have worked through the Local Radio Workshop to achieve this. West German feminists have tried to get West German television to alter the allegedly sexist nature of much TV advertising and many entertainment programs. Japanese parents and teachers have been laboring for the past two decades or more through parent-teacher associations to achieve a reduction in the amount and intensity of violent programming on Japanese commercial television.

These groups have certain features in common. They are almost perpetually short of money, they rely heavily upon volunteers for their staffing, and they are quite dependent upon the media to bring wider public attention to their causes. Some also would claim that they have unrealistic views of how broadcasting works, but that varies a good deal: Many of the groups have enlisted the aid of producers, researchers, and communications lawyers to help them in the formulation of realistic calls for change. Those groups that appear to have been most successful have been persistent, realistic in the sense of not expecting total transformation of the existing system, limited in their aims (usually restricting themselves to very specific types of programs, e.g., children's programming, morality, etc.), and resourceful, especially in knowing where to bring pressure for change, and when and how long to apply it. Unfortunately for these groups, money is a necessary element in their effectiveness, and public memberships do not seem to have generated much of it. Support by various foundations (e.g., Ford and Markle in the United States) has helped but cannot be relied upon from year to year.[15]

The groups often face one further problem: dealing with the regulatory systems of their respective countries. Broadcast law, as with any specialized body of law, has its own jargon and its own sets of procedures. Usually the legal system for broadcasting has not been designed to make it easy for the public to become involved. The United States Federal Communications Commission set up a Consumer Assistance Office during the 1970s, but staffing was minimal and public knowledge of its existence not very high.[16] The Australian Broadcasting Tribunal appears to have discouraged public involvement in its processes on occasion.[17] The many countries without administrative agencies for broadcasting virtually compel their citizens to turn to the general legal system for addressing grievances, with the attendant time, money and effort involved in presenting a court case. Most citizens probably don't wish to go to the trouble. And, while one certainly can argue that it should not be possible for every citizen or citizen's group to demand the right to be heard by the legal system or the broadcast system for every single element of programming that annoys or offends, it remains true that those citizens do pay for broadcasting in one way or another and are entitled to have at least some effective influence on the medium.

Communications Policy

The various agencies involved in control and supervision of broadcasting function as part of an interconnected whole, but it is an uncoordinated whole, for the most part. As Krasnow et al. have pointed out in their study of the dynamics of the governance of U.S. broadcasting, those interconnections can be diagrammed, but the strength of specific interconnections fluctuates over time and varies according to the nature of the situation.[18] That also characterizes broadcast systems in other countries and is quite natural and even desirable for a medium of communication that both influences and is influenced by the society within which it functions.

However, some governments, citizens, and broadcasters have wondered whether it might not be better to have a little more stability in this respect, particularly in planning for the future. With the expansion of possible uses for broadcasting during the 1970s — cable, satellites, multipoint distribution services, and so on — that idea seemed to be prudent. Furthermore, many of the developing nations, feeling the need to expand their broadcast systems so as to better serve national development, were considering the possibility of doing so in a more orderly and more cost-efficient way than had most of the world's developed nations. In the early 1970s, UNESCO (United Nations Educational, Scientific, and Cultural Organization) commissioned a set of studies of communications policy in several countries, about half of them developed, and half developing, nations. The organization's hope was to discover what already had been accomplished by way of communications policy, so that other countries about to consider the subject might be helped. Also, the attention on communications policy might inspire those nations that had no policy to consider whether they should.

What UNESCO discovered was that there were few common denominators in policy development and implementation. Most nations had evolved policies piecemeal, and few ever had stepped back to consider whether those policies still were relevant or whether they might profit from better coordination. Where the developed nations were concerned, the chief obstacle to orderly planning seemed to be that so many interests — business, government, and public — were involved in the mass media, and that their involvement had continued over so many decades, that it was impractical to redesign a total system along more rational lines. Some governments had studied communications policy from time to time, but often such studies examined only one segment of the whole, for example, cable TV or frequency spectrum use.[19]

With few examples of concerted attempts at the formulation of communications policy to guide them, and with little money of their own for implementation of such policies as they might devise, developing countries generally dabbled with the concept but did little to implement it. Indonesia and India, faced with common problems of large geographical areas, difficult climatic conditions, multilingual populations, and widespread poverty, disease, and illiteracy, did develop and attempt to implement wide-spanning communications policies, especially involving a high reliance on satellite technology and the expansion of broadcasting.[20] Few others followed their example.

Why have attempts at coordinated communications policy-making been so few in number and generally so abortive, when many authorities on broadcasting see such policy-making as economically, technologically, politically, and culturally better than a lack of coordination? The degree of financial investment in the older and more highly developed media systems is one explanation: It is one thing to argue that, with today's technology, one could have a far better system, but it is another to find the money to construct such a system *and* to protect the interests of those who have a stake in the present system. There is also the old adage "Better the devil you know than the devil you don't." Broadcasters, governments, and the public learn to live with imperfect systems and may feel threatened by proposals for change that look good on paper, but that are untested. And developing countries where the existing systems have not been around long enough to have fossilized nevertheless face tremendous pressures from developed countries that want to sell them something less than state-of-the art broadcast equipment and less than culturally relevant broadcast programming, usually at prices more in line with what the country feels it can afford.

There are several ways of considering communications policy-making, however, and many of them acknowledge that policy-making needn't necessarily be along the grand design lines that UNESCO appears to favor. In fact, most nations can offer several examples of broadcast policy-making along more modest, but nonetheless important, lines.

For most purposes, policy-making can be considered as attempts to make more economical and/or socially desirable use of the broadcast media. Usually it involves public deliberation and decision making by the major parties that will be affected by changed or new policies: The government (national, state, and/or local), the broadcast industry (broadcasters, advertisers, and/or manufacturers), and the public (whether general or special-interest groups), all may (and probably should) take part in the process. And finally, it may take the form of short-term, medium-term, or long-term policy, although, as we shall see, short-term policies sometimes have a way of becoming long-term ones, and long-term policies may disappear from view in a year or so.

SHORT-TERM POLICIES   Sometimes broadcast systems are faced with problems that must be addressed immediately with mechanisms that, once they have cleared up the problem, can be abolished. An example of that would be the intention of the United States Congress to create the Federal Radio Commission as a body that would bring order to the chaotic conditions of U.S. broadcast licensing, then disappear, with responsibility for the further licensing of broadcasting to be returned to the Department of Commerce, from whence it had come. The FRC had its term of service extended twice, after which the commission became a "permanent" administrative agency. It was enlarged and retitled in 1934, when passage of the Communications Act of 1934 saw the transformation of the FRC into the Federal Communications Commission, which certainly has the look of permanency! The chief advocates of this policy were the more professional (as opposed to amateur, or hobbyist) broadcasters, the Department of Commerce, and the United States Senate. The public had little involvement or even apparent interest in the development of this policy.

MEDIUM-TERM POLICIES   There are problems that may require several years to solve, thus necessitating medium-term policies. When their solution takes even longer than anticipated, or when attempts to solve them lead to new problems, the structures or approaches created by the policy may become more permanent. A possible example of a medium-term policy (although it is difficult to know whether it really was intended that way) is the FCC's policy toward the regulation of cable television, as set forth in three reports and orders in 1965, 1966, and 1972. It seems clear that the major purpose of this policy was to protect over-the-air broadcasting from cable; it also seems quite possible that the FCC saw this as a medium-term policy in that cable eventually would have to be given freer rein, but only after over-the-air broadcasting had had time to adjust to that likelihood and take measures necessary to deal with it. That particular policy thrust ended in the mid-to-late 1970s with a series of court decisions and FCC actions favoring the growth of cable. Chief advocates of the initial policy were the broadcast industry and the FCC; again, the public had little to do with its development.

LONG-TERM POLICIES   Most policy-making seems to be intended for long-term service, although changing governments, changing technologies, and changing economic circumstances may bring a halt to a given policy. In the late 1970s Iran was developing an "open university" along British lines, with degree-related courses offered through a combination of radio, TV, and correspondence. Then the Shah of Iran fled the country and the Ayatollah Khomeini's anti-western government took over. The open university having been associated with the Shah and with western technology and education, it was dropped. (Its high cost probably told against it, as well).

The FCC's development of the all-channel (VHF and UHF) TV receiver policy in the late 1950s and early 1960s was an attempt to set long-term policy that would promote use by broadcasters of a portion of the frequency spectrum that already was available but was underutilized because so few people had sets capable of receiving UHF. The FCC hoped that the all-channel receiver bill would lead to the growth of broadcast outlets, thus promoting competition. The bill was necessary because otherwise few investors would consider UHF stations profitable, whereas the guarantee of large numbers of VHF-UHF receivers within a few years would make such stations potentially lucrative. That has, for the most part, turned out to be the case. The FCC, the then-existing UHF station owners, and certain manufacturers were the initial advocates of the policy; Congress eventually supported it. Once again, the public had little to do with the process, whether through ignorance of its implications, indifference to the outcome, lack of knowledge as to how to make its opinions known, or some combination of these.[21]

The nation-specific chapters that follow contain many examples of policy-making. Most of them fit into the long-term category. There is another way of categorizing them, however, and that is in terms of their purpose. That purpose might be "pro" or "anti," supporting a positive development or avoiding a negative one. The list that follows is intended only to be suggestive of the ways in which types of policies might fit into one or the other of these kinds of purposes.

Positive

The greatest possible program diversity for the greatest number of people (this could include local and regional broadcasting, multicultural broadcasting, broadcasting to ethnic minorities and/or the handicapped, etc.).

The greatest possible availability of clearly receivable broadcast signals.

The greatest possible opportunity for the expression of viewpoints.

The greatest possible availability of broadcast receivers (this could include the removal or reduction of taxes and import duties on sets, the manufacture of inexpensive receivers, etc.).

The greatest possible use of broadcasting to provide positive guidance to society.

Negative

Protection from unfair or unbalanced reporting.

Protection from possible harmful effects of programming, including advertising.

Protection from excessive amounts of certain kinds of programming (usually advertising and imported material).

Protection from monopolization of broadcasting by governments, businesses, religious organizations, and so on.

Protection from unfair competitive practices within the broadcast industry and between broadcasting and related media.

Broadcaster-Audience Interaction

In the final analysis, broadcasting does not exist to serve governments, businesses, or other abstract entities; it exists to serve listeners and viewers. If it fails to do so, governments, businesses, and others will not have their particular purposes met. Furthermore, the audience pays in one way or another to receive broadcasting. In fact, no broadcasting system anywhere in the world totally ignores its audience, although some appear to have precious little regard or respect for its opinions.[22]

You have already seen how the public may become involved through various committees, councils, and groups, most of these established and appointed by broadcasters and governments. Aside from such mechanisms, broadcast systems usually have other methods for establishing contact with audiences, many of which are, again, initiated by broadcasters and/or governments; some are continuous, some are sporadic, some have permanency, some clearly are designed to deal with crises. These methods fall under the major categories of audience research; solicitation and/or reception of audience mail, telephone calls, and visits; public meetings with the audience; and public use of the media.

AUDIENCE RESEARCH   Almost every broadcast system (but not necessarily every individual station) in the industrially developed world makes at least some use of audience research, although for some of the systems in communist countries this research occurs only on occasion. Probably the most common form of audience research is *survey research,* which the United States, Canada, and a number of European nations have carried out on a regular basis since the mid-1930s. Most surveys seek to discover how many of what kinds of people are watching or listening, but many European countries also want to know whether the audiences liked the broadcasts or not, so they employ a numerical "appreciation index," which invites listeners and viewers to rate programs on a letter-grade or a one-through-ten scale (the latter is widely used in European schools for the grading of schoolwork, so audiences are very familiar — and perhaps unhappily familiar — with it). The great advantage to appreciation indexes is that they yield data that allow broadcast staff to argue for the continuation of programs that attract small but highly devoted audiences.

Appreciation indexes could be considered a form of *qualitative research,* in that they tell those who wish to know (broadcast staff, advertisers, advertising agencies, and sometimes the public) something about audience reactions to specific programs. However, that term usually is reserved for more highly detailed, interview-based studies in which listeners and viewers are asked sets of general and specific questions about specific programs, categories of programs, the perceived influence of programs on their daily lives, uses made of the media, perceived accuracy of the media, and so on. Such studies are widely and regularly conducted in most Western European and North American countries, Japan, Australia, and some of the communist countries. Japan's NHK and Great Britain's BBC are famous for the number and quality of their research studies, and the public broadcast services of West Germany, Italy, Sweden, and Finland are not far behind.

In the United States, however, qualitative research in broadcasting is far more likely to be conducted by social scientists at universities who are working with university, foundation, or federal government financial support than it is by broadcasters. The latter seemed indifferent to the need for such research until the 1970s and the rising tide of public opinion and congressional pressures concerning violence on TV and its effects. Some networks also claimed that they had little faith in the accuracy of existing methodologies or stated that, if they themselves supported or conducted such studies and the results turned out to be favorable to them, those results would not be accepted by the scientific community. Universities also are important centers for audience research in Canada, Australia, Great Britain, Japan, the Scandinavian countries, and West Germany. Advertiser-supported broadcast systems in general seem far less likely to feature qualitative research than do license-fee-supported systems. (Great Britain's IBA is a notable exception.) Perhaps that is because advertisers do not really care what the audience thinks of a program, so long as it continues to watch or listen in large numbers; or perhaps the license-fee-supported systems feel a greater sense of obligation to know more about public reactions to programs when that public pays directly for them.

SOLICITATION/RECEPTION OF AUDIENCE MAIL   Broadcasters vary in their practices of soliciting mail from the audience. Some seem to think it beneath their dignity, while others engage in it regularly. Some use it to generate data with which to impress advertisers or government officials, while other analyze it carefully for such clues as it might yield to audience reactions and tastes (in which respect it may be used as a supplement to or substitute for survey-based qualitative research). Several communist systems have regularly scheduled programs in which broadcast staff react to listener letters, and some of the Western European systems feature readings of excerpts from those letters, but usually not reactions of staff members.

Such programs themselves serve to induce the public to write, but the public also may write without any urging. Such unsolicited mail is unlikely to have much impact on programming policies, because, unlike most solicited mail, it usually has no focal point and thus lacks the force of numbers to carry any weight with broadcast staff. Sometimes, however, there are letter-writing campaigns generated by television critics writing in newspapers and/or by public interest groups, and sometimes those campaigns generate enough mail to influence policy-making: Several entertainment programs on U.S. commercial TV have been saved from elimination by such campaigns, which have given the broadcasters a further set of data with which to convince advertisers that there *was* an appreciative and sizable audience out there, and which also has allowed them to claim that they *were* responsive to public demand.

In any case, no social scientist is willing to accord audience mail the scientific respect received by properly planned and executed surveys. On those occasions when audience characteristics can be discerned from the letters (and that is rare), the letter writers turn out to be unrepresentative of the audience as a whole. It takes a certain amount of drive and a certain amount of confidence in one's ability to write to engage in such an act. It also requires a certain amount of leisure time and disposable income. Many audience members lack one or more of those characteristics, and in developing countries large segments of the audience often lack all four of them. Thus, while letters may be a useful (not to mention interesting and colorful) form of audience feedback, one must bear in mind that that audience is a limited one.

Telephone calls and visits to the broadcast system share in the disadvantages just mentioned, and the latter also includes the need for transportation and even larger amounts of leisure time. However, license fee and government appropriation supported systems often feature regularly scheduled or specially arranged station tours, at the end of which the tour group members may gather in a room and share their views on programming with members of the staff. This is a fairly common practice in communist broadcast systems. Such meetings, however, are far more likely to be organized by the broadcast system to take place outside the station, in the form of general public or special group meetings.

PUBLIC MEETINGS   Many Western and Eastern European broadcast systems hold regular or irregular public meetings at which one to several broadcast staff members answer questions put to them by the public. More often than not, the "public" will take one of two forms: (a) heterogeneous group made up of those who are anxious to have the opportunity to see what a particular broadcaster "really looks like" and those who have a particular complaint to voice; or (b) a very homogeneous group, for example, schoolchildren, old-age pensioners, factory workers, and so on. The Western European systems tend to favor the heterogeneous approach, while the Eastern European systems generally opt for homogeneity. Japan's NHK also has open meetings with the public, usually on a more frequent basis than do the Western European systems. The United States National Association of Broadcasters also has held them on a few occasions.

Public meetings seem to function more as an arm of public relations than as a meaningful source of feedback. Meetings with the general public often are so brief (usually two hours or so) and so crowded (a few to several hundred people in the audience) that it is almost impossible to tell whether there is much agreement among audience members as to whether a given concern is widely shared or not. It is also quite easy for a few dominant individuals to concentrate their fire on one or two issues and to monopolize the meeting time with their concerns. But what often happens is that the audience wants the broadcast staff to tell them what "really" goes on in the making of programs, so that a fair amount of any given meeting may be taken up with informal talks by the staff.

A few broadcast systems require reports on the meetings, with precise indications of the sorts of concerns expressed by the group. More often, however, such reporting as occurs is limited to anecdotal statements shared with colleagues. There are few indications that feedback gathered through public meetings has any real impact upon the decision-making process, the more so because different sets of staff members usually preside at each meeting, which minimizes the possibility that any one staff member will acquire a broader sense of the issues that arise.

PROGRAM-MAKING BY THE AUDIENCE   To some individuals, the ultimate form of feedback is to permit and even encourage members of the audience to make their own programs. In theory, that would allow audiences to make the sorts of programs that they would want to see. In practice, such an approach seems unreasonable where the vast majority of programming is concerned: entertainment, sports, and the news, at least as intended for the general public, are too expensive and too complex for most audience members to produce. However, it is possible to consider approaches that leave the actual production of programs to professional broadcasters but give members of the audience relatively free rein in determining program content. Also, with the spread of cable TV, cable systems in the United States, Canada, Great Britain, West Germany, and the Netherlands sometimes have made available not only airtime, but also equipment and professional advice that would enable individuals and groups to make their own programs.

In fact, participation in program making usually is a group, rather than an individual, activity. Most individuals do not have the time required to make a program, although the German Democratic Republic experimented in the early 1970s with radio "access booths," which allowed interested individuals to operate tape recorders and microphones capable of recording "broadcast quality" statements, which might or might not be broadcast. Great Britain's IBA tried the same sort of thing with television in the mid-1980s: People could enter video booths (only three cities had them) and record statements, which were then edited and used in a sort of "voice of the people" TV program. Groups often have more time, as well as the motivation and resources required to prepare a program. But *a* program usually is what it amounts to, since either the airtime or the production facilities or both are limited and have to be shared among groups.

There is another factor that limits the growth of audience-produced programming: "professionalism." Most broadcasters in most countries look upon themselves as "professionals," which to them usually means that it takes a certain level of skill to produce a program worthy of being broadcast to the public. Skills demanded probably will include the ability to compose, present, and record one's message in a professional manner, but the criteria for "professional manner" will be those set and defined by the professionals themselves. In some (perhaps even most) broadcast systems, that will include the use of "correct" speech (and many broadcast systems look upon themselves as upholders of the proper standards of speech), "correct" dress, "correct" recording levels and balances, and so on. Again, "correct" usually is defined by the broadcasters, and usually does not encompass what most members of the public might prepare.

A few broadcast systems, or stations within them, have taken a slightly different approach to the problem (if it is one) of helping elements of the public to express themselves through radio and television. Broadcast professionals have worked with groups, making programs about the groups, their perceptions of society, and their perceptions of society's perceptions of them, but guided through every step of the production process by the views of the group members themselves. In that way, the messages that emerged would be professional in their production techniques, yet reflective of the groups' self-perceptions. This has been done in Canada (for native American peoples) and in the Netherlands (for the working class), and it was proposed in Great Britain, albeit by some "concerned individuals," and not by the broadcasters themselves. Its failure to materialize in Great Britain is instructive: One of the chief sources of the failure was the very entity that in fact should have been speaking for the people, notably labor unions. Whether the unions had little knowledge of, or contempt for, broadcasting, or whether they regarded programs made with the active collaboration of their members as a threat to their own power is hard to say.[23] It is true, however, that little of what appears over most national broadcasting systems would inspire most special-interest groups to feel that broadcasting could render a true picture of either their activities or their views on society. National programming, especially on television, tends to generalize and simplify.

Finally, a few nations (New Zealand, Great Britain) recently have begun to authorize citizen-operated stations for brief periods of time (a day or to up to a month) and usually in conjunction with a local event, such as a fair. Such an approach should help citizens to gain more experience with broadcasting and at less cost than is the case with *närradio,* where groups must commit themselves to the project for a full year.

Programming

As one listens to and views broadcasting around the world, it is interesting to note that broadcast schedules tend to bear a great deal of resemblance to one another. News and public affairs, sports and game shows, "light" and "heavy" fictional entertainment, all are present in considerable quantity in television schedules around the world, and in radio schedules too, *if* television hasn't been introduced yet, or is still in its early stages of growth. The evening hours tend to include the most mass-oriented entertainment, and newscasts tend to come on the hour, albeit not every hour (although that, too, is becoming increasingly common in systems with several radio services, where one of them generally will provide brief newscasts hourly). Sports and action-oriented fictional entertainment tend to be most popular, but newscasts are not far behind in most countries. Even styles of presentation tend to resemble one another, whether because of the modeling effect of imported programming, the influence of broadcast training classes taught by foreigners, perceived limitations of the media themselves (how many ways can one manipulate a camera or microphone?), or some combination of these factors.

But there are differences, as well, and these take two forms: the balance between domestic and imported broadcast material; and the balance and timing of presentation of program types. Many studies have been conducted on patterns of program importation and exportation, the most notable being the Nordenstreng and Varis 1974 UNESCO study,[24] the Guback and Varis 1982 UNESCO study,[25] the Varis 1985 UNESCO study,[26] and the 1986 Chapman et al. study.[27] None are definitive, inasmuch as gathering accurate data for such studies is extremely difficult, but all suggest that most of the world's television systems import more programming than they produce.

Those studies deal with TV only. If radio were to be studied in this manner, I suspect that it would reveal some quite distinct patterns of importation of popular music from the United States, Great Britain, and perhaps France by other American and European systems, but also a fairly heavy reliance by most radio (and TV) news operations on five or six major wire services, all of them in Europe (including the USSR's Tass) and the United States.

Whether imported programs are good or bad is an unanswerable question. In attempting to answer it, one should take into account not only the quantity of such importation (which may be the least important factor), but also the types of shows imported, their placement on the schedule, and the state of homogeneity/heterogeneity between the cultures of the exporting and importing systems, if that can be defined without reference to the influence of broadcasting. While the first three factors may be quantifiable, the fourth is not, which is what makes the question unanswerable.

But it is possible to make a rough estimate of homogeneity/heterogeneity by examining the cultural traditions of nations to see whether they include genres of entertainment, information, and education that resemble or differ from those of other nations. For example, the cultures of many of the Arab world nations include a tradition of very physical comedy routines, much in the manner of slapstick comedy in the western world. Thus, the U.S. situation comedy *I Love Lucy* did not violate many cultural norms and was quite compatible with others when it was broadcast on Egyptian TV. Similarly, there is a tradition of physical comedy in Thai culture, and many U.S. situation comedies find ready acceptance there. Drama portraying extreme and very realistic violence, however, may find no domestic counterpart in nations such as China, where the portrayal of violence in drama does not occur all that often, and where its presentation on those occasions is highly stylized.

There is more than the presentation of basic themes involved here, however. One of the touchiest aspects of the debate over "cultural imperialism" is the possible role of television in contributing to the "revolution of rising expectations." Schiller, Wells, Nordenstreng, and other writers have expressed the fear that TV programs imported from the western world (and from the United States in particular, since it exports more television entertainment than does any other country) will show viewers in developing nations a range of goods and services (dress, housing, diet, etc.) that are far beyond their personal or national means. Such portrayals may cause them to be dissatisfied with their lot in life, may bring them to reject much of what is good in their own traditions, and, in extreme cases, may lead them to revolution to address those perceived needs.[28]

Broadcast systems in many nations have erected various barriers against what they consider cultural imperialism. The most common is refusal to purchase "offensive" programs in the first place. That is not as simple as it sounds, however. First of all, imported programs almost always are much cheaper than those made by the domestic system. Second, neighboring countries may import and then broadcast some of those offensive programs, which may attract many domestic viewers. And third, there is great pressure on a broadcast system to make programming available for as much of the day and night as possible; given the first factor, imported programs appear to be a logical answer to meeting that demand. A second barrier is internal censorship, which can be used to eliminate anything from a five-second glimpse of an improperly dressed (by domestic standards) actor or actress to an entire episode from a series. Such prescreening takes time, money, and effort, as well as the guidance of a clearly articulated set of cultural standards, and some of the developing nations possess few or none of these.

A third barrier, seldom used, is the presentation of potentially offensive imported programs within a broader framework, where explanations before, during, and/or after the program are intended to help the audience assimilate the program within the domestic cultural context. Some of the communist systems have introduced certain U.S. programs at times with explanations that indicate that they are portrayals of life in the United States and worth seeing as examples of how materialistic or violent conditions are over there. There is a story (perhaps apocryphal) that a Thai television station introduced the U.S. situation comedy *Laverne and Shirley* to its audience by stating that it took place in an insane asylum! The devising and presentation of such explanations takes time, money, effort, and a set of cultural standards, too, and might or might not have the desired effect upon the audience.

Barriers notwithstanding, there is a great deal of imported programming on television stations in most countries around the world — more in the developing nations, to be sure, but plenty in the smaller nations of Western Europe and even quite a bit among the Eastern European nations. Much of it is entertainment, but much of it is information, too, through the largest wire services and through special television services such as UPITN (United Press/Independent Television News) and Visnews, or through the Eurovision and Intervision news exchange services. Only educational programming seems largely domestic, and even there many developing countries import the *Let's Learn English* (French, German, etc.) series from the United States, Great Britain, France, West Germany, and so on, as well as other categories of in-school and adult education programs, the latter very often from their former colonial mentors (e.g., Great Britain or France).

Whether imported programs are "bad" or "good" is a personal value judgment and has been subjected to very little empirical testing. It is safe to say that such programs have brought images of a much wider world to viewers than most of them ever had seen before the advent of television. It is also safe to say that patterns of importation/exportation are unlikely to change much over the next decade or two, if only because the alternatives—more domestic production or shorter broadcast hours— seem unattainable or unthinkable to most broadcast systems, their financiers, and/or their audiences.

Just as there are differences in patterns of importation and domestic production of programs, so are there differences in scheduling practices. If there is a norm for scheduling and for programming in North American broadcast systems, it is for a radio broadcasting day that begins at 6:00 A.M. and ends in the late afternoon or evening hours if a station is licensed to broadcast only during daylight hours, or a day that often does not end at all if the station is allowed to broadcast after dark. Television stations, none of which have "daylight hours only" restrictions, usually begin around 6:00 A.M. and stop around midnight or 1:00 A.M., although increasing numbers of stations in large cities are telecasting around the clock, too.

Most radio schedules are filled with popular music, with individual stations specializing in one category of popular music (e.g., country and western) and offering brief hourly newscasts, most of whose items come from the wire services. (The U.S. radio stations that belong to National Public Radio or that operate noncommercially on limited power [community radio], and Canada's CBC networks, offer greater variety, although even they often play large amounts of music.) Most TV stations feature light entertainment during the daylight hours; even the two-hour-long information shows provided by the U.S. commercial networks at the beginning of the day (e.g., ABC's *Good Morning America*) contain many entertaining items. Quiz and game shows, soap operas, talk shows (e.g., *The Phil Donahue Show*), and reruns of old network entertainment series abound on U.S., Canadian, and Mexican commercial stations, while educational material, sometimes directed to school, sometimes to adults at home, generally is relegated to the public stations (the CBC, Mexico's Television Cultural de Mexico, and U.S. public TV), which often are not as widely available to the public as are the commercial stations.

It is hard for someone who never has seen television or heard radio outside North America to realize that there is any other way of scheduling programs. In fact, there are a few systems in other countries whose practices do resemble those just presented. The Australian and Japanese commercial systems look and sound a good deal like their North American counterparts, aside from all-night broadcasting, which some of their radio stations, but fewer of their TV stations, attempt. Some South American commercial systems, especially Brazil's, also bear a close resemblance. In the developing countries, where money is in short supply and where a given system may have to supply broadcasts in a dozen or more languages, one would not expect radio and TV schedules to resemble those of North American stations, and generally speaking, they do not. But Europe, one might think, would be a different proposition. Certainly people must want to have radio and television available most of the day and night.

It is quite possible that people *do* want more broadcasting than they get, but the prevailing philosophy among European broadcasters and their governments usually has been to provide programs, both in general and in particular, on a more limited basis than what the public might want. Twenty-four-hour-a-day radio services are largely a phenomenon of the past ten to fifteen years (Radio Luxembourg and Radio Monte Carlo, both of them commercial enterprises, offered such services earlier than that), and many European nations still do not have them. The typical television day in the smaller European nations offers little but educational programs in the morning, a brief newscast and possibly a talk show or a household hints program during the noon hour, programs for children in the late afternoon hours (and possibly some light entertainment, often syndicated U.S. situation comedies), news around 6:00 P.M. and a mixture of light entertainment, documentaries, interviews, serious drama, cultural productions (operas, symphonies, etc.) and the major newscast of the day during the evening hours. There are feature films on some nights, but more often than not these will be aired after 10:00 P.M. Advertisements are usually clustered and presented during an early evening hour and do not interrupt programs or, for the most part, appear between programs. If there is only one national TV system, programs may begin and end at odd times, rather than on the hour or half hour, as there is no need for a rigid schedule that enables local stations to schedule their own commercials or insert their own programs.

European broadcast systems in the larger nations are beginning to expand the TV schedule a bit, partly in response to popular demand. For example, some of them are repeating some of the previous evening's programs on the following morning for those whose schedules did not permit viewing at the original time of broadcast. Great Britain's BBC and IBA introduced breakfast-time television in late 1982 and early 1983, respectively, and *Good Morning Britain* and *The Breakfast Show* both bear strong resemblances to the National Broadcasting Corporation's (NBC's) *Today* and comparable programs in the United States. France and Spain followed suit in the mid-1980s. Even with those changes, however, most national-system TV schedules in Europe include small to large blocks of time during the morning and afternoon when only TV test patterns fill the screen and/or when only highly specialized programs (e.g., adult or secondary education) are on the air.

There are financial reasons for those differences in scheduling, of course, but it would be possible for most of the European national systems to fill the gaps in the television day with more repeats and with syndicated material, which would not add that much to the cost. Something else is at work, and it appears to be this: that the prevailing European public broadcasting philosophy of providing limited amounts of programming has an underlying social philosophy of providing what is best for the public. *Best,* of course, has different definitions among the various systems, but the idea is generally to provide a wide variety of programs and to present a good share of that variety at times when most people will be available to see it (or hear it, since the philosophy applies to certain types of radio services, too), whether they choose to do so or not. In that way, the public's tastes and levels of information might be broadened, and most European public broadcast administrators see that as an essential function of broadcasting. It also is important for that wide variety of programs to be as well produced as possible, so that programs are not "ghettoized" in scheduling or in quality. This in turn means that financial resources and studio time probably will not be sufficient to fill the entire broadcast day and night.

There is also the feeling among European public broadcasters that they should produce as much of their own material as possible rather than rely upon imported programs. (The fact that most European public broadcast systems play roles as patrons of the arts, commissioning various original works, is important, too.) And finally, paternalistic as it might sound, most European public broadcasters feel that their audiences should not depend upon broadcasting for an unbroken flow of programming but should be able to find other leisure-time pursuits.

For, in the final analysis, listening to radio and watching television usually are seen as leisure-time pursuits, first and foremost. National laws of broadcasting may call upon the media to inform, educate, and entertain, and there are very few nations where any of the three is missing (although different parts of the overall system may serve as primary or exclusive channels for one or another of those functions). However, entertainment usually receives the lion's share of airtime. Of course, that entertainment also may inform, educate, shape peoples' understanding of prevailing social norms, convey some sense of social, political, or cultural history, and so on, but at least one of its functions will be to allow people to relax, sit back, and enjoy what comes out of the speaker and over the screen.

One nation that started out with a very different view of the functions of television was India, where for the initial years of TV, entertainment as such had no place. The medium was to be used to inform and educate; while that information and education might be presented in an entertaining manner, this was not the primary purpose of the broadcasts.[29] But as television signals covered more and more of the country, and as more and more people began purchasing sets, pressures mounted for longer broadcast days and more entertaining programs. The result is that Indian television as of the mid-1980s carries more entertainment than anything else, although its use for educational purposes still receives a great deal of governmental support. It may be that television is especially well suited to the transmission of entertainment, but it also may be that the citizens of any country just beginning to develop the medium already know that it is being used for that purpose all around the globe and expect the same for themselves.

Another way in which broadcast programming practices differ is in the extent of local and regional, as contrasted with national, programming that is allowed, encouraged, or even required. Because of their depressed economic conditions, many developing nations cannot even consider the development of regional and local broadcast services, although Indonesia, India, Nigeria, and several others do have services at those levels. But many industrially developed nations did very little or even nothing along those lines during most of the history of radio, and some have only begun to develop regional and local radio services over the past decade, while relatively few Western and Eastern European nations have regional or local television services of any size. Instead, broadcasting usually has been developed as a national service, with brief periods each day for regional news and public-affairs programs (entertainment seldom appears on the schedule). While Sweden, Finland, Norway, Denmark, France, Great Britain, West Germany, and Italy all have promoted the development of regional (and sometimes local) radio stations with greater program diversity, often including more regional and local entertainment, television at those levels usually remains restricted to news and public affairs. (Italian and British commercial TV services are exceptions.) The national service may provide regionally based entertainment (although a frequent criticism of such programming is that it is too "big-city" or "capital" centered). These programs may be useful as a way of reinforcing the cultural diversity of a nation, allowing all viewers to share in that diversity, but it is those in charge of the national service who usually decide how much and what sorts of regional culture are displayed.

Such national systems may operate in this manner because the financial base, usually license fees, cannot be expanded sufficiently to make possible highly developed regional and local broadcasting. But there also are fears on the part of some national governments that national unity might be harmed by too much emphasis on regional and local broadcasting, and some European nations (e.g., France with Corsican nationalism, Spain with Basque nationalism) are vulnerable in that respect (although there are regional radio and television services for both the Corsicans and the Basques).

The coming of cable TV to parts of Western Europe, along with the "privatization" of broadcasting in a few nations — Italy and France in a major way, West Germany, Finland, Iceland, and Denmark to a more modest degree — is beginning to change the shape of TV scheduling. Imported TV entertainment predominates, and some of the new services are on for eighteen to twenty-four hours a day. Ads sometimes interrupt programs. It still is too early to tell how much effect these new services will have on the older national systems, but some of those older services already are fighting back, chiefly by making every effort to bring in the best of imported entertainment themselves, often at a hefty price and therefore at some cost to the overall budget for programming, which of course includes domestic programming. Videocassette recorders, too, are making their presence felt in many nations,[30] although their major impact in Western Europe seems to have been to slow the growth of cable.

Conclusion

Can one consider the host of factors presented in this chapter and select any that are especially well suited to serve as common denominators through which any broadcast system can be better understood? Certainly the basic factors of geography, population characteristics, economy, cultural and political makeup of the nation have influence upon all broadcast systems, but the specific influence of any one of them will vary over time and from country to country. The manner in which systems are financed, administered, governed, and influenced likewise varies a good deal among nations, and while some individuals claim that their broadcast systems come as close to perfection as humans can expect, none of those claims has gone unchallenged. Modes of interaction between broadcast systems and their audiences vary just as much, and so do approaches to programming, although there appears to be increasing homogeneity in television program scheduling.

Actually, all of the factors presented here should help to increase one's understanding of broadcasting, if one seeks to learn how broadcasting has been, is being, and might be used to serve society. The factors themselves are common to all broadcast systems; an understanding of them should make it easier to observe how and why systems resemble each other and differ, and what each might profitably learn from another's experiences. Some nations, faced with the challenge of reformulating a system or introducing a new element (television, cable, videotext, DBS) into the existing one, have examined other systems in order to avoid repeating their mistakes and/or to profit from their successes. The old adage that those who will not learn from history are doomed to repeat its mistakes applies just as well to broadcasting as it does to any other human venture. The six broadcast systems presented in the following chapters do not run the entire gamut of experiences, but for various reasons they have had influences extending far beyond their national boundaries.

2

France

From Competition to Monopoly and Back Again

FOR many years the French broadcasting system was dismissed by most scholars as unworthy of emulation in any respect. That was primarily due to the chaotic nature of French broadcasting throughout most of the 1950s and to the often heavy-handed political interference with it during the terms of President Charles de Gaulle and his successors, Georges Pompidou and Valery Giscard d'Estaing. But those very problems can serve as object lessons of how a broadcast system should not operate. Furthermore, the French system, thanks to the size of France's colonial empire, has reappeared to a greater or lesser degree in many of the former French colonies and protectorates in Africa, so that its influence has been pervasive. And finally, the French system underwent a number of rapid and fundamental transformations in the early to mid-1980s — an experience that serves as a case study of how a change in political leadership can alter an established system of broadcasting in a major way.[1]

Basic Factors

GEOGRAPHIC   France is the largest country in Europe, excluding the Soviet Union. Its unified land mass covers over 580,000 square kilometers (about four-fifths the size of Texas). Most of the northern half of the country is relatively flat, and the major mountain ranges lie on the eastern and southwestern borders. There is a large and fairly high plateau in the center south, the *massif central,* but it rises gradually. The French terrain in general presents no overwhelming problems for broadcasting.

France has several neighbors, but three of the four larger ones lie behind barriers of one sort or another. Spain is almost completely screened off by the Pyrenees Mountains, Italy likewise by the Mediterranean Alps, and Great Britain by the channel. West Germany shares a rather long section of border with few barriers, and Luxembourg, Belgium, and Switzerland also share relatively barrier-free borders, although the Swiss border is quite mountainous in places. The bulk of the country, excluding the Breton Peninsula, fits quite nicely within a circle and includes little of the territory of its neighbors within that circle. Its geographical shape is conducive to broadcasting, and a powerful radio transmitter set up near the center of the country can reach its borders quite comfortably and without too much spillover into adjoining nations.

The country is not very densely populated by European standards. There are about one hundred inhabitants to the square kilometer, far lower than West Germany, Great Britain, Italy, and certainly the Netherlands. While the vast majority of the French live in towns and cities, there are fairly few really large cities: Only six had populations in excess of five hundred thousand as of the mid-1980s, and only one metropolitan area, Paris, was much over a million — 8.7 million at the time. Those larger cities are scattered around the country, but they are linked with Paris far more efficiently than they are with one another. The major rail lines and the road and airline networks all converge on Paris, and often it is quicker to travel from one large city to another via Paris than it is to use a more geographically direct route. That centralizing tendency has had its impact upon broadcasting, as well.

DEMOGRAPHIC   It has been of great value to France that the country has had one language and one basically universal manner of using that language for several centuries. It has been of equally great value that the country has had relatively stable borders for a similar period, although wars at various times have brought foreign invaders onto French soil. For the most part, France has been able to develop as a nation with a strong national language and widely shared national culture since the mid-1400s. France contrasts strongly with Italy and Germany, and to a lesser extent Great Britain, in those respects. Even if the French often are depicted as a highly individualistic people, they are very homogeneous in many respects.

In recent years, that homogeneity has been compromised somewhat by the influx of guest workers, who now make up about 9 percent of the French population, and who largely come from North Africa and Portugal. Most of the guest workers are in the larger cities, entire quarters of which may be virtually dominated by them. Little was done to provide them with broadcast services until the advent of local radio in the early 1980s, and even then there was little systematic encouragement of such services. Much the same has been true for the country's minority-language speakers (Breton, Provençal), although it is doubtful that any speaker of Breton or Provençal would not be capable of speaking fluent French, as well.

ECONOMIC   Like most other Western European nations, France has become heavily industrialized during the twentieth century. However, it continues to have a larger percentage of its population engaged in agriculture than is typical of Western Europe: as of 1984, roughly 8 percent of the overall population. The agricultural sector often is criticized for inefficiency, but it is jealously protected by the French government, which has engaged in countless battles with other European Economic Community members over what those members see as agricultural protectionism. French broadcasting has served the agricultural community since the 1920s with market reports and information on new agricultural techniques and products, and the first concerted attempt to utilize television for rural development came in France in 1952.[2]

Industrialization in France in the first half of the twentieth century took the traditional form of manufacturing: steel, automobiles, and appliances, some of which were exported. Most of that industrialization could be accomplished by the country's own citizens. In the 1950s, industrialization expanded into other spheres, and a generally booming European economy brought French industry increasing orders, so more and more of the work force had to be recruited from outside the country, bringing cities such as Paris, Lyons, Lille, and Clermont-Ferrand their first sizable agglomerations of Southern European and North African residents.

The 1950s also saw French industry, and not least of all the service industry, hampered by frequent strikes, as workers sought what they regarded as a fairer share in the country's prosperity and in some cases a more powerful voice in the management of business enterprises. Broadcasting frequently was a target of those strikes, either on the part of workers protesting government censorship of information or on the part of broadcast staff protesting that same censorship as well as working conditions and pay. Yet France is not a particularly heavily unionized country; less than 20 percent of the labor force belongs to unions, and that percentage is dropping.

CULTURAL   The French are justly proud of their cultural achievements, which include the work of some of the greatest painters, poets, philosophers, sculptors, composers, musicians, and architects in western civilization. They also are proud of their educational system, which is mandatory until the age of sixteen and which includes a heavy emphasis on those cultural achievements—some would say to the point of cultural chauvinism. The educational system is centralized to the point where, for certain subjects, every student throughout France who happens to be enrolled in a given course will be studying the same material on a given day of the week. It is not a system that encourages individualism or innovation, and certain French critics, such as J. J. Sevran-Schreiber, have blamed it for hindering French economic development in the postindustrial age. That same uniformity and lack of individualism have made it possible to utilize radio and television in education on a broad national scale, but there is little that one would call progressive or innovative in that utilization.

Manifestations of French national culture are famous the world over, but the country also possesses a rich regional and local cultural heritage. It may be rare these days to see "the locals" in country towns wearing wooden shoes or lace bonnets every day of the week (although it wasn't all that rare as recently as the 1950s), but folk dancing and singing still occur spontaneously, and there has been a revival of interest in regional languages and literatures, aided in some cases by the creation of local commercial and noncommercial radio stations in the early 1980s.

Religion is a force in French cultural life if for no other reason than the sheer magnitude of cultural enterprises represented within the Roman Catholic Church, to which approximately 90 percent of the French belong, at least nominally. The church operates educational institutions, sponsors cultural activities, participates actively in political life, and is engaged in various welfare enterprises. Its influence on broadcasting is indirect, in that it operates few stations of its own and does not enjoy any formal rights of participation in broadcast advisory councils, but station administrators are well aware of its presence and take its sensitivities into account in making programming decisions. For example, birth control was a virtual taboo subject for French broadcasters until the late 1970s, which accounted for the large audiences attracted by Radio Luxembourg's programs on sex education (the station is received easily in northern France, including Paris).

POLITICAL   France has been a parliamentary democracy for well over a
century, but there have been periods of time during which political
parties followed each other in rapid succession as governments rose and
fell several times a year, and others during which a strong political leader
held and exercised power with little reference to the parties. Since 1958,
France has had a popularly elected president who also serves as chief
executive; before that date, the chief executive was the prime minister,
chosen by whichever party, or more likely, coalition of parties, could
command a majority in the House of Deputies, the more powerful by far
of the two branches of Parliament. (The other branch is the Senate.)

French politics features a number of political parties, most of which
ally themselves with other political parties in order to obtain enough votes
on a given issue at least to make their voices heard, if not to pass or defeat
the issue. As of 1987, there were five political parties represented in the
House of Deputies, displaying political philosophies that ranged from
extreme right to extreme left. Representatives are popularly elected, and
elections are held every five years. Votes of no confidence can result in the
dissolution of a government but would not result in the resignation of the
president.

France is a highly centralized nation in political terms, and the regions and departments into which the country is divided have little real
power of self-governance, although the Socialist government of François
Mitterand conferred more power on local governments in the early 1980s.
It is possible for a politician to rise to prominence from a local or regional
power base, and several mayors have done so, but that has been more a
case of individual charisma and, most often, the advantage of being
mayor of a large city with consequent media attention. Until the very late
1970s, however, that media attention would have been in the form of
newspaper or magazine attention, because radio and television either were
largely apolitical or were in the service of whichever political party was in
power. The history of French broadcasting, as you will see, is heavily
influenced by politics, but the ways in which that political influence has
manifested itself have varied a great deal over time.

A Brief History

The early history of French broadcasting closely resembles the early
history of broadcasting in most industrialized nations: a good deal of
activity on the part of radio amateurs using homemade equipment, little

interest on the part of the government in setting up its own radio service, and considerable interest on the part of manufacturers of sets and parts in establishing their own stations. There had been experiments in radio transmission from the Eiffel Tower in Paris as early as 1906, and meteorological reports were broadcast daily from the tower starting in 1921. When the first regularly scheduled radio broadcasts began in November 1922, they came from a Paris-based station (Radio Paris) operated by a company that manufactured radio equipment and saw the station as a way of promoting set sales. The station was licensed by the government through the PTT (posts and telegraph), had some very general program standards as a condition of its license, could not carry ads, and had to pay an annual license fee to the government.

Several months later, the French government enlarged the scope of programming offered over its Eiffel Tower station, making it sound much more like Radio Paris: concerts, readings, interviews, sports, radio plays, and so on. In 1924 the Eiffel Tower station added a daily newscast; Radio Paris already had occasional news bulletins and in 1925 reached an agreement with the French news agency Havas (which also was an investor in the station) that gave the station and any further stations founded by its parent corporation, the Companie Française de Radio (CFR), exclusive rights to use Havas material in their broadcasts. Thus there was competition of sorts between public and private radio almost from the beginning of regular service.

A decree passed in 1923 had granted concessions for private radio stations for a period of ten years, but the decree also mentioned the possibility that the government would take over those stations sometime during the ten-year period. A 1926 decree reaffirmed that limitation, but it did permit private stations and the PTT station to carry ads, and most stations quickly began to do so. Private stations sprouted up in other parts of France—by 1926 Lyons, Montpellier, Toulouse, Bordeaux, and several smaller cities had them—and CFR proposed the creation of a private network. Most of the other private stations were uninterested in or even hostile to the idea, but some French government officials thought it a viable approach for the government to take. They were intrigued by the possibility of employing radio as an instrument of national unity, and from the early 1920s on the various decrees made it a condition of licensing that stations use "proper" French in their broadcasts and avoid slang and regional dialects. However, the government was unwilling to provide the PTT with much of a budget for radio (funding for the station came directly from the government, and listeners had no license fee to pay), and radio did not become a separate administrative unit within the PTT until 1927. The private stations clearly had the upper hand in providing broadcasts to listeners throughout the country, simply because they were available in many places where the PTT station was not. But they were not unified—indeed, many of their owners were bitter enemies—and eventually the PTT came out on top.

The major shift in power came in 1933, a year when, as some previous decrees had stated, private broadcasting was to cease. (The 1926 decree had set 1931 as the termination date.) In the early 1930s, the PTT had raided and closed a few of the smaller unauthorized private stations, most of which never were on the air for more than a few months, anyway. The year 1933 did not bring the cessation of private radio, but the PTT was able to use that limitation to justify its purchase of Radio Paris and to place further restrictions on the development of the remaining private stations (thirteen by this time). The PTT also acquired a new form of financial support in 1933, when for the first time French listeners were required to pay annual license fees for the privilege of receiving broadcasts. None of the fee money went to private stations; none went directly to the PTT, either, but it could be used as a basis for requesting annual appropriations from the government. Those appropriations now increased and allowed the PTT to expand its services and create a genuine national network—something the private stations never had managed to achieve. In 1935 a new decree gave the private stations the exclusive right to carry ads but placed further restrictions upon them that would insure the primacy of the PTT network.

As the PTT system became more important, government officials began to take more interest in it. The director of the PTT radio station reported directly to the minister of posts, and there was a direct telephone link between the two offices, which high government officials did not hesitate to use. Some of the private stations were owned in part by leading politicians, and some of those politicians used the stations to support their own views and to ignore or oppose the views of other politicians and of the government. To help counteract such usage, the PTT, which licensed all stations, placed a new condition on them in decrees issued in 1934 and 1935: Each would have to have councils of management directly elected by the listeners. The councils would have some power in deciding broadcast policy. They rapidly became very political, and in 1937, elections to them became a straightforward contest between government and opposition.[3]

The mid-1930s saw some hotly contested national elections, and political parties sought more and more to express their views over radio. Both private and PTT stations broadcast speeches and news items about the campaigns, as well as election results. The use of radio during the

1936 election campaign was especially widespread at a local level, and the party coalition that finally emerged victorious decided that henceforth it would be better if all radio news reporting were done from Paris, so the PTT decreed a ban on local news broadcasts. That was one more link in the centralization and consolidation of control over radio by the government, and it was followed by a 1936 decree creating a Conseil Supérieur des Emissions de la Radiodiffusion to supervise the preparation of network broadcasts from Paris.[4] A 1938 decree established strict surveillance of programs on economic, financial, and political topics. And in July 1939, radio was made a separate administrative operation under the direct supervision of the president of the council (prime minister), the better to function as a "powerful instrument of moral defense," presumably against Nazi propaganda. The private stations, now twelve, continued to function but had to broadcast official news bulletins at fixed times and saw a decrease in advertising revenue as the war drew near. One of them, Radio Normandie, was taken over by the French government in 1939 presumably to assist in the war effort but, according to René Duval, in part because of some personal grudges.[5]

In June 1940 the French government surrendered to the Nazis and the four-year occupation of France began. The country was divided in two, the northern half administered directly by the Germans and the southern half by a French government acceptable to the Germans. The German occupation government took over all stations in its area, using some of them for domestic broadcasts and others for broadcasts to other parts of Europe. The French had been experimenting with television several years before the war; this, too, was taken over by the Nazis, who produced and regularly broadcast TV programs in the Paris region, to their own personnel and to the French, until shortly before the liberation of Paris in 1944.[6] The French government in the south (the Vichy government, named after its capital) continued to operate the PTT-founded system but became more and more involved with the private stations, as well: Lacking advertising revenue, the latter became dependent upon government subsidies for their continued existence, and in 1943 the government bought up the hitherto private Société Financiére de Radiodiffusion (SOFIRAD), which in turn bought up 50 percent of the shares in the newly created (largely by the Germans and Italians) Radio Monte Carlo.

Furthermore, a law of November 1942 gave the national (government) radio operation the power to buy shares in private stations. The Vichy government made heavy use of radio to propagandize, and the only counterweights to its messages came from outside the country— London, Brazzaville, New York, Moscow, and, later in the war, North

Africa. By 1944 the private stations had been absorbed completely into the national system. Their owners may have hoped for better things to come as the liberation of France began in May 1944, but if so those hopes soon were dashed.

MONOPOLY IN THE FOURTH REPUBLIC (1944–58)   The allied forces liberated Paris in June of 1944, and most of the remaining parts of France were freed from the Germans by the end of the year. The new French government, functioning under the leadership of Gen. Charles de Gaulle, set to work bringing order out of relative chaos. Where radio was concerned, the Germans had left much destruction in their wake, and allied air raids and ground attacks had added to that destruction, but there remained a fairly viable nucleus of facilities, public and private. A March 1945 ordinance revoked all private licenses; some private station owners were compensated, others were not, and a few even were jailed as alleged collaborators with the Nazis — allegations that may have stemmed from personal grudges.[7] Vichy government laws pertaining to radio were abolished, but some elements from them began to appear in new legislative proposals. In November 1945, a decree established the Radiodiffusion-Télévision Française (RTF), but on a temporary basis. However, attempts of other groups to get the government to consider alternative approaches proved futile.

Thomas indicates that there were more than a dozen statutes on alternative forms of broadcasting proposed between 1945 and 1958, but none received serious consideration. The French government — or rather governments, as coalitions moved in and out of power frequently during that period — seemed satisfied to let the monopoly stand, and even coalitions that might have been expected to favor the rebirth of private broadcasting stood pat with the RTF.[8]

Staff members of RTF found plenty of grounds to express their dissatisfaction, however. The period 1944–59 saw over eighty strikes, sometimes regarding salaries but at least as often over questions of editorial and artistic freedom. The RTF remained firmly under the government's control; the director general of RTF was selected by the French cabinet and reported directly to the minister of information (a wartime office that persisted in peacetime), while the director of radio news was directly appointed by that minister. The RTF operated as a civil service department, which meant that its annual budget was voted by Parliament and that its accounting practices had to follow civil service rules dating from 1862. Virtually all financial operations required prior consent of the Ministry of Finance. The structure was an administrative nightmare, and the modest budgets approved by Parliament added to the frustration.[9]

The fact that governments came and went with such rapidity meant that almost none of them tried to use radio and, later in the 1950s, television to support their particular policies. Presumably none of them wanted other political coalitions to use radio to support *their* positions should *they* come to power. Instead, they interfered chiefly by "asking" RTF not to cover or at least not to emphasize certain events, for example, North African resistance to French colonial rule there. As the conflicts in North Africa became more numerous and violent, the various governing coalitions clamped down on RTF even harder, but domestic events occasioned pressures from the top, as well: In 1957 the government suppressed a broadcast declaration by Fréderic Joliet-Curie against nuclear weapons, and an RTF interviewer faced threats of dismissal because he had interviewed politicians who opposed the then prime minister, Guy Mollet.

Television mattered little to any political party at first. Television broadcasts resumed in 1947, though not on weekends, but by 1950 there still were only four thousand sets in the entire country. By 1954 there were sixty thousand, and finally by 1958 over a million, but that was in a nation of perhaps 12 million households. Television news at first was considered unimportant, and it was controlled by the director of television. By the mid-1950s, it had come under the control of the director of radio news, who reported directly to the minister of information. Henri Spade suggests that the practice of holding daily conferences between RTF and the Ministry of Information on the makeup of each day's TV newscast started them.[10] (The head of radio news had been conferring daily with government ministers on news content since 1948.)[11] Some producers resented what they saw as censorship, especially of news about developments in North Africa, and a few refused to continue producing their programs. There was no alternative source of television, either for producers to express their points of view or for audiences to receive them. Unlike radio, where stations from around the periphery of France (Radio Monte Carlo in Monaco, Europe No. One in the Saar, Radio Andorra in Andorra, and, largest of all, Radio Luxembourg in Luxembourg) sometimes provided contrasting material, few foreign TV stations could be seen by any French viewers. Even at that, the government seemed anxious to insure that those viewers in areas able to receive outside signals (Strasbourg from West Germany in particular) have French TV as soon as possible, and indeed the second TV transmitter outside of Paris was in Strasbourg (1953).

THE FIFTH REPUBLIC BEGINS (1958–64)   A 1958 statement made by a
former director of RTF makes it quite clear that the state and those
who run it are in the best position to judge how broadcasting should be
used for the benefit of the people. After Gabriel Delaunay had attacked
television systems that were "over-responsive to immediate public demand," he went on to say, "A modern state has the duty to consider
radio and television as an essential element of its domestic life, as a
necessary expression of its radiance, as the best means of making last
that which continues to give it its grandeur. France, and France more
than any other nation, since it has an exceptionally radiant past to defend, would thus commit a serious error if, faced with a thing so excep-
tional and so revolutionary, it were to abandon itself to empiricism,
being content to follow and imitate, not setting a policy and defining the
means to realize that policy."[12] Complaints about the quality of broadcast services, and especially about the censored newscasts and the many
dull discussion and talk programs, appeared regularly in the press, and
listeners frequently turned to the peripheral services in Monaco, the
Saar, Andorra, and Luxembourg for alternatives to the RTF services.
Those services also profited from their ability to handle live reporting
better than did the rather traditional and less well equipped RTF staff.[13]
Occasionally RTF reporters appearing on the street were booed and
hissed and even pelted with rotten fruit.

The coming to power of Charles de Gaulle in 1958 did not bring
with it any marked degree of liberalization. For one thing, de Gaulle
believed in the need for a strong hand to "guide" (some would say "order") French broadcasting, which could play in important role in reinforcing French culture at home and spreading it abroad. For another, he
felt that radio and TV could be useful politically and soon set about
using it to "personalize" the French presidency. Stiff and seemingly un-
sure of himself at first, de Gaulle evolved into a skilled performer, especially on television. He developed a more informal style of speaking,
often delivering his remarks while seated (rare for a French politician on
TV in those days). He also appeared on TV frequently.

The daily conferences involving RTF staff and ministerial representatives became a more formal institution soon after de Gaulle took office.
The Interministerial Information Liaison Service (SLII), set up by and
under the Ministry of Information, undertook the planning of each day's
news programs. According to the then assistant director of television,
Jacques Thibau, the meetings centered on items that should *not* be covered and on inaugurations and ceremonies that should receive maximum
coverage.[14] The new government passed a statute in 1959; under it, RTF
became an autonomous public institution, but the government named its

director general, and it was not to have its own board of directors. If anything, the statue increased the degree of governmental control.

De Gaulle and his political followers ignored criticisms of their heavy-handed treatment of French broadcasting. He is alleged to have claimed on more than one occasion, "My opponents have the press. Why shouldn't I have television?" The 1962 election saw a tremendous imbalance between appearances on TV of the Gaullists and appearances of opposition candidates. Protests of that imbalance were widespread in the press, and even within RTF, where there was a protest strike in October 1962. But the government dealt with such internal opposition by asking RTF management (itself thoroughly Gaullist by then) to suspend or dismiss protestors, and many had to leave.[15] When Alain Peyrefitte took over as minister of information in 1962, his predecessor showed him a row of buttons at his desk, which were to be used to call the heads of radio and TV news "just like calling in the cleaning woman" in order to eliminate whatever might be displeasing in the evening news.[16]

There was enough ill feeling over this abuse of power to lead the French National Assembly to pass a law in November 1962, followed by a decree in March 1964, which guaranteed opposition parties, as well as the parties involved in the governing coalition, the right to equal amounts of airtime in election campaigns. Furthermore, a national commission composed of senior magistrates was to supervise RTF's practices in order to insure fairness. But some politicians felt that more sweeping reforms were necessary. André Diligent, a deputy and member of a political party that had broken away from the Gaullist coalition, proposed in 1962 that there be a new administrative structure that would include an administrative council made up of members of the public and of the government, and that the council should select the director general of RTF. His proposal was adopted unanimously by the Assembly's Cultural and Social Affairs Committee but never got beyond that stage. Prime Minister Georges Pompidou promised Parliament in October of 1962 that the government would propose a new statute, but that did not emerge until 1964. In the meantime, the Assembly debated what to do about broadcasting, the press continued to criticize its rival media, and there were further strikes at RTF, partly in order to press home the need for a new statute.

The bill regarding broadcasting was debated intensely in May and June, and both houses of the Assembly passed numerous amendments; the Senate, the weaker of the two bodies but the one in which the opposition was in the majority, rejected most of the major points in the government's proposal. A joint committee worked out a compromise, but the government would not accept it and forced the Assembly to approve the original bill.[17] On 27 June 1964, the statute became law, the RTF was abolished and the new Office de Radiodiffusion-Télévision Française (ORTF) took its place. To the audience, the change would prove to be almost unnoticeable.

THE ORTF (1964–74)   The one change in the broadcast organization's initials — O for Office — was supposed to be significant. It would mean that there would be an administrative council and a director general. Furthermore, the administrative council would be made up half of representatives of the state and half of representatives of viewers and listeners, the press, ORTF itself, and "highly qualified persons" (usually people who were well-known artists, diplomats, etc.). The council would approve and supervise the ORTF budget, would examine the quality and moral tone of broadcasting, would assure objectivity and accuracy, and would see to it that "principal trends of thought" could find expression through ORTF broadcasts. On the surface, all of that sounded like André Diligent's 1962 proposal. Beneath the surface, the government was as involved as ever. It appointed all members of the council; "representative organizations" could submit lists of qualified nominees, but the government made the final choice, and it chose individuals who were favorably inclined toward its policies. The government also retained power of appointment of the director general and the two deputy directors general. In theory, the council and the director general shared power, but the arrangement was not clearly defined in the new law, and it soon became evident that the director general held the balance of that power.

The annual license fee continued to supply most of the annual budget, but it was still up to the minister of information and the National Assembly to decide the size of that budget, although the onerous system of control that had required prior approval of expenditures in the RTF was modified to cover "only" recruitment, pay, and promotion of permanent staff; program expenditures themselves could be approved after the fact. Program advisory committees now were authorized, and covered music, science, literature and drama, and light entertainment. But their membership, too, was appointed by the government. As the old French saying goes, *Plus ça change, plus c'est la même chose.* (The more things change, the more they remain the same.)

It wasn't long before the implications of that saying became evident to viewers and listeners. A second TV channel came on the air in 1964, but it offered few real alternatives. There was a temporary flourishing of magazine programs, and some of them presented the views of political opponents of de Gaulle and dealt with hitherto little-covered subjects such as unemployment and prejudice (the ending of the Algerian War in 1963 saw an influx of French citizens living in Algeria and of Algerians who chose to leave their native land, but neither group found a very warm welcome in France). Already by 1965 there were governmental pressures on producers of those programs to tone them down. The 1965 presidential election campaign saw scrupulous adherence to the principle of fair and equal division of airtime among the six main parties, but that pertained only to airtime set aside for political campaigning during the official election campaign. De Gaulle had decreed early in 1964 that broadcasting would be closed to all presidential candidates until two weeks before the election,but that limitation did not apply to himself.[18] Nor did it apply to other members of the Gaullist coalition when they ran for office: They were frequent guests on interview and talk shows. Television reporters covering opposition candidates were instructed to shoot them from the back, so that their faces would not be visible.[19] Newscasts showed opposition party members in the Assembly stumbling over their words.[20]

There was a spate of current-affairs programs in 1966 that showed some promise. Not only did the political opposition obtain frequent and fair coverage, but Gaullist politicians sometimes faced tough and even hostile questions from journalists. That may have been a welcome change to viewers hoping for more balance from broadcasting, but as the 1967 legislative elections drew nearer, government control tightened. In November 1966, the cabinet decided that there would be an equal division of campaign broadcast time between the two Gaullist parties and the four main and several smaller opposition parties—hardly the sort of "equal time" principle covered in the 1963 statute. Then, on the eve of election day, and after formal campaigning had closed, President de Gaulle came on TV to make a special appeal to the nation for its electoral support. Political parties from right to left, excepting of course the Gaullist parties, condemned the move—the Communist paper *L'Humanité* called it "a characteristic rape" and the leader of an extreme right-wing party called upon the ORTF technicians to strike (they didn't)—but their condemnations had no effect. The Gaullists won the election.[21]

As blatant as was that interference by the government, it paled by comparison with what happened in May 1968. Ironically, the Senate had released a report by a special Senate commission on the ORTF only weeks earlier. The commission was chaired by the same André Diligent who had submitted a proposal for the reform of broadcasting in 1962. The 1968 Diligent Report was highly critical of the ORTF, although it acknowledged that there had been some improvement. It saw the administrative council as largely ineffective because the Gaullists controlled it and because there were no clear lines of authority for it. The report also noted the increasing sense of professionalism within ORTF but added that that professionalism was coupled with a growing sense of frustration on the part of staff members, especially journalists. The report recommended that the ORTF function through the minister of culture rather than the minister of information, that the administrative council should be appointed in a more democratic manner, and that there should be a higher council to insure impartiality and to protect journalists against "unjustified sanctions." It condemned political interference and in particular the SLII.[22]

Then came what U.S. novelist James Jones called "the merry month of May." Student riots broke out early in the month, barricades went up, some workers joined with the students, and a confrontation with the government was joined. The ORTF waited for about a week, and then the Panorama program staff prepared a report on the riots. The ministries of information and education ordered it cut, and it was. On 11 May a number of ORTF TV producers demanded a full documentary on the student problem. Instead, the assistant director of TV news broadcast an edited version of the Panorama report, but without the consent of the journalists involved. That led to a twenty-four-hour strike at ORTF. On 16 May riot police took up positions around the ORTF headquarters. Personnel at ORTF set forth a list of demands, including resignations of the administrative council, director general, deputies, and heads of TV news, annulment of the 1964 statute that had created the ORTF, plus preparation of a new statute.[23]

A general strike at ORTF started on 20 May. It was followed by a strike by nearly one hundred TV journalists on 25 May, angry with the director of television because he would not allow the airing of reactions from other political figures to de Gaulle's speech to the nation on 24 May (his first broadcast about the crisis). There were roughly forty members of the news staff who did not go out on strike, most of them staunch Gaullists, and it was they who put together the news for the next few weeks. The strikers and the Ministry of Information negotiated for reform, but as they did, a group of radio news journalists who had been attempting to put out impartial news bulletins in the meantime went out on strike in response to a 3 June gag order by the minister of information. Negotiations continued over the next few weeks and ultimately resulted in a few reforms, but little that would change broadcast policy. Splits developed in union ranks. Radio journalists voted to return to work in late June, TV journalists in mid-July. Both groups were told by the ORTF administration to wait; broadcast journalism was being "re-formed." In August 1968, ORTF announced a "reduction in manpower," under which most of the striking TV journalists were suspended, trans-ferred, or dismissed — a violation of government promises of "no retalia-tion."

What effect those events had on public opinion of ORTF credibility is uncertain, since the ORTF did not conduct public-opinion surveys on any regular basis and rarely released any details from the surveys it did conduct. But France's most popular weekly television magazine, *Télé-7 Jours,* asked its readers in late July about the need for reforms in broad-casting. There were over fifty thousand replies; nearly 90 percent wanted to see the statute governing ORTF modified, about 85 percent said that broadcast news should become more independent from the government, and almost 95 percent wanted more audience representation on the ad-ministrative council, when at the time there was only one audience repre-sentative.[24]

The government announced its reforms on 31 July. They included enlargement of the administrative council from sixteen to twenty-four members. Audience representation did not increase, but ORTF staff rep-resentation did, to five members. But the government still appointed sixteen of the twenty-four members directly and chose the remaining eight from lists supplied by various organizations. The council thus got bigger (and somewhat younger), but not much more independent. The SLII was replaced by the Interministerial Information Committee, which was not to have any direct links with the ORTF. The director general also now became president of the administrative council; since council mem-bers were appointed for three-year terms, that could have given the president–director general a bit more job security, but it didn't: The government still could "unappoint" any council member that it had ap-pointed whenever it wished.

The puny character of those reforms attracted some attention in the press, but another government reform move drew far more criticism. Various government officials had discussed the possibility of limited ad-vertising on ORTF over the previous few years. In the spring of 1968, some of them began to mention it as if it were fait accompli. When the list of reforms came out, there it was. Advertising was to be limited to twenty minutes a day, on TV only, but many newspapers saw it as the opening wedge in the government's attempt to draw advertising revenue away from the press, and especially from some of the smaller, financially weaker newspapers that were more or less anti-Gaullist.

The next four years brought few changes of any note, although a referendum held in 1969 caused President de Gaulle to retire from office, since he had staked his political reputation on a positive outcome and treated the vote as a rejection of his leadership. In summer of that year, there was a presidential election, and the candidates all made promises to develop a more objective ORTF. All of them also promised to abolish the Ministry of Information. Georges Pompidou, a Gaullist, won the election. He abolished the Ministry of Information (although it returned a few years later) and placed the ORTF under the prime minister, who soon announced plans to reform ORTF. The most notable aspect of the reform was the creation of two separate and competing news teams for the two television channels, one team to be headed by a noted Gaullist, the other by a noted liberal journalist.

The two-team concept indeed seemed to produce a more independent brand of TV news, although Gaullist political figures continued to find it easy to get on the air, while the opposition had far less opportunity. But it also proved to be very costly, with journalists from the two teams sometimes covering the same foreign news story, and not always with a discernible difference. A special governmental commission (the Paye Commission) reported in 1970 that more needed to be done to insure objectivity and proposed some changes in the administrative structure, but the report never was taken up by the Assembly. President Pompidou stated in a press conference in July 1970 that the ORTF was the "voice of France," and that in itself meant that ORTF journalists had to accept some restraints. In December 1970, an ORTF staff directive indicated that politics should be kept out of entertainment programs. There had been a well-established tradition of political satire during the 1960s, especially as practiced by producer Jean-Christophe Averty in a program entitled *Les Raisins Vertes* (Sour Grapes), which for example lampooned government policy on birth control by putting on a modern version of Jonathan Swift's "A Modest Proposal." Since such programs were regarded as entertainment, they either escaped the notice of sensitive government officials or were passed off as harmless diversion. Now there would be more attention paid to such programs.

Then in November 1971 a financial scandal broke. A number of ORTF staff were working with a state-operated advertising and public relations agency to insert commercials in noncommercial programs, generally by slipping in mention of brand names. Both houses of Parliament appointed commissions to look into the allegations. They found plenty of proof. The government reacted by discharging the director general of ORTF and drew up a proposal for yet another reform of the organization.

The 1972 statute turned out to be longer than the 1964 act creating the ORTF. It was no more liberal, however. The composition of the administrative council underwent a few changes—listeners and viewers now would be represented by two individuals instead of one, and fewer council members would be appointed directly by the government—but its functions remained basically the same. The posts of president of the council and of director general of ORTF were combined, but the new president–director general still was appointed by the government of the day. There was specific emphasis on ORTF's role as "guardian of the purest standards of the French language," and there was a new "right of reply" article—something that long had been sought by broadcast reformers. However, right of reply was limited to persons as individuals, and not as members of groups or parties. There also was to be a new High Audiovisual Council to advise the government on the implications of new technologies.

Members of left-of-center parties were disappointed because the new statute did very little to encourage greater freedom of expression for diverse points of view. Members of right-of-center parties were disappointed because there was no place under the new statute for private broadcasting, although one article did note the possibility of developing separate program services for "particular audiences." Still, it would be up to the government to decide whether to issue such permission, and that permission would be temporary. The Senate voted down the statute, but the government pushed it through the Assembly anyway, and it became law.

One small element of the statute, Article 4, addressed an issue that many members of Parliament and some government officials had raised on several occasions, but especially following the 1971 advertising scandal. Those individuals saw the ORTF as overly centralized and felt that decentralization might make the organization more efficient financially, administratively, and programmatically. Article 4 created a more subdivided ORTF, with various large units (e.g., radio) having slightly more autonomy, and with an indication that the degree of autonomy might be increased. It was this element that became the core of the next reorganization of the ORTF, scarcely two years later.

Meanwhile, it was business as usual, meaning that government officials still felt perfectly free to call ORTF studios directly to voice their objections to programs, even as those programs were being broadcast and even to the extent of demanding that they be cut off immediately. Journalists continued to be sacked, transferred, or encouraged to leave, and a total of roughly two hundred departed shortly after passage of the new statute. The new president–director general, Arthur Conte, once a Socialist but now seen by some of his former Socialist colleagues as a turncoat for having accepted appointment by the Conservative government to this sensitive post, appeared to be responsible for causing the departure of the liberal head of TV news on Channel 1, Pierre Desgraupes. Conte defended the action in indirect terms in a speech to the ORTF staff.[25] Conte also appeared to regard television as well suited to entertain but not to raise questions about troublesome issues in French society. His predecessor had banned from ORTF a documentary (*The Sorrow and the Pity*) made for the ORTF by Marcel Ophuls, because the documentary brought up the subject of French collaboration with the Nazis during the occupation. When asked whether he planned to unearth the documentary, Conte was reported to have said, "I don't sense any impatience on the public's part to see it." That attitude coincided nicely with the feelings of the minister of information, Philippe Malaud, to whom Conte reported; Malaud often had criticized French TV for its "pessimistic image of society."[26]

Beneath the surface, there were problems between Malaud and Conte, and they erupted when the authoritative newspaper *Le Monde* published excerpts from a letter from Malaud to an old friend who also happened to be assistant director at ORTF. Malaud called one of the radio services, France-Culture, a "permanent Communist pulpit," said that some TV news coverage had "a leftist bias," and accused Conte of financial irresponsibility. (There were rumors that there would be a deficit of Fr 150 million [roughly $35 million] for 1974).[27] Conte replied publicly that the ORTF had been subjected to "intolerable political pressures" by Malaud. Conte was replaced in late October by a "nonpolitical" appointee, Marcel Long, and Malaud was demoted to a lesser ministerial post.

Long quickly announced that a certain amount of administrative reorganization was in order, and that it would take the form of greater autonomy for major units within ORTF: radio, the three TV channels (the third channel had come on the air in 1973, mainly to serve France's regions), possibly production, and the foreign radio service. The trade unions did not like the look of the new system, still felt concern over government pressures, and called a twenty-four-hour strike on 6 November. Journalists at ORTF called a three-hour sympathy strike. Further strikes came in ensuing weeks, but they did no good; Long's plan won cabinet approval in March 1974. Meanwhile, Conte attempted to tell his side of the story through publication of his memoirs,[28] but when he was to discuss those memoirs on television, the government barred him from appearing.[29]

One element in Conte's accusation was that President Pompidou was so ill that others were running the government, and with it the ORTF. Pompidou died in April 1974, forcing a new election and delaying consideration of the latest ORTF reform. The three major candidates all had different views on broadcasting: François Mitterand came out strongly opposed to any form of commercial television (his position was considerably different ten years later); Jacques Chaban-Delmas seemed favorable to a "liberalization" of TV news; and Valéry Giscard d'Estaing, whose brother had proposed a bill favoring commercial TV (as did Giscard's own party), said very little about broadcasting. Giscard won the election, abolished the Ministry of Information, and promised that ORTF would display a more highly diverse set of viewpoints. But ORTF's financial situation was bleak, and in June there was a lengthy strike by technical and administrative staff over the issue of salary increases. There was widespread speculation that TV Channel One might become semiautonomous and more heavily commercial. The speculation—and ORTF itself—ended when the government announced that, on 1 January 1975, the organization would be split into six separate establishments, each with its own administrative structure. Characteristically, the government rushed the bill through Parliament in late July, amid complaints that there was not enough time for proper consideration, that there were too few details on how the new system would function, and so on. But both houses approved, and French viewers and listeners received their new year's present with little expectation that the results would be much different. They were correct in most respects, but few could have anticipated the cost in terms of financial inefficiency.

THE DECENTRALIZED ORTF (1975–81) The new law actually came into effect in 6 January 1975, and it did so accompanied by twenty-five decrees (not subject to passage by the French Parliament) to flesh out its slender skeleton. In the place of the dismantled ORTF arose seven separate companies, each with its own president, administrative council, and director. All of those individuals ultimately were chosen by the government, although many administrative council members were nominated by various groups, usually on lists of several possible candidates. Three companies dealt with television programming; two of them were responsible for the two national channels, the third for regional TV and France's few overseas territories. One company handled the four radio services. One company was responsible for major TV productions (drama, variety, etc.), and the three television program companies were to order their productions from it, although they also could place orders with private production companies. One company was in charge of certain common services: research, in-service training, archives. The seventh company took care of broadcast transmissions and the maintenance of the transmission system. There was to be a High Audiovisual Council with forty members, six appointed by Parliament, thirty-four by the government, to advise the government on the development of audiovisual technology, but also on ethical issues and on right of reply.[30]

Such an organizational framework was not likely to make must sense in terms of administrative efficiency, but it did have the virtue (from the government's standpoint) of reducing the power of the trade unions, which now had to work through seven companies rather than one. On the other hand, it had the drawback of compelling the government itself to work through seven companies, although the fact that the government itself appointed the directors of the companies probably helped to keep some order in the ranks. Also, each administrative council contained a member of Parliament, and those M.P.'s usually came from the majority party. As Jean Diwo explains, "Everything is decided by the Minister of State [for the Interior] and by his principal private secretary. . . . Every name, down to the heads of department, has been carefully scrutinized. It is most unfortunate for anyone whose past record is not entirely reassuring."[31]

Still, matters improved to the point where major-party politicians, whether in the majority or in the opposition, found airtime much more readily available. Usually they appeared in current-affairs programs, sometimes in debates. Minor political parties (extreme right, ecologists, etc.) had little opportunity to be seen or heard, although France Regions 3 (FR3), the regional TV service and probably the least widely viewed of the three TV services, carried a fifteen-minute "open forum" program five nights a week. A right of reply bill finally was passed in 1975 but applied only to individual persons; in 1976 the Socialist party proposed a law that would give that right to trade unions and political parties as well, but it was not adopted.[32]

Some government officials continued in the long-established tradition of interfering with program decision making when it suited their purposes. *Les Dossiers de l'Ecran,* a popular program that covered sensitive topics, introducing them with a film and following the film with a debate, was pressured into dropping proposed programs on crime (1975) and on the army (1976) by the ministers of the interior and of defense.[33] Politicians from the opposition parties continued to claim that their views were underrepresented on TV, and that the ruling coalition exerted pressure to insure that minority-party viewpoints would be distorted.

There was an interesting provision in the new system with implications for program quality. Some members of the public and many newspaper critics had complained about poor production standards, especially in television entertainment. United States–made shows may have struck the critics as deplorable on moral grounds or for their weak story lines, but critics also acknowledged that they were a good deal more attractive to look at than was the homemade product. Now the distribution of license-fee money to the program companies would be based on a formula that would take into account both the size of the audience and the quality of the programs. A twenty-seven-member committee "representing the geographical and social diversity of the country" would carry out the evaluation.[34]

The financing of the new system remained a problem. Indeed, in some respects the problem became far worse. Parliament continued to set the size of the license fee and exercised general supervision over its expenditure. It also had the power to vote for or against collection of the succeeding year's license fee, and in 1973 and again in 1975 the Assembly nearly refused to authorize the following year's collection because of its dissatisfaction with the fiscal management of broadcasting and with the broadcast administrators' incomplete and possibly even deceitful presentation of the budget. Budgetary matters went from bad to worse as the 1970s wore on. There were allegations of gross inefficiency in the "official" production company, Société Français de Production (SFP). (One French producer told me in 1981 that most major TV programs could be and sometimes were produced by private companies at a third of the cost that the official company charged—and were produced more skillfully, at that.) Furthermore, it appeared that the three TV companies were expected to give a large share of their production business to SFP regardless of cost effectiveness. Occasional license-fee increases offset some of the broadcasting companies' budgetary losses, but the losses never disappeared.

The political opposition led the way in calling attention to the problems of the new broadcast setup, but there were no prospects for any real reform, since the government of the day did not wish to relinquish its control over the system. Public opinion concerning broadcasting still was largely unknown, both because of the relative scarcity of surveys and the tendency of the broadcasters not to release any data. Magazines, newspapers, and various organizations conducted their own polls, most of which showed a fairly high degree of dissatisfaction with informational broadcasts (but some improvement in that respect compared with the pre-1974 era); however, most of those polls did not use accepted survey techniques, and their questions sometimes were quite biased.

All during the 1970s, the system remained a monopoly in law, but less so in fact. In 1977, union groups and political parties began to experiment with *radio libre*—"free," or pirate, radio (independent of government control, but also unauthorized). Steelworkers in the province of Lorraine set up Radio Coeur d'Acier, ecologists in Alsace Radio Verte Fessenheim, and there were several others, some of them on the air very briefly, others for years.[35] Following a legal challenge to the government's licensing authority by a Montpellier commercial station, Radio Fil Bleue in 1978, the government passed legislation later that year that specifically forbade such transmissions, as there had been an ambiguity in the 1974 law on that point. However, in most cases the inhabitants of the communities or districts from which the free stations broadcast alerted station staff whenever government inspectors came around. The Socialist party, frustrated perhaps more than any other party by the Conservative coalition's hammerlock on political power ever since 1958, ventured forth with Radio Riposte in 1979. It attacked government policies directly and quickly was jammed. At one point the police blockaded a building from which Socialist leaders were broadcasting. That leadership stood trial for its illegal act in August 1979, and the party leader, François Mitterand, said, "We wanted a political trial, and now we have one." One observer was cynical that any of this would have a lasting effect; she stated, "When the dust has settled, it appears sure that the old arrangement will remain unchanged, the state monopoly secure and the Socialists in quest of another issue."[36] In two years' time, Mitterand had won the presidency, and the state monopoly was broken. For the first time in over forty years, there would be a private alternative from within France.

THE SOCIALIST REFORM (1981–86)   For all of their campaign rhetoric about the need to liberate broadcasting from close government control, to make it more objective, to decentralize it, it took the victorious Socialists a while to change the law, and some of the political moves that accompanied the process were reminiscent of the "good old days." In his second month in office, president Mitterand appointed a study commission (the Moinot Commission) to examine broadcasting and come up with proposals for a new system. The report came out in September. But several months passed before the government, and chiefly the prime minister and the minister for communications (a newly created cabinet post, and supposedly symbolic of the new administration's intent to reform all communications enterprises), had a proposal ready for Parliament. In the meantime, reports began to surface that the minister for communications and other government officials were calling on news and current-affairs staff in particular to pressure some of their colleagues to resign. The administration, which had pledged that there would be no witch hunts to cleanse broadcasting of some of its allegedly anti-Socialist staff, nonetheless sought the resignations of the directors of the three TV companies. Prime Minister Pierre Mauroy stated in a June 1981 press conference, "We haven't asked anyone to go. But it is true that we are not asking anyone to stay."[37]

When Parliament finally received the government's proposals in April 1982, there were some interesting changes between what the Moinot Commission had recommended and what the proposals contained. The commission had recommended several specific steps to be taken in distancing the government from broadcasting, so that the latter could broadcast more independently. It also had recommended the rapid development of local radio. And it particularly wanted to see the budget for broadcasting dispersed through a new body, the Haute Autorité (High Authority), which also would license all new broadcast operations that were not part of the national system. The HA, as it came to be known, would be a nine-member body, with three members appointed by the president and three by the chief French legal/constitutional bodies; those six in turn would choose three members from a list prepared by the National Audiovisual Council. That, the commission felt, would help to minimize direct political influence over the HA, which also would be empowered to hear complaints regarding objectivity.

The government's proposals said little about the development of local radio, nor would the HA have any control over broadcasting's finances. Georges Fillioud, the minister for communication, stated during the National Assembly debate on the bill that "as public funds are at stake, there can be no question that the state [government and Parliament] could delegate this responsibility to the Haute Autorité." Furthermore, the HA itself would have nine members, but three would be appointed by the president, and three each by the speakers of the Senate and the Assembly. Thus, politicians would be in charge of all appointments, and the ruling party or coalition probably would be able to control the majority of them. The president also would choose the HA's president. The structure that had been in place since 1974 largely would remain intact, although regional TV stations were to have more independence from the national system and greater financial support.[38]

There was little in those actions to cause most people to expect radical changes in the broadcast system, but changes were taking place even before the bill passed later that spring. Political figures who had not been seen or heard over French broadcasting for years began to reappear; some were appointed to administrative positions in broadcasting. Those appointed generally were Socialists or favorable to Socialist policies, and it seemed to some audience members and critics that the Socialists were getting more than their fair share of broadcast time.

Also, some TV entertainment shows were dropped from the prime-time schedule in favor of educational programs, discussions, and other fare designed to enlighten viewers, rather than simply distract them. Angry viewers began to express their sentiments — one report noted that half the mail received by Mitterand consisted of complaints about programs influenced by the government[39] — but they also began to listen more and more to the hundreds of pirate radio stations springing up across the land.

The pirates had existed since the mid-1970s, and the government had managed to shut most of them down in short order. But because the Socialists had used pirate radio to strike back at the government in the late 1970s, and because they had promised a more liberal policy with respect to independent radio, it was difficult for them to silence such stations now that they held power. At first they didn't even try, but so many stations came on the air in Paris that it was evident that there would have to be a modicum of regulation applied to them. They certainly represented a variety of opinions and styles. Some were run by minor political parties, others by homosexuals, still others by foreign communities such as Arabs. A number of them were strongly antigovernment; I once heard one in Rouen do a satirical skit on the government's proposed tax increase, which suggested that listeners should liken paying taxes to having an orgasm: the more, the better. The station followed this with a reading of a letter allegedly received from a French paratrooper temporarily on duty in the former French African colony of Chad, helping the government there to suppress the rebels. Most of the "letter" was a thinly veiled indictment of the Socialist government's Chad policy.

The government announced late in 1982 that it would grant licenses to radio stations, subject to two major conditions: that the stations operate on low power (five hundred watts) and that they not finance themselves by selling advertising time. Also, there would be limited frequency space for the stations, so it was suggested that those located in the same community consider making joint applications. Many hundreds applied. In some of the larger cities, there were far more applicants than the frequency spectrum (FM only) could hold, so the Haute Autorité, which granted the licenses, issued some with the condition that the frequency be shared by two or more stations. Some stations were willing to go along with the decision, but others refused and continued to broadcast illegally. Many of the stations began almost immediately to violate the no advertising rule, simply because they could not make ends meet otherwise, and in April 1984 President Mitterand announced that the stations could carry ads, after all. A number of stations sought to increase their audience size by transmitting at more than five hundred watts. One of them, Radio NRJ (Paris), was banned from broadcasting for thirty days because it transmitted at thirty thousand watts, interfering with emergency services. The station owner refused to abide by the decision, and thousands of protesters turned out in Paris to denounce the action.[40]

The Mitterand government's authorization of private radio was the first major sign that broadcast policy under the Socialists was going to be substantially different from what it was under the Conservative coalitions. It is difficult to say whether the Socialists' own use of pirate radio while in the opposition virtually forced them to open up radio to private operators, but it probably hastened the process, at the least. That step soon was followed by others: The government announced in mid-1983 that there would be a new over-the-air pay TV service, chiefly featuring movies but with provision for program sponsorship by advertisers, as well. This new service, Canal Plus, required a special decoder (to descramble the signal) and aerial, and thus was costly enough that few but wealthy households were expected to subscribe to it – hardly the sort of enterprise supported by traditional Socialists! And cable TV, which had been the subject of experiments in a few French cities in the 1970s, but which never had really amounted to anything, now received strong support from the government, which hoped to have 1.4 million homes served by fiber-optic cable by the middle of the decade. Direct broadcast satellite service was to begin by 1986.[41]

The driving force behind this radical shift in communications policy was economic. The major manufacturers of communications and space technology were government owned, and the Socialist government did not care for the prospect of losing out to other European and North American nations, not to mention Japan, in the race to secure markets. The government also was willing to throw a few roadblocks in the way of those competitors, as it did early in 1983, when it began to require that all Japanese videocassette recorders pass through customs inspection at Poitiers (a city with special symbolic value, since it was near Poitiers that Charles Martel stopped another foreign invasion, that of the Arabs, in 732 A.D.). The inspection added to the cost of the recorders and delayed their progress to retail stores. Inspections ended just a few months later when the Japanese reached an agreement with a French electronics firm to allow the latter to manufacture up to a million Japanese VCRs per year.

Then in January 1985, Mitterand announced the authorization of private, commercial television. Ironically, he did so in the course of a televised speech in which he praised the public broadcast service as a "guarantor of quality"; just after that remark, his image faded from the screen, thanks to a technical disruption. As one French critic remarked, "The breakdowns have come to symbolize the badly-run, overstaffed, and under-efficient . . . state controlled French television channels."[42] The president claimed that there was room for eighty to eighty-five local television stations. Actually, some were on the air already, operating illegally: Télé Alphonse Jouy, for example, served a number of Paris city council apartment blocks for the poor with community programming delivered by cable. Several cities and towns across the country were at work on private projects, some of which were supported by opposition political parties. Again, Mitterand appeared to be bowing to the inevitable, perhaps hoping to win a bit of public favor by supporting diversity in broadcasting. Some of his aides reportedly opposed his proposal, partly because they feared that the political opposition would be able to take advantage of the new outlets, partly because they thought that investors would be drawn away from the cable and satellite systems being pushed by the government.[43] There were well over three hundred applications for new licenses in the first four months following Mitterand's announcement.

Certainly the government continued to use its own political influence on broadcasting, although not in as obvious a manner as had its predecessors. Ever since the founding of the Haute Autorité in 1982, it had been rumored widely that, even though the HA was to choose the directors general of the program services, nominees had to meet with Mitterand's approval first, usually through personal interview.[44] Gradually, all of the program services came under directors general who were aligned with the government; Mitterand's appointment of a noted Socialist, Jean-Claude Héberlé, as head of Antenne 2 (TV) in October 1984 seemed to some observers to show clearly how little say the HA had in the appointment process.[45] Still, the Autorité received praise from some normally critical sources for having prepared a number of excellent reports on needed changes in broadcasting, and for not having become the servant of the Ministry of Communication.[46]

Early in 1985, the government asked a distinguished lawyer, Jean-Dénis Brédin, to prepare a report on possible future directions for audiovisual communications media. Brédin submitted his report in May 1985, and it drew heavy media attention. The report urged the continued development of privately financed television but spoke to the need for a complementary approach, in which the public broadcasting system would continue to play a strong role and where private broadcasting would have certain public-service obligations, such as 60 percent European program content for private TV. Media reaction generally was favorable, but some critics wanted full-blown competition between the public and private systems, partly on the grounds that this would create more jobs in TV. Government officials, too, were satisfied with Brédin's recommendations, Mitterand remarking that it would be necessary to place some obligations on private operators through the licensing process.[47]

In November 1985 the government signed an agreement with a private consortium to permit the latter to place a private network on the air, probably by late February 1986. Here, too, politics was supposed to have played a role. Sixty percent of the shares in the new company were to be owned by a group headed by a "wealthy industrialist with left-wing sympathies," but the remainder were to be held by Italian commercial television magnate Silvio Berlusconi. Furthermore, the new channel (La Cinq, or Channel 5) would begin its broadcasts a few weeks before the next national election, which presumably would help to remind voters of how mindful the Socialists were of their wishes.[48] (Various surveys had indicated that a majority, and sometimes a large majority, of the French thought that commercial TV would improve their range of choice significantly.)

The March 1986 election resulted in a moderate loss of seats in the National Assembly for the Socialists—just enough to allow a conservative coalition to take over the reins of government (although Mitterand remained president) and to overturn many of the major changes that the Socialist government had brought about in media policy. A few weeks after the election, Conservative government officials announced that they would abolish the Haute Autorité and replace it with a national commission on audiovisual communication that would have broader powers than the Autorité. Those officials also announced their intentions to revoke the license of La Cinq, to break the previous government's agreement with the European Consortium regarding operation of a communications satellite, and to convert one and possibly two of the three public TV services to private networks. New legislation for broadcasting was to be introduced in late April or early May, with passage probable by June 1986.[49] While French broadcasting clearly had become far more diverse and objective during the five years of Socialist rule, the Conservative victory served as a fresh reminder of the ephemeral character of French broadcast legislation. Diversity was to increase under the new government in the sense that there probably would be more TV stations authorized, but what would happen to objectivity was anyone's guess, and past experience under Conservative governments was not very reassuring.

THE "NEW CONSERVATIVE" ERA (1986–1988)   The broadcast law that
finally passed in September 1986 in some ways was a matter of old
wine in new bottles. The Haute Autorité would be abolished, but the
National Commission for Communications and Liberties (CNCL) that
would replace it bore a marked resemblance to it. The CNCL would
have thirteen members, six of them appointed in much the same political
fashion as had been all appointees to the HA, three more to be appointed by and to come from the judiciary, one member of the prestigious Académie Française (chosen by the Académie), and three members
representing audiovisual creation, telecommunication, and the print media (chosen by the ten other committee members). Members would have
nine-year terms, which would be neither renewable nor revocable, and
they would elect their own chair.

The CNCL's duties extended a bit beyond those of the Autorité.
They included the licensing of private broadcasting and cable networks,
the appointment of senior personnel in public broadcasting, the monitoring of advertising, the overall scrutiny of children's programs, and the
safeguarding of public interests in the form of election broadcasts, anti-
competitive practices, and equal treatment of users of telecommunication services. They also would advise on numerous aspects of telecommunications policy.[50]

Whether the CNCL could play a truly independent role remained to
be seen. On the one hand, it had more power at its disposal than had the
HA. On the other hand, it was subject to political appointment, for the
most part, and the new Conservative government could prove just as
loathe to give up real power as had the old Conservative governments. A
test case arose quite soon: The new government had announced its intention to sell off one of the three public TV services, TF1 (Télévision
Française 1). That announcement itself provoked a May 1986 strike by
some public broadcasting staff and many discussions in Parliament and
in public forums, such as correspondence to newspapers, as to whether
this was a good idea and whether it was legal for a government to sell
something that had "belonged" to the public. The legality of the sale was
confirmed, and the CNCL had the duty of examining bids, taking testimony on the merits of the proposals, and then deciding who would be
the winner.

The process ended in April 1987. In the meantime, several bids had
appeared, some were withdrawn or were merged with other bids, and
finally there were two combatants left to battle for a prize that would
cost the victor Fr 3 billion ($.5 billion) for 50 percent ownership. One
was a consortium headed by the Hachette publishing firm, which already

operated a TV production house, had part ownership in the French-language commercial station Europe No. One, and enjoyed close ties with Conservative politicians. The other consortium was headed by Bouygues, France's largest construction firm, with Robert Maxwell, an English "media baron," as a 10 percent investor. Betting was on Hachette, with its Conservative connections, and the chair of the CNCL, Gabriél de Broglie, had even given Hachette some advice regarding ways of making the application stronger.[51] But when the vote came, a majority favored the Bouygues application. One reason appeared to be that Bouygues indicated more of a commitment to domestic program production than did Hachette, and another that awarding TF1 to Hachette would give it an even more dominant position in the mass media, but commission members also may have been put off by Hachette's seeming assumption that it obviously was the stronger candidate and enjoyed support in politically influential quarters. In other words, the commission did not care for the idea of being regarded as a rubber stamp and showed it in the clearest way possible.[52]

The privatization of TF1 was part of a larger preelection promise made by the Conservatives. It had bothered them terribly that Mitterand and the Socialists had authorized private television shortly before the general election of 1986 and thus had been able to award licenses for the two services to their own "deserving" friends. The Conservatives almost immediately promised that they would withdraw those license grants, but they soon discovered that the licensing terms included a provision that would force the government to pay a considerable sum in compensation to the two groups that held the licenses if they were withdrawn. When the CNCL considered the relicensing issue in February 1987, it awarded the license for La Cinq to a group made up of Conservative publisher Robert Hersant (who really had wanted TF1, but who withdrew from that race) and Berlusconi-Seydoux, the majority owners of the old La Cinq. That settled that compensation issue. Le Six was less of a problem, since there was a much smaller investment in it, and it was reawarded to the Companie Luxembourgeoise de Télédiffusion and to Lyonnaise des Eaux, a major utilities group, which also was involved with cable. (The company's chairman, Jerome Monod, was a close personal friend of Conservative Prime Minister Jacques Chirac.) In both awards, there also were several smaller shareholders, primarily banks.[53]

The political independence of CNCL was called into question when the French press revealed in November 1987 that its relicensing of FM stations in the Paris region seemed to have been influenced by political and economic factors, for example, licensing a new Arabic-language station (France Maghreb Media) because one of its backers was "close to" the office of the mayor of Paris. Several stations lost their licenses in the process, but the CNCL gave no specific reasons for its decisions. Some of the losers brought a court case against one member of the CNCL; the case was pending as of early 1988.[54]

Finally, the new government announced late in 1986 that it was reconsidering policy on cable and satellite development, and that it was not prepared to subsidize the development of either or both to the extent that the Socialist government had been. Cable could develop freely, but the government would not insist upon widespread installation of two-way cable, which the Socialist government had supported. Satellites could go ahead, but the financial risks clearly would have to be those of the potential users. Both moves were consonant with a free enterprise philosophy, but both also removed France from the ranks of those nations seeking to develop fiber-optic cable and satellites to result in foreign sales of technology and thus a boost for the domestic economy.

Financing

The state-run system in France derives its financial support mainly from license fees and from advertising, but it also earns modest revenues through sale of its programs abroad, mainly to other French-speaking nations. (Many programs, however, are free of charge to former French colonies in the Third World, since the French government feels that those programs help to maintain the French cultural presence abroad.) The private sector relies almost entirely upon advertising to generate its income.

License fees have been a part of French broadcasting since 1933. They are set by Parliament, although broadcast administrators are free to suggest increases whenever they choose. Increases come about, on the average, every four years. As you have already seen, Parliament is quite willing to use license-fee revenue as a club to hold over the heads of those in broadcasting. As of 1988, owners of black and white TV sets pay Fr 333 a year, while color-set owners pay Fr 506 a year. There is an 18.6 percent value added tax (VAT) on the license fee, as well. Sets in public places bring a much higher fee: just over Fr 2,100 for a color set intended for public viewing in a bar, restaurant, or similar place of business. Over 2.4 million households with black and white sets are exempt from paying the fee on grounds of war injuries, old age, and so on; that figure represents about one-third of all black and white–set households. There are no exemptions for color TV set households, on the grounds that anyone owning a color set cannot be all that economically disadvantaged. There are no license fees for radio sets.

There have been ads on French TV since 1968 — twenty minutes per day per channel at first, rising slightly to the present twenty-four minutes per day. But they have been a major source of income for the two national channels, TF1 and A2, partly because there was no real competition until early 1986. In fact, while the quality-points system described earlier was in force, those two channels paid little attention to it, because the amount of money they would receive for putting on high-quality shows paled in comparison with what they could make by putting on highly popular shows.[55] One reason the Mitterand government dropped the quality-points system in the early 1980s was that it seemed to make so little difference in program quality, especially in view of all the effort that went into making the quality assessments.

Both public TV channels (three until TF1 was privatized) carry advertising, and so does the France Inter radio service. Ad time is sold by the Régie Française de Publicité (RFP), which also places the ads on the various channels. Fifty-one percent of RFP's capital is held by the state, and part of the remaining 49 percent is held by another state corporation, SOFIRAD. Because airtime for ads is so limited, the two major TV channels, TF1 and Antenne 2, often have not been able to accept all demands for ad time; a 1982 estimate for Antenne 2 indicated that the channel had to turn away 70 percent of all requests.[56] What made ad time especially attractive before the establishment of private television was that it was sold mostly for the early to middle evening time block (6:30 to 8:30 P.M.), when the largest audiences would be present. Furthermore, the price per second was the same whether the ad ended up next to *Dallas* or next to a low-rated show. (Ads cannot interrupt shows on public stations; they are clustered in short blocks between them.) But if a show *did* receive consistently low ratings, advertisers placed their ads on one of the other channels for that time block.

The first two private stations to be licensed did not affect that situation, because the stations started out small, covering only Paris and its environs. La Cinq grew faster than did Le Six (it was better financed), but by early 1988 still reached only about half of the nation's TV households. However, the privatization of TF1 should bring profound changes to television advertising practices. The TF1 service already has full national coverage, and now it will have to subsist on advertising, with no license fee to offset expenses. That will give advertisers access to more airtime. The continued growth of La Cinq and of Metropole TV (the new title for Le Six) will do the same. Antenne 2, and to some extent FR3, are almost certain to request greater freedom to advertise: more time, fewer product restrictions, and so on. As of early 1988, certain products may not be advertised: alcoholic beverages (including beer), tobacco products, tourism, jewelry, retail stores, building societies, publishing, and computers. Most of those restrictions are designed to protect print media ad revenues. Also, toys and pharmaceutical products require special authorization. Sponsored programming has not been allowed on the public channels, but Canal Plus can and does accept it (the channel has a noontime talk show program which is advertiser-supported and which is not "scrambled," so that anyone can watch it), the private stations certainly want it, and the remaining public channels probably will wish to follow suit. If restrictions are dropped for one sector of broadcasting, other sectors almost certainly will demand equal treatment. All of that in turn is bound to have some effect on programming, with an increased need for cheaper programs that please a larger audience.

The introduction of TV advertising on the regional service, FR3, came in January 1983 to a few of the twelve regional TV services, although it was to expand to most of them by the end of the 1980s. It was highly controversial. The regional press, most of which is much weaker financially than its Parisian counterpart, worried that this would bite deeply into their already none-too-substantial revenues, and some critics claimed that the Socialists would profit from a weakened regional press because so many of the papers were anti-Socialist—in other words, the same argument that was applied against the Conservatives when TV advertising was introduced in 1968. But so far there has been no great exodus of advertising money to regional TV, where the ads are very simply produced and where regional and local advertisers still seem uncertain as to whether broadcast advertising is a good investment. After all, they have had little previous experience with it. Local private stations carry ads for a wide variety of local and regional products and services, usually for very low rates. Private station staff have told me that business is slow because local advertisers are conservative, and so far the regional and local press do not appear to have lost much business to radio.

The HA and the CNCL had the legal right to monitor broadcast advertising, but did not exercise the right very often. With some fifteen hundred local radio stations around the country and roughly two hundred staff members, regular monitoring is not likely. Also, there are few stipulations regarding broadcast advertising in the legal frameworks of French broadcast regulatory agencies, so enforcement would be a real problem.

Many French broadcast ads would seem quite familiar to U.S. audiences. Techniques seem much the same, as do appeals used. But ads for brassieres, toilet paper, and other intimate products often receive bold treatment by U.S. standards. A brassiere ad will contain such lines as, "Yes, you too can have breasts this big!" and will feature a live model demonstrating the product. A toilet paper ad will show a small child perched on a potty, then getting off and dragging the toilet paper down a long hall (to show the length of the roll) and into a living room where the parents are hosting a party, which the child interrupts by demanding to be wiped. Some ads use what I find to be typically sly Gallic humor: One shows a man being annoyed by a fly. He says, very solemnly, "Here's another use for Fly-Tox [a popular insect spray]" and swats the fly with the can. By and large, French audiences seem not to mind broadcast ads, and some profess to like them, although so far their ad diet has been a restricted one.

Canal Plus carries ads, but derives most of its revenue from the roughly eighteen-dollar-per-month fee paid by the 2.3 million house-holds (as of early 1988) subscribing to it.

Governance and Administration – Internal

In sharp contrast to most of the other systems covered in this book, the internal governance and administration of French broadcasting is quite simple to describe. The six companies of the national public broad-casting organization (the old ORTF) all are headed by a president ap-pointed by the government, and all but one of the companies has an administrative council of five to ten members, chosen variously by the National Assembly, the Senate, and the chief executive (president of the republic). Most of the high administrative positions in the companies also pass under government review, but the broadcast regulatory agency ultimately approves them. Administrators had greater freedom to make decisions under the Socialist government than they did before, but gov-ernment officials of whatever political party still feel freer to intervene in broadcast decision making in France than they do in any other Western European country. Nor do they intervene solely in the case of news and informational programs. In 1982, Regis Debray, cultural advisor to Pres-ident Mitterand, told a press conference that he felt that a highly sophis-ticated (and very popular, often drawing 5 million viewers) book-review show *Apostrophes,* was being run too dictatorially by its host. Debray stated, "We have some plans to relieve that program of its monopoly on the choice of titles and authors."[57] As it turned out, President Mitterand was a devoted fan of the show, and nothing happened to it, but Debray was operating on the basis of a long-standing assumption that it was perfectly normal for government officials and advisors to tell broadcasters what to do.

Up until 1981, almost all decision-making power resided at the national level, but the new Socialist government had featured decentralization as one of its campaign pledges, and that applied to broadcasting as well as to many other enterprises. The considerable increases in amounts of airtime for regional TV productions, plus the creation of several new "local" (really subregional) public radio stations, expanded the possibilities for local decision making. The station managers would be appointed by radio or television administrators in Paris and usually would be drawn from the ranks of those who had had experience in the national public system, but they might well come from the regions or cities served by the stations, and they would have to be prepared to make decisions without referring them back to Paris. My visits to regional and local stations in 1983, 1984, and 1986 revealed that local station managers were reasonably autonomous, although they were unlikely to program material that challenged the establishment point of view.[58] Broadcasts by avid Breton nationalists, for example, would be a rarity over Radio Bretagne Ouest, although there could be news items about some of their activities, and they might appear on discussion programs.

Where production of programs is concerned, French public broadcast administrators have other problems. The first is lack of money, or at least lack of money to spend on production. Most government commissions on broadcasting have concluded that the system is top-heavy with management, and commissions reporting since the 1974 reform have concluded that the division into separate companies probably has added to economic inefficiency. Each program company may produce a fair share of its own programs, so long as they can be produced in the small studios and with the modest technical facilities of the company. News programs, interviews, talk shows, and so on, all fall into that category. Larger productions must be put up for bids, and the "official" TV production company, SFP, is expected to be chosen often enough that it at least will spend its own budget—this despite allegations that the productions of the official company often cost two to three times what an independent production company would charge for the same product.[59] That situation leads to a second problem faced by administrators: lack of control over program costs. There is little that an administrator can do to spend production money wisely when a large amount of it is outside her or his control. In short, this is not an administrative system in which its staff will find much scope for the exercise of traditional administrative talents.

Yet another problem is the relationship between management and production staff. The French broadcast industry is highly unionized, and strikes are frequent, although they have been far less so since 1981. Nevertheless, there was a twenty-four-hour strike by journalists and technicians in November 1982, and the first broadcast of the new breakfast-time TV service in early January 1985 failed to go on the air because of a technician's strike in which the demands were for extra staff and more pay. There also was the May 1986 strike in protest over the sale of TF1. Since so many management staff are chosen by the government in one way or another, the adversarial relationship between the two sectors — present in most systems — is likely to be even more hostile, and especially in those cases where administrators seem to know little and care less about broadcasting. The Mitterand administration had a better record than did its predecessors in appointing and approving appointments of administrators who had had backgrounds in broadcasting and who seemed to take a genuine interest in what they did, but still there were individuals who received their appointments as rewards for faithful service to the party and with the understanding that they would not be expected to do a great deal of work.

That is less likely to be true of the private TV stations, although, as politics continue to play a role in the licensing process, it certainly could enter into staff appointments. The unions are likely to find it much more difficult to negotiate with the private TV stations than with their public counterparts, since there is every indication that the former will be far more cost conscious than the latter, and probably more antiunion, as well.

In theory, the administrative councils associated with the public services (they aren't required for private stations) could act as a force for improvement, but in practice most council members have not seen themselves in the role of whistle-blower or efficiency expert. Most are in political sympathy with the company president, and in personal sympathy from the standpoint of acknowledging the lack of money and/or power to change things in any fundamental way. There have been changes, to be sure, and council members and presidents have helped to bring about some of them, but the scope for change is decidedly limited.

Governance and Administration — External

GOVERNMENTAL   As should be amply evident by now, the French
government, and the executive branch in particular, has a great deal
to say about the way in which broadcasting operates. There are direct
appointment powers, held by the president, the National Assembly, and
the Senate. There is also the unofficial power of approval of still other
appointments, which is exercised chiefly by the president and/or the
prime minister — the former if the president and the parliamentary majority are from the same party, the latter if they are not. Thus, there is a
virtual guarantee that any individual who occupies a high-level position
within French public broadcasting will be at least mildly favorable to the
majority party of the moment. The 1982 Broadcast Law contained provisions designed to help make certain appointments somewhat less political — members of the Haute Autorité were chosen for nine-year, nonrenewable terms and could not be removed from office for other than
serious crimes — and the 1986 Broadcast Law took the same approach.
Still, the Socialists lost little time in replacing broadcast administrators
sympathetic to the Giscard administration with administrators who
would be more in tune with the Socialist philosophy, and the Conservatives returned the favor shortly after the resumed power.

The National Assembly continues to exercise considerable control
over broadcasting through the budget. It approves the annual license fee
and also approves the annual budget for the public-service broadcasting
system. The Ministry of Finance also is involved in approval of the
annual budget. The days of line-by-line approval of specific expenditures are long since gone, but it is a rare year that passes without pro-
longed hearings on the broadcast budget. Furthermore, both the Assembly and the Senate can and often do appoint special committees to
examine in detail one or another aspect of broadcasting, and financial
aspects have been the subject of more committee investigations than any
other aspect of broadcasting. Unfortunately for the broadcasters, those
examinations often have turned up evidence of carelessness, wasteful-
ness, and even improper handling of finances, and with such a legacy it
will take broadcasters some while to reassure government officials that
they deserve still greater fiscal freedom. The National Assembly and the
Senate also have the power to approve or disapprove laws relating to
broadcasting, but the government, if it so wishes, is able to push through
laws that it desires and to remove "unfriendly" amendments to those
laws. The government also can proclaim decrees that have the force of

law, and that often have much more influence on the workings of the broadcast system than do the laws of broadcasting themselves. Those decrees can be discussed by the Assembly and the Senate but cannot be modified or repealed by them.

The judicial system in theory plays a role in broadcast regulation, in that it is possible for individuals to bring right of reply cases to the courts for possible redress, if the special right of reply commission did not produce a satisfactory (to the plaintiff) decision. Before 1982, they had to do so as individuals, not as members of larger groups, and the "offensive" broadcasts had to have been directed against them personally. Given those conditions, it was not surprising that few cases were brought to the courts. The 1982 law granted right of reply to "legal persons" as well, so that groups, organizations, and corporations could be covered. So far, there have been few instances of requests for right of reply, which also is incorporated with the 1986 law.[60]

There have been several court cases involving rights of transmission and rights of compensation. Before La Cinq came on the air, its owners got authorization from the national government (in this case, from the president) to use the Eiffel Tower as a transmitting tower. That enraged many people, including then mayor of Paris (and after March 1986, prime minister) Jacques Chirac. The city of Paris took the case to the Constitutional Court, where it argued that the city had sovereign rights over the use of the Tower, which belongs to Paris. The Constitutional Court ruled in December 1985 that the national government's action was unconstitutional, mainly on the grounds that the basis on which it took the action did not sufficiently protect the rights of owners of other tall structures. In less than two months, La Cinq gained access to the Tower, although only with the help of police, and even then it took several weeks more to clear away the remaining legal obstacles.[61] In a compensation case, the Council of State ruled in February 1987 that the former owners of La Cinq and Le Six were entitled to recompense for at least part of their investment; the national government had argued that the owners had been awarded the license illegally, and that no compensation was due.[62]

There is no exact equivalent of the United States Federal Communications Commission in France, although the Haute Autorité and the CNCL bear some resemblance to it. The HA was the first quasi-independent French regulatory agency for broadcasting, and its powers were quite broad, at least on paper: licensing of all private stations, appointment of top-level public broadcasting administrators, monitoring of "fairness" in broadcasting, conditions for allocation of airtime to politicians, promotion of regional languages and culture through broadcasting and so on.[63] The nine-member council (all full-time, and paid quite well) was hampered in carrying out that sweeping mandate by three factors: a small support staff, a limited budget for travel, and the political process that appointed them in the first place. From the start, there were questions as to how independent it could be of political control.

The first president of the HA, Michele Cotta, had excellent credentials as a broadcast journalist (France Inter, Luxembourg) and good connections with a wide assortment of politicians, and several other council members had had media experience, but accusations of political bias arose almost immediately: When the council announced its decisions on the first round of licensing for private radio stations in 1983, there were some complaints that the Autorité had been pressured by politicians not to award licenses to some of the fringe political groups seeking them. (However, there also were examples of such groups receiving licenses.) Furthermore, President Mitterand in effect told the council to approve his nomination for president of A2 in 1984, and the council complied. On the credit side, the council warned TF1's director general in May 1985 to make certain that the prime minister's monthly program be matched by time for the opposition. That warning was upheld as a proper exercise of its powers by the French Council of State.[64]

The National Commission for Communications and Liberties took up its duties late in 1986, with much the same mandate as had been conferred upon the Haute Autorité. Its initial action—the appointment of new administrative heads for the public broadcasting services—was not promising: Political "payoffs" appeared to govern the choices, which were criticized even by the minister of culture and communications for their uninspired quality.[65] There was a greater show of independence in the awarding of TF1 to the Bouygues-Maxwell consortium, although that award, as well as the licenses for La Cinq and Le Six (Metropole TV), went to acknowledged supporters of the Conservative coalition. Also, the CNCL appears to have paid no more attention to what private radio licensees broadcast than did the Autorité: Although such stations are required to serve to some extent as community voices, many of them, by my observation, do little but play recorded music (sometimes supplied by satellite—several radio "networks" such as NRJ operate that way). News is a rare commodity on most local private stations, and news about the particular community where the license is held even rarer. It is still unclear, then, whether this relatively new form of broadcast regulation will result in much independent judgment, and the November 1987 case referred to on p. 90–91 raises further doubts.

It is possible for citizens and groups who feel that they have been treated unfairly in broadcasts to take their cases to the courts. In addition, a law passed in 1984 makes it illegal for the media to present images deemed to be degrading to women—more specifically, images that constitute "incitement to discrimination, hatred, violence, insult or defamation." A person or institution found guilty of violating the law could face a prison term of up to a year and fines of up to several thousand francs. So far, no cases have been brought to the courts, perhaps because of the difficulty of proving whether a specific image contained in a specific medium of communication actually incited the specific act.

NONGOVERNMENTAL   Citizens' groups concerned with one or another aspect of broadcasting have been active in France since the 1930s, but they have no legal standing and most of them suffer from a lack of continuity, funds, members, or all three. Certainly none has achieved the visibility of Action for Children's Television in the United States or the Viewer's and Listener's Association in Great Britain. When broadcast bills have been considered by the Assembly or Senate, or when those bodies have appointed special commissions to examine one or another facet of broadcasting, a number of representatives of the groups have appeared to give testimony, but most of the groups appear to be active only at such times, and it is doubtful that they have made any lasting impression upon the consciousness of the general public. A French scholar conducting her dissertation research on the activities of such groups told me in 1972 that many of them in fact had no continuing existence, and that some didn't even have members![66] More recent discussions with French scholars indicate that the situation has not changed.

At moments of crisis—usually when the government and a particular staff group, (e.g., journalists, producers, etc.) are in conflict—statements opposing the government's action will appear in some of the leading newspapers, signed not only by the staff group, but by some of the leading French intellectuals. So far, no one group has managed to attract the ongoing support of enough of those intellectuals to give itself the aura that might make it truly effective. Perhaps the problem is that intellectuals do not have a particularly high opinion of broadcasting. They come to its defense when there is a specific freedom of speech issue but take little interest in pushing for any fundamental reform to the system. It also may be that they, or any other citizens who criticize broadcasting, doubt their ability to influence any fundamental reform. It seems clear enough that the impetus for reforms of broadcasting can and has come from both the legislative and executive branches of government, but that the executive branch almost always has ended up dictating the specific nature of reform. It may not be easy for citizens to influence legislative decisions, but it is even harder for them to influence executive decisions. Hence, why bother trying?

In the past, unions played a major role in French life, but their influence appears to have diminished greatly over the past two decades. I have already noted the specific influence of broadcasting unions, but they too seem to be losing some of their power. Broadcast administrators certainly have not gone out of their way to be favorable to unions in programming about their activities; as George Ross notes of the French mass media in general, "The media originally tried to ignore unions. When unions, for whatever reason, became strong enough to achieve certain of their objectives, the media tended to portray them as one major cause of French difficulties. When unions plunged to the depths of weakness and ineffectiveness, as they seemed to with cyclical regularity, the media played up the 'crisis of unionism.' "[67]

Programming

PHILOSOPHY   Early in the history of French broadcasting, there were individuals who felt that broadcasting had a certain role to play in French society. Some looked upon it as guardian of language standards, and as already noted, many of the decrees passed in the 1920s required that stations avoid the use of slang and dialect. That concern has carried through to the present day; part of the CNCL's mission is to insure the usage of "proper" French in broadcasts. Similarly, most French ministers of culture have spoken of the need for French broadcasting to give a prominent place to the display of French culture, past and present. To that end, French broadcasters traditionally have set self-imposed limitations on the use of foreign programs. That has not kept shows such as *Dallas* from appearing in prime time and outdrawing most other programs on French TV, and it has not kept United States–made movies from appearing two or three times a week on public stations (more often on Canal Plus and the private stations) in prime time, either; but it *has* meant that there has been money available for the production of some relatively lavish entertainment series, for example, *Châteauvallon* (see p. 111).

Some of the concern over the issues of safeguarding the language and promoting French culture probably stems from the fact that France exports many of its programs to its former colonies and protectorates, especially in Africa. Since the citizens of those countries do not enjoy the benefits of total immersion in French life, it is especially important that whatever they receive from France be the best possible representation of that life.

As for informational broadcasts, again it is quite clear that the government has taken a great interest in such programs from the first decade of radio's existence to the present. During the initial period of coexistence for public and private broadcasting, it was harder for the government to achieve total compliance with its wishes, but by 1938 it had gained control over several types of informational broadcasts, and in 1939 it restricted private stations to the transmission of an official news bulletin (see p. 68). Subsequent creation of a broadcast monopoly made the task of supervision easier, and as we have seen, the pattern of direct ministerial involvement in shaping the contents of daily newscasts began at least as early as 1948. The Socialist government that came into office in 1981 removed the direct ministerial controls over newscast content, but not the indirect controls; just as its political predecessors had done, it took special pains to see that the "right" (but not in political terms!) people were appointed to head the news departments.

The authorization of local private radio stations in 1982 broke the monopoly, and the authorization of private television in 1985 completed the break. However, the radio stations initially lacked a network structure that might allow them to develop informational programs that would be competitive with the public system on a nationwide basis. By 1986, a few of the largest stations in Paris (NRJ, RFM) had begun to use satellites for distributing their music programs to local stations throughout France, and news services sometimes were part of the package, but the local stations seldom supplied news to the "network." The two initial private television stations were almost completely entertainment oriented at first, but the relicensing of February 1987 brought promises from the new owners that news operations would be developed, and La Cinq quickly established a news production facility. Still, entertainment is far and away their major function, and though the CNCL made the domestic production of entertainment a condition of licensing for both stations — within three years, 50 percent of the programming must be French made and only 40 percent can be non-European[68] — the temptation will be strong to make lots of inexpensive programs, such as quiz shows, and place many of the non-European programs in prime time.

The peripheral stations all carry newscasts, but they too were subject to government pressure during the 1960s and 1970s. The Socialist government did not face a crisis comparable to the 1968 strike, so whether it would have come down as heavily on the peripheral stations as did de Gaulle's government is difficult to say, but the prevailing tendency over the decades for any French government in a crisis situation has been to place tight controls on newscasts, peripheral or domestic. A Senate committee sent the then three public TV networks a questionnaire early in 1987 in which the networks were asked to furnish information on which crew members covered the student demonstrations in Paris of November 1986, what their journalistic briefs were, which freelancers (including some working for peripheral stations) contributed to reporting the riots, and so on.[69] And Hachette, which purchased the controlling block of stock in Europe No. One early in 1986, fired one of the station's commentators a few months later, allegedly because he was a cosponsor of an "antiprivatization" (of TF1) petition.[70] Francis Bouygues, president of TF1, sacked Michel Polac, producer/host of TF1's *Droit de Reponse* (Right of Reply) in September 1987 because Polac criticized the CNCL for a licensing decision and a week later criticized Bouygues for asking him to apologize for the attack on the CNCL.[71]

RADIO   The French public radio system, Radio France, features three major national services and three specialized services, as well as thirteen regional and thirty-five "local" radio stations. The three major national services resemble the major national radio services of many large European countries. France Inter is on the air for twenty-four hours a day, with brief and longer newscasts hourly (and sometimes on the half hour, as well), several interview shows, and a great deal of music, most of it popular (including a fair amount of jazz) and most of it on disk-jockey-hosted programs. The tone for the most part is light and chatty, there are few talk shows that permit audience interaction, some of the disk jockeys run on in lengthy and at times nearly incomprehensible soliloquies, and although France Inter easily outstrips the other French public and private stations in numbers of listeners, Luxembourg and Europe No. One draw half again the number of France Inter listeners. France Musique also is on the air for twenty-four hours a day, carries seven five-to-ten-minute newscasts, but devotes most of the remaining time to classical music, although there are presentations of jazz once or twice daily as well. France Culture broadcasts from 7:00 A.M. to midnight, with seven newscasts, daily radio dramas, discussions of books, the arts, the sciences, and four to five hours of music, mostly classical but again with some jazz. France Culture emphasizes French culture almost exclusively: reviews of French books, presentations by French scientists, performances of French music (with some works from other countries) played by French musicians. Some of the programs are quite imaginative; for example, an 18 September 1984 episode of the series *Nuits Magnetiques* (Magnetic Nights) dealt with walking, as viewed by athletes, stage directors, blind persons, city planners, and for a grand finale, someone who had walked around the world!

The specialized services are Radio Bleue, on from 8:00 A.M. until noon and consisting of news, music, interviews, commentary, and advice programs, and intended particularly for older listeners (retirees or those near retirement); a twenty-four-hour-a-day news service, which in 1987 replaced Radio 7, a pop music/informational service for younger listeners; and France Inter Regions (FIR), serving Paris and ten other large cities (e.g., Lyons) and a few regions from 7:00 A.M. until 9:00 P.M. over FM (Paris and Marseilles have AM transmitters as well), with brief newscasts, lots of popular music, and frequent traffic reports. France Inter Regions was one of the few experiments with specialized radio initiated during the Conservative government's pre-1981 period of control; it started in 1970. (There had been a brief experiment with a youth-oriented radio service in the 1960s, and there were radio services for summer vacationers in certain resort cities, e.g., Biarritz and Cannes, starting in 1960.)[72]

There are eight further regional services (e.g., Radio France Normandie), but they play a less important role now than they did up until the early 1980s, when the local public radio stations became widespread. Those eight stations broadcast for about four hours each day, but my visits to them indicate that they are not as well staffed or well financed as they had been, and some of those staff members wonder whether there is much of a future for their operations. Much of the French listening public does not seem all that inclined to think of radio in regional terms.

The local public stations first began to come on the air in 1980, some claim as a belated bid by the Giscard government to show that it was interested in decentralizing broadcasting. Only three such stations were in existence by the time of the 1981 election; the Socialist party, making good on its announced intention to decentralize broadcasting, increased their number to fifteen by 1983 and proclaimed that there would be over ninety by 1988. As of 1987, there are thirty-six. Most have eight journalists, and most have well-equipped studios, although few are in buildings designed originally as radio stations: warehouses, floors of apartment buildings, and other structures have been converted for the purpose. Each is on the air for twelve to eighteen hours a day, starting around 6:00 A.M. and signing off anywhere from 6:00 P.M. to midnight. There are local disk jockeys for the many popular music programs, but most of that music can be heard over most other stations broadcasting to or within France, although occasionally a local rock group, municipal band, or school or civic choral group will perform. But the news has a decidedly local flavor: Radio Périgord concentrates heavily on agricultural activities, Radio Bretagne Ouest on fishing, and so on, because those activities are the lifeblood of the area. Some programs, both news and interviews, may be done in the regional or local language or dialect. Radio Bretagne Ouest carries one to two hours per day of programming in Breton, and Radio Périgord features ten to twenty minutes a day in Occitan, although few listeners speak it with much fluency. Many programs encourage phone-ins, and to judge from my own listening experience, a wide variety of listeners take advantage of the opportunity. A majority of station staff come from the regions to which they broadcast, and both ratings figures and personal messages from listeners indicate that the stations have large and devoted audiences. A July 1984 survey in the Dordogne ($N = 3,100$) showed that Radio Périgord, the chief local public station in the area, drew an average of nearly 40 percent of the total available listenership, and there were from seven to ten French-language stations from which a Périgord listener could choose.[73]

The officially licensed local private stations numbered over fifteen hundred as of 1988, but it is difficult to get a precise count because some go off the air temporarily or permanently and do not always notify the authorities. They exist even in towns of several hundred people, and there may be as many as one hundred in the Paris region alone. By law, they are not to exceed five hundred watts, but many go beyond that limit, and few are punished for doing so because, unless someone complains, the authorities do not investigate, and routine patrols by signal detection trucks are few in number and generally limited to major cities. Cross-channel interference among stations in the major cities, especially Paris, often is incredibly bad, but the authorities rarely interfere—the more so as some of the stations are run by politically influential people. Some groups share frequencies with one or more other groups. Most are on the air ten to twelve hours a day, but a few operate twenty-four-hour services. Most feature lots of popular music (a few began to specialize in "100 percent" French music in the mid-1980s, most of it from the 1950s),[74] much of it by request, because that is the least expensive program format: Most stations rely heavily upon volunteers and on individuals willing to work for next to nothing. Sometimes the amateurism shows, as I have witnessed in listening to broadcasts where it took a staff member five minutes to get on the right microphone.

The stations do their utmost to elicit telephone calls, because this is about the only tangible evidence of listenership that most of them can present to would-be advertisers, but often their efforts go unrewarded despite the offers of small cash or other prizes for giving the correct response to quiz questions: In September 1983, I listened to Radio Lorient, a small station in Lorient (south coast of Brittany) and nearly twenty minutes elapsed before anyone bothered to call the station to answer a simple question about a film star. There are local private stations that provide some unusual, provocative material, particularly the "gay" station (Fréquence Gaie) in Paris, Radio Pays in Paris (seven French minority languages such as Basque and Provençal), certain religious stations (four representing various facets of Judaism in Paris, and sometimes at odds with one another;[75] the liberal Catholic Radio Frontiére in Lyons), and the politically oriented stations (one or more in all of the large cities) of the sort described in Rouen (see p. 85). However, they are in the very distinct minority, and most of their confreres sound much alike and not particularly local.[76]

There probably are a few hundred illegal local private stations in France, most of which sound like most of their licensed counterparts. Those outside the large cities generally go unmolested, but those in the cities often must dodge the authorities, moving their equipment from place to place, usually on the warnings of neighbors that the detection team is in the neighborhood.

Despite the proliferation of radio outlets in France over the past several years, the overall amount of time that the average listener spends with radio remains pretty constant: roughly 2½ hours per day as of 1987. But the local public stations and some of the local private stations have cut heavily into the time people once spent listening to the national services, and, to some extent, the peripheral stations. Before the 1981 election, France Inter had an average of 22 percent of the audience listening at any given time; a year later, it had 14 percent.[77] A spring 1981 survey showed that the average daily (Monday–Friday) time spent by a listener to France Inter was just over 113 minutes, while for Europe No. One listeners it was 125.6 minutes, for (Radio-Télé Luxembourg) RTL 155.5 and for Radio Monte Carlo 158.8; other stations, most of them illegal, were not measured, but were so few in number that their audiences could not have been very sizable. By spring, 1984, the figures were France Inter 92.9, Europe No. One 123.7, RTL 155.8, and RMC 153.8, with "other stations," most of them local, now obtaining a collective average of 159.5 minutes per day.[78]

While national radio services retain some measure of importance, particularly to the small audiences for classical music, drama, and jazz fans and to the larger audiences of motorists who can listen to traffic reports frequently and just about anywhere in the country, it seems clear from my discussions with officials at the national, regional, and local levels that most people think of local radio as the most significant and worthwhile use of the medium. Whether this will be as true once local radio has ceased to be a novelty is anyone's guess, although most of the local public stations seem bent on involving the listening public as much as possible with the broadcasts, albeit rarely to the extent of setting up community advisory boards: Professionals by and large still feel that they know what's best. Local private radio is another matter; unless most of the stations can solve their financial problems—and there is a special but quite modest government grant program to which noncommercial stations may apply—there seems little prospect for them to develop much truly local programming.

TELEVISION   The two national public services of French public television really are one national service (A2) and one service divided between national and regional programming (FR3). Furthermore, the A2 and the recently privatized former national service, TF1, are almost indistinguishable in their program formats, although traditionally there has been some attempt to provide viewers with a genuine choice at any given hour. Whether this will last as TF1 more fully assumes its private identity remains to be seen. So far, the major evening newscast, which is different for the two channels, comes on at the same time on each (8:00–8:30 P.M.). The three services TF1, A2, and FR3 all have followed the usual European practice of broadcasting little or nothing during the weekday morning hours, although A2 has a cartoon show for children on Wednesday mornings because school is not in session then. Antenne 2 also carries breakfast-time television, which first came on the air in January 1985, running from 6:45 to 8:30, but it has had a hard time establishing itself in the daily lives of the French because they are not used to sitting down to a leisurely breakfast, and because the TV set usually stays in the living room. The afternoon hours on TF1 and A2 are filled with a mixture of short (fifteen- to thirty-minute) and long (forty-five- to fifty-minute) episodes of drama series, talk shows, documentaries, and, at the end of the afternoon, cartoon shows and minidocumentaries for children, as well as frequent offerings of popular music, often with rock videos. Game and quiz shows are relatively rare on French public TV, but A2 has a daily series, *Des Chiffres et des Lettres* (Numbers and Letters, 6:50–7:10 P.M.), that has been on for many years and seems to retain its popularity.

The evening period (prime time in France starts around 7:30 P.M., due to the late dinner hour, and lasts until 10:00 to 10:30 P.M.) is likely to contain lavishly produced variety shows, documentaries, nature programs, dramatizations of novels (usually by French authors), feature films (often French, and if not, sometimes dubbed) and, although rarely, a sports event (sports are more apt to be carried on weekends; soccer, rugby, and cycling lead the list). There is a brief newscast shortly after 11:00 P.M. on TF1 and A2 (again, separate newscasts), followed by a talk show on TF1 and *Bonsoir les Clips* on A2, then sign off around midnight.

The FR3 service follows a rather different schedule. A few of the dozen or so regional TV stations come on the air as early as 12:00 noon, but most begin their broadcasts at 5:00 P.M. Many of the stations draw from the same pool of cartoon shows (e.g., *Inspecteur Gadget*), documentaries and drama series (e.g., *Belle et Sebastien*), but schedule them differently. All FR3 stations carry regional newscasts and newsmagazines sometime between 6:00 and 7:55 P.M. At 6:55 FR3 becomes national, with one program lineup for the entire nation, for five minutes, with *Juste Ciel* (a horoscope program). From 7:00 to 7:55 P.M. there is *Magazines Informations,* a mixture of national and regional reports. The FR3 service again goes fully national at 7:55 with *Les Entrechats* (a ten-minute cartoon series), followed by a game show, either *Les Jeux de 20 Heures* or *Les Nouveaux Jeux de 20 Heures* ("new 8:00 games," with people from various French cities invited to participate). A feature film often follows at 8:35; usually it will be an "art" film, and quite often it will bear the equivalent of an *R* rating in the United States. After this comes a brief newscast, then often a minidocumentary (about five minutes) on one or another interesting development in France (e.g., architectural developments in the ancient city of Nimes), a classical music selection, then sign-off around midnight. Weekends on FR3 usually see the presentation of somewhat lighter fare, including such imported series as *Dempsey and Makepeace* (United Kingdom detective drama) and music videos.

The private television stations initially were quite different in their programming lineups, in that La Cinq broadcast little but imported drama and situation comedy, plus quiz shows, while Le Six broadcast little but music videos. Both began to diversify slightly toward the end of 1986, putting on some "blockbuster" feature films such as *Les Charlots Contre Dracula,* probably in hopes of improving their chances for renewal of their franchises. Neither service produced news or sports; they operated on a financial shoestring, and although they were supposed to produce original shows as a condition of their franchise, that obligation remained largely unfulfilled.

With the rewarding of the two licenses came the aforementioned programming obligations, which may not be easy to fulfill, now that La Cinq and Metropole TV (Le Six) will be pitted against a privatized TF1. Early indications are that both continue to rely heavily upon imported material, although La Cinq has developed its own news program, and both are obligated to do so. Certainly the owners of La Cinq are willing to spend quite freely to strengthen the station: A "talent raid" in April 1987 brought two of the most prominent TF1 light entertainment stars (Stephane Collaro, whose mildly satirical, *Muppet Show*–like *Cocorico-coboy* usually is in the weekly top ten, and Patrick Sebatier, host of the popular variety show *Grand Public*) and TF1's head of light entertainment, who had brought a French version of the U.S. game show *Wheel of Fortune* to TF1 only three months before. (As of early 1988, *Wheel of Fortune* regularly claimed three or four of the top-ten program listings.) Salaries were not the only consideration: There were some fears that the privatization of TF1 might compromise creative freedom and some expressions of anger that TF1's new owners did not seem all that anxious to bid for their services.[79] But the bidding itself shows quite clearly La Cinq's major priority: light entertainment.

Light entertainment apparently is becoming a greater priority for TF1, as well. About a fourth of TF1's news reporters quit during summer and fall of 1987, most of them because of what they saw as the network's reduced commitment to the news operation.[80]

Canal Plus, the private scrambled-signal channel, carries little besides entertainment, most of it in the form of feature films, but also some old U.S. series (e.g., *Batman*), some sports (including U.S. professional football), and a few talk, game, and variety shows, plus three or four brief news flashes a day. It broadcasts for twenty hours a day (7:00–3:00 A.M.), and some of its early and late afternoon offerings are descrambled.

A foreign viewer watching French television entertainment over an extended period would become aware of three things: first, that there are many repeats; second, that there are many feature films in prime time; and third, that there are few original (French-written, French-produced) prime-time dramas by modern writers, whether written for TV or not. (Traditional writers such as de Maupassant and Hugo fare better; there were excellent productions of *Toilers of the Sea* and *Les Miserables* in the fall of 1986.) Lack of money, or, to be more specific, lack of money for original productions, seems to be the root cause, but it also may be that, unlike the situations prevailing in Great Britain, West Germany, and Japan (for NHK, at least), serious creative artists do not find it particularly rewarding to express themselves through television. There are exceptions — the satires of Jean-Christophe Averty are very creative, and some of the documentaries show considerable inventiveness — but the usual program is no more than competent. The often meager production budgets don't help, nor does the long-established reputation of television as "servant of the government," but there is also the long-standing rejection of television by intellectuals that has nothing to do with budgets or with government interference. It may be that intellectuals simply cannot conceive of an instrument of mass communication as a suitable vehicle for the transmission of what they judge to be material of artistic merit.

Some of the more popular shows on French TV probably reinforce that opinion. The variety shows usually are colorfully costumed and staged, but performances often are wooden and lifeless. Historical dramas will be set with great attention to authenticity, but at times feature highly stylized acting that is more suitable for the theater than for television. Some of the comic sketches rework the same themes season after season: Stephane Collaro's various comic series (e.g., *Cocoricocoboy*) are sure to contain intellectual-but-sexy females whose bodies will be subjected to pinches and pats by various lecherous males, although his muppet-like figures representing President Mitterand (a frog) and Prime Minister Chirac (a pig) show some nice satirical touches. The game shows are more challenging than their U.S. counterparts, but not by much, although they are generally free of screaming and jumping contestants, flashing lights, and obtrusive hosts and hostesses.

Still, French television does devote considerable airtime to the display of French culture, and the typical evening lineup on the two public channels and on TF1 usually is heavily French. Imported drama series are rare, although *Dallas* and *Dynasty* achieved considerable popularity (and notoriety — newspaper critics and intellectuals loved to whip them for their mindlessness). Imported films are more common, and few days of the week pass without one or more on one or another of the channels. The few classical music programs, too, are just as apt to come from other European nations as from France. The various French-produced movies will have settings in various parts of the country, but the dramas are more likely to have a Parisian setting, although an increasing number are being produced by the regional stations in FR3 and broadcast nationally over that channel or over one of the other channels.

As already mentioned, sports is not a major element in the French public TV program lineup, nor are situation comedies, nor are game shows, although the latter are becoming more common on the private stations. The relative infrequency of sitcoms might seem surprising in a nation with a strong comic tradition and many performers skilled in comedy, but again, it may be that creative comic artists do not find the medium sufficiently challenging to try their hands at such endeavors. Interestingly, the one success in recent years, *Maguy*, was based on the U.S. 1970s sitcom, *Maude*, and the French producers paid for the rights to use the idea. On the other hand, satire is quite frequent, although often it appears as one segment of a variety show.

Soap operas also are rare on French TV, although Canal Plus introduced the half-hour daily *Rue Carnot* in 1985. Initial ratings were poor, so the producers followed the usual U.S. practice of spicing up the plot: they added a homosexual, a "bitch," and a terrorist, and had a romantic involvement between a Nazi and the lead character.[81] There also was the mid-1980s prime-time soap *Châteauvallon,* which some TV executives hoped would rival *Dallas*. It represented the power struggle between a rich, traditional family and a poorer, but more ambitious, family in a fictional city somewhere along the Loire River. There were roles for Germans, Italians, and other Europeans in the series, and they spoke in their own languages, with subtitles in French. Because the coproduction was with other European nations, and because other languages were used, the French hoped that the series would find a ready market outside France. However, a second season for "CV," as it was dubbed, had to be scrapped when one of the series' female stars was injured in an auto accident. The series was panned by most French TV critics as representing a pale imitation of *Dallas* but sometimes achieved respectable ratings.

News and public affairs, too, have a heavily French flavor. Documentaries almost always are French produced and usually deal with domestic subjects. Some of those subjects are highly controversial — divorce, abortion, racial prejudice — and often the controversy will find full expression, with analyses by experts sometimes following the documentaries. There has been a trend in recent years to make more minidocumentaries (three to five minutes in length) on specific subjects and problems, and often these are included with longer shows that present advice to viewers, depict life in other parts of the country, and so on. Documentaries are as educational as most of French TV ever gets; in contrast with the situation in the 1950s and 1960s, where there were several hours per day of educational radio and TV, there is currently little in-school programming. Institutes of education place little emphasis on the uses of the media in the classroom, and most French teachers appear to have little respect for television or for radio as educational media.

Newscasts were a part of French television almost from the beginning, but early TV newscasts were brief and uninteresting, and the de Gaulle era saw the credibility of TV news greatly diminished. Several French magazines published articles during the 1960s and 1970s comparing French TV news with what other European systems provided,[82] and the French product always suffered by comparison: It was less free, less interesting visually, and the presenters were boring. The presentation of news improved considerably during the early to middle 1980s, although lack of an equivalent to the satirical weekly newspaper *Le Canard Enchainée* probably meant that few intellectuals found it all that rewarding. The biggest improvement was in the relatively greater freedom to cover stories unfavorable to the government, although French mass media scholar Claude-Jean Bértrand observes that investigative reporting is not a strong suit for any of the French media, TV included, and that reporters generally lack much sense of professionalism.[83] There also was the creation of teams of news presenters who seemed at one and the same time to be knowledgeable and attractive. This was particularly true of the A2 team of Patrick Poivre d'Arvor and Christine Ockrent, which in late December 1982 raised A2's ratings for the 8:00 P.M. *Journal* (newscast) above those of the TF1 *Journal* for the first time in French TV history. Although theirs was not the "happy news" approach followed by so many U.S. stations, they did emerge as distinctive and attractive personalities. Ockrent felt so strongly about her identity as a journalist that she resigned from A2 in 1984 in protest over what she regarded as the politically inspired appointment of A2's new president. She was hired as assistant director general of TF1 shortly after its privatization, along with Michele Cotta, former president of the Haute Autorité, who became TF1's director of news.

The hiring of Ockrent and Cotta, as well as the retention of two of TF1's most prominent news anchors, Yves Mourousi and Anne Sinclair (who received large salary increases, although Mourousi's roughly six hundred thousand dollars per year leaves him some distance behind the most highly paid U.S. network news anchors), was a strong indication that TF1 did not intend to completely give up the long-running battle with A2 for leadership in broadcast journalism, and that it would not let La Cinq mount a serious challenge in that respect, either. (There were rumors that TF1's competitors had tried to woo Mourousi and Sinclair.)[84]

The Audience

Anyone who has visited the research divisions or offices of such broadcast organizations as Japan's NHK or Great Britain's BBC or IBA will experience a considerable letdown where French broadcasting is concerned. Traditionally, the public-service broadcasting system has not emphasized audience research, and until the 1970s it seemed to be more interested in the regular analysis of listener and viewer mail than it did in the collection of data through more rigorous, scientifically respectable methods. Some of the mail was elicited through panel members appointed by ORTF, and it contained indications not only of who viewed or listened, but also of what they thought of the program, as expressed through a ten-point scale (awful to excellent) and through narrative comment (sometimes pretty brief, as evidenced by one disgusted viewer's appraisal of a J. C. Averty program on Salvador Dali: "a nut depicted by a nut"). But panel sizes often were small for a given program, and selection of panel members not random, yielding inconclusive results.

Interest in more systematic audience research picked up during the 1970s, as TF1, A2 and FR3 all appointed directors of audience research. Not all were of top quality, but TF1's Michel Souchon came to the job in 1984 with an excellent academic reputation. Antenne 2 developed a simulation system to aid in scheduling programs to maximize audience size and began to use some research data to help sell advertising time.

Because of some of the obvious deficiencies in RTF and ORTF audience research, and because most of the data were not available publicly, other groups began to enter the field in the 1950s. Chief among them is the Centre d'Études des Supports de Publicité (CESP), founded in 1956 and still very active. It is a nonprofit organization supervised by an administrative council made up largely of its various mass media users. The CESP has been particularly useful for the peripheral radio stations, who in the earlier years covered a good share of its annual budget. Generally speaking, CESP designs studies but has them carried out by other organizations such as IFOP (Institut Français d'Opinion Publique). Its questionnaires often have been highly detailed—a typical questionnaire on radio listening in the mid-1970s sometimes had eleven pages[85]—although more recent efforts show fewer pages, perhaps to help combat a refusal rate that averaged about 20 percent. Panel members, usually around 1,750, are randomly selected, although there are the usual criticisms of underrepresentation of certain groups, especially the urban poor and rural dwellers in more remote parts of the country.

Up until 1976, there was another criticism of CESP's practices, and one that will sound very familiar to anyone who has studied audience research practices in U.S. commercial broadcasting: The stations knew well in advance when CESP would commence another survey (there were four each year, each lasting about one month), and, they would flood the market during those times with billboard, bumper-sticker, and on-the-air announcements and self-promotions, such as "Never alone with RTL." Since 1976, CESP has kept the dates of the survey periods secret, which has driven the peripheral stations at times to conduct their own surveys on their own schedules, although they continue to subscribe to CESP. Also, with the commercialization of ORTF in 1968, CESP became more deeply involved in audience research for television. It continues to make use of the aided recall method, whereby an interviewer will ask a respondent to look at a list to TV programs and check off those that she or he has viewed — a method discarded by most research organizations as too much subject to the fallibility of human memory.

The other major organization involved in audience research is the Centre d'Études d'Opinion (CEO), formed at the time of the breakup of ORTF in 1974. Originally, its research was intended chiefly to serve the public-service broadcast organizations, but within a few years Europe No. One and RTL both subscribed to it. The CEO developed a national random sample-based panel system with a fourteen-hundred-member panel; panel members were to fill in questionnaires on their daily listening and viewing and mail the questionnaires back to CEO at the middle and end of their particular sample week, and there were new panels each week.

Both CESP and CEO frequently were criticized for their secrecy and for questionable application of research methods. The sweeps held three times a year by CESP have drawn much the same critical reaction they have drawn in the United States: The networks load their "blockbuster" programs into those periods, so that data gathered in such circumstances tell little about a service's real ability to attract audiences week in, week out. A further problem with the CESP sweeps is that the sample size for each sweeps period is just over forty-four hundred individuals, and each individual responds only on the basis of what he or she recalls having viewed the previous evening. The CEO was accused in late 1984 of using faulty black boxes in which to collect data on the use of TV sets; the boxes were said to be so fragile that only four hundred out of the total six hundred boxes were in working order. At that point, the three heads of the public networks threatened to cut off their funding of CEO unless things changed.[86]

The CEO did change. It became a new operation, called Médiamétrie, in April 1985. It was dissociated from the prime minister's office and set up as a private corporation, although its funding would continue to come mainly from the three public networks. Starting in September 1985, Médiamétrie released to the public the ratings for the three public networks. The data revealed that the average French family spent about three hours and thirty-five minutes a day watching TV, and that TF1 was slightly ahead of A2 in viewer preference. Médiamétrie also had installed about one thousand well-constructed black boxes by January 1986 and now was able to provide reliable overnight ratings. Médiamétrie also has undertaken a nationwide telephone polling service, featuring interviews on program preferences and reactions to commercials for 185 TV viewers daily. As telephone service now is claimed to be available to just over 90 percent of French households (although some of this probably includes small apartments with one telephone for several households), Médiamétrie feels that the sample is quite representative.

The privatization of French broadcasting has begun to change the ratings system somewhat. Ratings rivalries now are more intense, and so are criticisms of methods used to determine ratings. New firms have sprung up and are bidding for contracts; one of them, Sofrés-Nielsen, already measures smaller samples of TV households and had hoped but failed to receive a CESP contract to conduct overall national surveys starting in January 1988. AGB received the contract, Nielsen brought suit against CESP, and as of March, 1988, both firms were installing "Peoplemeters" to collect ratings data. Médiamétrie has been criticized by TF1's director for leaking a confidential report to its chief rival, La Cinq, while La Cinq has accused Médiamétrie of incompetence and use of outdated methods.[87]

Problem Areas

It may be stating the obvious to say that political bias is a major problem area in French broadcasting, but it is worth noting again nonetheless, because five years of Socialist government lessened but certainly did not eliminate it. That government itself, as we have seen, acted at times as if it had learned little from its predecessors, although on balance broadcasting is far more open to the portrayal of divergent points of view than it had been before 1981. President Mitterand drew heavy criticism and opposition party complaints to the Haute Autorité for having been interviewed on TF1 in March 1986, during the three-week campaign period when there is supposed to be no political advertising (political ads appear in the press, but not on the electronic media). The Haute Autorité seemed uneasy in deciding that this was neither an advertisement nor a "communication of the government" (which would have opened it to right of reply), but it did take the unusual step of requiring the network to broadcast opposing politicians' reactions to the interview. Criticisms of bias in broadcasts sometimes have emerged when there seem to have been no real grounds for them, but that may be in part a reflex action based upon the conditioning that took place in the fifties, sixties, and seventies, which the Haute Autorité acknowledged in deciding on the 1986 Mitterand case.[88]

A second problem—the foreign cultural invasion of French television—may be more in the minds of certain TV critics, intellectuals, and the Socialist-era minister of communications and culture, Jack Lang, than in the minds of the public. The public stations do not carry very many foreign television programs, although imported feature movies (especially U.S.) are very common. The private stations do use far more imported material, but most French households at first were not able (or, in the case of Canal Plus, have not chosen) to receive them. The privatization of TF1 and the expansion of La Cinq changed that situation, but both have pledged to produce substantial amounts of domestic programming, and Minister of Culture François Leotard committed the government to spend 10 percent of the over $800 million it expects to receive for the sale of TF1 to the production of domestic programs "in the public sector."[89]

Certain of the foreign TV programs, especially *Dallas,* have been very popular, despite (or because of) the denigrating comments of the critics. So far, there have been no absolute quota restrictions on the amount of foreign material that can be shown on public television, although the new commercial TV services, as noted earlier, do face certain limits. Figures on the amounts of TV drama broadcast over the three public channels for the period 1980–84 showed that French productions outstripped foreign productions by fairly wide margins up until 1984, when the imported programs showed a slight lead. French television critic Raymond Kuhn sees the situation in more pessimistic terms, predicting a marked increase in imports and noting a growing tendency to imitate the U.S. product, especially such things as "the horrendous American practice of breakfast television."[90]

A third problem, and one common to most countries, is the relative lack of attention to regional and local cultures. That problem may be particularly acute in France, however, because the Socialist government made regionalization and localization among its top priorities. Thus, people may expect more regional and local broadcasting, and TV in particular, than they have received in the past. Also, France has some particularly rich and old regional cultures, with bodies of literature that could, and sometimes do, make good broadcast material. The Breton, Provençal, and Alsatian regions are particularly well endowed in that respect. But bringing such material to the screen, and encouraging modern regional writers to think of broadcasting as a natural outlet for their talents, takes money, and little of it flows to the regional and local levels (although certainly more than did in the past). And how far should the central government go in encouraging regionalization, when there have been rather strong separatist movements in Corsica and Brittany?

A fourth problem is serving France's immigrant and guest-worker communities. By the mid-1980s, those communities accounted for about 9 percent of the total population, and thanks to larger than average birthrates, that percentage is bound to increase in years to come. The advent of local private radio gave some of them a voice of their own, at least in the largest cities, but there is almost no foreign-language programming for such groups on the national stations. Their access to television, public or private, is almost nil. That pretty much sums up their portrayal *on* television, as well: It is a rare drama or even newscast item that shows them to the rest of France, although they are the subjects of occasional documentaries. Yet the average French viewer finds them more and more a part of urban life, without knowing much about the sorts of lives they lead.

Women suffered much the same treatment in and on broadcasting until the 1980s, but now they are quite prominent: One of the leading TV news anchors in the early 1980s was Christine Ockrent, and Michele Cotta was appointed first head of the Haute Autorité, while Jacqueline Baudrier was president of Radio France for several years. Furthermore, one can find women in a number of midlevel decision-making positions. Marie-France Briére was credited with revitalizing light entertainment on TF1 in the mid-1980s, and Pascale Breugnot, director of production at A2, has popularized such potentially difficult subject matter as economics (in the series *Vive la Crise*).[91] Whether any of this affects the portrayal of women through broadcasting is another matter. The ads and many programs reinforce long-standing stereotypes of woman as mother, housekeeper, and sex object, but women's liberation groups either are not as active in France as they are in West Germany, Great Britain, and the United States, or they are less concerned about their portrayal.

Foreign Influences on Programming

While there may be disagreement on whether or not it is a problem, most French certainly are aware of the foreign influences on their broadcast services, television in particular. As I have already noted, *Dallas* and other U.S. shows have done quite well in the ratings, and also seem to have influenced the creation of an imitator, *Châteauvallon*. Coproductions, too, have served to present French viewers with some non-French ways of looking at things and probably have caused French producers to rethink some of their concepts. News producers and presenters, too, are well aware of how newscasts are done in other European countries, Great Britain's BBC and IBA being cited as particularly good models. As private broadcasting brings more and more imported material to the screen, foreign influences may increase.

But much of French broadcasting still appears to be a law unto itself. Many of the variety and quiz shows and dramas I have seen over the years bear little resemblance to their counterparts in other broadcast systems, at least in style of production. There is a combination of formalism (in settings and in acting/performing) and slowness of pace that seems typically French, and outside any foreign influence. The themes of the crime shows and domestic dramas are little different from those same genres elsewhere, but they seem almost easygoing compared with British, German, Japanese, or U.S. productions. Antenne 2's *Télématin,* the breakfast TV show (6:45–8:30 A.M.), is even more casual than are its U.S. and British counterparts.

It may be that the French policy of maintaining the "Frenchness" of its former colonies, through television as well as through other means, has led TV producers to develop and maintain a unique style—one that is easily and immediately identifiable as French. It would be fascinating to study the domestic television production styles of former French and former British colonies, to see whether they reflected identifiable colonial origins. And certainly the French government spends a great deal of money both to export French broadcasts and to bring broadcasters, particularly from former French colonies, to France for further training.

Relations with Other Media

During the 1920s and 1930s, there was a close relationship between the press and private radio, since newspapers frequently were part or full owners of such stations. That relationship ended early in World War II, and despite numerous attempts on the part of several French newspapers to reinstate private broadcasting after the war and on up through the 1970s, it was not resumed. With the reestablishment of private radio in the early 1980s, some newspapers did choose to invest in the medium. However, less than 5 percent of all private radio stations feature any degree of press ownership.

Television has been a much more attractive proposition. As soon as the Socialist government announced its proposal to license private television, several press and publishing interests announced their intention to be among the investors. Two of the major figures were the press baron Robert Hersant (owner of the French pro-Conservative daily *Le Figaro*) and the Hachette publishing firm (which once had been a major shareholder in the Companie Luxembourgeoise de Télédiffusion), while Les Éditions Mondiales also expressed its interest. All of those groups already employed individuals who had worked in French television, several of whom had been top-level executives with TF1. The largest private ad agency in France, Publicis, also announced its intention to seek a license in cooperation with Europe No. One, which long had wanted to obtain a license and which already was involved in producing and distributing TV programs. The first TV license went to the Berlusconi-Seydoux group, as you have seen, but Publicis, Gaumont, and commercial radio station NRJ obtained the license for Le Six shortly thereafter.[92] In the 1987 relicensing, Publicis, NRJ, and Gaumont failed to retain their shares in Le Six, but Hersant acquired a large block of La Cinq, and a financial newspaper also acquired minor share blocks in it.

Aside from press and publisher ownership of broadcast stations and cable operations, the press has played a role in the development of French broadcasting by acting as a gadfly. Over the years, the general tone of French press comment on broadcasting issues has been highly critical. Even newspapers such as *Le Figaro* which were known to be favorable to the centrist coalition led in turn by de Gaulle, Pompidou, and Giscard d'Estaing often criticized the government for its various abuses of broadcasting. Newspaper critics writing about individual shows were very likely to take a condescending attitude toward them, treating them as second-class entertainment or information. If certain newspapers do acquire ownership in functioning private television stations, that might have some effect on the present adversarial relationship (although it is a one-sided relationship, in that the press does most of the criticizing), but if so, it would mean a major readjustment for TV critics, who have become accustomed over the years to looking down their noses at almost anything appearing on "le tube." It did not help matters that the French press saw public television in a particularly negative light once the government had authorized the sale of ad time in TV in 1968. Television news may not have been much of a competitor for print journalism, but advertising certainly was a competitive arena.

Ad agencies and broadcasting also have had an interesting relationship over time. Agence Havas, one of the world's largest ad agencies, was involved in broadcasting before World War II and continued its involvement after the war, albeit in different forms. It became a major investor in RTL, and when advertising was authorized for French TV, it claimed a considerable share of the business. And when the Socialist government decided to allow advertising on FR3 as well, Havas and Publicis divided the business between them. Though not officially an agency of the French government, Havas *is* closely connected with it, and the Havas president holds that position only with the blessing of the French president. The government sees to it that Havas is well provided with business, and the agency already is acquiring holdings in cable. It also acquired responsibility for Canal Plus in late 1983, after Canal Plus initially had been placed with the State Secretariat for Communications.

Relations with the film industry have been, to say the least, uneven. For many years there was a legal requirement that French television not show movies (unless made specifically for TV) until three years after their debuts in cinemas. Because Canal Plus was to base its schedule on feature films, it needed a smaller interval between cinema release and release on Canal Plus. Initially it negotiated for a nine-month interval, but eventually it settled for twelve months. Another part of that negotiation with the film industry involved determining the numbers of movies to be shown on Canal Plus—it wanted 375 films a year, while the industry proposed 250—and the price, with the industry pushing for a minimum price per film and Canal Plus offering a collective price for all films produced each year.[93] Eventually the two sides compromised: There would be 320 features a year. That figure was raised to 364 in 1985, partly because Canal Plus was not attracting as many subscribers as it had projected. That situation prompted Canal Plus to seek further investors, and in March 1986, one of Great Britain's largest commercial television companies, Granada TV, acquired a roughly 5 percent share in the venture.

All in all, the film industry received something of a financial shot in the arm through this transaction, but its concessions represent a recognition that TV is a more important customer than are cinemas—a recognition that seems to have taken longer in France than in most western nations, despite the clear evidence of declining cinema attendance. (The growth of VCRs in France also has opened an important market.) However, those concessions also led the Berlusconi-Seydoux group to demand concessions for La Cinq, and it negotiated a two-year wait, rather than the three-year wait on public television.[94] Actually, "negotiated" is something of a misnomer: The government simply conceded the point during contract negotiations, and the film industry was powerless to do anything about it.

The FR3 service was allowed from its debut to enter into coproduction agreements with movie producers, as were TF1 and A2 starting in 1980, and it quickly won critical acclaim for those productions. (French critics are far more kindly disposed toward film, which they treat as an art form, than toward TV.) Many were exported, especially to French-speaking nations, and children's shows have become quite important in the export market. Much of the production has been done in sixteen millimeter, and all of it is conceived in terms of what will work on television, not on the movie screen.[95]

As the film industry has recovered some degree of prosperity through the support of television, it has become increasingly vocal about what it feels are abuses by almost all of the television services, public and private alike, of various agreements to hold down the broadcasting of theatrical films so that cinema houses can continue to attract audiences, too. The industry wants reductions both in the numbers of movies broadcast overall and in the number of movies broadcast in prime time. The increased competition brought on by privatization has made films an especially attractive and inexpensive programming element that hurts cinema attendance. (A decline of some 10 percent was anticipated by the end of 1987.) But the Conservative government's minister of culture, François Leotard, seemed unresponsive, and the industry was considering a cinema campaign, including an anti-Leotard commercial, to call public attention to what it considers "nonassistance to a culture in distress."[96]

International Cooperation

France is a very active exporter of radio and television programming to its former colonies and protectorates, as well as to other French-speaking European nations and to Canada. Most of that export trade is in the form of entertainment programming and is on videotape, but in 1984 France linked up with Switzerland and Belgium, and later with Canada, to develop a jointly programmed service for distribution to cable TV outlets via satellite. The service, TV5, contains a mixture of information and entertainment from the four nations, but France supplies over three-fourths of the material.

One aspect of French TV program distribution that used to limit the size of the export market was the small amount of programming available in other languages besides French, but in 1979 the Ministry of Foreign Affairs created a special department to increase the dubbing of programs into English, which has facilitated sales abroad. That move is indicative of the view of past and present French governments that French television can serve as a useful form of cultural propaganda; as such, it is perfectly proper that the government be involved in the activity.[97] Private firms become involved, as well: Télé-Hachette has produced *Life of Hemingway, The Dreyfus Affair* and *Mother Teresa*, Hamster has done *L'Heure Simenon* (stories by France's most famous writer of detective novels), and Telecip the adventure series *Scorpio*. The government also helped to subsidize an ill-fated attempt to supply French TV programming to the U.S. cable market, through TeleFrance USA. There were hopes that the organization could distribute to many of the larger cable operations on a daily basis, but TeleFrance USA never made it past New York and Boston or beyond a few days each week.[98] TeleFrance folded in 1982.

France has entered into coproduction arrangements with most of the other major European broadcasting organizations and several of the smaller ones at one time or another. *Châteauvallon* was a notably ambitious example of such an undertaking—it is rare to have a series produced through coproduction—but each year sees a number of documentaries, cultural programs, and children's programs (e.g., the U.S. series *3-2-1-Contact*) done as coproductions. Belgium and Switzerland are natural partners because they are in part French speaking, but West Germany, Italy, and Great Britain also have been frequent collaborators. For example, French public TV and a West German private production house teamed up in 1987 to produce a series on French teenagers during World War II.

The official production house for public television, SFP, is making major efforts to coproduce and otherwise internationalize in part because the privatization of TF1 means that that station no longer has to give SFP the lion's share of its production business.[99] The private stations also see some prospects for coproduction: Berlusconi and Seydoux, together with West Germany's Beta Film and Great Britain's Robert Maxwell, formed the European Consortium for Commercial Television in 1987 and announced plans to produce miniseries such as Thomas Mann's *The Magic Mountain*.[100]

France is a member of the European Broadcasting Union and an active participant in the Eurovision news and program exchanges. In 1986, French public television and Canal Plus contributed almost 250 hours to the program exchange and received just over 825.[101]

In addition to these more standard forms of international activity, the French government early established an organization that either controlled or strongly influenced several foreign broadcast stations, three of them just outside the borders of France and with French audiences as their primary targets. The organization is SOFIRAD, or Société Financiére de Radiodiffusion, but its informal title is "the octopus," for reasons that will be evident. The predecessor to SOFIRAD came into being in 1942 as the result of a cooperative arrangement between the German government and the government of Vichy France and controlled the newly created (by the Germans) Radio Monte Carlo. It became SO-FIRAD in 1945; the French government took over full responsibility for its financial support.[102] Its twelve-member administrative council was appointed by the French government, and it had partial or total owner-ship of Sud Radio (Andorra based, directed to Southwestern France), Radio Monte Carlo (Monaco based, but with its transmitter on French soil and directed largely to France), Europe No. One (transmitter based in the West German state of Saar, studios in Paris and directed to France) and several overseas operations: Radio Monte Carlo Middle East (Cyprus based, directed to the Middle East), Afrique No. Une (Gabon based, and directed largely to central and west Africa), Radio Mediterranée Internationale (Morocco based, and directed largely to North Africa), and Radio Caribée Internationale (Dominica and Saint Lucia-based, and directed to the Caribbean). It also had been financially in-volved in Télé-Liban (a television station in Lebanon), Télé Monte Carlo, and Télé-France Internationale (a supplier of prerecorded French programs for overseas distribution; TeleFrance USA was a part of it).

Clearly SOFIRAD has been an operation of major proportions. Whether it has exercised control over the programming of its many "tentacles" is more difficult to discern, and whether that control has been the result of pressures from the government still more difficult. Inter-views with SOFIRAD officials[103] elicited strong denials that the company had anything at all to do with program content; officials say that their role is strictly financial. However, certain crises within France have led to specific acts of censorship of broadcasts and punishment of broadcas-ters that clearly have been inspired by government displeasure at mate-rial carried by the peripheral stations with which SOFIRAD is con-nected. Notable examples are the firing of several of Europe No. One's broadcast journalists following the 1968 disturbances (see p. 75–76) and the sacking of Maurice Siegel, Europe No. One's director general, in 1974, on the pubic grounds that he had been there too long, but with the accompanying statement by Denis Baudouin (SOFIRAD's then director) that he (Baudouin) was tired of the station's "bantering tone" toward the government.[104]

On the whole, the two other peripheral stations under SOFIRAD's influence, Sud Radio and Radio Monte Carlo, caused fewer problems for the government than did Europe No. One, and found themselves rewarded on occasion for their "good behavior." When Sud Radio lost its access to its transmitter in Andorra in 1980, the French government allowed it to use a French transmitter until access was regained in 1983, although the station could not carry commercials during the time if broadcast from within France. And when Radio Monte Carlo wanted to increase the range of its transmissions in 1974, which could be done only by finding a more suitable transmitter-antenna site, the French government arranged for the lease of land within France itself—a move that angered officials at Radio France tremendously, since they had been struggling to keep the peripheral stations from taking away even more of their audience.[105]

Once the Socialists had come to power, they indicated that the peripheral stations, too, would see changes. Whether all of the changes are to the stations' tastes is another question—the increase in competition through the licensing of local private radio definitely has hurt the peripherals[106]—and the French government remains securely in control of SOFIRAD, but at least there have been no recent cases of open interference with program content to match those of previous decades. Still, there always is the possibility that *any* government could shape or block future peripheral broadcasts, so whether the stations offer French listeners a genuine alternative to Radio France will continue to depend very much upon the prevailing circumstances. The peripherals were allowed to acquire local radio frequencies in 1986, which Luxembourg, Europe No. One, and RMC all have done, so they now benefit from FM outlets in several large French cities.

In early 1986, the French government began to sell off parts of SOFIRAD. The first major element to go was Europe No. One; the giant publishing company Hachette acquired controlling interest in the station for over $70 million, and most of the stock it bought was what had been held by SOFIRAD. Whether other parts of the SOFIRAD empire will be sold off by the Conservative government remains to be seen, but SOFIRAD had been having financial problems for some time before the sale of its stock in Europe No. One, and Sud Radio, one of its weakest revenue producers, was sold in the summer of 1987. The SOFIRAD shares in Radio Monte Carlo, too, were up for sale starting in 1986, with no takers by early 1988.

Radio-Télé Luxembourg has no SOFIRAD investment, but the French government-connected ad agency Havas owns stock in it and wields even more influence over the financial affairs of the station than its shares (about 8 percent) would seem to warrant.[107] In addition, some French publishers with ties to the government (e.g., Hachette) own shares in the company, so the opportunity for influence exists, even if it is not as direct as is the case with SOFIRAD-connected stations.

The New Media

If France had been able to capitalize upon the implementation of several domestic technological developments during the 1970s — videotext, fiber optics, multichannel cable TV— by now it would have had a commanding lead over other Western European nations in exploitation of the new media. But the economic problems that beset French industry in general during the middle to late 1970s[108] also afflicted the French telecommunications industry, and the experiments remained few in number and were exploited to only a fraction of their potential.

By the end of the 1970s, the French government had decided that it was time to intervene in the languishing telecommunications industry, which then began to receive some government assistance. If that industry could be stimulated, so the reasoning went, France might have a strong entry in the export market, especially in Western Europe where various trade agreements gave Western European products an edge over those produced in North America and in Japan, the two major telecommunications exporters. The Mitterand government continued that stimulation policy, and also erected further trade barriers of the sort described earlier for Japanese-made VCRs, but the Chirac government dropped the barriers in 1987.

Fiber-optic cable was one of the first beneficiaries of the stimulation policy, and in mid-1985 the government approved a plan that called for cable service to some 450 cities and serving over 15 million people, to be accomplished by the end of the decade. Not all of the services were to be of equal complexity, but most were to provide the full set of domestic TV services (often with greatly enhanced picture quality) and videotext, and some would provide one or another of the peripheral services (Télé Monte Carlo, RTL) and one or more of the services of neighboring countries (Belgium, Switzerland, West Germany), as well as some of the services available by satellite (e.g., Sky Channel). Some also would provide two-way services. The 1982 Audiovisual Communications Law required that private investment in cable not exceed two-thirds of the capital; the remainder was to be held by the city council, which also selected the chairperson of the company actually operating the cable installation. The French PTT would own and operate the technical facilities.

Still, if the Biarritz experiment in fiber-optic cable is any guide, development of fiber-optic cable on a wider scale may take quite a while. The Biarritz experiment was begun in 1981; by 1985 it had six hundred subscribers, and by the end of that year a little over a thousand. French industry was not geared to mass production of fiber optics. Subscribers had a limited choice of programming fare by North American standards: ten TV channels, including the various French services, two Spanish services, one Belgian, one Swiss, and BBC1. A local channel commenced service in late 1985, for an hour or so each day, and Sky Channel also was available. Subscribers paid Fr 55 (about $9.25) a month, with various additional services (videotext, videophone) carrying supplementary charges.[109]

Most cable service currently available in France is through coaxial cable (about 5 percent of all French households) or through master antenna TV service to apartments (about 30 percent of all households). The coaxial service in Cergy-Pontoise, near Paris, is quite typical: twelve channels, most of them over the air, a few satellite delivered. French observers are divided in their opinions as to whether most French really want to see that much more television than they already receive; and if Canal Plus and the new commercial networks establish nationwide distribution soon, there may be little interest in cable. A steady increase in VCR ownership—about 25 percent of all French households had one or more of the recorders by mid-1987—also makes movie-oriented cable TV services less attractive. However, the government's announcement in January 1987 that it would drop the Socialist project of wiring the nation with fiber-optic cable, but would encourage French investors to wire individual communities with coaxial cable, could stimulate the more rapid development of cable service, since coaxial is so much cheaper than fiber optic.[110] Local authorities initially decide whether to authorize cable for their communities, although the broadcast regulatory agency has final licensing approval and sets general licensing terms (usually but not always including retransmission of all regularly available programs, provision of an access channel, etc.).

Potentially the biggest stimulus to the further development of cable TV in France is Paris Cable, owned in part by Lyonnaise des Eaux, which also has invested heavily in Metropole TV (Le Six). Two hundred homes signed up for Paris Cable in December 1986, with company predictions that there would be 1.3 million homes hooked up by 1992. However, the fourteen-channel system, which offered subscribers the usual French channels plus BBC1, Italy's RAI1, Télé-Luxembourg, Télé Monte Carlo, Turner Broadcasting's Cable News Network (in English), a new children's channel operated by Hachette, and a new local channel called Paris Premiere, was off to a slow start: fewer than ten thousand subscribers by mid-1987. If the operation was to expand more rapidly, it could stimulate the development of cable throughout the nation.

Direct broadcasts from satellites to home receivers had been one of the great fascinations of the Socialist government during the early 1980s, and in 1984 the French and Luxembourg governments signed an agreement to finance and jointly program a DBS operation. Such an approach had been discussed by the then Conservative-led French government and the Luxembourg government in the late 1970s, but the Socialists had to reconcile themselves to the demand on the part of Radio-Télé-Luxembourg (RTL) that it carry commercials on its two DBS channels. In early 1986, the Socialist government altered the conditions somewhat: It now offered two of the four DBS channels to a European consortium made up of investors from Great Britain, West Germany, Italy, and France (the latter two were Berlusconi and Seydoux, who were responsible for the newly licensed commercial TV station La Cinq), with possible further investment from Spain. Luxembourg now was to be offered one channel. Some observers saw this as an expression of distrust by the Socialists of certain investors in the Belgian-based Groupe Bruxelles-Lambert, the major investor in RTL.[111]

The return to power of the Conservatives in the mid-March 1986 elections threw the DBS picture into further confusion. Conservative spokespersons for communications policy announced in early April that they were annulling the existing DBS agreement (largely because they disagreed with the Socialist government's choices of participants) and would reopen the bidding process (which probably would favor RTL). Launch of the first French DBS satellite was scheduled for November 1986, but it remained an open question as to whether there would be many of the required dish antennas and converters available by then. In any event, the launch problems that had plagued so many nations in the mid-1980s also hit France, and now the satellite, TDF1, probably will not be launched until late 1988. Some of the cabinet ministers have argued against its deployment at all, on the grounds of the enormous cost and questionable benefits, but the 1988 policy of the Conservative government appears to favor the launch, so long as private investors will meet its expenses. By mid-1988, Luxembourg may have launched its own satellite, Astra, so one important customer may have vanished, leaving the newer French private TV services as the major backers of the TDF1 – provided, of course, that they haven't gone over to Astra![112]

In short, French policy toward the new media has been as politicized as has policy toward conventional broadcasting. Both Socialist and Conservative governments have agreed that rapid development of the French telecommunications industry could give the French economy a shot in the arm, but weaknesses in the French economy and transfers of political power have hindered development to the point where, if the new media finally do take hold, they are likely to have more European, Japanese, and North American technological and program components.

Conclusion

French broadcasting has been dominated by political pressures throughout most of its history, to a degree remarkable among European nations. The electoral victory of the Conservative coalition in 1986 and the ensuing "media reforms" showed once again how difficult it is for any long-range planning to be accomplished where broadcasting is concerned, since a new government is almost certain to undo much of the work of its predecessor. Still, the opening up of broadcasting to more licensees, and the greater degree of freedom of expression enjoyed by broadcasters, are likely to remain as legacies of the Socialist government; the Conservatives are not about to attempt to restore the monopolistic system or the tight controls over broadcast content of the pre-1981 era.

France also has emphasized its own culture in its broadcast output over most of the history of broadcasting, sometimes to the point of seeming overly chauvinistic, especially by comparison with other European systems. The licensing of commercial radio and TV stations in the early to middle 1980s brought with it larger amounts of foreign program material, and some of it seems to have been quite popular, but government officials remain wary of foreign incursions, and French talent unions have lobbied for tighter controls on imports. The intellectuals, too, have expressed alarm over the prospect of a cultural invasion through TV. French officials are aware that the new technologies make it almost impossible to restrict the flow of foreign programs into France in any major way, but they do seem determined to support French production so that at least French programs will be able to compete on a reasonably even footing.

Clearly, too, economic considerations are becoming more important in shaping French broadcasting. The development of cable (especially fiber-optic cable) and satellite technology was a high-priority item for Conservatives and for Socialists alike in the early to middle 80s. Even as the government subsidized work in those fields, however, it expressed concern over the rising costs of production, the need for increases in the annual license fees, and possible inefficiency in the administration of the public broadcasting services. Those concerns have been present over the past few decades, but they seem to have become more serious within the last few years. It was not surprising that the newly elected Conservative coalition announced in April 1986 that there might be privatization of one or two of the public TV services, and that in fact no public broadcasting service was sacred. Nor was it surprising to learn that some government officials were considering the removal of advertising from public television so as to provide more revenue for private TV.[113] It may have been more surprising to see the Conservatives back off from the subsidization of fiber-optic cable and DBS, given their earlier support for both, but that action was consistent with the new economic conservatism of the middle to late 1980s, which was finding expression in many parts of Europe.[114]

Whether France can maintain a high level of domestic cultural TV production in a large privatized broadcast system is another question, as is the question of political control or influence over such a system. Whatever its faults, the French public system exhibited the dubious virtue of being amenable to the influence of the government of the day, even under the Socialists. Reconciling political, cultural, and economic considerations in the more complex dual (public-private) system that has developed in the 1980s is bound to be a more difficult task.[115] It remains to be seen what sort of system of control ultimately will evolve to meet that task, presuming that it is still possible to do so, but it seems clear that the evolution is not likely to stop anytime soon.

NETHERLANDS

Leewarden

NORTH SEA

Amsterdam

Hilversum

Rotterdam

FEDERAL REPUBLIC
OF GERMANY

BELGIUM

FRANCE

LUX.

0   25   50 miles

3

The Netherlands

Plurality with a Vengeance

T HE broadcasting system in the Netherlands often has been acclaimed as a model of how broadcasting can be structured to serve society (as opposed to serving government, advertisers, media managers, the "power elite," etc.). Certainly that structure is very different from any other in the world, but there are some doubts on the part of several Dutch observers as to whether the system merits the praise it has received, or whether it will be able to adjust to changes in society and in technology. A combination of physical and societal factors has helped to shape the present system, but recent changes in some of those factors may have weakened its foundations.[1]

Basic Factors

GEOGRAPHIC   It would be hard to imagine a geographical situation more conducive to the growth of broadcasting. The Netherlands is almost as flat as the proverbial pancake and is the most densely populated nation in Europe (423 inhabitants per square kilometer). It is approximately 150 miles long and 120 miles wide at its broadest points, and its major population centers all lie within a 30-mile-wide, east-west band running through the middle of the country. It has two other nations on its land borders: West Germany to its east and southeast, Belgium to its south. England lies some 50–150 miles across the channel. While the nation is not really circular in shape, it is possible to broadcast from a central point and cover the entire nation with a 75-mile radius signal, with little spillover into the neighboring nations.

Those neighbors also play a role in shaping Dutch broadcasting. The northern half of Belgium, which borders the southern Netherlands, is Flemish (Dutch) speaking. Broadcasts from Belgium may be heard throughout the Netherlands and seen in much of the country. The same is true for West Germany, and many Dutch citizens can understand German quite well, although those with memories of World War II often prefer not to speak it. Radio broadcasts from England also can be received throughout the country, and television comes in along some parts of the Dutch coast. Since most Dutch citizens have studied English in school for several years, they can follow British broadcasts with relative ease. The spread of cable TV in the Netherlands also has helped to bring television from each of these countries to Dutch viewers. Broadcasts from the Netherlands can be heard in parts of all three countries, as well, but only in northern Belgium is there likely to be much of an audience for them, few Germans or English being fluent in Dutch.

DEMOGRAPHIC   Not only is the Netherlands densely populated, but its people are remarkably homogeneous. Most of the 14 million Dutch were born and raised there, and their family trees go back for centuries. This has led some observers to claim that the Dutch are overly class-conscious,[2] but it also enables broadcasters to assume certain shared national traditions. When broadcasting began in the early 1920s, that homogeneity was almost total, and broadcasters had little concern for such few non-Dutch speakers (aside from Frisian, which is linguistically related to Dutch and which is spoken by perhaps 250,000 people living in the north) as there might have been in the audience. Regional dialects are spoken in the home and among friends, but rarely appear on national broadcast services.

However, the past few decades have seen some marked changes in that situation. Although precise figures are hard to come by, there may be some 35,000 Moluccans, 180,000 Surinamese, 40,000 Antilleans, and 350,000 "guest workers" from southern Europe, Turkey, and Morocco living in the Netherlands. Some estimates double those figures. The Moluccans are there because their island home, once part of the Dutch East

Indies, was incorporated into Indonesia in 1950; many did not welcome the change and left. The Surinamese came from former Dutch Guiana and the Antilleans from the Netherlands Antilles, on and just off the northern coast of South America. Their major reason for coming was to escape the poverty of their native lands. The guest workers came during the economic expansion of the 1960s, when there were too few Dutch citizens willing to take or to continue on in some of the really grimy, physically exhausting jobs that opened up during that period. Members of those groups keep largely to themselves, and few speak or understand Dutch all that well. Most are to be found in the larger cities, but it is not unusual to see Surinamese and Moluccans living in smaller towns.

ECONOMIC The Netherlands is a prosperous nation, although the worldwide recession of the late 1970s and early 1980s had a dampening effect on the Dutch economy. Certainly the country has a high enough per capita income (Fl 23,416 [Dutch florins], or about $10,000, in 1983) to be able to support with relative ease what is, as you will see, an expensive broadcasting system. Almost every Dutch household has a number of radio sets and one or more TV sets. Most Dutch citizens are urban dwellers, working in businesses, the professions, for government, and in manufacturing. However, some 6 percent of the population is employed in fishing and agriculture. Broadcasting pays special attention to the latter two through detailed marine weather forecasts and early-morning radio programs on agricultural development.

POLITICAL The Netherlands is a constitutional monarchy, in which the sovereign (currently Queen Beatrix) has little to do with the governance of the nation. Ten political parties are represented in the Dutch Parliament as of 1987, but most are involved in coalitions in order to gain more voting strength. Coalitions generally are responsible for the formation of governments: In 1982, a coalition of Christian Democrats and Conservatives was called upon by the queen to form a new government, with specific implications for broadcasting policy. In 1964, a government even fell from power because of its inability to present to Parliament a suitable proposal for an additional television service — probably the only time in history, Dutch or anyone else's, where a broadcast problem caused the downfall of a government. Major political parties also are involved with the country's major broadcasting organizations, and all political parties represented in Parliament receive equal amounts of airtime for party political broadcasts.

CULTURAL   The Dutch are able to draw upon a rich cultural tradition
going back to the Middle Ages and including such figures as Rem-
brandt and Escher. Thanks to the presence of a universal and high-quality
system of education, literacy is very high, and many works of Dutch
novelists and playwrights who are unknown outside the country are widely
known and appreciated within it. Some of those works have become popular favorites when adapted for television, such as the late nineteenth-
century novel *De Stille Kracht* (The Hidden Force). But there also is a
considerable following for foreign culture, ranging from avant-garde theater and painting to rock and roll and TV series such as *Dallas*.

   Religion plays an especially important part in Dutch culture, although surveys indicate that nearly one-third of all Dutch citizens do not
consider themselves to be affiliated with any organized religion, and
church attendance is dwindling. According to a 1975 survey, some 30
percent considered themselves to be Roman Catholic, another 30 percent
Protestant, and about 8 percent various other denominations. However, a
1987 survey showed that nearly half of the population considered itself
unaffiliated with any organized religion.[3] Still, the largest groups — Roman
Catholics and Calvinists — continue to exercise considerable influence in
Dutch society. They operate their own school systems from kindergarten
through university and have their own newspapers, political parties, and
broadcasting organizations, in addition to sports clubs, youth groups, and
even for Catholic farmers a goat-breeders association. This pervasive involvement by organized religion in the life of the nation often has been
called the "pillar" concept, with each organization seen as one of the chief
pillars supporting the national structure. Where broadcasting is concerned, three main religious organizations (Roman Catholic, Calvinist,
Liberal Protestant) became involved in the middle to late 1920s, and were
joined by a sociopolitical organization, the Socialists.

   But Dutch culture is very encouraging of the expression of minority
opinion, and dozens of artistic and social reform groups bring their viewpoints and works before the public. Associations and foundations for
sexual reform, moral rearmament, free thinkers, Freemasons, Christian
Scientists, Humanitarians, and many others flourish in the Netherlands,
and many receive continuing allocations of airtime to present themselves
over Dutch radio and television. It is not unusual to hear a Dutch citizen
complain about the "kooks" and "oddballs" one sees and hears, especially
in the larger cities, but the same person is quite likely to observe with some
pride that tolerance and even encouragement of such activity is what
makes Dutch society different (meaning "better"). As a specific manifestation of that spirit where broadcasting is concerned, consider the situation
of the most radical of the broadcasting organizations, VPRO (Liberal

Protestant). Often, its dues-paying membership has come dangerously close to dropping below the minimum number specified by the Media Act for the lowest category of organization entitled to major blocks of airtime. When that has become known, VPRO regularly has received membership dues from people who state that they do not agree with its programming but respect and encourage its right to continue.

A Brief History

Some Dutch historians have claimed that the world's first regularly and continuously scheduled radio broadcasts for the public came about in the Netherlands in November 1919.[4] An engineer, H.H.S. à S. Idzerda, began to broadcast from the Hague laboratory of his company, the Netherlands Radio Industry. His broadcasts were financed out of his own pocket, and on occasion, by listeners from as far away as England responding to his appeals for funds. The next few years saw several manufacturers of radio equipment initiate their own broadcast services, presumably in hopes of stimulating the sale of radio sets and parts. By 1923, the minister of public works attempted to bring a greater sense of order to the situation by calling for formal applications for franchises to broadcast, but there were too many to accommodate, so, much as had been the case in Great Britain, the minister called upon applicants to submit a joint application. Only one company, the Netherlands Transmitter Industry, followed through. (Idzerda's company was nearly bankrupt by then.) The company was allowed to lease airtime to interested organizations, and by 1928 there were five of them, broadcasting on two transmitters. They were:

NCRV (Netherlands Christian Radio Association) 1924
VARA (Workers Radio Amateurs Association) 1925
KRO (Catholic Radio Broadcasting Foundation) 1925
VPRO (Liberal Protestant Radio Broadcasting Association) 1926
AVRO (General Radio Broadcasting Association, originally made up of people who had constructed their own sets and wanted to promote their hobby by making broadcasts) 1928

From the beginning, then, the government made two important decisions: first, that it would insure some degree of order and stability in broadcasting, and second, that it would not operate broadcast services itself. However, no single organization would be permitted to claim exclusive rights to operate such services, either. Organizations that did claim airtime were required from 1923 on to provide a reasonably complete range of programming, not only for their own particular supporters, but also for the Dutch citizenry in general. This concept of broadcasting might be called "pluralism within a monopoly," since the government decided who was entitled to broadcast and what the general shape of the program schedule would be but permitted several quite diverse groups to exercise that right.

Under the terms of a 1928 ministerial order, the groups also had to agree to share the two transmitters. In 1927, KRO and NCRV had co-financed the construction of the second transmitter, which they then reserved for themselves. The General Radio Broadcasting Association (AVRO) claimed near-exclusive rights to the first transmitter, leaving little time for VARA and VPRO. All this now changed: The four largest groups were given equal amounts of airtime on the two transmitters, while the smaller VPRO received a lesser amount. Size of membership thus became a criterion for amount of airtime and remains so to this day.

It is difficult to determine just why those particular organizations received airtime, although their size, and their prominence in Dutch political, social, and cultural life, certainly were factors. There was only moderate support at that time for a national system of broadcasting along the lines of the BBC, and little for a government-run service.[5]

The various broadcasting organizations were responsible for raising their own finances. Voluntary contributions from listeners, as well as support from the parent organizations (e.g., the Roman Catholic Church), formed the not always reliable mainstays of that support. After the first few years, no advertising was allowed for Dutch audiences, although a few English firms sponsored popular music programs in order to reach British listeners (the BBC did not broadcast ads), and a few Dutch firms furnished gifts to be given away on programs so long as the brand name of the gift was mentioned.[6] Advertising stopped altogether in 1935. There was no license fee for listeners to pay, either, even though that practice already was widespread in Europe.

During the first decade or so of Dutch broadcasting, the government did not concern itself overmuch with specific broadcast content. The need for each broadcasting organization to present a balanced service never was governed by set percentages of program categories or standards for program content; however, general regulations concerning public order and other related matters were issued in 1930, and smaller organizations (e.g., the Radio People's University) were authorized small amounts of airtime. But in the early 1930s, the government showed that it was quite ready to express concern over content, even without specific standards. In 1933, the Socialist broadcasting organization, VARA, observed a minute of silence after the execution of van der Lubbe, the man the Nazis had accused of setting fire to the Reichstag building in Berlin. The government felt that this was prejudicial to its policy of political neutrality and withdrew one hour of broadcasting time from VARA as "punishment." As a gesture of solidarity, the other broadcasting organizations mutually agreed not to use that time themselves, so the hour went unfilled.[7] In 1934, with the depression causing high unemployment and with Naziism growing in Europe, the Dutch Communist Party, Dutch Nazi Party, and several other parties became involved in various disturbances; at one point, the Communists declared a "Red front" and made illegal broadcasts over a transmitter in "the heart of Red Amsterdam,"[8] but they soon went off the air. And in 1935 the government created a "mixed" company called NOZEMA (Nederlandse Omroep Zender Maatschappij), which was to handle all transmission facilities; the four largest organizations held 40 percent of the stock, the government the remaining 60 percent.

When the Netherlands was occupied by Nazi Germany in 1940, all of the broadcasting facilities came under Nazi control. The various broadcasting organizations ceased to function, although many of their staff members continued to work for the German occupation government. Also, that government instituted a license fee for listeners; the Dutch government had drafted legislation approving a fee in 1939 but had not passed it by the time of the occupation.[9]

When the occupation ended in 1945, the broadcasting organizations were anxious to get back in business and immediately sought to move into their former buildings. However, the Dutch government did not turn control of the facilities back to them immediately. It wanted to discuss the matter of whether the prewar system should resume, or whether it should be replaced by a national system of some sort. There was some criticism of the prewar system on the grounds that it was not very open to the expression of minority viewpoints from within the various organizations. The Labor Party adopted resolutions calling for a more truly national system. But leaders of the Catholic and Calvinist "pillars" pushed for a return of the old system, the Socialists gave it grudging support for fear of being left out, and back it came.[10]

The license fee that had been passed by the occupation government was continued by the postwar government, and its proceeds were divided among the various organizations according to their transmission time (still equal for the four largest organizations, with a much smaller amount for VPRO), with a sum set aside for fee collection and for transmission. Even with this additional revenue, the organizations could see the wisdom of pooling their resources, particularly for studio utilization, news coverage, broadcasts of large musical groups, and so on. All five of them agreed in 1947 to form the Netherlands Radio Union. The organizations retained their autonomy but worked cooperatively through the NRU Board. The minister of education, arts, and sciences approved the creation of NRU, stated his ministry's jurisdiction over broadcasting, and appointed a commissioner to serve as liaison between the ministry and NRU. While the commissioner could pass along to the minister any and all board decisions for review and possible annulment, the latter never occurred. The minister also decreed that airtime be allotted to the various churches, reflecting a traditional Dutch concern for freedom of religious expression. Mainline religions had been broadcasting for some time but now were joined by smaller groups with brief periods of airtime.

This cooperative atmosphere also brought about renewed attention to educational broadcasts, which had begun in 1926 with broadcasts by the Educational Foundation of Inland Navigation to children of families living on barges that plied the country's many waterways. Broadcasts for Protestant and for Catholic schools began in 1947 and 1948 through NCRV and KRO, and in 1951 AVRO, VARA, and VPRO combined their resources to begin broadcasts for nondenominational schools. The Radio People's University had been broadcasting adult education programs since 1931; in 1946 it began to receive a small share of the license fee.

THE GROWTH OF TELEVISION Experimental broadcasts with television took place throughout the 1930s, but the occupation put an end to them. They began again in 1948, with the Philips Company (electronics manufacturers) conducting them. The radio broadcasting organizations feared the high costs of television, but pressure from Philips helped to lead in 1951 to the establishment of the Netherlands Television Foundation—this despite a government report that had concluded the country could not afford TV yet. The radio organizations agreed that they would have to cooperate to an even greater degree than they already were doing through the NRU. They also agreed to finance television out of their existing revenues for a further two-year experimental period. The Philips Company furnished most of the technical gear, some of the staff, and the transmitter, while the post office (PTT) covered transmitter operating costs. Parliament debated the future of TV in 1953 and decided to make the service permanent, although it wasn't until 1956 that it approved a separate license fee for TV set owners that would help defray the added costs of the new service. The Ministry of Education and Culture was made responsible for television, drew up regulations for it, and created a Television Advisory Council to assist in keeping track of how it performed.

While the 1950s saw a continuation of cooperation among the organizations, there were incidents that revealed just how far apart they remained in some respects. The most striking example was a pastoral letter from the Roman Catholic bishops in 1954: It forbade Catholics membership in the Socialist trade union movement, attacked the Socialist party, and warned Catholics against "frequent tuning in to Socialist broadcasts." It is doubtful that many Catholics took it seriously, but it did cause the near rupture of the Labor-Catholic coalition. (A 1965 press release from the bishops reaffirmed most of those bans, including that on broadcast listening and viewing.)[11]

An incident in 1956 revealed something of the government's attitude toward the mass media. Stories were appearing in the British and German press about Queen Juliana's use of a faith healer to treat her daughter. The Dutch prime minister called a meeting of the chief editors of newspapers and radio services. No TV editor was invited, TV apparently being considered too insignificant (and in truth its news service was minuscule at that time). The editors were asked not to print or broadcast anything on the story in view of "possible constitutional consequences," and they complied, despite the fact that there was considerable public knowledge of it. Broadcast journalists in the Netherlands had little experience with objectivity or comprehensiveness, thanks to the "pillars," and the government was not about to encourage them to acquire it.

As Dutch society moved into the 1960s, there began to appear evidence of a more liberal spirit, often in ways that shocked many Dutch citizens. Amsterdam became known as the "hippie capital of the world," and traffic in drugs was common. The Beatles gained many Dutch fans, partly thanks to the broadcasts of the Dutch and British pirate radio stations operating in the channel, and several Dutch Beatle-like groups sprang up. The Dutch television service, unable to afford the heavy costs of broadcasting only Dutch material, carried large amounts of foreign programming (particularly British and American), and some of it presented new ways of looking at society. The marriage of Princess Beatrix to a German commoner who had done military service in World War II, and the revolutionary pronouncements of Pope John XXIII, added to the sense of turmoil, excitement, and discovery.

The pirate radio stations carried little but popular music, and music of a sort unlikely to be played often over the Dutch system. They soon acquired large audiences. The stations also broadcast ads, but most listeners did not seem to mind them, and some said that they even enjoyed them. In 1964, a pirate TV station joined the radio services: Broadcasting from an offshore platform, TV Noordzee provided a heavy diet of imported light entertainment; again, there were ads, and again, viewers seemed not to mind them. The government, after considerable debate, sent in a military force by helicopter in December 1964 to put the station off the air.[12]

All of this illegal activity helped to spark a major debate in Parliament over the future of broadcasting. Various proposals came up, including a national system (no pillars), an advertiser-supported system, a renewal of the existing system, and modifications in the system to allow a wider range of organizations more ready access to airtime. A second TV service started in 1964, programmed jointly by the five broadcasting organizations, but the costs involved in operating it highlighted the need for additional revenues. Raising the license fee was not a popular option for Parliament, which would have to approve any such increase.

To add to the complexity of the situation, the International Telecommunications Union authorized a third television frequency for the Netherlands, and some Dutch commercial interests applied to the government for permission to operate and finance such a service through sale of ad time. (Ad-supported TV had been considered as early as 1953, and it was one of the earlier applicants for such a service, REM, that had set up TV Noordzee after having had its application turned down.) The Dutch government already had presented proposals to Parliament in 1961 and 1963 that would have authorized Dutch firms to establish a second television service that would be ad supported. Parliament had turned down both proposals, partly because of strong opposition from the existing broadcast organizations—themselves linked with various political factions.[13]

In 1964, the coalition government again presented a proposal for an ad-supported television service, this time along the lines of Great Britain's Independent Television Authority (ITA), but again Parliament refused to accept it. The coalition resigned, a new coalition was formed, and a new broadcast law was its first major order of business.

THE NEW BROADCASTING ACT AND ITS EFFECTS   As legislation was being drafted for the new act, various political factions and other interest groups reached agreement on the introduction of advertising into Dutch broadcasting. They created an organization known as STER (the Broadcast Advertising Foundation), which would preview all ads for acceptability of content (the foundation was to develop content regulations), set rates, and place limits on allowable amounts of advertising time (ninety-five minutes a week for TV starting in January 1967, twenty-six minutes a day for radio starting in 1968; both have been increased since then). The broadcasting organizations would have nothing to do with advertising, which in theory meant that their programs would not be influenced by it, but they would receive proceeds from the sale of ad time in rough proportion to their overall airtime. In order to protect newspapers that might be harmed by losses in advertising revenue, 40 percent of the proceeds was set aside in a special fund to aid them. (This was reduced in 1970 and replaced in 1974 by the Trade Fund for the Press; however, part of the money for that fund came from a 5 percent increase in STER's advertising rates.)

Meanwhile, new proposals for broadcasting indicated that Parliament seemed ready to allow other sorts of groups besides the "pillars" to apply for major blocks of airtime. That concept became known as the open door, and Parliament approved its inclusion in the Broadcasting Act in 1967, amidst sharp debate. Although the act was not to come into effect until 1969, one new broadcasting organization and several small groups were authorized to begin operations immediately. The organization, Televisie Radio Omroep Stichting (TROS), had been formed chiefly by supporters of TV Noordzee, and in no sense was it a "pillar" of Dutch society.

The Broadcasting Act of 1967, then, did not do away with the "pillar" system, since the five original broadcasting organizations remained on the air, but the act did make it awfully difficult to determine whether the character of a would-be broadcasting organization could be taken into account in deciding whether to allow it to broadcast. The act contained a provision that organizations "must aim at satisfying cultural, religious or spiritual needs felt among the population, to such an extent that their transmissions may on that account be deemed as serving the public weal" (Chapter 2, Section 13.2), but those were very loose criteria. The existing organizations lobbied hard to obtain postponement of the act but were unsuccessful. One of their worries—and a worry of many observers of Dutch broadcasting—was that still more organizations without any special character and with little but light entertainment to offer would join the Dutch system, taking up precious airtime (precious to those who already had it, certainly!).

Furthermore, because the act did specify numerical (membership) criteria for four categories of broadcasting organizations, because airtime increased as one moved up in the categorical list, and because ad revenues and proceeds from license fees also were apportioned on that basis, an organization that could appeal to mass audiences would realize several financial benefits from so doing. As the "new kid on the block,"

TROS stood as a primary example of what the older organizations feared. Without waiting very long to see whether their fears were justified, three of the older organizations began to popularize themselves, a process Dutch critics called "trossification." The organizations of VARA and VPRO resisted the temptation to a greater degree; each had set ideas as to how broadcasting could serve its members and society in general, VPRO was too small to aspire to huge numbers (although it did begin to recruit "culturally progressive" members), and VARA felt that its members were particularly loyal.

The early 1970s saw the creation of two more broadcasting organizations. The EO, or Evangelical Organization, was more or less in the tradition of "pillars," although there was some concern that its broadcasts were too narrowly devoted to the interests of its members—and there *is* that requirement in the act that speaks to serving the public weal, meaning the broader public. But the second organization, Veronica Omroep Organisatie (VOO), posed more problems. Much like TROS, it had been formed by the followers of an outlawed pirate station, in this case Radio Veronica. The act had set specific criteria of size for broadcasting organizations but also had created a candidate status, which would allow aspiring broadcast organizations to come on the air for three hours a week on radio and/or one hour a week on television. Such status would last two years, during which time the organization had to increase its dues-paying membership from the forty thousand required for candidate status to the hundred thousand that was then the minimum for a Class *C* (smallest) regular broadcasting organization.

A list of forty thousand VOO members was presented in 1974, but VOO also indicated that its program policy would place almost exclusive emphasis upon popular music. The minister of culture (the government minister responsible for broadcasting at that time) decided that VOO was not sufficiently broad in its programming to warrant candidate status. That ruling was contested by VOO, and the Council of State, which is the highest court of appeal under the terms of the act, reversed the decision. The organization went on radio in December 1975 and on TV in April 1976. In June 1976, it submitted lists with names of one hundred thousand members, but irregularities (more than half of those listed had not paid their dues yet, and the act counts only dues-paying members) delayed VOO's acceptance into Category *C* until late 1978. Clearly, size of membership had become increasingly important as a criterion for who was to broadcast, and just as clearly programming that catered to mass tastes would have advantages in increasing that size.

One other very important result of the 1967 act was the strengthening of the centralized program-making bodies. The NRU and the

Netherlands Television Foundation (NTS) had been formed by the broadcasting organizations themselves. Because of the heavy expenses of television, the foundation had been responsible for a good deal of centralized program making, and even though it was the creation of the organizations, it had acquired something of a life of its own. The Radio Union had done the same, to a smaller degree. The act created a new body, the Netherlands Broadcasting Foundation (NOS), that would combine the functions of the old NRU and NTS. It would receive a guaranteed share of airtime (minimum of 15 percent of total radio time and 25 percent of total TV time, maximum of 40 percent for each medium), a share of license fees and ad revenues, and would be governed and advised by various boards and committees whose membership would come from government appointees and from the other broadcasting organizations. In other words, the NOS now would become a competitor for money and for airtime, and no longer would it be the creation of the broadcasting organizations or so much under their control. The NOS also was given the task of coordinating the overall broadcast schedule and of administering TV and radio studios (the latter only when organizations lacked their own).

The NOS was to function under a broad mandate. The act stated that it was charged with "looking after affairs which are of interest to radio and television as a whole" (Section 39, Part 2a), and NOS consolidated its hold on such categories as newscasts, actualities, and sports—the latter highly popular among Dutch viewers—but also broadcast children's cartoons, jazz, original drama, and other entertainment, as well as documentaries. It did not compete with the other organizations in providing serialized entertainment or "mass appeal" feature films, however.

Thus, while the 1967 act did not represent an attempt to create a new broadcasting system, it did weaken the "pillarized" concept in several ways: by encouraging the establishment of nondenominational, nonpolitical broadcasting organizations (whether that was the intent of Parliament is another question, but that was the net effect) and by strengthening the centralized portion of the system (NOS) and at the same time giving the other broadcasting organizations less control over it. However, it did not appear to be a case of the government wanting more control.

As the act was debated, passed, and put into effect, the broadcasting organizations themselves were reacting to the climate of questioning and challenging then abroad in the Netherlands. The Catholic KRO aired interviews with Catholic leaders in which interviewers sometimes were skeptical or even caustic; VARA did a program on abortion at a time (the mid-1960s) when that topic was considered off-limits for public discussion; VPRO frequently broadcast speeches of and interviews with the radical *provo* and *dwarf* political movements. The government generally kept its hands off such programs, although there sometimes was plenty of opposition to them within the organizations themselves, and several instances of self-censorship. However, in 1963 the government warned KRO that it was prepared to take the picture off the air if KRO broadcast an interview with Georges Bidault, head of an illegal (in France) French "terrorist" opposition group known as the Organisation de l'Armeé Secrète (OAS), and KRO backed down. Both VPRO and VARA were "deplored" by the government on several occasions in the late 1960s and early 1970s for "tasteless" programs, among them an impersonation of the queen and a composite image of the pope standing among some attractive women in an item about a literary ball.[14] However, in no instance could the government take effective action against the broadcasters because the only legal grounds were "danger to the security of the state, public order and morality" (Paragraph 4, Section 10.2). "Morality" is almost impossible to define, and application of the other grounds in the KRO case resulted in the passage of a motion of censorship against the government by the Parliament—in a televised debate.

AFTER THE ACT—THE 1970S AND 1980S   In the 1970s, the broadcasting
    organizations began to face more competition from broadcasters outside the country. Some Dutch viewers already could receive Belgian, West German, and British television stations, depending upon the part of the Netherlands in which they lived. As cable TV spread throughout the country (to improve reception in cities, to broaden program choice, to eliminate unsightly rooftop antennas), all of those stations became more widely available and diverted some viewers away from Dutch TV. In 1979, an Amsterdam cable TV firm, Kabeltelevisie Amsterdam (KTA), became the unconscious purveyor of yet another form of programming when illegal operators began beaming signals carrying illegally acquired tapes of first-run movies, some of them pornographic, at the KTA master antenna; the antenna then automatically passed the signal along to its viewers over a channel that had signed off for the evening. The illegal operators sold ad time at bargain rates, and as the ads went only to the local area (legal Dutch TV ads go nationwide only), meat markets, furniture stores, and other places of business found the new service very attractive. Such operations sprouted up in other Dutch

cities, and some became very specialized: One offered a twenty-part course in black magic![15]

Feature-film distributors and exhibitors claimed to be hard-hit by these pirate activities (one TV guide for the illegal services even called itself De Piraat), and in late 1981 the Motion Picture Association of America won a suit in a Dutch court banning such exhibition of MPAA films. The Amsterdam Court of Justice decided that cable transmission was a new form of publication for which copyrights were due and required that the cable companies themselves close down a channel as soon as a pirate transmission broke into it. Also, those who advertised over pirate transmissions could be prosecuted. The net effect of all of those measures was to sharply reduce pirate TV activity.[16]

Land-based radio pirates, which had been around in small numbers in the more sparsely populated northern and eastern parts of the country during the fifties and sixties, also became very active in and near major urban centers during the late 1970s. Most were low-power, had highly irregular broadcast hours, and were run as hobbies. However, a few became more powerful and regular, whereupon they became more attractive to local advertisers but also more of a threat to other forms of radio communication that had the legal right, as the pirates did not, to operate on certain frequencies. As of the late 1980s, there may be as many as ten thousand to twenty thousand of these stations, which is far too many for the small force of detection crews to locate and to remove from the airwaves, besides which the Radio Controle Dienst (the government detection service) has no investigative authority but may act only on the basis of complaints. The radio pirates, too, have their own magazine, a monthly publication called *Free Radio,* which has been around since 1973.

There was yet another newcomer to the media mix in the early 1980s. Some of the Dutch cable systems began to receive broadcasts from satellites (Optical Technology Satellite [OTS], ECS-1, Soviet). The ECS-1 service (Sky Channel, a Rupert Murdoch venture), an ad-supported British venture that programs mostly U.S. and British TV entertainment for several hours a day to cable operations in various parts of Europe, seemed to some Dutch critics a harbinger of worse things to come. Direct broadcasts from satellites (DBS) to home receivers had been under discussion in Western Europe for several years, and finally in 1981 the Western European nations agreed on an allocation plan for DBS frequencies.

Luxembourg seemed likely to initiate such a service along the lines of Radio Luxembourg: mostly light entertainment interspersed with ads

placed by firms in countries such as the Netherlands where various restrictions discouraged them from advertising over their own systems.
Radio Lux had had a Dutch service since the 1930s, and critics wondered
whether a similar TV service would add further impetus to the process of
"trossification."

That discussion came at the same time as a major review of the
future of Dutch broadcasting undertaken by the Scientific Council for
Government Policies (an advisory body to the Dutch government). Unlike the British system of broadcasting, there is no provision for periodic
review in the Netherlands, so reviews usually arise in response to actual
or anticipated problems. The council was asked to undertake its investigation in 1979 and released its report in 1982. There were several reasons
for conducting the review: the advent of the new technologies, controversy over just how open the system should be to what sorts of organizations (including pirates), and cost effectiveness of the present system (widely held to be inefficient and even wasteful).

Already the "trossification" of Dutch broadcasting had resulted in
an amendment to the Broadcasting Act that would make it more difficult
for new organizations to be admitted to the system. The amendment
came into force in 1980 and set the following membership standards for
size of organization:

Category A	450,000 or more (formerly 400,000)	5 units of airtime
Category B	300,000–450,000 (formerly 250,000)	3 units of airtime
Category C	150,000–300,000 (formerly 100,000)	1 unit of airtime
Aspirant	60,000 (formerly 40,000)	1 hour TV and/or 3 hours radio per week

Aspirants would have up to three years to reach Category *C,* but would
have to show that they offered programs that "differ from those already
available." A few new organizations have applied (e.g., an Islamic
group, a Hindustani group), but none has been granted aspirant status.

The council's report dealt with "trossification" from a different
angle. It advocated a high culture service for TV, to be run by a new
organization. If the old organizations insisted upon continuing their pursuit of high ratings through mass appeal programming, at least there
would be one reliable source of high culture. But airtime for the new
service would have to come from the existing two-channel service, as the
council rejected suggestions for a third channel on the grounds that it
almost certainly would have to be supported by advertising. Yet it argued
that more airtime should be devoted to commercials, both to help offset
the rising costs of TV and to further encourage Dutch companies not to
advertise over foreign stations viewable in the Netherlands. The council

also called for an opening up of cable TV so as to allow local cable franchises to offer a wider range of services (e.g., subscription TV) and perhaps to interconnect as networks. The press would be allowed to invest in cable, as would existing broadcast organizations. Local cable could carry commercials but could not claim any portion of the annual license fee.[17]

The government responded to the council report in a White Paper issued in August 1983. By that time, the governing coalition was Christian Democrat–Conservative and favorable toward private enterprise (deregulation, reductions in public sector spending). The White Paper went far beyond the council report in proposing revisions. It advocated allowing subscription TV, but not allowing the broadcasting organizations to operate it. It advocated cabletext and cable newspapers (including ads), but only the press was to operate them. It also advocated breaking up the NOS: There was to be a facilities department (studios, etc.), which was to become an independent company whose shares were to be held by the state (a majority) and the broadcasting organizations (a minority); there would be a program service for "centralized" programs (news, sports, etc.), which also would be an independent company, governed by a board on which the broadcasting organizations would be in the majority but with government representation as well. The coordination and planning of the overall broadcast schedule, an NOS function, was not covered in the White Paper. The foundation itself would cease to exist.

One of the government's intentions seems to have been to reduce the cost to the public of what admittedly was an expensive system. Even before the White Paper, it had proposed both budget cuts and a cancellation of projected increases in the annual license fee. It also favored a limitation on the proposed expansion of broadcast advertising time, so as to minimize harm to the press. The various new services (teletext, etc.) would have to be paid for by individual users, and not by the general public through increased fees.

But deregulation would have its limits. The White Paper stated that the four radio services were not distinctive enough in their programming and raised the possibility that the government would do something about it if the broadcasting organizations could not. Also, the organizations were given a program formula for the first time in Dutch broadcasting history: 20 percent culture, 25 percent information, 25 percent entertainment, and 5 percent education (various categories make up the remainder). The categories were not tightly defined, largely because they resisted definition. The minister of culture was to enforce them.

The NOS reacted with dismay, of course, but the other organizations were not very happy, either, since they had hoped to be allowed to compete in providing the new cable services; nor were they particularly pleased about the plan for fiscal austerity. The White Paper was debated in Parliament in early 1984, the final votes coming during the spring. The paper passed largely intact. In July 1984, a steering committee and seven working groups were established to carry out the paper's proposals. They reported at the end of 1984 and recommended that the NOS be divided into a limited company for the provision of production facilities and a foundation for producing limited amounts of broadcast programming. Its other functions were to be handled by a commissariat for the media, headed by five government-appointed commissioners. There also was to be a new media council to replace the existing broadcasting, press, and (in part) advertising councils.

The fact that the broadcasting organizations were unable to influence a majority of Parliament to change those aspects of the government proposal that the organizations disliked showed that the "pillar" system had lost some of its power. In fact, the history of Dutch broadcasting could be described as a fairly rapid rise of "pillar power," followed by its gradual decline, although certainly not disappearance. The changing character of Dutch society, whereby religious and political organizations clearly became less important in people's everyday lives, undoubtedly played a role here. (Ironically, broadcasting probably had much to do with that shift, by increasing people's access to a range of entertainment and information.) But so did the coming of cable, teletext, and other new media. And so did the recession of the late 1970s and early 1980s, coupled with the replacement of the Socialist-dominated coalition government by a Christian Democrat–Conservative coalition government.

Some of that complex reform never came to pass, for a reason that is quite common in European broadcasting: There was a national election in May 1986, and since the parties backing the proposed broadcast reform had not been in any particular hurry to pass a new media act, they were overtaken by the election. The same thing has happened twice in Great Britain, and once or twice in several other European nations. In this particular instance, the outcome was not affected radically by the election, since the governing coalition was returned to power. However, the Liberal party lost some of its strength, and since it had been the coalition partner that had pushed the hardest for greater commercialization of television, its hopes for a new, fully commercial third TV service vanished. The government soon announced that there would be a new third service (recall that a third channel had been available for about twenty years by now), but that it would not be commercial. Instead, it would accommodate NOS services and most of the very small broadcast organizations, such as the Humanists, SOCUTERA (social-cultural welfare), and so on.

That proposal itself showed that NOS would not be totally abolished, but simply segregated. Nederland 1 and 2 would accommodate the eight "pillars": The "entertainment" companies—AVRO, TROS, and VOO—would go on Nederland 1, while the three larger "ideological" companies—VARA, KRO, and NCRV—would go on Nederland 2. The smaller ideological companies, VPRO and EO, would have small amounts of time on each of the two channels. The redivision of channels was scheduled to occur in the fall of 1987 but later was put off until the spring of 1988. The companies almost immediately began to wonder where they would find the money to fill the increased airtime that most of them would have. Amounts of advertising time could be increased, but the press objected to that strategy, and the press still represents a powerful lobbying force. Nevertheless, Parliament decided to increase the allowable amounts of ad time but also required the broadcasters to share their extra revenue with the press.

As for the other White Paper proposals, some appeared in modified form, while others failed to appear in the 1988 Media Act. The NOS "hived off" its production facilities, which now would be handled by an independent, limited liability company, the Netherlands Production Broadcasting Company (NOB). However, the various broadcast organizations, including the NOS program departments, are required to use NOB for 75 percent of their TV production requirements and 100 percent of their radio for the next few years. The NOS Research Department might or might not be privatized. The NOS itself would continue to coordinate the overall schedule and would act as collective representative of Dutch broadcasters in international forums, for example, the ITU and European Broadcasting Union (EBU). The Commissariat for the Media would take over most of the broadcast supervisory functions of the Ministry of Culture. The new act came into effect in January 1988. As with so much else in the history of Dutch broadcasting, the act represents a compromise rather than a wholesale revamping of the broadcast structure.

Financing

Dutch broadcasting organizations receive their financial support from several sources. The annual license fee assessed on all households with radio sets (Fl 46, or about $21 as of 1987) and TV sets (Fl 158, or about $70) is divided among the organizations according to their airtime;

also some of the fee money supports transmission operations and a small share goes to the post office for costs of license fee collection. The process of division is not by rigid formula — the organizations submit their annual budgets to the minister in charge of broadcasting and to Parliament — but there is no indication that minister or Parliament manipulate the budget in order to reward or punish organizations. The advertising revenues collected through STER are added to the license-fee money and divided together with it.

The broadcasting organizations also earn money through the assessment of membership fees, which must be a minimum of ten florins for basic membership and thirty florins if there also is a subscription to the organization's weekly program guide. No one is compelled to belong to an organization, but only they are allowed to publish detailed guides, as in Great Britain. Each organization may highlight its own programs but does list all programs on the air. Up until 1982, newspapers carried only brief daily listings, but then a Dutch newspaper began to print detailed listings, claiming that it was reprinting them from Belgian guides that listed Dutch programs. The lower court accepted that defense, and several other Dutch newspapers began the same practice. The higher court ruled in 1983 that the practice was illegal because it went beyond using the program information supplied by the NOS on behalf of all Dutch broadcasters to the NDP (Netherlands Daily Press, the umbrella organization for Dutch newspapers). But NOS also agreed to supply NDP with somewhat more detailed program information for the use of its members.

Not only do the guides generate revenue by attracting members; they also provide space for sale to advertisers, and ads placed in the largest circulation guides (e.g., AVRO's *Televizier,* the largest weekly magazine in the Netherlands) bring in tens of millions of florins each year. Some of the organizations have attempted to make their guides as much like general-purpose magazines as possible, despite a ministerial order that limits nonbroadcasting editorial matter to a maximum of five pages, and there are occasional ministerial reminders that one or another organization is exceeding the limits. By the same token, organizations may spend a few minutes of airtime each month promoting themselves and soliciting new members; this too occasionally becomes excessive and results in warnings.

All broadcast advertising is handled by STER, which has the unchallenged power to accept and to reject ads and even to take them off the air if it feels that an ad has been on long enough, or if STER's standards change. Ad time is limited to about sixty minutes per day for radio and thirty for TV, but that may be increased in 1988. There is over forty percent more demand for TV ad time than there is time available, and over 65 percent more demand for radio ad time. Ads must appear in blocks and not within programs, as in the West German TV system. Television ads had occurred only during the early to middle evening hours, just before and after the newscasts, but that period was increased when the new Media Act came into effect in 1988. In 1976, Parliament passed a resolution calling for the elimination of ads around the 7:00 P.M. newscast, in order to protect children from "undue promotional influence." Starting in April 1978, the 7:00 ad block was eliminated and later blocks made longer. Advertising is not permitted on Sundays (another influence of religion; there are also no Sunday newspapers). Satellite-delivered cable services may not carry ads directed specifically to Dutch audiences. Ads for tobacco products are not permitted, ads for pharmaceuticals have to be approved by an expert panel, and ads for sweets must be displayed with the superimposed outline of a toothbrush! Many of those restrictions are designed to protect the newspaper industry.

The financing system does lack flexibility where the organizations are concerned. Aside from increasing memberships and selling more ad space in the guides, or charging more for them, they have no power of their own to increase revenues. The government sets license fees and amounts of ad time, and STER sets advertising rates. And the system is expensive. Centralized studios have helped, but the existence of a full complement of administrative staff for each organization drives up the cost, as does the seeking of new members, work on program guides, and other matters not directly related to program production. As one observer put it, "Instead of all this money filtering out and providing a breeding ground for programme makers, directors, writers and actors, it has been sucked in by a swollen bureaucracy. Far too much of television's resources are eaten up in fat salaries and office furniture."[18]

The "closed shop" situation of Dutch broadcasting also is a factor: Few productions can be made by anyone outside the broadcasting system (documentaries are the major exception), so there is no particular pressure to economize in order to meet competition. Also, the Dutch trades union system makes it extremely difficult to discharge nonproductive staff or to hold down the numbers of people needed for studio or remote productions. The government's latest reforms are intended to help cut costs, but a number of the cost factors simply are not amenable to reduction. A "plural" system seems to have a particular disadvantage here, in that it is bound to lead to some duplication of effort and therefore is bound to be more costly to operate.

Cable television charges vary slightly throughout the Netherlands, but average around ten to twelve dollars per household per month for a twelve-channel service. The one remaining add-on (pay cable) service as of 1988, Filmnet, charges about ten to seventeen dollars per month, according to level of service, but its roughly sixty thousand subscribers hardly make it profitable.

Governance and Administration — Internal

THE DECISION-MAKING STRUCTURE   Dutch broadcasting features two sorts of overall decision-making bodies: the NOS and its various committees, and the individual broadcasting organizations and other groups that are allotted smaller amounts of airtime (Humanitarians, Freemasons, etc.). As the NOS is responsible for a larger portion of the broadcast schedule than is any other single organization, and as its administrators decide (in consultation with administrators of the other organizations) what it will broadcast and when, much of the schedule is built around NOS programming. There are NOS program boards and program coordination committees for radio and for television; all eight broadcasting organizations are on the two boards, but only two serve on the two committees, and in both instances they are in the minority. The boards and committees report to the NOS executive board, a body that once had thirty members — hardly conducive to speedy decision making! Under the terms of the 1988 Media Act, it has thirteen members, eight chosen by the organizations, four by the minister of culture from various sociocultural organizations, and a chair appointed by the government of the day through the queen or king. The executive meets every month to make final decisions on broadcast policy; its meetings are open to the public and often are very lively, although it sometimes is accused of hamstringing the NOS by not approving potentially positive NOS proposals, yet being unwilling to see to it that one of the other broadcasting organizations will undertake them. A seven-member Board of Management, composed in like fashion, is responsible for policy preparation and reports to the executive. Under the terms of the 1988 Media Act, the eight "pillar" organizations became a majority on the various NOS boards, although the chair still is appointed by the government.

Program coordination is a sensitive subject. Most of those in the organization want to place a number of popular programs in the prime-time periods, but pressures from NOS and government are in the direction of a more even mix of mass and specialized programming. Coordination does work reasonably well for scheduling between channels: A listener or viewer generally can count on having a genuine choice between what is on each of the five radio services (although the government announced in 1983 that it wanted even greater choice) and two (soon to be three) TV services, for example, a popular music show opposite a documentary or religious talk. A "claim" system operated by the NOS allows the organizations to register the sorts of programs they intend to make and to purchase from abroad. If two organizations appear to be duplicating, there is an arbitration committee to resolve conflicts (which are rare).[19]

Within the individual organizations, there also is a decision-making structure. There will be a board of directors and a full-time administrative staff for each. For certain of the more ideologically oriented organizations, such as VARA, VPRO, NCRV, and EO, decisions will be taken with an eye to satisfying the perceived programming needs that are in harmony with the world outlook of the members, for example, pro-Socialist programming for VARA. For the more mass-audience-oriented organizations, such as TROS, AVRO, and VOO, decisions will be taken with an eye to increasing membership as much as possible. Something of an anomaly is KRO, as it seems to be striving to reach both sorts of audience. However, increasing competitive pressures are forcing two of the larger ideological organizations, VARA and NCRV, to become less overtly ideological and more popular, and VARA announced in 1987 that it no longer considered itself obliged to serve as the "Socialist megaphone."[20]

While all of the broadcasting organizations aside from NOS have dues-paying members, that does not mean that members necessarily have any influence on program decision making. The VPRO and VARA organizations do make special efforts to involve their members in decision making, VPRO by encouraging members to write, telephone, or visit its offices in Hilversum (where all of the organizations are located, and which is no more than a few hours' drive or train ride from any part of the country). Many do, and many have very specific suggestions to offer. Furthermore, they expect to be listened to, and often they come up with useful suggestions, although some VPRO producers and directors do not care for this kind of "interference" with the creative process. At VARA's local, regional, and national conferences members discuss program policies, pass along comments to VARA's board of directors, and elect delegates to the annual meeting of the organization. At that meeting, members propose resolutions and speak up freely about their likes and dislikes. If a majority of the members approve a resolution, the board must attempt to carry it out. More often, the board presents resolutions to the members, as it did in 1972 when it proposed banning boxing from the VARA schedule on the grounds that a Socialist organization should not be promoting violence. The members rejected the proposal, apparently because they felt that boxing at least had rules to govern its violence![21]

The other organizations do little to promote member involvement, aside from printing occasional surveys in the programming guides, asking members to send them in, then publishing the results in a subsequent issue. There is no requirement in the act that an organization maintain contact with its members, much less be obliged to heed their comments. Keeping members content certainly is important to an organization, since membership has so many financial implications, but apparently most of the organizations are general enough in character that their members do not expect or desire involvement in program decision making.

Governance and Administration — External

THE NATIONAL GOVERNMENT   There are two major sources of government involvement in broadcasting: the minister responsible for broadcasting (usually, but not always, the minister for culture, welfare, and recreation) and the Lower House of the Parliament. The minister may propose amendments to the Broadcasting Act, but they must be approved by Parliament. She or he also may take specific actions with respect to broadcasting, but these may be challenged by the broadcasters through Parliament or in the court system. The minister is advised by a broadcasting council of thirty members, who are appointed by the minister with parliamentary approval. The council meets fifteen to twenty times a year, publishes an annual report, and sometimes disagrees openly with the minister's recommendations and actions, but it has no power other than moral ("Why did you appoint us if you won't take us seriously?") to stimulate action. The minister also is advised by a commissioner for broadcasting, a full-time ministerial appointee. The council's functions will be carried out by the new Commissariat for the Media starting in 1988, but the appointment system will remain the same.

Parliament may discuss and vote upon broadcasting issues whenever it feels so moved. Broadcasting falls under the purview of the standing committee on welfare and culture, but any member of Parliament may raise questions concerning it. Parliament also votes upon ministerial recommendations and approves the annual budget for broadcasting derived from license fees and STER revenues. Neither Parliament nor the minister seem willing to use the power of the purse to pressure broadcasters, although the minister did delay approval of VOO as a Category C organization for a few years, which certainly had an effect on VOO's budget.

The minister also functions as one member of the Dutch cabinet, and is subject to the influences of other ministers, her or his political party, and the ruling coalition. As coalitions occasionally change composition, and as governments move in and out of office with some frequency, there seems to be a tendency not to let party and coalition politics play a large role in broadcast regulation; an incoming coalition or party might turn an outgoing coalition's or party's actions against it.

By long tradition, the minister is not supposed to be very active or particularly public in regulating broadcasting, but in 1985 Minister Elco Brinkman was both. Under the general terms of the Broadcasting Act of 1982, he imposed heavy fines on several of the organizations for spending too much airtime promoting themselves so as to increase their memberships and for carrying "hidden" ads (e.g., performer or host mention of some product or service during a show). Parliament rescinded some of his decisions and cut back the amounts of the fines, but the organizations still were shocked that he would have the temerity to take such a step in the first place.[22]

REGIONAL AND LOCAL GOVERNMENT   Even in such a small country as the Netherlands, there are regional and local differences. However, it was only after World War II that there was any broadcasting at the regional level, and even today it consists of no more than one to two hours of radio a day. Until 1987, regional governments had nothing to do with its financing or supervision: It was financed through the NOS or by special government appropriation. But local broadcasting is a different matter. Local radio generally has been supplied by pirate stations, but with some local services appearing as experiments in the mid-1970s and coming on cable beginning in 1983. Local TV always has been an offshoot of cable. The first local cable TV service appeared in 1971; local demand for it in a small community in Limburg Province, plus some support from the Philips Company and from a large Dutch publishing firm, brought it about. However, the minister of culture claimed that it was illegal: Communities could grant franchises for cable but did not have the right to initiate their own services. Only the minister had the power to allow the latter. In 1975 and 1976, six communities set up two-year experimental services through cable, with the permission and financial assistance of the minister. In no case did the minister attempt to dictate broadcast policy or program content, and the six services differed widely in what they offered, but they had only 3½ hours a week apiece in which to do it.

Both local and regional broadcasting have sought to move beyond their modest limits, but financing has been a problem. In the late 1970s, the minister of culture stated that she no longer was prepared to request that government money be used to support such broadcasting. By then, the six regional services had formed an association and lobbied for the expansion of regional broadcasting to twelve (one for each province) or even twenty-three stations. However, they wanted a continuation of national government support, which in their opinion would minimize regional government interference. The minister felt that the regions themselves should provide the money. The stations were not allowed to broadcast commercials and could not solicit memberships, although they could accept donations. The recession of the late seventies and early eighties made matters worse, as few at any level of government were enthusiastic about supporting them, but all of them continue on the air with money from NOS and from the minister. Five of the local cable operations have managed to stay on as well, raising money in a variety of ways.[23]

The 1984 White Paper did not give high priority to regional broadcasting, but there was a provision in the 1985 amendments to the Broadcasting Act for a supplementary license fee to be assessed by regions wishing to expand their broadcast activities, and that became law in 1987. Regional governments now may add a maximum ten-florin surcharge to the license fee and use that money to help develop regional radio and television. Theoretically, the regional governments would not have any additional control over regional stations through the surtax, but some regional broadcasters with whom I spoke in October 1986 thought that some individuals within regional governments might find the prospect of such control (or at least influence) tempting.[24]

There is specific evidence to indicate that their fears may not be unwarranted. The Limburg Provincial Council, displeased with what it felt was the overly leftist tilt of the regional station, Radio Limburg, threatened to set up a second station in the province so as to better reflect a more traditional viewpoint (Limburg is a strongly religious province). And when Radio Limburg announced in December 1985 that it would broadcast a lengthy report about what some of the leftist groups proposed to do in the following year, and to broadcast it on Christmas Eve, the station's broadcast council (which all regional stations have) expressed its strong objections to the coordinator of regional stations at NOS, who persuaded Radio Limburg to call off the broadcast.[25]

NONGOVERNMENTAL Because so many organizations and groups have access to broadcasting, it is not surprising to find that very few citizen involvement groups exist in the Netherlands. Most people find that the system is more or less open to them. The minister receives proposals for airtime from groups wishing access; if a group wants that access on a continuing, scheduled basis it must present evidence that its programming will be important to a reasonable number of people (no number specified) and that such programming is not already provided. Groups may be dropped from the authorized list if they turn their time over to others, as one group did in the mid-1970s, or if they fail to use continually the time they are allotted, or if they become too small to seem to require a broadcast outlet. It is not particularly difficult to obtain airtime on a one-time basis, and not even all that difficult to gain continuing access. The relative ease with which small, land-based pirate stations operate also answers the apparent needs of some who are dissatisfied with the official system, although in November 1987 the government announced a higher level of penalties for those operating and those advertising over such stations.

There have been protests about some aspects of programming policy, however. Parents, teachers, and religious leaders from time to time have decried the immorality of television, and feminist groups have criticized the image of women as presented by TV. Members of ethnic minority groups, the Moluccans in particular, pressed for the creation of special broadcast services in their own languages, but there were none on TV until 1976 (radio had carried very limited services from 1966), and then in very small amounts. There was an expansion of such services in the early 1980s, in some cases only after settling out internal dissension within the groups as to whose voice should be heard. That was a particular problem within the Moluccan community, which really was several more or less warring factions.

Programming

PHILOSOPHIES   The history of Dutch broadcasting reveals above all
    an attempt to create and maintain a system that offers access to a
variety of organizations and groups. That was part of the broadcast
regulation of 1928, and it has been part of the Dutch system ever since.
There also has been the continuing requirement that organizations provide programming for their own members but also for the larger public,
and that the programming be a mixture of information and entertainment. A few of the organizations, particularly TROS and VOO, have
tried to blend the mixture with as much entertainment as possible, including informational programs that tend to be light features about personalities, but most organizations do make an effort to attain some
balance.

Whether the organizations truly have philosophies of their own is
another question. The chairman of TROS was reported to have said,
"The essence is to give the people the programmes they want to see. . . .
The viewer is the boss."[26] That *is* a philosophy, but it comes close to
avoiding responsibility: Any "bad" program can be excused by saying,
"But just look at the size of the audience!" In the battle for members,
some of the older organizations appear to have moved in TROS's direction. Still, most of them do wish to reach certain sorts of audiences with
specific programs some of the time. The religious organizations broadcast not only church services and discussions of religious issues, but also
claim to select their entertainment programming with some regard for
what will contribute to (or at least not work against) the moral development of the audience. For example, NCRV states that "when acquiring
foreign productions, the NCRV fully applies the standards of quality
and ethics it is committed to by the 'C'[hristian] in its name."[27] That may
be good business: Why risk offending members? But programs transmitted by those organizations sometimes *do* offend, anger, or upset, and
usually that is deliberate. Most often VARA and VPRO do this, but
KRO sometimes has done likewise, particularly in broadcasts made by
Monsignor Bekkers, who called among other things for a more open
attitude toward birth control.[28]

Because its mandate is quite different, and because it does not have
members in the usual sense, NOS might be expected to have a different
philosophy than do the other organizations. In a way, it does: It presents
current-affairs programs on touchy topics, features spokespersons with
very strong viewpoints, and so on. But it does all of this within an
overall framework of balance. After all, it is financed by the Dutch
people in general through the license fee and ad revenue and should not

show quantitative or qualitative favoritism or approbation. Also, the other organizations and the government serve on NOS's boards and committees and must be assured that NOS is not showing undue bias.

RADIO   As has happened over much of the world, radio has become increasingly dominated by music in the Netherlands. That already was occurring in the early 1960s, as TV claimed a larger and larger share of the budget, but it received further encouragement through the "non-stop pop" provided by the offshore pirate radio stations. The broadcasting organizations proposed a third radio service, which would be largely pop music with appropriately informal disk jockeys. The service would be legal, of course, and Dutch artists and recording companies would receive fees—something the pirate stations rarely paid. In other words, the situation was much like that in Great Britain at the same time, and the solution was similar. The third service came on the air in October 1965, became a twenty-four-hour service in 1973, and was cut back to seventeen hours a day in 1979. But classical music fans were unhappy with the prominence this gave to pop music and lobbied vigorously for a "serious" radio service along the lines of the Third Programme services in Great Britain and West Germany. They were successful: In December 1975, Hilversum 4 came on the air.

Almost predictably, complaints began to appear about the programming on Hilversum 1 and 2. According to some listeners, they seemed to have little distinctive character, so the organizations (with some ministerial pressure) made Hilversum 1 a family-oriented service and Hilversum 2 an informational service starting in 1979. Hilversum 5, a target-group station (for ethnic and linguistic minorities) began service in 1984 for about one hour per day. It had grown to nearly fourteen hours a day by 1987, but most of that expansion was in Dutch-language programs, health programs, children's programs, and so on. There was a daily ninety-minute block divided among four linguistic groups, but they were not always the same groups each day. Turkish, Moroccan Arabic, and Spanish were daily features, but Portuguese, Italian, Serbo-Croatian, Greek, and Mandarin Chinese came once a week. There also was a Saturday afternoon block of ten- to twenty-minute programs for Moroccans, Surinamese, and Turks.

All five radio services provide news and music (but rather little of the latter on Hilversum 5 so far), and Hilversum 1 and 2 have several discussion programs, many of them presented by NOS and featuring in particular the viewpoints of "nonmainstream" individuals and groups. The NOS also plays the role of promoter of the arts as do the BBC,

ARD, NHK, and French radio: It supports various orchestras and choruses, commission new musical works and radio plays, prepares documentaries, and so on. A few of the other organizations do so, too, but more rarely. The NOS also broadcasts daily summaries of parliamentary activity, and occasionally parliamentary debates. A little over three hours each week goes for educational (in-school) radio broadcasts, about a third of them prepared by NCRV, KRO, VARA, and AVRO, and about two-thirds by NOS. Many recordings and much newscast material comes from abroad, but program production generally is local.

Younger listeners sometimes criticize the formality that characterizes so many radio programs, even presentations of pop music (where, to be sure, there is some informality, but not the sort that one gets from the land-based pirates or even Radio Luxembourg's Dutch service). And because so many broadcasting organizations and groups have to be accommodated, the schedule for each of the five services looks, on paper, like a patchwork quilt, although they don't *sound* that chopped-up most of the time, as most broadcasters follow similar presentational styles. Hilversum 1 and 2 are 24-hour services, with 10 hours daily of simulcasting; Hilversum 3, 17 hours; Hilversum 4, 16 hours; and Hilversum 5, 13½.

The regional radio services broadcast two or three times a day (generally early morning, noon, and late afternoon). All of them emphasize news and interviews of regional interest. Radio Fryslan broadcasts almost exclusively in Frisian, and Regional Omroep Zuid broadcasts for ten minutes once each week in Arabic and ten minutes in Turkish. Most of the local pirate stations feature popular music, very informal and even amateurish announcers, and appeals to the audience for mail and phone calls, which shows just how much they fear detection by Dutch authorities!

Cable radio stations are most numerous in Amsterdam and Rotterdam; in the former, there were a dozen stations sharing time on three FM frequencies at the end of 1986. No organization can broadcast for more than twenty hours a week, but each has great freedom to broadcast what it wishes. There are several more or less conventional services, such as classical music, easy listening, Dutch old-time popular music, and religion, but also a homosexual service (M/V Media), a service for the "counterculture" (Radio X), and one for Hindustanis. None may carry ads, but clearly a few of them are on cable in hopes that private commercial radio will be authorized sometime in the near future and that they will be in on the ground floor when that happens. (I attended the dedication of an "easy-listening" service, Radio Unique, in October 1986 and heard the station manager make a speech in which he looked forward to the time when the government finally would license what he called "American-style radio," which he thought of as mostly music and very little news.)

The biggest problem faced by cable radio is that many households on cable do not know that they can receive radio through it. When households are connected, often the service personnel fail to explain its availability, and estimates are that probably no more than 20 percent of all cable households are hooked up to receive it. Also, cable radio is not well suited to households where most or all of the radios are portable. The classical music station (de Concertzender) seems to fare best in attracting listeners, perhaps because its listeners hook the cable up to a fixed-location, high-fidelity system.[29]

TELEVISION   As of April 1988, there are three television services. Ordinarily, there is only in-school educational television in the morning and early afternoon hours, aside from a five-minute subtitled newscast at 1:00 P.M. for the hard of hearing. Those limitations generally hold true for weekends, as well, giving Dutch viewers fewer hours of domestic TV service per day (eight to nine hours per channel) than just about any other medium-sized or large European nation. Expansion of the schedule has been slow, and when it has come in recent years, much of it has been in the form of repeat programming and feature-length movies.

The third TV channel came on the air in April 1988. The NOS programs and programs of the small broadcasting groups (SOCUTERA, IKON [religious], and other "nonpillar" organizations) appear on that channel, while the first channel is devoted to the programs of the more religious pillar organizations (VARA, KRO, EO, NCRV) and the second channel displays programs of the nondenominational pillar organizations (AVRO, VPRO, VOO, TROS). Presumably that will make it easier for viewers to select the types of programs they enjoy, and it may lead to larger quantities of the types of programs they enjoy, *if* the organizations can afford to produce more. There are some fears that the shift may result in more, but also more cheaply (in both senses of the word) produced Dutch material. There also are fears that the shift will make it easier for viewers to disregard the sometimes challenging and even upsetting material produced by NOS and the small groups.

If radio's schedule looks like a patchwork quilt on paper, TV's schedule looks like one on the screen. Because so many organizations and groups must be fit into so few hours, most TV programs are no more than thirty minutes long. The U.S. concept of block scheduling (e.g., a full evening of situation comedy) simply does not work on Dutch television, where a typical prime-time period will be programmed by a mixture of "pillar" organizations and smaller groups. The NOS presents three newscasts each evening (fifteen, twenty-five, and five minutes). Most evenings also have short programs (often of the "talking heads" variety) by smaller groups such as IKON, SOCUTERA, and TELEAC (adult education). Sports broadcasts and artistic feature films presented by NOS also appear in the prime-time schedule. Certainly viewers do not lack for variety, and usually there is considerable choice between what the three channels offer at any one time.

Much like other European systems, the Dutch system has a stipulation (here embodied in the 1988 Media Act) that adult fare should not be presented until 9:00 P.M. Late afternoon hours on weekdays are more or less reserved for younger viewers and include a daily newscast for them. Early evening hours feature many programs about pop music. The mid-evening period is likely to offer just about anything: sports, nature, and political documentaries, occasional feature films (most of them made for cinema rather than for TV), situation comedy and drama series (about 90 percent of them from Great Britain and the United States), variety shows, quiz shows, and so on. Roughly half of the prime-time schedule is made up of imported programs.

Drama programs made in the Netherlands generally are well produced. Sets and costumes for period dramas are authentic and detailed; actors and actresses are highly skilled; writers are at least competent, although there is little original TV drama; more is based upon novels and stage plays. A good example is KRO's October 1986 presentation of a four-part dramatization of novelist Piet Bakker's *Ciske de Rat* (Ciske the Rat), the story of a depression-era street urchin in Amsterdam. It was beautifully staged and acted (it's not all that easy to recreate depression-era grime and style in the prosperous Amsterdam of the mid-1980s!), but it was originally shot as a film with financial support from broadcasting and shown in cinemas two years before coming to TV.

The many quiz shows look much like their U.S. counterparts, which is not surprising, since many of the ideas are packaged and sold to Dutch TV organizations by U.S. firms.[30] Variety shows feature top-quality Dutch and foreign performers. Both quiz and variety shows are far less lavishly produced than are dramas and sometimes look absolutely spartan, which doesn't appear to hinder their popularity: The Dutch top ten for any given week usually contains one or two of them, and sometimes more. Shows in which people imitate famous performers are especially popular, and there is one with children and one with adults.

Newscasts, current-affairs programs, and documentaries likewise are well produced, although the typical current-affairs program is likely to be of the "talking heads" variety. The Eurovision daily news exchange has helped to provide a far wider variety and depth of coverage than Dutch TV could do on its own, and in the early days of the exchange, Eurovision items provided something of a model to Dutch broadcast journalists for coverage techniques. Investigative reporting has progressed over the past decade or two; although NOS is not at liberty to do much of it within the country (foreign situations are something else), VARA, VPRO, and KRO often prepare penetrating investigative reports on Dutch society and political life.

Educational television productions tend to be somewhat unimaginative, although some of TELEAC's work for adult viewers is attractive. There is a Dutch Open School for which TV is used; it hasn't any degree-granting authority, as does the British Open University, but a Dutch Open University with such authority was started late in 1984.[31] Adult viewers pay for all printed materials used in connection with educational TV.

All political parties represented in Parliament have access to television, as they do to radio, but the amount of time available is limited: one ten-minute period per week on TV while Parliament is in session, to be used in rotation by each of the fifteen or so parties. (Radio has six ten-minute periods each week.) The total amount of airtime increases in the three-month period just before elections. The prime minister is interviewed on TV every Friday, except for public holidays. The NOS carries up to eight one-minute spot announcements on TV each week for government public service messages. The government may request airtime whenever it wishes, but it rarely exercises that privilege.

There are no regional television services in the Netherlands, although there are brief educational broadcasts in Frisian. The five remaining local cable TV operations generally offer an hour or less of programming each day, usually news and current affairs. Two of them carry city council sessions.[32]

The Audience

In the days before advertising, Dutch broadcasting organizations had little need for continuous audience research on the size, composition, and program preferences of the audience. Membership payments, as well as letters, telephone calls, and personal visits seemed sufficient measures. Even the advent of commercials did not increase the need for audience research that much; the more popular a program, the higher the ad rate for that time period, but ad revenues were divided among the organizations according to their total amount of airtime per organization and not on the basis of audience size for a given program.

In the mid-1960s, the broadcasting organizations pooled their resources in order to conduct continuous audience research, and with the creation of NOS, audience research became part of that organization. The other organizations retained small research offices in order to maintain liaison with NOS's audience research department, to interpret research results to staff colleagues, and in a few cases to conduct projects of their own.

The NOS has several methods of gathering data: telephone calls, electronic measurement of set usage, and, more rarely, face-to-face interviewing, laboratory viewing, and content analysis. Diaries were used until 1987; viewers from age three on up had their own diaries (parents assisted young children) in which they indicated programs watched and an "appreciation" score of 1–10 (a marking system used in Dutch schools) for each. The diary was replaced by a "people meter" type of electronic interactive measurement device in 1987, which yields overnight data on viewership and appreciation scores (the average TV program receives a score of just under 7) and results appear on teletext the following day.[33]

For more specific qualitative data, the research department conducts twenty-six sets of telephone interviews in the October-April period; sample size is seven hundred viewers aged twelve or older. One problem here is that only about two-thirds of all Dutch households have their own telephones; the more transient and those lower in the economic scale tend to be underrepresented. There is a similar set of telephone interviews for radio listening, carried out yearly from January through April. Topics covered generally concern size of audience and enumeration of preferred programs.

As with audience research departments almost everywhere, the NOS department does not have a particularly easy time of it convincing producers, directors and administrators that they should treat results of studies seriously. The problem is compounded because the various broadcasting organizations tend to see that department as part of NOS, not of themselves; thus, they feel perfectly justified in ignoring what they do not like or understand.

Several of the departments of sociology and political science in Dutch universities also conduct research projects on listener and viewer reactions. Most are conducted at the university's expense, as there is little tradition of governmental or private foundation support for such activities. Frequently the Dutch press will publicize such studies, for example, a 1984 University of Amsterdam study of the popularity of the Sky Channel service for cable TV.

Research studies conducted by NOS over the years have revealed moderate audience satisfaction with Dutch broadcasting. Some of the more specialized programs and services, especially Hilversum 4 ("serious" programs), show a very predictable profile: small audiences, high degrees of satisfaction. Programs attracting large numbers of viewers often receive appreciation scores in the 6–8 range. Quiz shows bring both large audiences and high scores, as do sports events and as does the VARA-produced situation comedy, *Say Ahhhh!*[34] (featuring husband-and-wife doctors and their extended, sometimes klutzy or odd, family). Pop-music programs do especially well among younger viewers. When asked what they would like more of, many viewers say feature films, sports, and nature documentaries. They also would like to see more Dutch-produced drama, but seem to realize that the high cost (and lack of prospects for overseas sales) of such drama makes it difficult to produce more. Radio and television newscasts produced by NOS have high credibility, as witness a 1983 NOS survey ($N = 1500$): When answering the question "Which medium brings the most reliable news and information?" 29 percent said radio, 27 percent newspapers, 2 percent illustrated journals, and 43 percent television.[35]

The impact of broadcasting on Dutch society is more difficult to assess. There have been several NOS and university studies that have revealed that certain programs intended to reduce people's negative feelings toward immigrant groups in the Netherlands, or negative feelings about traveling to parts of neighboring countries not usually visited by tourists, actually have heightened those negative feelings. However, violence on television has not been as much of an issue as it has in Great Britain, the United States, or West Germany.

Certainly viewing and listening are popular activities: Figures for early 1987 show that the average person listens to radio for about three hours per day and watches TV about two hours and fifteen minutes per day. Cable households, which account for about 70 percent of all TV households in the country, view slightly more per day than do noncable households, but that may change as cable increases the number of program sources available; up until 1984, it served mostly to improve signal quality of existing stations. Sky Channel is the most widely viewed foreign-originated service on cable: It commands about 7 percent of viewer time. West German TV stations seem to be the most widely viewed of all foreign channels receivable by both cable and noncable households in the Netherlands: About 10 percent of all TV households are tuned to them at any given hour during prime time, although that seems to stem more from a desire for program variety than it does a wish to learn more about Germans and Germany.

Problem Areas

Aside from the problems of not having enough of certain types of programs, wishing for livelier presentation styles, and occasional reactions against some "radical" program (usually VARA or VPRO, and often satirical), problem areas seem few and mild. Not only is it relatively easy for groups to secure airtime for themselves or to be interviewed, but also it is a fairly simple matter for those who feel that their interests have been harmed through a broadcast to seek airtime for a correction or rebuttal. The 1982 Broadcasting Act states that "every institution having obtained transmission time may be obliged, in the event it has transmitted any factual data which is incorrect or misleading through incompleteness, to transmit a rectification upon the demand of someone directly concerned in such communication, if the latter has a sufficient interest in such rectification" (Section 38). The president of the District Court of Amsterdam sets the manner and time of reply on the advice of the minister's commissioner for broadcasting. Few such cases arise in a given year; most are objections by cultural and religious groups, or by manufacturers, concerning the portrayal of these groups in consumer-protection programs such as VARA's *De Ombudsman* and in documentaries, minidocumentaries, and newscasts such as the NOS *Journaal* and TROS *Aktua TV*. The broadcasting organizations try to handle such complaints themselves, so that they will not go to court. When they do, the decision more often supports the broadcaster than not.[36]

There remain complaints from feminist organizations that women hold few decision-making positions in broadcasting, and that the portrayal of women in drama programs and in ads is stereotyped and even demeaning. The broadcasting organizations appointed an "emancipation worker" in 1980 to help identify and rectify problems encountered by women working in broadcasting but also to sensitize programmers to the need to improve their portrayal of women.[37] Immigrant groups sometimes complain that certain factions within their ranks receive more airtime and/or more favorable treatment, and no immigrant group feels that it has meaningful, direct access to TV. To help answer that latter complaint, the Ministry of Culture financed a set of experiments in "migranttelevision" (Immigrant TV) in five Dutch cities starting in 1983. Professional broadcasters worked with Surinamese, Moroccans, Turks, Italians, Spaniards, Portuguese, and Latin Americans. A three-year training and production cycle has given various immigrant groups the ability to make their own programs; however, few of the groups get to show their work on cable TV more than once a month. Some of the trainees have entered further training programs with the national broadcasting organizations.[38]

Blue-collar workers sometimes complain that the general public sees very little of what a worker's life is really like, although VARA in particular has attempted to involve the workers themselves in producing programs that come closer to real life. Throughout the 1970s the VARA series *Van Onderen* (From Those Below) showed viewers the lives of the workers themselves: Producers talked with workers, shot material segment by segment, then showed each segment to the workers and elicited suggestions as to how the portrayal could be made more accurate. It was a slow and costly process, but it won the praise of workers and of many VARA members for its authenticity.

Foreign Influences on Programming

The large proportion of imported programs in the prime-time TV schedule, coupled with the ready availability of broadcasts from neighboring countries, means that Dutch listeners and viewers have plenty of exposure to foreign broadcasting. Foreign popular music places prominently in the Dutch top ten, foreign TV dramas do the same, foreign news (often supplied through foreign wire and telefilm services, as well as Eurovision) takes up a large portion of the main evening newscasts. Quiz shows often are prepared according to U.S. formulas. Does such a seemingly heavy dependence upon foreign sources concern Dutch viewers and listeners?

There is no absolute answer to that question, as audiences differ in their tastes and tolerances, but in general it does not appear to be a matter of great concern. Dutch audiences are accustomed to a heavy diet of imported programs, and much of the obviously sexual or violent fare that is controversial within its country of origin does not appear on Dutch TV. Also, the broadcasting organizations do manage to produce a few TV dramas each week, some of them one-time shows, some of them miniseries. A number of them have been produced at great expense, for example, a miniseries on William of Orange, coproduced with Belgian

Radio and Television. Some have probed sensitive areas in Dutch society, such as personal relations between Dutch and Surinamese.

But many dramas are based upon plots that would be recognizable to any viewer of U.S. or British prime-time soap operas and raise the question of whether foreign influence has penetrated Dutch productions themselves. This is a description of the second of a two-set miniseries entitled *The Factory* (TROS):

> Dries has gone to Portugal, overworked after the events of the first series. There he is visited by his secretary Jannie with the request from the company board to return and take over the factory again. Dries confesses to Jannie that he is in love with her. An attractive new laboratory worker at the factory turns out to be a protégée of Campers, the competitor. An act of sabotage ordered by the same Campers leads to the destruction of a large part of the factory. Dries' estranged wife Mary has fallen into the hands of porno producers. She goes into hiding with a barkeeper named Jack, and witnesses the killing of Jack, who thus pays the price for his willingness to help. When Dries returns from Portugal, he is suspected by police of being the man behind the arson at the factory. In the end Dries manages to expose Campers as the source of all the trouble.[39]

But Dutch viewers are likely to be thankful enough that Dutch actors and actresses are performing in Dutch settings and speaking Dutch (almost all imported programs are subtitled) and will not be all that concerned over possible foreign influences. Furthermore, many of the dramatic elements in Dutch and foreign TV programs are common to western civilization: jealousy, greed, loyalty, expressions of love, all have been staples in western literary traditions long before TV. Aside from a few Dutch newspaper critics, religious figures, and politicians, there seems little public fear that Dutch culture might be "lost" because of foreign domination of broadcast programming. Still, to better insure balance between domestic and imported programming, the new Media Act requires that, beginning in 1988, there be at least 50 percent domestic production in all program categories.

There is a pragmatic factor at work here: Many of the Dutch with whom I have spoken seem aware of the high cost of producing original drama, unless artistic standards were to be lowered. They seem to prefer having a smaller number of well-produced productions — and often those productions also place in the Dutch top ten. Also, they realize that their country is small and probably does not have the breadth of artistic resources to turn out vast amounts of TV entertainment. And they do find entertainment value in Archie Bunker, Fred Sanford, and J. R. Ewing,[40] who don't really seem all that foreign to them. As citizens of a small country, the Dutch are used to interacting with many foreign cultures; broadcasting is only the most recent mode of interaction. If the 50 percent domestic content rule is to be observed, it will take considerably more money or considerably lower production standards, and the audience might not look too kindly on either option.

The importation of Sky Channel, Music Box, and other satellite-delivered cable services certainly has increased the amount of foreign programming available to Dutch viewers, but here too the government has set up a semiprotectionist barrier: Such imported services cannot be subtitled in Dutch. Given the ability of the average Dutch citizen to speak two or three languages fluently, however, that probably does not amount to more than a minor hindrance.

Relations with Other Media

The relationship between broadcasting and the press in the Netherlands is colored by the "pillar" system, since broadcasting organizations and newspapers often find themselves in the same "pillar." In some cases, that has meant that newspapers will not criticize their "fellow" broadcasting organizations too severely, although they feel quite free to criticize other organizations and the NOS. Most newspapers of any size have regular columns of broadcast criticism and also cover parliamentary debates and government proposals on broadcasting.

Newspapers see broadcasting as a dangerous rival for advertising revenue, which is why STER originally set aside a portion of broadcast ad revenues: It would help to cushion the blow by making available a source of financial support for the newspapers, particularly failing ones. That same protectionist spirit can be found in the 1988 Media Act, with its provision for sharing of increased ad revenues. Still, the press remains sensitive on that point, the more so because money from STER has been an "on again, off again" proposition. When the broadcasting organizations made a plea for fairly sizable increases in ad time in the late 1970s and early 1980s, intensive lobbying by the press led to a reduction in the amount of that increase.

Although newspaper circulation has dropped over the last two decades, broadcasting is not blamed for that situation as often as it is in many other countries. Newscasts on radio and TV are brief (the longest is twenty-five minutes), and regional and local news receives relatively little broadcast coverage. It is more likely that slumping circulation stems from declines in some types of ad revenue (e.g., job announcements), increasing distribution costs, and reader indifference to heavy concentration on party politics, although that is changing as some newspapers drop their party affiliations.

The Dutch film industry is tiny and, if anything, has benefited from the existence of television. Television documentaries in particular often are shot by or with film companies, and there are many on the air each year. Over the past several years, Dutch broadcasting organizations and film companies have agreed on a method of having TV contribute to the financing of feature films (usually 10–20 percent of the cost) in return for being permitted to show them on TV at some date agreeable to the film producer. In 1986 the government appealed to the broadcasting organizations for further help in strengthening the Dutch film industry. The VPRO responded by agreeing to employ a few directors and scriptwriters each year, leaving them free to produce feature-length films, helping to secure financing for the films, and then arranging that the films be shown first in cinemas.[41]

There also is a coproduction agreement between Dutch ballet companies and some of the broadcasting organizations; it calls for at least three coproductions a year. And Dutch broadcasters have been working on something similar with Dutch theater; there once were some forty TV productions done from theaters each year, but that number has dropped to around ten as more and more productions took place in TV studios. There may be a formal coproduction agreement sometime in the near future.[42]

International Cooperation

While coproductions are increasingly common in Western Europe, the Dutch broadcasting system is less able to avail itself of this method of sharing production costs than are the larger systems. Part of the problem is a lack of money to invest in such productions: Cost savings arise because a coproduction usually falls into the "spectacular" category, which no one broadcaster could fund; and with little enough to spend on its own domestic productions, Dutch broadcasters would find it hard to justify investing in elaborate coproductions. But there have been several cooperative ventures nonetheless, especially with Belgian Radio and Television (BRT). Here, the common cultural heritage and common language make coproduction easier.

Eurovision provides a very important avenue for cooperation, and the Dutch system has taken full advantage of it. As is usually the case with the small to medium-sized European nations, the Netherlands is far more a taker than a giver where Eurovision's daily news exchange is concerned. In 1986, the Dutch system originated 155 programs for the exchange (a slightly smaller number than Austria's ORF), while it received over 9,000 items (almost twice as many as the BBC and about the same as Sweden and Switzerland). The Dutch originated 67 programs of other types (mostly sports) for the Eurovision exchange, and received 333, again mostly sports.[43]

It is unlikely that the situations for coproduction or exchange through Eurovision will change in the future. The Netherlands is not at the center of European activity in the sense that Switzerland and Belgium are; it is not a major financial center, it is not home to NATO or to the European Community, and its cultural productions, aside from certain classical-music ensembles and the Royal Dutch Ballet, are not in high demand in other parts of Europe. Its position in those respects is much like that of Scandinavian countries, which nonetheless exchange a fair amount of material among themselves.

The New Media

The Netherlands was one of the first countries in Europe to adopt cable television on a widespread basis. However, it would be a mistake to assume that the country also was early to recognize the many possibilities of cable transmission and reception. Dutch cable TV remains to this day a largely passive, limited-channel capacity medium, with very few (and severely limited in transmission time) instances of local origination. The 1982 report of the Scientific Advisory Council devoted more than a fourth of its space to consideration of future uses of cable, including viewdata (already available experimentally), cable newspapers, interactive services, pay cable, and so on.[44] Even with the over 70 percent level of cable penetration in the Netherlands, however, there would be a very high investment in reequipping the existing franchises, most of which operate as privately owned individual units and not as cable networks. Few of the operations can handle more than twelve channels, most of them one-way. The government did begin a $21 million five-year pilot project for interactive cable in Limburg Province late in 1986, but it had been cut back from an original $35 million project that was supposed to involve forty thousand homes. The final version covered twenty thousand homes, with two-thirds of the money coming from the national government and one-third from the provincial government.[45] The government has made it clear that it will do little to subsidize the upgrading of cable, and there are strong doubts as to the willingness of the general public, and therefore private industry, to spend money on most of these extra services, at least for the immediate future. (There are private companies that handle videoconferencing, high speed data communication, and video telephony services.)

Even where conventional cable services are concerned, cable households spend the vast majority (over 80 percent) of their viewing time on the two Dutch TV channels, and Sky Channel appears to be losing viewership.[46] The other services usually available on cable—Music Box (English), the three West German public channels, the two Dutch-language and two French-language Belgian services, BBC and ITV from Great Britain, TV-5 from France, Belgium, and Switzerland—all have low levels of viewership.

Videocassette players have sold moderately well in the Netherlands—as of 1987 nearly 30 percent of all Dutch households had them—but that is a somewhat lower level of penetration than one finds in Great Britain, Sweden, or West Germany. The most popular items are feature films, and, to a far lesser extent, soft-porn material, but time shifting accounts for 85 percent of VCR use.[47] Growth projections are modest. Apparently a fair share of the public is unwilling to invest the money or the time to expand its viewing choices in this manner.

Pay cable services also have been a disappointment, at least to their investors. The government began to license them in 1985, and ten applicants received authorizations to begin service later that year. Three actually did so. As of early 1988, only Filmnet remains, and with only sixty thousand subscribers, one wonders how long it can stay in business. It offers little besides feature films, and the market for that product appears to have been covered by VCRs. The Media Act of 1988 permits anyone to start such a service without governmental authorization, although notification to the Commissariat for the Media is required; but that is not likely to produce a flood of business, given Filmnet's dismal record, and despite its strong financial base.[48]

Direct broadcast satellites (DBS) are not likely to become an attractive alternative source of television, either. Most of the country is so densely populated that conventional over-the-air TV brings a wide range of choice to such rural areas as there are, and the larger cities all have cable TV. Satellites have been used to bring signals to cable TV operations for several years now: A number of the Dutch cable firms began to bring in the signal from a Soviet TV satellite in the early 1980s, until the Dutch government objected on the grounds that the Soviet satellite was not a broadcast satellite. A few Dutch cable firms continue to bring it in, but it has been dropped by most of them because it had little more than short-term novelty value for most viewers. There was a brief experiment with the European Orbital Test Satellite (OTS) in 1982 in which several European countries prepared special programs for reception throughout Europe, presumably through satellite-to-cable, since very few Europeans have satellite reception equipment. The Dutch were leaders in that experiment, as they were in its successor, the Europa project, which started in 1985 but went off the air late in 1986. I watched it shortly before its demise, and if my viewing during a several-day period gave me a representative sample, it probably died because a large share of its material consisted of reruns, including Dutch reruns. Increasing financial conservatism within the five to six nations that participated in it probably hurt, too: Its founders had hoped to sell ad time on it but had few takers. The Dutch government's ban on advertising in Dutch to Dutch audiences over satellite-delivered cable services certainly did not help matters. (That ban was successfully challenged by advertisers in a case decided by the European Court of Justice in April 1988.)

Conclusion

The latest government actions with respect to broadcasting make it clear that the Dutch system of the next decade or so will be somewhat different from what it has been thus far. Yet, with the many changes, there remain certain elements that have been around from the early days and seem destined to remain for some time to come. The "pillar" organizations are still in place, although they are not quite so narrowly defined now, and they have been joined by other organizations that are not very pillarlike. Smaller groups continue to have access to the air, and no one has suggested seriously that they should not. In fact, now that the third TV channel has materialized, they have even more airtime. It is easier for viewers to ignore them now that they are on one channel, but by the same token it is easier for interested viewers to know where to find them.

It has taken the system quite a while to provide much service for non-Dutch speaking listeners and viewers, but the situation slowly is improving. The efforts of Migranttelevision are limited by what the government will support financially—by their very nature, the immigrant and guest-worker groups will not be able to provide that support—and the present government's conservative economic policies are not encouraging in this respect. However, the commitment to provide such service does seem to be quite firmly established now.

Under the new Media Act of 1988, the government retains its traditional freedom to involve itself in the regulation of broadcasting but usually restricts itself to warnings and shows only occasional disposition to intervene in programming matters. The Commissariat for the Media may be able to establish itself as a buffer between government and broadcasters, but such a role is not as necessary (and, for that same reason, is not as difficult to secure) as it is in France. Perhaps the sorts of checks and balances that are built into the Dutch system of government – the many political parties, the shifting coalitions, the presence of the "pillars" – will act as a brake on major changes in the broadcast system.

If major changes were to come, the costs would be enormous. As I have already noted, there is little market for Dutch programs outside the Netherlands and Belgium, so overseas program sales will not be an answer. The license fee could be increased; it is one of the lowest in Western Europe. But the present conservative coalition is philosophically opposed to large increases, although the fee may go up by ten florins over the next few years.[49] Ad time will be increased, but not by much, so as to protect the press. The press itself has expressed considerable interest in investing in broadcasting, provided that ad time increases, and there were discussions between publishers and the more entertainment-oriented broadcast organizations (AVRO, TROS, VOO) during the spring of 1987 that raised the possibility of a third TV channel that would be a merger of those organizations and the press. But AVRO, the largest of the three, was cool to the idea, in part because the government had made it clear some months earlier that any such move, while it would be legal, also would result in all three losing any share of license-fee money.[50]

As for other potential sources of income, pay-cable services have done poorly, and there is little prospect for improvement. Some of the present costs could be cut if broadcasting were organized more rationally, but the "pillars" never would stand for that, and while they may be weakening, they remain a force to be reckoned with in political and cultural terms. What all of this means in terms of encouraging domestic production still is very unclear, although the present government, as we have seen, wants it to expand and also has attempted to protect Dutch cable TV viewers (and the newspaper and broadcast industries) from satellite-delivered ads coming from outside the country. Perhaps, to borrow a title from Arend Lijphart, the Dutch broadcast system is and will continue to be a reflection of "the politics of accommodation."

4

Germany

State's Rights, National Ambitions, and International Communism

ORE than is the case with any other major broadcast system, German broadcasting has undergone substantial restructuring since its earliest days. There have been five points in time when the system was altered in a fundamental way. Certain domestic developments, most of them political, have had a lot to do with this process of alteration, but so have influences from beyond the country's borders. And, although the West German broadcast system has won praise for the generally high quality of much of its programming, cultural material in particular, its record on political broadcasting has given rise to some concern. The East German system stands in strong contrast to its western neighbor; taken together, the two systems present a vivid portrait of the fundamental differences between broadcasting in communist-socialist and capitalist-socialist societies.[1]

Basic Factors

GEOGRAPHIC Germany presented many geographical difficulties at the moment of the birth of broadcasting there in 1923. As the map shows, the country had a most unusual shape, and was not even fully contiguous, since East Prussia was separated from the other German states (*Länder*). Despite the loss of about an eighth of its territory following its defeat in World War I, Germany still was the largest nation in Europe, and over seven hundred miles separated northern East Prussia from the southern Black Forest. Mountains were not a major problem since, aside from the Harz range, they lay at the country's edges. But population distribution was terribly uneven, with heavy concentrations in the Ruhr industrial area and in a few other major cities scattered around the country, and relatively light concentrations elsewhere. The geographic situation certainly did not favor the development of a highly centralized broadcast system, and at the same time made it virtually certain that, unless there was some measure of central pressure, some parts of the country would be poorly served or served not at all.

Germany had plenty of neighbors, as well: ten as of 1923. They ranged in size from Lithuania and Luxembourg to France and Poland. A few already were active in broadcasting, and their incoming signals had helped to stimulate German appetites for a broadcast service of their own. Several others saw Germany commence broadcasting before or at the same time as they did, and in some of those where German was spoken by a portion of the population (Switzerland, Austria, Czechoslovakia, Poland), the spillover of German signals had various influences, positive and negative, on their systems.

The division of Germany following World War II changed the geographic situation somewhat. Population distribution in West Germany was altered by the millions of refugees who arrived from East Germany and the eastern territories (now part of Poland and the Soviet Union), but there remain many thinly populated areas. East Germany's population changed very little; in fact, the·country occasionally has recorded negative annual figures for population growth. There now are fewer neighbors for each of the two Germanies, although there is considerable spillover of radio and TV signals between them and from West Germany into Denmark, the Netherlands, Luxembourg, France, Switzerland, Austria, and Czechoslovakia, as well as from East Germany into Czechoslovakia and Poland. Signals from West Berlin, an enclave in the middle of East Germany, reach western Poland quite easily. Inasmuch as German is fairly well understood by many people living just beyond Germany's borders, the potential for mutual influence through broadcasting definitely exists.

DEMOGRAPHIC   For a large country, Germany was and is very homogeneous. Its post–World War I losses deprived it of most of its non-German speaking minorities: Poles, Danes, French, Belgians, and Czechs. From that standpoint, broadcasting had an easier time getting established, since the system did not have to take into account the need for a multilingual service. That situation exists today: Aside from the guest workers who were brought to West Germany from Turkey, Greece, Italy, Spain, Portugal, and elsewhere in the 1960s to help supply factories with laborers during the economic boom, and who may number some 4 million today, West Germany is a German-speaking country. Granted, there are many dialects, and a Frisian fisherman and a Swabian farmer who attempted to converse with one another in their respective patois would not get very far. But neither would have much trouble speaking a standard form of German that is taught in all the schools and used in broadcasting. Thanks to its much smaller size, East Germany presents even fewer problems of dialect, although it does have one linguistic minority: the fifty thousand Sorbs, who speak a Slavic tongue.

Since the guest workers were not expected to stay in West Germany on a long-term basis, little was done at first to integrate them into West German society, and that included broadcasting. Brief broadcast services in their languages began to appear around 1964 and have been expanded somewhat since but still remain confined largely to radio. Some of the guest workers have learned to speak German more or less well, but many have not. Most live in the poorer districts of the larger industrial centers, and West Germany's economic slump in the early 1980s made their lives far more difficult, yet their homelands presented even worse prospects, so they attempted to stay on in Germany. The Sorbs of East Germany do not present the same sort of problem, since they continue to live in their age-old district in the southeast corner of the country. They receive schooling in German but are allowed and even encouraged to maintain their own language, in which there are daily radio broadcasts.

ECONOMIC   Germany became a major industrial nation in the late nineteenth century. At the time of Germany's emergence as a unified nation in 1871, some two-thirds of the population were rural dwellers; less than fifty years later, some two-thirds lived in cities. World War I crippled German industry, and war reparations to the allied governments also played havoc with the German economy, but by the mid-1920s the nation was regaining some measure of prosperity. The Great Depression proved a temporary setback, as the ascent to power of the National Socialist Party (Nazis) in 1933 was followed by increasing industrialization. Throughout the entire period of industrialization, agriculture lagged: Farming methods were not very progressive, and much of the soil was of poor quality.

The division of Germany exaggerated some of those conditions. The western part of Germany always had been more industrialized than the eastern part, which now had the additional burden of fulfilling some very stiff reparations claims by the Soviet Union. Thus, East Germany had to create an industrialized economy out of almost nothing, despite which the country now stands as one of the world's leading industrial powers and is recognized as having the highest standards of production within the Eastern Europe economic community (COMECON). West Germany, thanks in part to economic help from the United States through the Marshall Plan, rebuilt its industries and soon became a major industrial power, not only in Europe, but around the world.

Agriculture remains somewhat inefficient in both Germanies, at least when compared with some of the other nations of Europe and North America. Only some 3 percent of the population are engaged in it. They receive small amounts of radio programming about their particular concerns and interests. Mining, fishing, and forestry engage even smaller percentages of the population. Most Germans, West and East, live in cities and work in government, industry, businesses, and the professions. West and East Germans enjoy high per-capita incomes compared with their West Bloc and East Bloc neighbors, and both are major exporters of manufactured goods. Electronics is a major industry in both Germanies, and partly as a result the two German broadcasting systems are technologically advanced.

POLITICAL   Following the dissolution of the monarchy at the end of World War I, Germany embarked upon an experiment in parliamentary democracy. Many of the years of the Weimar Republic (1918–33) were marked by strife, but a democratic system of sorts seemed to have taken root by the mid-1920s. The coming of the Great Depression at the end of the 1920s and the resultant high unemployment helped to weaken the fragile democracy to the point where Hitler and the Nazis, who had come to power more or less within the democratic framework, soon were able to subvert the system to their own autocratic ends; radio played an important role in their consolidation of power.

By the end of World War II, there was little semblance of government in Germany, and the allied powers set about rebuilding a democratic system that would govern all of the country. It soon became apparent that the Soviet Union and the three major western powers (France, Great Britain, the United States) had widely differing ideas of what constituted a democracy, and the two segments of Germany moved farther and farther apart. The western powers moved toward a system with multiparty participation, a division of power between state (*Land*) and federal (*Bund*) government, a strong Parliament, and so on, while the Soviet Union shaped a system with one dominant political party (SED, or Communist), concentration of power in the national government (the *Länder* in fact eventually were abolished in favor of smaller districts, or *Bezirke*), and a rather weak Parliament. Today, both Germanies can claim to be democracies in some respects, with universal suffrage, various constitutionally protected freedoms, and so on. The exercise of those freedoms and that suffrage is another matter, and in most respects West German citizens have much greater freedom than do their East German counterparts, who face a visible reminder of one lack of freedom—to travel—in the presence of the Berlin Wall and the Iron Curtain of watchtowers, mined land, and electric fences that runs along the border separating the two Germanies. Still, some freedoms of choice are growing in East Germany; among them, there is the relative freedom to watch and listen to West German broadcasting undisturbed.

Certainly the various political parties in West Germany—two major ones, several smaller ones—have sought to use broadcasting to bring their views to the public, but they also have complained from time to time about the broadcasts of their political opponents, and there have been periods when West German broadcasting has taken on the appearance of a political battleground. East German political broadcasting presents no such problems: Although there are several political parties, the SED predominates, and the others support it rather than contend with it.

CULTURAL   The Germans have one of the greatest cultural traditions in
    Europe, stretching back to the early Middle Ages and embracing painting, poetry, music, drama, and other arts. Philosophers such as Hegel, Buber, and Kant, composers such as Bach, Beethoven, and Brahms, novelists, poets, and dramatists such as Schiller, Goethe, and Thomas Mann, and painters such as Dürer, Menzel, and Kollwitz were and for the most part still are major influences in European and even world culture. Broadcasting has played a part in the dissemination of that culture, but it also has brought foreign cultures to Germany in sometimes new forms, and *Dallas* and other U.S. (and occasionally British) TV series have many devoted viewers. United States-style fast-food restaurants have spread around West Germany, and blue jeans are common in both Germanies.

Religion does not appear to be a major influence in contemporary German culture, for various reasons. Although well over half of all West Germans profess to follow one faith or another, the churches have little influence over the educational system, in marked contrast to the Netherlands. Nor is there a state church. Churches certainly are allowed to exist in East Germany, but they hardly are encouraged, and most of their present leaders are prepared to cooperate with the government, which means not opposing it. There have been some small peace and antinuclear groups in East Germany that have been associated with churches, but most of the time they function under tight state control. Religious programs are broadcast over East German radio, as they are over West German radio.

The Germans themselves are voracious consumers of culture, at least according to certain indices. Their annual level of book reading is among the highest in Europe, they are frequent visitors to art galleries, they attend many concerts, and they seem willing to support state subsidization of the arts. They sometimes are accused of being highly conservative in their artistic tastes, and even intolerant of avant-garde movements or figures, yet Germany (and Berlin in particular) was home to some of the most active avant-garde movements and figures during the 1920s, and West Berlin has regained something of that reputation over the past two decades. Broadcasting has been the vehicle for some of that avant-garde expression: The playwright Bertolt Brecht was active in radio during the 1920s, and the composer Karlheinz Stockhausen has written many works specifically for transmission over radio starting in the 1960s. Both Germanies encourage their best writers to write for radio and television and give them considerable creative latitude. The public, too, appears to regard broadcasting as an important medium for cultural expression, although audiences for high culture broadcasts often are small. At the same time, German and other critics have pointed out that there is a considerable following for kitsch and low comedy in Germany, and one can discover many examples of each in the two German broadcast systems.

A Brief History

It is hard to imagine more difficult conditions for the creation of a broadcast system than those that existed in Germany in the early 1920s.[2] The country was emerging from World War I with its economy shattered, its monarchy gone, and its territory and population reduced. The war reparations obligations placed upon it by the allied governments were nearly impossible to fulfill and helped to lead to rampant inflation and to a devaluation of currency that must be unparalleled in economic history: The *Reichsmark*, which had stood at about nine to the U.S. dollar just after the war, fell to over 4 billion to the dollar by November 1923! Yet all during this period various German businesses, government departments, and individuals were busy experimenting with wireless transmission (Germany had made considerable progress on this before and during the war). There were experimental broadcasts of concerts and operas starting in December 1920, all carried out over the German Post Office (*Reichspost*) transmitter at Königs—Wusterhausen near Berlin, and radio amateurs all over Germany and beyond received them and commented on reception conditions. An Economic System Broadcasting Service was set up in 1920 but at first used telegraphy to convey economic data (stock-market reports, etc.) to its customers and did not utilize wireless telephony until 1922. Even at that, the public could not (or wasn't supposed to) listen to the service; it was to be received over licensed sets only, and the sets themselves were tuned to one frequency.

When broadcasting to the general public finally did begin, those who invested funds to establish the stations hoped for some financial return from them, perhaps through sale of airtime to advertisers, perhaps through increased sales of phonograph records (the Vox record company's headquarters in Berlin was the site of the first broadcast), perhaps through rising public demand for radio receivers (some of the investors were connected with radio dealerships). In fact, they received very little return at first: The government placed high annual taxes on radio receivers, which discouraged people from buying them (although it did lead to sharply increased, and illegal, home construction of receivers). The tax was reduced in March 1924, and just as had happened in Great Britain, the number of licensed sets increased enormously: Fewer than 10,000 registered and taxed sets as of April 1924, nearly 550,000 by the end of the year. The tax revenues themselves made the individual stations considerably stronger economically, and ad revenues increased as the economy improved.[3]

As radio grew in strength, the stations set up a cooperative association, partly in order to be able to protect themselves from the encroachment of the post office. That association lasted only a few months and was succeeded by the German Radio Society (Reichs Rundfunk Gesellschaft) in 1925. The society concept had been suggested by the German Ministry of the Interior, which remained quite distrustful of the idea of such a powerful medium of communication resting in private hands. The charter for the society granted controlling power to the post office—the private businesses saw little reason not to, since the post office supplied them with the major share of their revenue through the taxes it collected—but also made the society itself responsible for a wide range of functions, including regulation of program exchange among the stations. This meant that, indirectly at least, a government ministry would have some degree of influence over programming decisions.

That was not all. The radio stations now were required to accept the supervision of "cultural committees" that would be appointed by the respective state (*Land*) governments; those committees would examine the program output of each station to see that it was serving the cultural interests of society. In addition, there were to be supervisory committees at each station, one member appointed by the national government and two by the state government; those committees would attempt to keep radio from being used for partisan political purposes. The founders of the stations had not expected them to function as important sources of information, and the newscasts had been supplied through a governmentally supported wire service (DRADAG — Drahtlose Dienst A.G.), so the new restrictions were not all that bothersome. However, they did frustrate some of the more extreme political parties, the National Socialists (Nazis) in particular, and made the Nazis all the more determined to shape radio to their own purposes when and if they came to power.

For the remainder of the 1920s, then, radio served as a considerable cultural force by broadcasting German and foreign drama, some in transcription and some originally written for radio, talks on cultural subjects, and music, popular and classical. News broadcasts were brief, political discussion programs were rare, commentaries were nonexistent. And when in 1932 the government passed radio reform legislation, which further centralized control of the medium by creating the post of radio commissioner in the Ministry of the Interior to supervise informational broadcasting, the move brought some public criticism (especially from the radio periodicals) but little else. Even the states raised little protest, probably because by this time their status in the German political system was much weaker. It is doubtful that most of the public noticed the difference. Newscasts already were bland and supercautious; now they became more so. Those portions of the legislation that pertained to entertainment broadcasting were so general in tone, but so contradictory, that one writer for a radio periodical said, "How many questions of conscience must a [station] manager submit to himself and inwardly answer today, before he can label a program 'good,' if he does not want to be entangled in the mantraps of these definitions."[4] The chief outcome of that particular reform was a notable increase in last-minute cancellations and substitutions of entertainment programs. In a Germany rapidly descending into chaos, thanks to the depression and to the increasingly violent activities of some of the political parties, the government of the day, such as it was, wanted to guarantee the neutrality of radio in every way possible, wanted to avoid giving offense. Centralization made this easier to do. It also made things much easier for the Nazis when they finally came to power. Unfortunately, neutrality was the last thing they had in mind.

THE THOUSAND-YEAR REICH (1933–45)   The first head of radio in the
Hitler era, Eugen Hadamovsky, made his (and the Nazis') excitement at finally getting control over radio very obvious when he stated,
"While in the opposition, we wrote the word 'radio' with three exclama-
tion points. We still do it today, as well, for we are possessed by the
magic strength of electric sparks which open the heart and set the spirit
in motion, a strength which does not stop at city limits and is not turned
back from closed doors, which knows no boundaries and is able to draw
the people into the spell of one mighty spirit."⁵ That fascination with
radio's "magic strength" was shared by many Nazi leaders, German
chancellor Adolf Hitler and his propaganda chief Joseph Goebbels in
particular. They soon set in motion plans shaped many years earlier to
make radio serve as the instrument by which "the entire nation will be
drenched through and through with our philosophy."⁶ The 1932 reforms
had simplified their task, but due in part to economic conditions, radio
was not yet as all-pervasive as the Nazis wished. Therefore, they soon
implemented several steps that would bring the medium to virtually
every German citizen, and several more steps that would insure its
"proper" use.

Because many people could not afford to purchase radio sets, there
already existed in Germany many informal clubs and associations where
one set served a group of people. The Radio Participants' League was
the largest and most national of those associations, and the Nazis had
begun to infiltrate league groups even before 1933. Now such groups
were encouraged even further, because they had the added benefit of
bringing people together under conditions where trusted Nazi party
members could get the groups to discuss what they had just heard; hope-
fully, that would insure that the Nazi message was properly understood,
but also that "deviants" in the groups could be spotted, singled out, and
persuaded to change their thinking.

But people also wanted to be able to listen on their own, and for
this, too, the Nazis had a solution: an inexpensive radio receiver. The
People's Radio Receiver, as it was called, was inexpensive because it was
simple—so simple that it would receive only one or two frequencies,
which of course were those of the German broadcast service. Thus,
"alien" broadcasts from other parts of Europe (some of them in German, especially from the Nazis' sworn enemies in the Soviet Union)
would not reach the ears of at least some of the people. By the outbreak
of World War II, it became a crime punishable by a prison term or even
death to pass on to others what one had heard on those alien broadcasts.
The People's Receivers sold like hotcakes, and by the late 1930s, Ger-

many had the largest number of radio sets in all of Europe.

Although the existing broadcast system featured transmitters and studios all over the country, transmitter power was weak enough in some cases that not everyone could hear broadcasts clearly, so the Nazis strengthened transmitter power to the point where that no longer was a problem. (Such a move was especially important because the People's Receivers were not particularly sensitive, and a weak signal, even if on the correct frequency, would be almost inaudible.) And finally, even though the annual license fee for having a radio set in the household was quite low (twenty-four marks a year—which it remained until 1969), the Nazis allowed many exemptions to it, especially among war veterans, old people, and the physically handicapped.

It was just as important to insure that listeners received politically and culturally correct information, so the Nazis also remodeled the administrative structure of German radio. The advisory and supervisory councils were abolished. Radio stations throughout the country were placed under managers who would have total power over program content. Those managers were trusted Nazi party members, of course. Political and cultural elements deemed undesirable by the Nazis—meaning Jews and communists in particular, but also those whose approach to the arts, journalism, and so on was "decadent" or "negative"—had no place on the radio, although it took a few years to remove them altogether. That was made all the easier because one person, Joseph Goebbels, headed all three of the agencies that were most important to the functioning of radio: the Propaganda Ministry, the Nazi Party Office of Broadcasting, and the Reich Chamber of Culture (a "union" of producers, writers, etc.).

The Nazis also created new studios and transmitters in German cities which heretofore had not had them but gradually squeezed out regional programming by claiming more and more time for the national service from Berlin, which once again served as the German capital.[7] All of the important public speeches of Hitler were broadcast, of course, but so were those of other party leaders, including Goebbels himself. There were plenty of talks and other features about National Socialism, too, some intended for the general public, others for specific groups, such as housewives, factory workers, and so on. Music broadcasts increasingly took on a German character, with less and less time for foreign works. In October 1935, jazz disappeared from the broadcast schedule; it was considered to be too decadent for the new Germany.

One of the most striking demonstrations of the power of radio, at least as the Nazis wielded it, came in late 1934 to early 1935. The Saar, a small but industrially significant territory on the French-German border, had been placed under French supervision by the League of Nations just after World War I. The league decided to hold a plebiscite to determine whether the Saarlanders wished to remain under French jurisdiction, return to Germany, or opt for independence. The Nazis saturated Germany and the Saar with broadcasts urging a return to Germany: There were approximately a thousand separate broadcasts on the subject within a two- to three-month period. The persuasion was almost entirely positive, emphasizing the many benefits to be had through union with the new Germany. The vote, too, was overwhelmingly positive, and the Nazis credited radio for their success. In a way, the Saar campaign was a tune-up for the propaganda barrage the Nazis directed to Austria in 1937–38 and Czechoslovakia in 1938,[8] except that, in those cases, threats definitely were mixed in with promises. Both campaigns were successful.

The Nazis also were interested in television. Several German scientists had been working with the medium since the 1920s, and in 1935 the Nazis proclaimed the first "regular" TV service in the world — regular because it was on the air three days a week and on a fixed schedule. Most of the receivers were set up in public places, and none were available for general public purchase. The initial standard was crude (180 lines), but by 1937 there was a 441-line system, and shortly thereafter a few receivers were placed on sale at very high prices (RM 650). The outbreak of World War II halted the production of sets, but the transmission of a regular service continued until 1944.

The outbreak of war in 1939 brought other changes to broadcasting. Listening to foreign broadcasts became illegal. More and more airtime was taken up with patriotic music and with announcements of victories, which themselves were handled very cleverly: The national service would receive reports of military triumphs at various times during the day, but rarely announced them immediately; instead, it broadcast "special announcements," complete with trumpet fanfares, that indicated the coming of major declarations. In that way, people's curiosity would grow and word would spread, so that the audience would become as large and as attentive as possible. By 1943, defeats had become more frequent than victories, but even these sometimes served the same purpose, since they could be described as "strategic retreats designed to lure the enemy into a trap." Goebbels disclosed his increasing pessimism about the outcome of the war in his diaries,[9] but went on to note some of the new propaganda twists he was devising to keep the German people as optimistic as possible.

As the war continued, some listeners became disenchanted with the service provided by the national radio station. Regional services were on during the morning hours only, and in any case were no real alternative. There were enough listener protests over the almost incessant German marches and waltzes that the stations eventually cut them back to something more closely resembling balance in presentation. The accuracy of the newscasts was something else again; no one dared to protest openly in that case, but a fair number of Germans found ways of obtaining, rehabilitating, or modifying existing receivers (even the People's Receivers!) so as to be able to receive broadcasts from outside the country. That was risky, of course, and German jamming (electronic interference with incoming broadcast signals) made it difficult to listen, anyway. However, German morale remained remarkably high in the closing period of the war, and Nazi radio probably can claim some of the credit for that.

During the early and middle periods of the war, the allied forces were successful in bombing a few of the German transmitters, but auxiliary transmitters usually got stations back on the air within minutes, so technical services were maintained throughout the conflict. Late in the war, as the Allies pushed into Germany itself, the German military frequently blew up their own transmitters in order to keep the Allies from using them. The Soviet advance from the east was so rapid, however, that the Red Army was able to enter Berlin, capture the national station intact, and begin to broadcast from it in less than two weeks. The remnants of the German government fled to northern Germany and attempted to continue a national broadcast service from there, but the war was over within a few weeks. The Thousand-Year Reich had lasted barely twelve years, and for all its effectiveness as a propaganda instrument, the German radio service could do little to prolong its life. Its ultimate masters, Adolf Hitler and Joseph Goebbels, had committed suicide together in an underground bunker in Berlin, even as German radio exhorted the people to fight on.

BROADCASTING UNDER THE OCCUPATION (1945–49)   Germany's defeat at the hands of the Allies was followed by several developments that neither it nor they could have foreseen. Although Germany and its capital, Berlin, were divided into four zones (in Berlin, sectors) of occupation, that was to be a temporary measure, and the country and the capital would be treated as one entity, the four occupying powers coordinating their activities with one another. That was the plan. It did not work in practice, and the three western zones and sectors, under the French, the British, and the Americans, pulled closer and closer together and farther and farther apart from the Soviet zone and sector. The country's veins and arteries—its postal system, road, rail, and canal network, and its broadcast service—all were subdivided sooner or later.

Attempts to coordinate policy took place over many months and in many meetings, but their net result usually was the same. The Soviet Union seemed interested chiefly in extracting as much in reparations from Germany as possible, while the three western Allies worked toward the economic reconstruction of the country. Broadcasting proved to be an especially difficult matter: Many of the regional stations in the western part of the country had been destroyed or severely damaged in the closing months of the war and never were designed to be heard throughout the country, whereas the Soviet army had captured the national station intact. It mattered not at all that the station was located in what turned out to be the British sector of occupation in Berlin; the Soviet Union was able to treat it as an enclave and had full rights of entry and exit—rights maintained until the early 1950s, when a new broadcasting center was built in East Berlin.

It seemed logical, at least to the western Allies, that the Berlin station should be used by all of them to broadcast to all of Germany. The Soviets agreed in principle. It was not so easy to gain agreement in practice. At one point, as the western Allies pressed their claim for airtime, the Soviets offered one hour per day. When the western Allies stated that they did not think that an hour apiece was very much, they were told that they had misunderstood: It was one hour to be subdivided among themselves as they saw fit! At that point, the western Allies decided that their own efforts to reestablish broadcast services would have to go ahead without any assumption that they eventually might form part of a broad national service.

Already there were stations in several of the larger cities of western Germany: Munich, Frankfurt, Hamburg, and Stuttgart all had been placed in service again, although with staffs made up largely of print journalists and others inexperienced in broadcasting. Most of the experienced broadcasters were or were assumed to be Nazis or Nazi sympathizers and were on trial or in jail. German-speaking Americans, British, and French not only ran the stations but did some of the on-air work at first; soon, German staff took over all but the top management positions, and in the U.S. and French zones, those too went to Germans within a year or two. The Soviet Army had brought along with it a number of Germans who had worked for Radio Moscow's German service during the war; they now formed an important part of the Soviet zone broadcast management structure.

The occupation zones led to some peculiar results simply because of their peculiar geography. One commentator claimed that the British got heavy industry, the Americans got scenery, and the French got wines. There were more profound underlying reasons for the choice of zones, but the division created a need for broadcast facilities in places where there had been few or none up until then. For example, the French chose as their administrative center the spa and casino town of Baden-Baden, which never had had a station of its own. Now it had one. The United States needed an enclave in the British zone in order to handle shipping, since the main U.S. zone in southern Germany was completely land-locked; it got Bremen and Bremerhaven, and soon put in operation a station in Bremen, which had had no more than a small studio before that time. The Soviet Union had the main station in Berlin, but also one in Leipzig, and it soon added others in order to provide a small amount of localized broadcasting. In fact, until 1952 there were two networks in the region, a North German Network based in Berlin, and a Central German Network based in Leipzig, although the greater share of the program material originated in Berlin.[10] The merger of the two networks into one centralized service coincided with the abolition of states in East Germany and was part of an overall move toward centralization.

The military occupation governments were determined that another Hitler should not rise again, but West and East went about the task of preventing that in very different ways. The Soviet zone was to feature a strong national government with little power in the hands of the states (which eventually were abolished), but with a considerable amount of oversight by the Soviet Union itself. The western zones were brought together gradually (and not without some disagreement among the western Allies) into a federal structure, with certain rights guaranteed to the states and others to the federal government; there would be decreasing oversight by the allied occupation governments. Broadcasting was reserved for the states, with the hope that that would keep any demagogue from making effective use of the medium nationwide. Broadcasting was separated from the post office in all four zones; in the western zones, that move appears to have been taken because Germans were fearful that the national government could use the post office to influence broadcast policy, as it had done starting in the mid-1920s.

Some Germans agreed with the state's rights policy, while others saw it as wasteful, inefficient, and possibly unworkable. But the western Allies had agreed upon it, and although the provisional legislatures in the various West German states had to draft broadcast laws themselves, those laws had to win occupation authority approval. Therefore, all of them ended up bearing considerable resemblance to one another. And when a constitution was drafted for the federal government, it recognized states' rights in this and other domains. Thus, the western part of

Germany ended up with a broadcast system that bore very little resemblance to anything the country had ever had before: one in which there would be no nationally administered service.

Unfortunately, the states themselves had not been designed with broadcasting in mind. Some were quite small, others were large, and two of them — Hamburg and Bremen — were tiny city-states. Also, the occupation authorities had followed some of their own national tendencies in setting up broadcast systems within their respective zones of occupation. The British and French each developed a single major broadcast center (the British in Hamburg, the French in Baden-Baden), as was characteristic of their own national broadcast services. There were smaller stations elsewhere in their zones, but they were decidedly secondary. The Americans were less centrist: Each large city in the U.S. zone had a station, which meant that Munich, Stuttgart, Frankfurt, and Bremen all became broadcast centers, with some degree of cooperation among them but also a fair measure of independence.

When all of this came together in the new federal republic in 1949, it was not exactly a seamless robe. Barely sixty miles separated Hamburg and Bremen, yet each had a broadcast center. The states of Baden and Württemburg were joined together, giving the combined state two broadcast centers, in Baden-Baden and in Stuttgart (also about sixty miles apart). The station in Hamburg was to provide service to the city-state of Hamburg and to three other north German states, although in 1954 a subsidiary station in Cologne became a broadcast center in its own right and served its particular area. The Saar once again was under French administration, and by the time it rejoined Germany in 1957, once again through a plebiscite but without an intensive radio propaganda campaign as accompaniment, it already had a station of its own even though it was one of the smallest of the states. In other words, the system that evolved lacked geographical logic. It also turned out to lack economic logic, as we shall see.

One of the features common to all broadcast laws in the western zones also was one of the most revolutionary. The allied authorities wanted guarantees that the German people would become involved in the administration of broadcasting — again, in the hope that that would help prevent another Hitler from taking over radio. Few countries ever had tried to institutionalize citizen involvement, although one of the U.S. networks, NBC, had had an advisory council made up of leading figures in society, Great Britain had had more broadly based advisory councils for the BBC since 1935, and France had had citizen councils that actually wielded some power for a few years in the mid-1930s.

The modus operandi was quite interesting: attempt to divide society into interest groups (educators, labor, and religious groups, business and manufacturing, politicians, cultural organizations, etc.), then draw up a council that would represent those interests, without particular reference to their numerical strength. Each state broadcast law had to contain provision for such a council, although variations were permitted, as a result of which some councils were and are larger than others, have certain interests represented that others do not, and so on. The councils were to have real power in the administration of their respective stations — hiring and firing the station manager, examining the yearly budget and possibly even having limited veto power over expenditures — and the groups themselves would get to choose their own representatives; they would not be selected by the broadcasters or by the state governments (except for those council members who represented state governments). The councils were to be as independent as possible.

None of those features characterized broadcasting in the Soviet zone. Organization was at the national level, and there were no broadcast councils. There was no need for the latter, in theory: Communism followed the Lincolnesque precepts of government of, by, and for the people. Therefore, broadcasters were of the people and naturally would work in the people's interests. There was one respect in which broadcasting in the four occupation zones was very similar, however: Stations everywhere gave prominence to programs detailing Nazi misdeeds, called upon listeners to recognize their own roles in allowing and even encouraging that to happen, and urged them to be vigilant in the future so as to prevent any recurrence. That was a necessary part of the rehabilitation process that would lead Germany back to democracy and full sovereignty. By the time that finally occurred, it was clear that there would be two very different Germanies.

The names taken by the two new Germanies portrayed very clearly one of the most fundamental differences between them: The western portion called itself the Federal Republic of Germany, thus emphasizing a division of power between the federal and state government; the eastern portion called itself the German Democratic Republic, thus emphasizing an approach to governance that the other, not "truly" democratic Germany perhaps could not claim for itself. The broadcast systems displayed the same fundamental difference. However, while the East German system has remained essentially unchanged in its structure from 1949 up until the present, the West German system has undergone several changes, some by mutual agreement among the stations, some as a reaction to state and federal government pressure, and some as a reaction to changes in external situations.

THE REPUBLICS ESTABLISH THEMSELVES (1949–61)   In 1951, the federal government, then led by Chancellor Konrad Adenauer and the Christian Democratic (conservative) party, or CDU, made the first of several attempts to establish a national broadcast system alongside the state system. It was unsuccessful, but nothing daunted, Adenauer mounted further efforts. In 1959, the CDU-led government proposed an omnibus broadcasting bill that would establish a second TV service (the state system had begun to add television to radio in 1952), which was to be set up along the lines of the British IBA.[11] The bill also called for the federal government to take over the tiny international broadcast service (Deutsche Welle), which was being operated as a joint venture by the state systems, and to establish a new German-language radio service (Deutschlandfunk) ostensibly intended for German-speaking listeners outside the Federal Republic (East Germany, Switzerland, Austria, and various pockets of German speakers elsewhere). It soon became evident that the TV portion of the bill would not pass, so the two radio stations were made the subject of a separate bill, which did pass. Then Adenauer and a few of his close political associates worked with a group of businessmen to establish a second TV service that would come into being without federal legislation. A company was established during 1960 and was scheduled to go on the air in February 1961.

The states reacted predictably to the proposed TV service, took the case to the West German Supreme Court, and in 1961 received a favorable verdict, at least in part: The Court declared that the federal government had no right to establish a domestic broadcast service, as the federal basic law (constitution) reserved that power for the states.[12] The widespread discussion of the attempt to establish a second television service aroused public interest in having one to a sufficient degree that it emerged by 1963, albeit in a rather bizarre organizational form, about which more later.

The state stations already had taken steps to strengthen themselves, beginning with the creation of the Arbeitsgemeinschaft der öffentlichrechtlichen Rundfunkanstalten Deutschlands (Working Group of German Public Service Broadcasting Organizations, hereafter referred to as ARD) in 1950. The stations had exchanged ideas and programs with one another during the occupation period but felt the need for a more permanent organization through which to carry out such activities. Also, it was evident that furnishing a full range of broadcast programs would be difficult for any one of the largest stations, and almost impossible for the smallest ones. The stations soon established an ongoing program exchange service that not only took into account the financial ability of individual stations to contribute to a program pool but also recognized certain "spheres of influence"—specific kinds of programs that would come from certain stations because of their already-established expertise in that area. The stations also agreed to establish a news production center in Munich in order to serve all parts of the country with a more comprehensive national and international news service than any one of them could furnish. (All of them continued to cover local and regional news.)

The stations themselves financed the ARD, but they also worked through the organization to rectify some of the financial imbalances in the broadcast system. Since each station received license-fee money from listeners in its particular state, some stations had far larger revenues than did others. Hamburg's NWDR received revenues from an area with a population of over 25 million, while Radio Bremen's area had perhaps 1 million, and SR (the Saar) not much more. Therefore, the stations worked out a revenue-sharing scheme that would see the larger stations subsidizing the smaller ones—a scheme that continues to function to this day. The stations also agreed on some general limits for amounts of advertising to be carried (the Americans had introduced radio advertising on stations in their zone in 1948, mainly to help encourage growth in the economy), although a few stations, such as NWDR, that could afford such a policy declined to carry any at all. The ARD also allowed the stations to negotiate from a position of collective strength—important in dealing with unions and with state legislatures, since any increase in broadcast license fees must be approved by all of the legislatures. (Even with the ARD acting as coordinator, that is a clumsy, tedious, time-consuming process, which is the main reason why there have been only four increases in the license fee since 1949, with another small increase scheduled for 1988 and a larger one for 1989.)

Television presented another set of problems for the stations. Following a series of tests, the first regularly scheduled TV service by a state station came on the air in December 1952; by 1954, several other state stations had TV services, and they again pooled their programming resources. For TV, that was far more crucial than it had been for radio, since the costs were so much higher, and the stations devised a fixed exchange system that would see stations contributing specific programs and series on a regularly scheduled basis. Most of the prime-time schedule was and still is put together in that manner. Again, the stations developed a central news organization—actually an expansion of duties for the existing operation in Munich. While all stations contributed to the total program pool, obviously some were far better situated to do so than others, notwithstanding which all stations were and still are required to contribute a minimum of 3 percent of the program material for the collective program. (Individual stations also produce and purchase programs for non-prime-time hours, including local and regional news.)

During the first decade or so of its existence, the new West German broadcast system earned high marks for the quality of its productions, although some critics observed that the amount of programming about the Nazi past seemed to have decreased once the occupation period ended. Politics was a frequent program topic, and the system appeared able to defend itself against attempts at political influence. However, when NWDR was divided into two stations in 1954 (NDR in Hamburg, WDR in Cologne), politicians took advantage of the opportunity by changing the manner in which members of the broadcast councils were chosen; the new radio laws for the two stations specified that the state legislatures would appoint the members, and unlike the other state broadcast councils, there was no specific indication of which societal groups should be represented. Some critics have seen this as the first move in an increasing politicization of German broadcasting. Since appointments were based on political party affiliation, and council seats were divided roughly along the lines of political party representation, there certainly was the potential for greater political influence from the councils. The move also had its effect on the appointment of broadcast administrators: Increasingly during the late 1950s the councils — and not only those of the NDR and WDR — took the concept of *Proporz,* or proportional balance of political parties, into account when considering staff appointments. *Proporz* is now an accepted part of West German broadcasting, however much it may represent a departure from what the allied occupation authorities had in mind.[13]

Finally, some of the larger state broadcasting stations began to offer second and even third program services over radio during the 1950s, so as to provide some listening alternatives. While the first and second services usually were quite similar, the third services, where they existed, were far more specialized and closely resembled the BBC's Third Programme for that same period: lots of high culture, such as plays in their original languages, avant-garde musical works, and so on, and presentations of highly specialized cultural and scientific topics. The state stations saw themselves as patrons of the arts, and several of them created folk, jazz, chamber, and symphonic groups to play standard and specially commissioned music; they also commissioned some of Germany's best writers to write radio and television plays, and Heinrich Böll, Günter Grass, and others willingly did so because they saw that broadcasting was treated as a serious artistic medium.

The East German broadcast system remained monolithic throughout the 1950s, although a television service came on the air in 1952 and four more radio services were added during the decade. All services were under the control of the State Committee for Broadcasting, whose chairperson held cabinet rank and was a relatively senior SED party official. More regional stations came on the air in the 1950s, but they had only a few hours each day on their own and otherwise served as relays for the programs coming from Berlin. East German broadcasting, too, took upon itself the patron of the arts role, creating orchestras and commissioning music and plays, but both often had a strongly ideological flavor: Plays often were about the sacrifices that "good" citizens made on behalf of the nation and about the evil designs of West Germany and its U.S. supporters on East German society. Music often consisted of well-known works from the past, but commentary on them often would emphasize the difficult social conditions facing composers such as Beethoven or Mozart. There also were "popular" songs composed especially for presentation over radio or TV and with the lyrics, melody, and chords printed in the weekly radio-TV guide; they included such subjects as why bad drivers are a menace to society, why collective farms are good for society, and so on.[14] And in 1960, East German television introduced a program that still is on the air (although it was off during the mid-1960s), *The Black Channel,* which consisted of excepts from West German television, analyzed and placed in proper political perspective by East German commentator Karl Edouard von Schnitzler. East Germany was becoming more and more aware of the influence of West German broadcasting on its own listeners and viewers and was fighting back not only with *The Black Channel,* but also with improved programming (especially variety shows) of its own.

FROM THE WALL TO THE TREATY (1961–72)   The erection of the Berlin Wall in August 1961 did more than symbolize the division between the two parts of Berlin; it also cut off West Germany from continuing and easy access to East Berlin, making it that much more difficult for broadcasters, among others, to learn just what was taking place in East Germany, what East Germans thought about the issues of the day, and so on. Before August, it had been relatively easy for East Germans to visit West Berlin and to use it as a means to leave East Germany for good; some East Germans even worked in West Berlin, coming and going on a daily basis. East Germans also had fair access to information about the West, although radio broadcasts intended specifically for East Germans were jammed (RIAS Berlin, a United States-supported station, was the primary target of the jamming),[15] and the watching of West German television was discouraged by various means, including the use of "goon squads" that occasionally climbed up on roofs and twisted or tore down antennas that were oriented to receive western TV. At the same time, the East German broadcast system redoubled its efforts to present its viewers with interesting, high-quality programming.

The West German Supreme Court's 1961 decision upholding state's rights in broadcasting gave the states a renewed sense of their own strength but also thrust upon them further responsibilities. The West German public clearly wanted more broadcast services (especially TV) than the present system was providing. If the federal government was not allowed to provide service, then either the state broadcasting systems themselves or other systems licensed by the states would have to do so. There were several interested parties who wanted to set up private, commercial TV stations; most of them were publishers, who could see the opportunity both for profit and for protection of their publishing interests. But the states generally were opposed to considering commercial broadcasting of that sort. At the same time, setting up a second TV network through ARD seemed far too costly; license fees would have to be increased tremendously, and state legislatures did not care to consider that option. However, the state stations did patch together a second television service as a stopgap measure while a more permanent solution was being devised.

The second television service that finally emerged as a permanent solution in 1963 — called, not too imaginatively, Second German Television (ZDF) — was a strange compromise. All West German states were cosigners of the legal agreement creating ZDF, so in that way the new service was a state function. However, ZDF was a centralized organization, with its administrative headquarters and main production facilities in the neighboring cities of Mainz and Wiesbaden, and with very small studio facilities (enough for interviews, panels, etc.) in many cities throughout the country. Thus, its program output did not represent the collective efforts of individual state stations.

The legislation for ZDF embraced the concept of a broadcast council, but on a much larger (and national) scale: The ZDF council has sixty-six members (the largest ARD station has forty-nine, and the average size is a bit over thirty) representing various groups in society, selected by those groups on a national, rather than state, basis. It also includes representatives of the various state governments. The ZDf was to receive a share of the license-fee money, and the license fee itself, which had remained at two marks per month from the mid-1920s until

1959, was increased to take into account the higher operating costs of television. The ZDF also could advertise, but under the same restrictions as ARD had devised for its members: brief blocks of ads for nationally advertised products and services only, interspersed with other program material in the late afternoon to early evening hours, and with virtually no sponsorship of programs. Nevertheless, ZDF was an attractive buy for advertisers, because they had one station rather than several to deal with. The program mix was much the same as on the state television service, and the two services were required to coordinate their broadcast schedules for maximum service to the public, avoiding the simultaneous scheduling of similar programs and providing plenty of fare for "minority" tastes (operas, original plays on controversial topics, etc.).

The largest state stations were able to consider adding their own second television services starting in 1964, and several of them did so: NDR, WDR, Bayerischer Rundfunk (BR) in Munich, Sudwestfunk (SWF) in Baden-Baden. Eventually they were joined by the other ARD stations in regional groupings. For example, SWF, Süddeutscher Rundfunk (SDR) in Stuttgart, and Saarländisches Rundfunk (SR) in the Saar banded together, as did NDR, Radio Bremen, and Sender Freies Berlin. Hessicher Rundfunk (HR) in Frankfurt, WDR, and BR each provided their own second TV services. In each case, these services, collectively labeled the third service, featured more specialized fare: educational material, foreign films in their original languages, discussion programs involving specialized topics.

During the 1960s there were numerous political controversies. One of the largest involved East-West relations. While the Christian Democratic party remained in power (from 1949 to 1969, although in a coalition with the Socialist party, or SPD, for the three final years), there was little disposition to make overtures to the East, and especially to the Soviet Union, Poland, and East Germany. The West German media commonly referred to East Germany as "the so-called German Democratic Republic," and West German maps continued to show the former Reich territory east of the Oder and Neisse rivers as "under Polish administration," whereas Poland and its Eastern European associates considered it as an integral part of Poland. However, in some of the states there were Social Democratic party governments, and there one sometimes could hear and see commentaries, documentaries, and reports advocating changes in West German policy toward the East, discussing more frankly the Nazi past. One NDR commentator, Gert von Paczensky, did not have his contract renewed in 1963 because the NDR broadcast council and some NDR administrators, along with conservative politicians working through them, thought that he was going too far in airing such material.[16]

But when the Social Democrats came to power at the federal level in 1969, and former West Berlin mayor Willi Brandt became chancellor, there was a new era of *Ost-Politik* (East Policy). Derogatory references to East Germany did not cease immediately, but there were more and more programs about steps that could be and were being taken to bridge the East-West gap. Brandt visited Poland and declared that the western part of that country was an integral part of it, and not "under Polish administration." Discussion with East German authorities finally led to an interstate treaty in 1972, which among other things provided greater visiting rights for West Germans wishing to see relatives in East Germany and granting media personnel in both Germanies freer access to people and events in each.

The gradual thaw in inter-German relations and the signing of the treaty brought to an end the activities of two unusual East German radio stations. The Soldatensender had begun its broadcasts in 1960 and was intended for troops serving in the West German army. The Freiheitssender 904 (Freedom Station 904 — the number for its frequency) was the "unofficial" station of the West German Communist party and had begun operation in 1956, just one day after the West German Communist party was declared illegal. Both stations strongly denounced western political, economic, and military policy, criticized West German political leaders, and called attention to the Nazi-era activities of some of them. They would have been "undiplomatic" in this era of greater cooperation, and besides, the West German Communist party became legal again in 1971; immediately after that, Freiheitssender 904 went off the air, and Soldatensender followed in 1972.[17] The two major stations broadcasting from West Germany, RIAS Berlin and Deutschlandfunk, continued on the air. Apparently they were not considered to be as baldly critical of East German policy as the two East German stations were of West German policy, and besides, they functioned openly, rather than as stations pretending to broadcast from within West Germany, as Soldatensender and Freiheitssender did.

One East German broadcast activity for listeners in West Germany continued unabated. West Germany had experienced a large influx of guest workers from southern Europe and Turkey during the 1960s, and many of the state stations had begun to provide limited broadcast services in Turkish, Greek, Italian, and other languages. The East Germans also began to provide services in some of those languages, but of course the content of their programs was considerably different, with much emphasis on the exploitation of workers by employers and the hostility of West Germans toward the guest workers. East German services in Greek, Italian, and Turkish remain on the air.

POLITICS, THE ECONOMY, AND THE NEW MEDIA (1972–87) *Proporz*
first emerged as an issue in the late 1950s. During the 1960s, it grew in importance, and several German critics began to lament the disappearance of the "nonpolitical" broadcast system that the Allies and Germans had crafted so carefully in the pre-1949 days. Social Democrats often complained that commentaries on ZDF were biased in favor of CDU policies and personalities; CDU members often said the same thing about stations in states with SPD governments. The Young Socialists, considered more radical than the mainstream of their party, complained that their views did not get aired at all, and in the 1970s began to work in earnest to see to it that their adherents were employed in stations. Political discussions, long a prominent and popular feature of West German radio and television, seemed to some observers to be getting sharper, more contentious, and with moderators sometimes appearing to play favorites.

A related phenomenon was *Mitbestimmung,* which began around 1969 but became a major issue in the early 1970s. It involved attempts on the part of broadcast journalists to have more of a say in whether and how their stories would be used by their stations. it was a demand for codetermination of editorial decision making and extended beyond the newsroom to include representation on the broadcast councils. Not all stations were equally involved with this movement, which continues to the present, but most changed their procedures to some extent as a result of it. It is unlikely that it would have arisen with the strength it did if *Proporz* itself had not become so much a part of West German broadcasting.[18]

The West German economy boomed during the 1960s and into the 1970s, bringing with it increased purchase of color TV sets (color TV itself had been introduced in 1967). The demand for more and more productions in color placed a considerable strain on the state stations and the ZDF. However, there was no license-fee surcharge on owners of color TV sets that could help to meet the increased costs of programming in color. The state legislatures were reluctant to raise the basic license fee but eventually had to do so, in 1974, 1979, and 1983, always by less than the stations said was needed. That situation has meant that there have been deficits at most of the stations in almost every one of the past fifteen or so years. The would-be private commercial broadcasters continued to press their case, offering the argument that they could supply further television services without (direct) cost to the public, and indeed there were plenty of advertisers who were eager to advertise but for whom there was insufficient time on the two existing TV services. The states continued to control the licensing of broadcasting, but now a few of them were considering the possibility of licensing private services, in addition to maintaining the existing ones.

The Bavarian government gave such a proposal serious consideration in the early 1970s. That government was in the hands of the CSU (the Christian Democratic party in Bavaria calls itself the Christian Socialist party), and the CSU's powerful leader, Franz-Josef Strauss, felt that a private commercial service would be both good business and a useful counterweight to the state service (BR), which he and some other CSU members considered too liberal. Attempts to gain the approval of the Bavarian Parliament for such a service eventually failed, as did the CSU's attempts to radically restructure the BR broadcast council (although it was enlarged and in the process made more political).[19]

The next major move in that direction came in the late 1970s. The states of Lower Saxony and Schleswig-Holstein had been partners with the city-state of Hamburg in NDR. Gains in CDU strength in the two states, and increased tensions with SPD-governed Hamburg, led to calls for the withdrawal of the states from the NDR, together with the licensing of new broadcast stations in each. A 1980 agreement managed to hold the NDR structure together for the time being, but Lower Saxony and Schleswig-Holstein announced their intention to license new television and radio stations. That agreement also brought about a reorganization of the NDR broadcast council, making it conform much more closely with the model followed by the majority of states. Now a third of the council's members would be appointed by the state legislatures, instead of all, and nine seats on the council would be open to applications by groups that considered themselves representative of significant public opinion in any of the three states.

Although Lower Saxony and Schleswig-Holstein now had legal authority to set up new stations, they did not exercise that option immediately. Instead, both expanded the NDR facilities within their own states and also claimed more airtime for those expanded services. Two other states became the first to license private broadcasting, and in each case it represented an outgrowth of cable radio services set up in 1985. Early in 1986, both Bavaria and Rhineland-Palatinate licensed private, commercial radio stations. Schleswig-Holstein followed in mid-1986 and Lower Saxony in early 1987. In November 1986, the West German Supreme Court upheld the rights of states to issue "private" licenses, but only if licensing conditions included the same sorts of restrictions as pertained to public stations, for example, establishment of broadcast councils.[20]

There also was the matter of cable television. Many West German households had received their signals through cable for years, but over master antenna systems, which simply retransmitted existing signals, improving their technical quality but adding no new program services. The West German media were full of reports about the "cable revolution" in North America, and some Germans began to ask about such additional services for themselves. However, there were some knotty jurisdictional questions. States might be responsible for licensing broadcast stations, but was that true of cable? And shouldn't the federal post office be in charge of wiring the country? The former was resolved in favor of the states in the early 1980s, and in 1985 Bavaria licensed West Germany's first full-fledged cable system, complete with access cable and cable radio. As of early 1988 such systems are operating in Munich, Berlin, Ludwigshafen/Mannheim, Dortmund, and some smaller towns, but they have relatively few customers because there is not all that much available by way of additional material. The cabling of the nation (or most of it, at any rate) began in 1985 and as of early 1988 passed about 40 percent of the nation's households although subscribership was at about 15 percent.[21]

Satellite TV also became a public topic in the late 1970s, and in the early 1980s discussion of it increased because of Luxembourg's proposal to use its satellite channel to beam German, French, and possibly other commercial TV services into Germany and France. The French and German governments strongly protested, but there was nothing that either could do about it. Whether Luxembourg will go ahead with its plan is another question — its high costs present problems for such a small country — but already a ground-based satellite operation beams commercially supported TV from Luxembourg into nearby areas of West Germany. This service, called RTL Plus, currently must be received through a special dish antenna and decoder or through one of the four cable systems, and the signal is sent through microwave. But the reception technology is much like what would be required for satellite reception, and it must be considered as a sort of trial balloon. It has few subscribers, but appears to be gaining in popularity.[22] In 1985, a consortium of West German publishers developed a satellite-to-cable service, SAT1.

West German broadcasting, then, is entering another era of change, partly as a result of the new media, but partly also in response to long-present pressures from private industry to open the broadcast media to their investment and participation, whether any or all of those changes will take root and have lasting effects remains to be seen, but the states are being forced to rethink their policies with respect to broadcasting. They do not wish to be bypassed in any "march to the future," but neither do they find it easy to agree with one another on what sorts of actions they might take collectively—a situation made all the more difficult because of the disputes between the political parties, which form differing balances of power in the various states.

East German broadcasting has undergone no such sweeping changes. The State Committee for Broadcasting added a second television service, and the first to be in color, in 1969. Separate state committees for radio and for television were created in 1968. But the administration of the system remains the same, and the prospects for cable and/or satellite TV are very distant, aside from the installation of cable to improve reception. Large numbers of East Germans view West German television, and, although there are occasional newspaper and magazine articles warning viewers and listeners of the possibly harmful effects of consuming too much western programming, the "goon squads" and other crude methods of discouraging such viewing and listening are relics of the past.

THE FEDERAL REPUBLIC OF GERMANY

Financing

There are three sources of financing for West Germany broadcasting: license fees paid by households, advertising, and sales of programs abroad. Program sales account for less than 1 percent of annual revenues; aside from sports, West German programs generally are not all that attractive to non-German-speaking countries, and Austria and Switzerland cannot afford to pay all that much for what they use from their northern neighbor. Unlike Great Britain and the Netherlands, West German broadcasters do not sell radio-TV guides. Ironically, some of those firms that do, notably the Axel Springer publishing firm, also have been among the strongest advocates of private commercial broadcasting, and the Springer firm is one of the principal investors in SAT1.

License fees are collected by the GEZ, an organization created by the state stations and ZDF in 1976. (Before that time, the post office collected the fees and received a portion of them for that service.) The fee money is credited to the station serving the state in which a given household is located. It does not matter whether listeners and viewers in that household may receive better technical service from transmitters located in another state, or that they may spend little or no time viewing or listening to the station located in their own state. Each such area precisely represents one or more states, except for Baden-Württemburg, which is divided into two broadcast service areas, for SWF and SDR. Radio Bremen, Saarländisches Rundfunk, and Sender Freies Berlin (SFB), all serving geographically tiny areas, derive little income from license fees (each has less than a million households in its area) and must be subsidized from the license-fee revenue of the remaining states (mostly from WDR) as collected by GEZ. The SFB also receives extra money because it has the additional mission of transmitting into East Germany. Because it is a national service, Deutschlandfunk also receives a share of the subsidy money (about DM 45 million as of 1984). The ZDF, also a national service, receives 30 percent of the fee money earmarked for television — slightly under a billion marks as of 1984.

The GEZ also tries to track down households where the fee has not been paid (about 10 percent annually), and there are stiff fines for evading payment, but so many West Germans live in multistory apartment houses that electronic detection methods aren't of much use. Fees can be paid on a monthly basis, which helps to spread out payments, and they are slightly high by Western European standards: DM 199.20 per year per household for TV (with no separate fee for color TV), DM 61.92 per year for radio. (Separate radio fees continue to be levied in West Germany, in contrast with many other European nations.) West Germans seem to feel that they get good value for the money, but as already mentioned, state legislatures are reluctant to raise fees very often, and the procedure for doing so is time-consuming.

Advertising has become more and more important as a source of revenue for West German broadcasting. Between 1963 and 1967, ZDF saw its advertising income increase from just under $10 million a year to nearly $40 million a year. The state stations receive about 20 percent and ZDF about 60 percent of their annual incomes from advertising. There has been little increase in airtime for TV advertising; it has gone from eight minutes a day in the late 1950s to twenty minutes a day at present, and remains limited to the 6:00 to 8:00 P.M. period for state TV stations and 5:30 to 7:30 P.M. for ZDF. There are varying periods of time for public (ARD) radio, with some stations devoting as much as 18 percent of their broadcast time to advertising blocks, varying portions of which carry ads, on certain of their services. The third TV service does not carry ads, and WDR and NDR do not carry ads on radio. Neither medium permits advertising on Sundays or national holidays. Sponsorship is difficult to arrange, there is no political advertising, no advertising of tobacco products, and numerous other restrictions abound. Each state station has its own advertising code (although the codes closely resemble one another), and all advertising is handled by a separate organization located within the corporate structure of the station, which underlines the idea that, while ad revenues can be (and are) taxed, the rest of the station's revenues should not be. Everything possible is done to separate advertising from other program content, and even the groups of ads are broken up by short features, brief cartoons, and other devices designed to set them apart. The more recently licensed private radio stations operate on much the same principle, although there are slightly more ad blocks per hour on the private stations.

Because there is so little time available for advertising on the public stations (the limit of twenty minutes per day for TV is absolute), and because the West German economy is relatively healthy and its people prosperous, demand for ad time is very heavy, and there are waiting lists for most ad-time blocks. In fact, ad time can be purchased only once a year, in the fall. This "seller's market" has allowed the stations to set high rates, but advertisers are willing to pay the price. That situation also has made advertisers anxious to see the development of private commercial TV and, to a lesser extent, commercial radio. The few private radio stations on the air as of 1988 have not made a great difference in demand at the national level, but regional and local advertisers, who were not allowed to advertise on ARD or ZDF, seem to be taking readily to their new outlet, and the cable TV outlets also have attracted a number of regional and local accounts. A few of the ARD stations are beginning to request increased amounts of advertising time, in part as a reaction to their private sector competition, and it is possible that the restrictions on accepting local and regional advertising will be loosened or dropped.

Most of the ads run for fifteen to thirty seconds and use techniques and formats that sometimes seem dated by U.S. standards: lots of singing commercials on radio, some relatively unadorned settings on TV. Food, cosmetic, and cleaning products predominate, and there often appears to be a stronger tone of sexism to ads than in the United States. Housewives are shown as ready to bend over backwards to please their grumpy husbands, male and female children take "appropriate" male and female roles when imitating grown-ups, and so on. There has been a small but growing amount of protest over such ad content on the part of feminist organizations.[23]

Because of the manner in which it is organized, West German broadcasting—the state part of the system in particular—is bound to be expensive. Each station has a sizable administrative staff, whether the station's service area is large or small. The requirement that even the smallest stations contribute 3 percent of the total collective (evening) TV program schedule increases program diversity but is not very cost-effective. Broadcast union demands also have increased production costs, particularly in the area of broadcast journalism, where crews of three or four individuals may be sent out to record a very simple interview. Technical standards are among the highest, and most costly, in the world. Few West Germans seem ready to dismantle that system, but if license fees had to be increased sharply to offset that lack of cost-effectiveness, they might wonder whether perhaps a better way could be found. The handful of private radio stations seem to operate without the public objecting to the amount of advertising they carry, which is very little more than what is carried by the ARD stations. Since the private stations do not have license-fee support, it may be that German listeners will wonder why the ARD stations need license-fee money, but so far that has not been a public concern.

Governance and Administration — Internal

THE DECISION-MAKING STRUCTURE   The state stations and ZDF are quite similar in terms of their decision-making structures, which is not surprising given their origins: Both were created (with a lot of help from the allied occupation authorities in the case of the state stations) by the states. Each has a manager (*Intendant*) responsible for day-to-day administration of the station; each has a broadcast council (*Rundfunkrat*) responsible for some degree of supervision and/or advice regarding overall programming and administrative policy, plus an administrative council (*Verwaltungsrat*) drawn largely from the *Rundfunkrat* and responsible for specific budgetary and administrative issues; and each has a full complement of program, administrative, and technical departments whose heads usually are selected by the manager in consultation with one or both councils. Most of the broadcast councils have representatives from various groups (these are listed in the broadcast law of each state), and even the one broadcast council selected by the state legislature, WDR's, is made up of members who have widely varying interests and occupational backgrounds, although that is not a legal requirement. The state stations also work through the ARD, but there is no legal stipulation that they do so, and any station may opt out of a program feed coming through the ARD network if it chooses, as some have. (Radio Bremen and BR at times have found TV programs coming from other state stations politically or socially offensive — the Bremen area and Bavaria are quite conservative — and have replaced those programs with locally available material.)

How the manager, councils, and departments work together is another matter. Each station follows its own practices, and those may change over time. As the councils usually meet four to six times a year, and for one day each time, there are limits to their influence, although some council members visit their stations more frequently, and most councils have a few "movers and shakers" (*Königsmacher*) who wield a great deal of power. The broadcast councils generally hire, discharge, and rehire the manager, although the administrative councils perform that function at WDR, which also has program advisory councils to assist in that specific function. No manager ever has been discharged by a council, although a few either were not rehired or were given short-term renewals while the council searched for a permanent replacement. One of the two councils, and in a few cases both, approves the annual budget, accounts, and report. The broadcast council also deals with program content, but it is not always clear whether that is done on an advisory (to the manager) basis or whether the council has the right to require airing or cancellation of a program or series. It generally seems to be accepted by councils and managers that the role is advisory, but occasionally council members have felt that a manager's decision to drop a program was the result of their expressions of dissatisfaction, and that those expressions went beyond being advice.

The administrative councils, which usually contain a majority of members appointed by the broadcast council and a minority chosen by station staff, control the station's conduct of business and audit the annual budget, accounts, and report. In most cases, their power does not extend to rejection of specific items in the budget, although the NDR council was able to exercise such power if it involved free-lance work done for the station and if it were in excess of a certain sum. It used that power on one occasion in 1972 to attempt to block the making of a program that was judged by some of its members (and by politicians working through those members) to be politically sensitive — a program called *Bauern, Bonsen, und Bomben* (Farmers, Politicos, and Bombs) involving a violent uprising by Schleswig-Holstein farmers in 1930, but with some implications in terms of West German urban violence in the early 1970s. The money finally was made available and the program was made, but the NDR administrative council had shown its willingness to overrule the manager.[24]

The influence of the councils is reduced further by two factors: size and composition. Some of the broadcast councils are quite small (eighteen to twenty-five members) and can conduct a good deal of business in a one-day meeting, but others are large (thirty-five to forty-nine members, and for ZDF sixty-six), often causing decision making to be a lengthy process. Furthermore, the very diversity of council membership, ranging from educational groups to religious bodies to women's groups to business, labor, and political parties, is almost guaranteed to produce a certain amount of posturing for the public record. (Most councils release abstracts of their meetings to the media, which may or may not publish or broadcast them; often the council's particular station does not even broadcast them.) In short, many councils are quite inefficient, and a clever manager can have them tied in knots, or get them to tie themselves in knots, without much difficulty, especially if she or he has a few close allies on the council.

There is also the question of just who or what council members represent. Most organizations that are "represented" on the councils do not elect those representatives, and many of them do not even bother to inform their members that there is a representative on such a council. The representative has no legal obligation to report back to her or his organization, and even if an attempt is made to do so, there may or may not be adequate channels of communication between the organization and its members to get the message across. Furthermore, council members are encouraged to think of themselves to some extent as representing the general viewing and listening public, which may come in conflict with group loyalty. As representatives may be reappointed (the usual term of appointment is three years, and renewals likewise), there is a natural tendency for a person who enjoys this particular sort of activity to keep the interests of the organization foremost when making decisions.

It must be remembered, too, that most of the councils were created back in the late 1940s, well before the guest workers were a prominent feature in German life, and before some of the more militant women's organizations had become active. In other words, the councils are frozen in time. A state legislature may modify the composition of the council by amending the broadcast act, but that is not easy: Legislators generally recognize that the councils often are too large already and do not want to add members or create new categories by abolishing old ones. Even if those problems did not exist, many legislators feel that, by adding a new group to the approved list, there would be many more groups that would insist upon being added, too. As the *Länder* write new laws to deal with cable, they are including councils of slightly different composition, and some of those councils do take into account changes in society in a given *Land,* but there is a strong likelihood those new councils also will appear frozen in time within a few years.

But the councils do have some impact upon station decision making. Managers often have found that council members can supply useful insight on the wisdom of adding a new program or abolishing an existing one. Program directors often have found that councils are useful sources of reaction to embryonic program ideas. Station staff sometimes have found the councils a useful way of getting points across to otherwise unreachable senior administrators. Councils serve as a safeguard for fiscal responsibility. In each of those cases, the presence of a council, where there is the possibility of public disclosure of what goes on inside broadcasting and where the collective membership will raise a range of issues and opinions, gives the station something that it would not get from its own internal discussions and reliance on a few trusted advisors.

Unions can have a large impact upon broadcasting. The Radio, Television, and Film Worker's Union has some fifteen thousand members in broadcasting and represents a solid majority of those involved in production. Union demands regarding size of production crews for broadcasts or taping outside the studio have resulted in high production costs and, some claim, cutbacks in outside productions, to the detriment of the program schedule. The union also has worked hard for better benefits and more permanent employment for free-lance broadcasters and managed to convince the courts in the late 1970s that such broadcasters were entitled to both. This again has led to claims that the move only succeeded in causing the stations to cut back on their use of free-lancers, who often had brought fresh approaches to program-making.[25] There also is a union of West German journalists, the Bundeskorrespondent, working in Bonn, the federal capital, which seeks to insure equal access by media correspondents to politicians and government officials.

As the privately financed and operated electronic media gain a foothold in West Germany, the unions may find it more and more difficult to function. West German private enterprise is not well-disposed toward unions and has a powerful ally in the ruling (as of early 1988) Christian Democratic party, which does not much care for them, either. Production staff members with whom I have talked during my visits to West Germany in the 1980s seem by and large less interested in unions than they were in the sixties and seventies. Surprisingly, this is especially true of younger staff members, which is not a good sign for the future health of unions. Their feeling seemed to be that they belonged to unions (which not all of them did—membership is not compulsory) largely because they believed in the idea of unions, but they did not see them as particularly useful. A few even thought that unions were unnecessarily obstructionist in the adoption of modern technology, for example, electronic news gathering.

The ZDF and the collective television service (Deutsches Fernsehen, or German Television) of the state stations are required by law to coordinate their program schedules, the only situation in the world where that is a legal requirement. The two bodies conclude coordination agreements for two- to three-year periods, and a coordination committee with equal numbers of representatives from each body meets every six months to consider possible changes in the overall agreement. Also, representatives from each body meet every month to discuss specific program details before press releases announcing their respective schedules are sent out for publication. As West Germany has only three nationally available television services, there are limits to the amount of choice viewers can expect, but the coordination system at least maximizes that choice.

The administrative structures of the newer private station for the most part run along the same lines as are followed in the public stations. In part that is a consequence of the public service tradition in West Germany: Much like Great Britain, where the Independent Television Authority was expected to follow the path of the BBC in many respects (advisory councils, audience research department, etc.), West German private broadcasting has councils and internal administrative structures similar to those found in public stations. The private radio stations do appear to function with fewer production staff than do their public counterparts, which in part may be because the unions do not seem to play much of a role in the private stations.

Governance and Administration — External

THE NATIONAL GOVERNMENT   Compared with broadcast systems in other parts of the world, West German broadcasting is almost completely free from formal control at the federal level. There is a small measure of technical control in the form of post office operation of television transmitters for ZDF and for the state third-program services.

The post office also allocates frequencies, and can keep a proposed service from coming on the air if there is no suitable frequency available. Some of the private stations have claimed that the post office has been slow in processing their frequency requests, allegedly because the post office feels that handling the requests makes more work and risks cluttering the spectrum, all for services that do not seem particularly worthwhile.[26] But spectrum space now *is* available, thanks in part to a 1985 agreement among European broadcasters to use more of the UHF spectrum for radio broadcasting and in part to a willingness to consider licensing low-power (50–100 watt) stations for localized service.

The federal government may appoint commissions to study aspects of broadcasting and make recommendations for possible changes, and it has done so on several occasions. The second Michel Commission, for instance, studied in 1968–70 the possible duplication of services caused by having two stations (SWF and SDR) serving the same geographical area and made recommendations as to possible solutions to the problem. But it was up to the stations and to their respective state legislatures to decide whether to act upon any of the recommendations, and they did not. (The stations did agree to coordinate more closely, however, and to jointly operate a morning service on radio.) The federal government is not even involved in license-fee collection, so it cannot withhold or threaten to withhold license-fee money, as can (and as have) so many other national governments.

Certainly politicians at the federal level are interested in broadcasting, and every year they make plenty of comments about it, in Parliament, in press conferences, in interviews, and so on. Chancellor Konrad Adenauer, as we have seen, took a very keen interest in creating a second TV service. Chancellor Helmut Schmidt made numerous public statements about television, often criticizing it for its allegedly negative influence on young people, on the more traditional cultural activities (e.g., book reading), and on family life; he even proposed that there be a television-free day each week, but he had no power to create one.[27] The present chancellor, Helmut Kohl, reflects his CDU background in pressing for the development of alternative sources of television (cable and satellites) and would like to see them in the hands of private industry, but it is not up to the federal government to decide whether they should be authorized. That is the responsibility of the states.

STATE GOVERNMENT Nowhere else in the world do states possess the power (in theory) to regulate broadcasting that they enjoy in West Germany. The state legislatures pass and amend the laws establishing their respective broadcast stations, as well as the newer laws regulating cable. They have the power to amend those laws or even abolish them altogether and start over with a new system. They also enjoy a measure of financial power, since it is up to them, acting collectively, to decide when and by how much to increase license fees. Aside from the matter of fees, however, that power generally goes unused. For reasons already mentioned, legislatures have been reluctant to modify the membership structures of the broadcast councils, although the structure of Radio Bremen's administrative council was modified in the early 1970s to permit the addition of two broadcast staff as council members with full voting rights—part of the controversy over editorial codetermination— and Bremen also passed a new broadcast law in 1979 that enlarged the broadcast council from twenty-five to thirty-six members (since increased to thirty-seven to allow for representation of the Green [proenvironment, somewhat leftist] party).[28] In general, state legislators seem satisfied with the broadcast laws, which go into considerable detail on matters of administration and supervision, but which confine themselves to general, if lofty, statements on program policy matters. Laws passed to cover the newer private stations closely resemble the laws for public stations, although, as noted earlier, the councils for such stations (and for cable) are likely to include some of the newer public-interest groups, such as guest workers. Individual legislators often speak out on broadcasting, but seldom do they call for changes in the law itself.

The biggest problem facing the states is coordination of overall policy. When Adenauer made his bid to create a second national service, the prime ministers of the states met and developed a counterproposal. But political lines were not so firmly drawn then as they are now, which made it very difficult for the states to reach an agreement on an overall policy regarding cable and satellite TV services. They finally did so early in 1987, in part because they feared that the federal government, possibly supported by some degree of viewer agitation for the new services, would find a way to circumvent the law and sanction the establishment of such services itself.

LOCAL GOVERNMENT   The West German system makes no provision for local government involvement in broadcast policy making. A few local governments are watching the development of cable television experiments in their communities (West Berlin, Munich, Ludwigshafen/ Mannheim, Dortmund), but it is not clear at this time whether they will have any direct influence on policy making. Local private radio stations also have begun to appear in the late 1980s, but they too are subject to the jurisdiction of the state governments, as are the present private regional stations in Kiel, Munich, Ludwigshafen, and Hannover.

NONGOVERNMENTAL The broadcast councils are a form of institutionalized representation in station decision making, but there are many societal groups that are without representation (e.g., guest workers) and others that believe the organizations that might in theory represent them do not do so in practice (e.g., women's organizations, which tend to be represented on the councils by the more traditional, less militant Deutsche Frauenbund). There also are political parties (e.g., the Green party, identified with ecology, a nuclear-weapon-free world, etc.) and splinter groups within political parties (e.g., the Young Socialists) that do not believe their views and interests are reflected in the councils. One call for reform of council structures advocated that "a group's chances for gaining access to the broadcasting council should be inversely proportional to its chances for gaining access to public communication."[29] Only Bremen and Hamburg have followed the spirit of that recommendation, the former by making provision in its 1979 broadcast law for the appointment of five representatives from *schwer organisierbare* (difficult to organize) groups, the latter by opening nine council seats to applications from any group in its 1980 broadcast law.

Some groups have developed media interest sections and have made public statements of their views on broadcast policy. Often, those statements have appeared only in the group's own media outlets (magazines and newsletters), but occasionally the groups have commissioned studies that have been reported by some of the more "mass" media. One group particularly effective in raising issues involving ethics, freedom of speech, and so on is the Evangelical (Lutheran) Church, which operates its own press service and through it publishes a periodical, *Kirche und Rundfunk* (Church and Broadcasting). Its leaders often have spoken out on matters of broadcast policy and often have received media coverage of those statements. As in so many other countries, the newspapers in West Germany take a certain amount of delight in calling the public's attention to problems in the world of broadcasting.

Most groups have a relatively narrow focus for their broadcast-related activities, but Aktion Funk und Fernsehen (Radio-TV Action Group) takes on a much broader range of issues, particularly morality in television programming and the defense of conservative causes. In those respects, it is similar to Mary Whitehouse's VALA in Great Britain and to Accuracy in Media in the United States, although not as well organized or with as many members. However, West German television tends to be less sex and violence oriented than does British TV, so there is less to protest. Advertising that depicts women in highly traditional, subservient roles has been a frequent object of protest since the early 1970s, but so far the groups opposing it have not been able to muster enough support for their cause to achieve more than minimal change.

Programming

PHILOSOPHIES The post–World War II history of West German broadcasting is characterized by an unusually strong devotion to the principle of fairness. That is not to say that there is freedom of access to the airwaves for any person or group wishing to express opinions or beliefs; rather, fairness in the West German system involves protecting individuals and groups from harm. Given the nation's experience during the Nazi period, it is hardly surprising that there should be a desire to protect individuals and groups from attack or exclusion. East state broadcast law contains provisions guaranteeing this: Article 2.4.i of the law governing SDR of Stuttgart states that "no broadcast shall be permitted that might cause prejudice or discrimination against individuals or groups because of race, religion or color." Article 2.4.h, after guaranteeing the right of "democratically minded commentators and speakers" to criticize wrongs, goes on to state that those criticized also have the right to defend themselves. The federal constitution (Basic Law) goes even further; Article 5 states that "anyone has the right to freely express his opinion through the spoken word, in writing or through pictures. . . . There will be no censorship."

Limitations on broadcast frequencies, airtime, and money mean that not every voice will be heard, or at least not as often as some individuals and groups would like, but broadcasters do have an obligation to promote diversity of opinion. As a result, informational programs, and discussions in particular, often are very free-wheeling affairs in which one may see and hear a wide range of views on topics of the day. It isn't terribly difficult for an individual or group with an extreme point of view to receive airtime for its expression, although it may be broadcast over one of the less popular radio services and at an "off" time of day. However, there is no institutionalized access along the lines of the Dutch system, nor is there anything quite like the U.S. Fairness Doctrine. Political parties are another matter: They usually are entitled to airtime in proportion to their strength in the state and federal parliaments (although the two major parties receive equal amounts), and parties that are campaigning in all of the states, even if they are unrepresented in the state and/or federal parliaments, also may receive airtime. The time itself is used by the parties as they see fit, usually in brief blocks (two to three minutes), and always in prime time and at the same time on the first and second public TV channels. Radio has roughly similar arrangements.

Certainly West German broadcasting does not suffer from the apolitical blandness of German radio during the Weimar Republic. News broadcasts are as comprehensive and objective as possible, but political features, commentaries, and discussions abound, and some of them can be quite partisan: The ZDF's *Magazin,* hosted by Gerhard Lowenthal, is widely recognized as expressing the viewpoint of the more conservative wing of the CDU. That may rankle viewers who oppose those views, but it is perfectly legal so long as there is no evidence that ZDF allows *only* that point of view on its programs.

The philosophy underlying cultural programs is harder to discern. The concept of fairness to individuals and groups has some influence on it, but much more is involved. For example, despite the regional structure of the first and third television services, there is little evidence that the system is employed to promote regional cultures. Such cultures do exist; they are more prominent in some parts of the country than in others and exhibit varying degrees of difference, so one might imagine that it would be part of television's (and radio's) cultural mission to display them. Yet there is no legal requirement to do so, and the provision that all state stations contribute at least something to the collective service (Deutsches Fernsehen) of the first program does not involve a necessary guarantee that any part of what a station contributes be unique to its region, and usually it is not.

There is the expectation in West German television that the more violent and explicitly sexual programs be kept off the air until around 9:00 P.M. in deference to families with children. Because there are so few TV services available nationwide, that sort of expectation is easy to fulfill. But another expectation — that broadcasting serve as vehicle for the display of a wide range of German culture — is harder to fulfill, simply because it costs more money to produce one's own programs than to purchase them, especially when those production costs cannot be offset by large-scale sales to other countries. The German-speaking market *is* a limited one.

The newer private stations follow a roughly similar overall philosophy but on the whole provide a more specialized program service. The stations RTL Plus and SAT1 carry a large share of light entertainment, half or more of which comes from abroad (imports account for about 5 percent of the total on public television), and the private radio stations spend almost three-fourths of their program time on light music (pop and rock), about half of it German.[30] Clearly their predominant concern is to attract audiences that will be attractive to advertisers, although a number of their programs do deal with problems and concerns of individuals and groups, locally, regionally, and nationally.

RADIO   West German radio has undergone much the same sort of transition as has radio elsewhere in Europe and North America. The rise of TV in the late 1950s diverted more and more audience and financial support from radio and led to the decline and in some cases disappearance of such mass entertainment fare as quiz shows and popular serial dramas that had dominated radio schedules from the late 1940s to the late 1950s. That did not mean that all such shows were dropped, however. Radio plays continue to be presented by all West German public stations, and some offer them once a week. All public stations also provide broadcasts for schools, political talks, and discussions. There are serialized readings of novels, gymnastics exercises, religious thoughts for the day, roundups of world press opinion, and of course news, weather, traffic, and sports reports.

But music certainly predominates. Nearly 60 percent of broadcast time is devoted to it. Light classical and classical music make up almost half of that total on most public stations (Deutschlandfunk [DLF] and one of the Sudwestfunk services of Baden-Baden have a heavier load of popular music), and there are many musical request programs. German music and/or performers (most of the public stations have one or more orchestras, small or large, popular, classical, or folk) make up a fair share of the total for most music programs, but there also are many selections from other parts of Europe and from North America, and occasional presentations of Latin American music. Music of some of the guest-worker groups (Turkish, Italian, Greek, Portuguese, Arabic) receives little airtime on the more popular public radio services, but a bit more on the specialized ones. Two late-night/early-morning music services, one middle-of-the-road and the other classical, are offered through the ARD network, and the state stations take turns producing them.

All of the public radio stations except DLF broadcast two separate services, and seven of them operate three or more (NDR added a fifth service in 1984, and BR, SWF, Radio Bremen, and SR operate fourth services). The first and second services of each station usually bear a strong resemblance to one another and may include periods of simulcasting, especially in early morning hours. There also is a limited amount of program sharing between stations. The third service usually specializes in material for smaller segments of the audience; experimental music and radio plays, talks on unusual subjects, and so on. Most stations offer an early-evening program block for guest workers, with forty minutes to an hour in Turkish, Italian, Greek, Serbo-Croatian, and/or other languages spoken by sizable numbers of guest workers in the station's coverage area.

The private radio stations display some interesting differences among themselves. Radio 4, the service for Rhineland-Palatinate, actually includes four different (separately owned) operations, the two smallest of which have 1½ hours a day, the largest just over 17. Disc-jockey-hosted pop music shows take most of the airtime on all four operations, but the smallest ones, Linksrheinische Rundfunkunion (LR) and Radio 85, often devote from a fourth to a third of their airtime in a given hour to interviews with people from the region, for example, the head of a woman's institute talking about a new leadership program for women. On the other hand, Radio Schleswig-Holstein in Kiel broadcasts little but popular music, with very brief newscasts and few interviews with the public.[31]

Radio remains a popular medium, at least in terms of the amount of time people claim to spend listening to it. Figures presented by Berg and Kiefer indicate in increase in listening time for the average West German over a sixteen-year period: 1964: 1 hour, 29 minutes; 1970: 1 hour, 13 minutes; 1974: 1 hour, 53 minutes; 1980: 2 hours, 15 minutes. And figures for 1987 were even higher: 2 hours, 33 minutes, which for the first time in 21 years exceeded the figure for TV (2 hours, 19 minutes). Furthermore, listening appears to be distributed evenly over age groups and by sex.[32] The fact that most cars sold in West Germany come equipped with radios is a partial explanation for radio's popularity, as is the twenty-four-hour-a-day schedule that many stations provide, but the high technical quality of the service may help, too: Because Germany was still something of an outcast when the European nations met in Copenhagen in 1948 to reallocate radio frequencies, it received very few on AM. The FM broadcasting system, however, was not at issue in those deliberations, both because its signals do not carry as far and are not affected by time of day, and because few other European nations had much interest in utilizing it at that time. So West Germany moved quickly to develop and manufacture the necessary transmitters, receivers, and so on, and as a result soon had a heavily FM-based transmission system, with all of its advantages for static-free, high-fidelity reception.

In contrast with the Dutch and British experiences, West German radio largely has been unaffected by pirate radio stations. Land-based pirates have come along every now and then, usually in connection with Green party activities, for example, a 1979 demonstration against the construction of a nuclear power plant at Gorleben, when Radio Regenbogen (Rainbow) broadcast the demonstration. In most cases, the diligent West German authorities usually have tracked them down and put them off the air in short order.[33] Radio Luxembourg's German service, as well as the various American Forces Network (AFN) stations scattered throughout the country, are attractive to younger listeners, and the free and easy style of the disk jockeys on both has influenced some of their West German counterparts, but most of West German public radio remains quite formal, correct, and dignified. Even the disk jockeys on the private stations, while a bit less formal than their public counterparts, sound quite formal when compared with AFN or Luxembourg. Slang rarely is used, and broadcasts in regional dialects (*Mundart*) are rare, except over such subregional stations as Kurpfalz Radio, where brief remarks by dialect speakers on such subjects as the coming of fall will be used to provide a bit of local color. There is a rich tradition of radio plays in dialect running from the 1920s through the 1960s, but most of that has vanished by now.[34]

The greatest change occurring in West German public (and soon, perhaps, private) radio is in its localization. The major broadcast centers always have had branch studios within their coverage areas, but those were limited to supplying material (usually interviews) that would be broadcast throughout the region. They certainly did not function as local stations. However, beginning in 1975, the centers gave some of those studio operations small blocks of airtime, usually twenty to thirty minutes early in the day, and perhaps also in the afternoon, and the use of transmitters serving their particular areas. Some of those operations have become quite large: Kurpfalz Radio in Heidelberg (moving to Mannheim by 1988) now offers three program blocks per day, for a total of 3½ hours. Much of the material is news and interviews, especially with local figures and occasionally in dialect, but there may be music by listener request as well, and vignettes on the history of towns and villages. Station staff sometimes find that local government officials are not very radio-conscious, in the sense that those officials rarely if ever were interviewed by the state stations and sometimes do not know quite how to handle requests for information from the local stations. Still, more and more cities, for example Munich, with its *Citywelle* (city [radio] wave), are developing such services.[35] Money to support them comes from the overall license fee, which probably is not fair to the many license-fee payers who cannot receive such miniservices, but they cost very little and seem to be very popular with listeners in those communities that have them. While no one is predicting anything as extensive as the development of local radio in Great Britain, it is quite likely that this movement will grow in years to come, bringing most of the larger cities their own radio services for at least a few hours each day.

TELEVISION   West German public television follows a typical West European weekday schedule, in that the earlier morning hours (6:00 to 10:00 A.M.) either are devoid of programs or contain educational material, some of which is for adult education (the *Telekolleg* — mainly foreign languages, history, and various social sciences), some for primary and secondary schools (largely those same subjects, but with a differing lineup from one state to another — not all states have educational TV). However, there have been discussions of a morning news program along the lines of those on the U.S. networks, the BBC and IBA, and the French TV morning show. Also, starting in 1985, there has been a block of repeat programs from the evening offering of the previous day or week. The ZDF and the state stations, working through ARD, cooperate to provide this service, which is intended for shift workers and others who did not have the opportunity to see the shows the first time around. The block lasts from 10:00 A.M. until just after 1:00 P.M. It is not available on the third program service, which limits itself to occasional educational programs until 5:00 P.M.

Early afternoon hours generally are without programming, as well. Both ARD and ZDF offer a selection of videotext materials from 1:15 until 1:30, more as an advertisement for this service than anything else, and repeat it at 3:40 P.M. Each provides a brief preview of the afternoon and evening schedule, but programming for the general public does not begin until around 4:00 P.M. Thereafter, the state stations and ZDF provide a mixture of feature films, imported TV shows (e.g., *Simon and Simon*), children's cartoons, and brief newscasts, all scheduled so as not to duplicate one another. The third service offers educational material, *Sesame Street,* and shows for particular audiences, such as teenagers, or on unusual topics (an October 1984 program dealt with the role of garlic in promoting one's health).

Prior to the early 1970s, it was assumed that prime time began just before 8:00 P.M. and ran until 11:00, although the last program of the evening generally ended a little before or after 12:00. But in 1973, ZDF shifted its major newscast, *heute* (today), to 7:00 P.M., even though that meant that it would be surrounded by advertising (all of which occurs in the 5:30 to 7:30 P.M. block). Critics were afraid that, since the first channel offered entertainment at that time, viewers would attempt to avoid watching the news, which they could not manage as easily when both first and second channels broadcast their major evening news at the same hour. To some extent, that has happened, but there also are viewers who now watch both newscasts, so the net loss has been fairly small.

The prime-time schedules of all three channels represent a considerable mixture of programs, including feature films (usually no more than one per evening for all three channels; sometimes none at all); sports (Wednesday night is soccer night in Germany); *krimis* (crime shows); situation comedies; quiz shows (one of the great German national pastimes — even the TV guides promote the quality and number of their crossword puzzles); TV drama, much of it historical and classical and often in miniseries form; nature documentaries (usually of very high quality, with costs to match); round-table discussions of political, social, and cultural issues; symphony concerts and operas.

West German public television probably provides the greatest amount of program variety of any three-channel national system anywhere in the world and outdoes many systems with four, five, or more channels. Although the first channel schedule is the collective effort of the state stations, production quality is almost uniformly high and gives nothing away to the national ZDF. Third-service productions sometimes are more spartan but generally are well produced and offer opportunities for devotees of chess, gardening, jazz, and other "off the beaten path" subjects (for most TV systems) to indulge their tastes. And though there is no formal quota, imported programs make up a very small percentage of the prime-time schedule — usually about 5 percent — although *Dallas* and *Dynasty* (called *Der Denver Klan* in German) often are top ten shows. They are usually topped or equaled, however, by a sports event, quiz show, *krimi,* and/or one or two of the week's newscasts. They also are regularly topped by *Schwarzwaldklinik* (Black Forest Clinic), sometimes referred to as the German *Dallas* because of its high ratings (shares of audience in the 60 percent range are fairly common). This series, which began in October 1985, is an unabashedly sentimental glorification of hard work, loving care, and paternalism, all portrayed in a beautiful setting and with a lead figure, Professor Brinkman, who is as good at giving advice as he is at setting bones.

One highly unusual show (on the West German or any other TV service) is *Aktenzeichen: XY . . . ungelöst* (Case XY unsolved). On the air since 1967, and hosted throughout by Eduard Zimermann, this hourlong monthly program presents the facts of an unsolved crime, with as much visual depiction (including re-creation of some elements) as can be managed of what is already known, together with interviews of people who can shed some light on the crime. Viewers are urged to call law-enforcement authorities if they think they can add to the sum of information, and both the program and the TV guide entries for it furnish telephone numbers for the purpose. The program is presented with a good deal of drama. Some feel there is too much drama—that it encourages amateurs to transform too easily their own possibly doubtful pieces of information into "hard facts," sometimes to the detriment of innocent individuals. However, viewer information has led to numerous convictions (although one viewer failed to identify the swindler he had invited into his apartment at the very time the program was telling about the criminal activities of the selfsame swindler!), and the show is enormously popular, almost always placing in the top ten for its week.

Weekend schedules feature programming from the early-afternoon hours until after 1:00 A.M. on Saturdays, with the repeat block from 10:00 A.M. to 1:00 P.M. Even the third service is likely to offer something in the early afternoon, such as the Davis Cup (in tennis) elimination rounds. Sunday morning TV begins sometime between 9:00 and 10:00 for the first and second channels; the third service usually does not come on the air until 4:00 P.M. Sports and music are likely to receive heavy play on Sundays, and ZDF telecasts a church service in the morning. The broadcast day ends just before or after midnight. (In fact, surveys have revealed that the vast majority of Germans are in bed before 11:00 and nearly half by 10:00 P.M., which is one reason why ZDF moved the start of its prime-time schedule to 7:00 P.M.)

There are certain types of programs that do not appear very often on West German TV. Situation comedies are few; those that exist often resemble the socially relevant sitcoms of Norman Lear, especially the mid-1970s series *Ein Herz, Eine Seele* (One Heart, One Soul), with its Archie Bunker- (and slightly Adolf Hitler-) like main character, Alfred Tetzlaff. Single-parent families and high-school settings also are quite popular. Most of the state TV stations and ZDF broadcast relatively few programs about the Nazi past [36] until 1979, when a showing of the U.S. series *Holocaust* in West Germany prompted renewed viewer interest in the Nazi era. The series was particularly controversial because the state stations and ZDF turned it down at first, partly on the grounds that it lacked sufficient authenticity, then agreed to show it, but only over the minority third TV service, which promptly got its highest ratings ever: Some episodes scored in the 30 percent range. The past several years have seen several TV programs and series about the subject.[37] Programs about World War II, on the other hand, have had relatively steady popularity over the years, although there are not nearly as many of them as there are on Soviet television.

The national newscasts are comprehensive and feature sound reporting from ZDF and ARD correspondents all around the world, as well as items supplied through the Eurovision feed. However, the longest newscasts on ARD last only fifteen minutes, while ZDF's *heute* is on for thirty minutes. Newscasts tend to be heavier on coverage of German news than of international news. The regional newscasts often are light on visual documentation and heavy on items that smack of press releases. Neither is as lively or informal as are U.S. newscasts, and investigative reporting is a rarity. But documentaries can be very penetrating and often win critical praise, large audiences, and action on dealing with problems.

Most of the third TV services provide an unusual form of educational television. The *Telekolleg,* started in 1966, allows people who dropped out before completing their secondary education to finish the necessary coursework through a combination of television and correspondence. The course offerings are not as comprehensive as those offered through Japan's NHK Correspondence High School but do include physics, chemistry, foreign languages, history, geography, and a few other subject areas.

The private-TV services, as noted earlier, feature a great deal of light entertainment. Cable subscribers can receive both German- and English-language Music Box (music video) services, as well as several channels carrying many old British, U.S., and West German series. Also available only over cable, 3SAT contains a mixture of old and new ZDF, Austrian, and Swiss programs, again largely light entertainment. A few of these—the two Music Boxes, Sky Channel from Great Britain (mostly old U.S. and British entertainment shows)—are available throughout the day, but more are on the air from the middle or late afternoon through midnight, when almost all of them sign off. Pay-cable services of Home Box Office (HBO) or Showtime variety were introduced late in 1986 in one city (Wolfsburg, home of Volkswagen) on an experimental basis, and Hannover began to offer such service in 1987.

The Audience

The German broadcast system's interest in survey research dates back to the mid-1920s, when mail questionnaires, usually distributed by and through magazines for fans of radio, were used to learn more about audience reactions to programming. That interest continued during the 1930s, although surveys became less and less frequent as World War II approached, and the practice pretty well ceased during the war. During the occupation period, many surveys were conducted, and starting in the early 1950s West German broadcasters and academics became more involved in the practice than ever. Each state station conducted or commissioned others to conduct surveys, usually by mail or in person at first, but more and more by telephone as well, as telephones became more common.

Quite early on, however, the stations recognized the wisdom of working through a national organization in order to obtain listener and viewer reactions from all around West Germany. It was not all that necessary to have the data for advertising purposes, since commercial time was limited (ads did not appear on TV until 1956) and since advertising had no direct connection with individual programs, anyway. But programmers did want some indication of how many of what kinds of people watched and listened to which shows, and how much they appeared to like them. Therefore, both demographic and program quality data were gathered, the latter by asking people to rate the shows they watched and listened to on a ten-point scale.

The organization that conducted the national surveys was selected through a process of competitive bids, and the initial contract went to Infratest of Munich, in 1961. When ZDF came along in 1963, it joined in with the state stations on the arrangement. Infratest held the contract until 1974, when it lost out to *teleskopie,* which still holds it as of early 1988. Teleskopie conducts specialized surveys of TV viewing, but also uses meters (TeleMetron) attached to sets, much in the manner of A. S. Nielsen's Audimeter, for continuous measurement of viewing in some 1,400 randomly selected household (4,200 individuals) throughout Germany. There is one refinement, however: Each member of the household can register her or his viewing by pressing a designated button on the measuring device, thus allowing for far more precise measurement of who is watching TV at any given moment (provided that viewers remember to press their buttons!). In that respect, the German system, which has been around since the late 1970s, resembles the "People Meters" used by Nielsen and others in the United States from around the mid-1980s.

Survey research methods of all standard types are used: diaries, in-person interviews, telephone surveys, mail questionnaires, and mechanical devices. In addition to the continuous data gathered on TV viewing by *teleskopie,* there are many individual projects conducted by ZDF (which has a sizable research department), the state stations (which rarely have research departments, but which employ or contract individuals for such work), various institutes (e.g., the Institute for Research on Children, in Munich), and certain of the universities (e.g., the Hans

Bredow Institute at the University of Hamburg); there also are several independent organizations that conduct advertising research, such as the Broadcast Advertising Association.[38]

According to data gathered through various means, West Germans are interested but not addicted radio listeners and TV viewers. Their average viewing and listening times of roughly two and a half hours a day for each medium hardly are excessive. Radio stations carry large amounts of popular music coupled with brief news, weather, and traffic reports command the largest amount of listening time. Variety and quiz shows, detective drama, family drama such as *Schwarzwaldklinik,* and major sports events head the popularity list on TV, often attracting 40–50 percent of the audience. Newscasts are not far behind; one or two usually manage to attract 30 percent or more of the audience each week. Adaptations of novels and plays, particularly by famous writers (Theodor Fontane, Jack London), also often score in the high 20, low 30 percent range. But operas, symphony concerts, ballet, and experimental drama usually attract no more than 5 percent of the possible audience and often enough pull 2 to 3 percent, even though most of them are presented in prime time and over the two major services and are lavishly produced. Political discussions, interviews, and call-in shows, however, do quite well—usually between 12 and 25 percent. *Aktenzeichen: XY . . . ungelöst* generally draws 30–40 percent of the audience. Most programming on the third service is seen by less than 10 percent of the potential audience, but the various episodes of *Holocaust* were seen by 30–40 percent of it. Children's shows, which occupy much of the late afternoon period, are watched by 5–15 percent, with adults often far outnumbering children, especially when a feature film for children is on.

Several of the university and private institutes and research organizations have conducted research on the influence of television on its audiences. In relative terms, there is as much research on the influence of TV on children in West Germany as there is in the United States, and just as much contradiction in its results, some studies showing that certain kinds of TV viewing seem to encourage criminal behavior, lead to poor performance in school, and so on, while other studies show that there are very few measurable effects.[39] Studies of bias in television news have become quite numerous in recent years, and also have been contradictory, although results in general show relatively little measurable bias for either ARD or ZDF.[40]

Research appears to be regarded as a necessary evil by many broadcast staff members, especially producers and program planners. A strong audience appreciation (ten-point scale) figure for a show with a small percentage of viewers can help to save it from cancellation, and occasionally the *teleskopie* data will be used to help rearrange the program schedule, but there is little evidence that survey or laboratory research will have much influence on the content of specific programs or will lead to their cancellation, if that research shows possibly harmful effects on viewers.

Aside from audience research, there are other feedback mechanisms that allow for assessment of audience likes and dislikes. Although West German broadcasters do not specifically encourage letter writing and telephone calls (aside from musical requests, quiz show entries, and information on upcoming events), West German listeners and viewers write tens of thousands of letter every year and call stations by the hundreds every day with reactions to everything from technical problems to "offensive" programs. Also, special-interest groups (morality in media, women's rights, political factions) have sought to influence programming by developing protest campaigns of various sorts, but broadcasters usually disregard their efforts on the ground that they represent only a tiny fraction of the total audience.

West German TV schedules at times include programs designed to educate the audience as to what goes on in television: how programs are made, what sorts of problems arise, and so on. The aim appears to be to make the viewers become more discerning consumers of television. Some programs, for example, ZDF's long-running *Glashaus* (Glass House), permit a studio audience to criticize various aspects of television programming.

Problem Areas

Most aspects of West German broadcast programming arouse little controversy. There is some expression of concern over the possible harmful influences of television on young viewers, although they are not exposed to anything like the quantity of violent or sexually explicit material that reaches the eyes and ears of their U.S. counterparts. Women's groups have protested the sexist portrayal of women on television, especially in advertising. Avid sports fans feel deprived because public TV devotes only about 5 percent of its total schedule to sports. Popular music fans would like to have far more time given over on TV to their music and far less to classical music; classical music fans do not seem to feel quite so strongly the other way, perhaps because they are aware that, by the general standards of television around the world, they fare quite well.[41] The relatively small amounts of locally and regionally oriented material on radio and TV do not seem to bother that many people, perhaps because they are not in the habit of thinking of broadcasting as an important source of such material.

But the subject of politics and television amounts to a national preoccupation, at least on the part of politicians, the media, media scholars, and various public-interest groups. Few of them seem satisfied with the present state of affairs, and most of them claim that the problems have been increasing almost from the start of the Federal Republic. Some of the specific instances that they cite have been mentioned already: Adenauer's attempts to set up a national TV service; the change in the manner of selecting members for the broadcast councils of NDR and WDR; the von Paczensky and *Bauern, Bonsen und Bomben* incidents at NDR; the CSU attempt to set up commercial TV and to "pack" the broadcast council at Bayerischer Rundfunk; the breaking apart of the three-state agreement that governs NDR. There are many more; the following are a brief but reasonably representative sample:

1. The WDR license-fee case: When it considered the proposed license-fee increase in 1973, the state Parliament of North Rhine–Westphalia engaged in a sharp debate over it, and political lines were firmly drawn. The fee increase finally passed, but a number of the more conservative members of the Parliament pressed for greater control over the liberal WDR, particularly financial control. In 1974, the Parliament passed an amendment to the broadcast law that gave the state *Rechnungshof* (audit bureau) review power over WDR's annual expenditures, thus treating the station as though it were a state agency.[42]

2. The 1973 election of NDR's manager: The NDR broadcast law specifies the date for the election of the station's manager and deputy manager (the two must be chosen at the same time). In late 1973, the date came and went without such an election because the SPD and CDU could not agree on a suitable candidate, and the NDR administrative council, which was politically appointed, reflected that stalemate. Since the broadcast law makes no provision for an interim manager, a solution had to be improvised, and during that period (which lasted fifteen weeks), the three states directly involved with NDR agreed upon a statement in which they claimed the right to "take further supervisory measures if an election has not been held by 31 December 1973, *and the functioning of the station makes this seem imperative*" (italics mine). Since the station continued to function normally, there was no state intervention; what form it might have taken is unknown, but the case is a graphic illustration of just how powerful political influence could become.[43]

3. The 1977 "Save freedom of broadcasting" movement in WDR: The television news staff of WDR long had had a reputation for (alleged) left-wing sympathies. In 1977, the television controller, Werner Hofer, retired; he was replaced by a CDU member, Theo Loch, and very soon complaints began to arise within the editorial staff that Loch was seeking to interfere with their work. Within a few weeks, trade unionists, some politicians (generally associated with the left), and a mixture of intellectuals had organized a citizen's initiative group called "Save freedom of broadcasting in the WDR" to prepare for the passage of protective legislation if the situation did not improve. There were some informal concessions by Loch, the group did not have all that much staying power, and the controversy continued to simmer, but at a sufficiently low level that no legal action was taken.[44]

4. The mid-1980s cable access cases: As each state licenses broadcasting, so also it licenses cable and even controls which specific cable services a cable authority may carry. As cable experiments were set up in various states, and as smaller cities and towns began to acquire "passive" cable, which would allow them to bring in outside services from satellites, politics once again played a role. The Bavarian government, dominated by the Christian Socialist Union (conservative), forbade the reception of the ARD satellite service, Eins Plus, on the grounds that it was "too liberal." The state of Hesse, dominated by the SPD (liberal), forbade reception of SAT1 on the grounds that it was "too commercial," by which the government seemed to mean "too mindless, too anti–social activism." Both states had dropped those restrictions by 1987, when the states concluded their agreement on the licensing of the new media, but their initial actions were symptomatic of a deep philosophical division between the CDU/CSU and the SPD, one seeing every good economic reason for introducing more broadcast services, the other being wary of such a move on the grounds that additional services could harm society, perhaps by making it more dependent on the products of foreign cultures, perhaps by making people too self-satisfied or self-indulgent.

How much effect the increased politicization of broadcasting has had on actual broadcast content is difficult to tell. There are frequent accusations that a given station treats politician or political party X favorably or unfavorably, but those accusations themselves often come from partisan quarters, as they generally did when the ARD broadcast a tape of Prime Minister Kohl's 1986 New Year's Day address to the nation on New Year's Day, 1987; the mix up appeared to be an honest mistake, but a number of CDU officials and journalists favorable to the party saw it as an act of political sabotage. There does seem to be general agreement that ZDF is more favorable toward the CDU than toward the SPD. Since ZDF is a single national service, and since the prime-time schedule of the state stations represents all of them, there is a more natural tendency toward diversity in political viewpoint on the latter. There also seems to be general agreement that there has been a greater tendency for TV commentators to be more cautious over the past fifteen to twenty years than they were earlier, although that could be the result of a keener recognition of TV's power. Where entertainment is concerned, some of the state stations certainly have not hesitated to opt out of the prime-time schedule when they felt that a program contained morally offensive material. The fact that that has occurred most often in states where the CDU was in power may or may not indicate that the decision was politically motivated.

Foreign Influences on Programming

Although West German TV uses relatively little imported material during prime-time hours, aside from feature films, it uses quite a bit in the late-afternoon to early-evening block, largely U.S. and British series. Detective shows (*Hart to Hart*), children's programs (*Sesame Street*) and adventure series suitable for family viewing (including such ancient fare as *Lassie*) are the leading genres. Most of them are dubbed, rather than subtitled, as surveys have revealed that West Germans are not particularly fond of subtitles. Some programs have been based on foreign models, as was *One Heart, One Soul* (noted earlier) and *Traumschiff* or *Dream Ship,* based on the U.S. series *Love Boat.* Many items on the nightly newscasts will come from Eurovision's news exchange, and sports events, too, often originate elsewhere and come to German viewers through Eurovision.

It is a rare weekly top ten that includes more than one or two imported shows, however. Germans show a strong preference for their own material. The week of 1–7 February 1988 is typical:[45]

1. *Tatort* (adventure)
2. *Schwarzwaldklinik* (family drama)
3. *Donnerlippchen* (comedy)
4. *Tagesschau* (news)
5. *Derrick* (adventure)
6. *Superlachparade* (comedy-variety)
7. *Tagesschau* (news)

8. *Der Grosse Preis* (quiz)
9. *Ein Naheliegender Mord* (adventure)
10. *Die Wicherts von Nebenan* (comedy)

Radio plays a large number of U.S. and British pop music selections, U.S. jazz, and a great deal of classical music from other European nations.

It is more difficult to judge whether foreign radio and TV have had much effect on the nature of West German programs. Radio disk jockeys often sound a bit livelier and more informal now than they did twenty years ago, which some have attributed to the influence of American Forces Network stations. Certain West German detective and police shows bear some resemblance to their British and U.S. counterparts (although without such heavy reliance on auto chases as the U.S. shows often display), and the numerous quiz shows feature much the same sort of bubbly, extroverted male host and attractive female assistant as do quiz shows in other parts of Western Europe and North America; but at least the formats are not purchased from the United States, as is the case in Dutch TV, and on most of them the intellectual level of the questions seems considerably higher than on U.S. TV. Newscasters have not yet begun to exhibit the informal, almost conversational approach that characterizes their U.S. colleagues; in fact, the tone is even more formal and sober than it is on British television.

Even the plots of the more popular prime-time West German TV dramas seem to exhibit particularly German characteristics, although the themes may be familiar enough: divorced or divorcing parents having problems with each other and/or with their children, people frustrated in their ambitions to rise higher in society or at work, family members not understanding one another. But the characters themselves often appear to be far less exaggerated than they are in U.S. TV series, and the frequent resort to hard work and more effort as a solution to problems may be especially Germanic. The following is an example of a fairly typical West German TV drama: "The journalist Manfred Krupka has just about managed to clear up the puzzling events that have given him so many headaches. And Marianne Hohmann is happy to finally have found in the young man someone who is willing to help in finding her vanished father. Their search leads them to Genoa, where terror awaits them." (*Babeck*, 4 November 1986, ZDF)[46]

Relations with Other Media

Newspapers and magazines in West Germany furnish considerable coverage of broadcasting. All major papers, and many smaller ones, have broadcast critics who write daily columns. Controversies within stations, which are frequent and which often have, or are alleged to have, political origins, sometimes receive front-page treatment. Condensed broadcast schedules appear in most West German newspapers, and there are four major and very competitive TV guides, all published by private concerns; they carry far more detail on programs than do the papers but rarely provide critical commentary on programs, station politics, or any other broadcast-related issues. Instead, their features deal with the lives of stars, how certain programs were made, and so on — all "safe" and entertaining topics.

Newspapers long had an abiding fear of broadcasting, and TV in particular, as a source of competition for advertising revenue. Even though broadcast advertising on the public services was restricted to national products and services only, the newspapers feared that this might change, largely for two reasons: Public radio and TV were quite attractive to advertisers, and the stations were in frequent financial difficulty thanks to the high costs of their operation. Fears of competition for advertising revenue were strong enough just after the creation of ZDF that they became the subject of investigation for a federal commission, the first Michel Commission, which reported in 1967. The Michel Commission found those fears to be exaggerated, and strongly recommended against one of the solutions the press had proposed: to be allowed to invest financially in broadcasting.

With the coming of private radio in 1985, the press finally had its opportunity, and most private radio stations licensed thus far feature very heavy investment by the press. The TV services RTL Plus and SAT1 are almost 100 percent press investments. Whether this has meant that those services are controlled editorially by the press is another question. Initially, some of the programs on SAT1 reflected those press interests; for instance, a program on fashions was backed by Burda, West Germany's largest fashion-magazine publisher. Most of those "publisher's programs" had vanished from SAT1 by mid-1986 because they failed to draw and hold viewers, but some publishers would like to see them reappear, if not on SAT1, then on another satellite service.

A major West German publisher, Bertelsmann Verlag, got involved in broadcasting even earlier. In 1983 it invested in the development of a special German-language TV service transmitted from Luxembourg into West Germany on a UHF transmitter. (About 60 percent of all West

German TV sets can receive UHF.) Only 10 percent or so of the population were within receiving range of RTL Plus, but Bertelsmann's long-range plans were to make it into a DBS service or get it onto cable through DBS, which began to occur in 1985. Most of its programming consists of cheaply produced quiz shows and reruns of old German and foreign TV entertainment, and it still is losing millions of marks a year. It may do better if and when cable expands, but it is also attempting to be licensed as an over-the-air TV station in Bavaria. The SAT1 service was able to procure a UHF frequency in West Berlin in early 1987, so there is a precedent.

Most of the new private TV services show little inclination to produce daily newscasts of any real magnitude; As of mid-1987 the longest newscast on any of them was less than ten minutes, nor were there more than two of them per day. Still, they gave those households that could receive them a real alternative in the form of briefer items and a breezier style.

The West German film industry has achieved a reputation for provocative, well-produced films in recent years, thanks to the efforts of Wim Wenders, Rainer Fassbinder, and Werner Herzog. Those films represent a small percentage of the total output, and in any case are not the sort of fare one expects to see on television. Their themes and styles generally have appeal for select audiences. However, Fassbinder's *Berlin Alexanderplatz* is an outstanding example of a film made for television but clearly just as viable for cinema, which is where it was shown in the United States.

There is not a great deal of TV free-lance work available on a scale and with a continuity that would be appealing to most film producers, and there is not a lot of time given over to feature films on public television. Nevertheless, ARD and ZDF have signed five-year agreements with the Filmforderunganstalt (FFA) in 1974, 1979, and 1984. In the 1979 agreement, they pledged DM 56.5 million for coproductions over the next five years, plus DM 17.5 million for FFA's own projects.[47] The 1984 agreement called for subsidization of approximately DM 42 million per year. Those agreements are voluntary, but the film industry long has been protected under the terms of the Cinema Promotion Act where cinema owners are concerned: A levy on ticket sales brings in about DM 30 million a year. In the mid-1980s, the industry began to lobby to have the act applied to the new private television ventures and to distributors of videocassettes.

One respect in which the film and television industries do not appear to agree is on the place of film critic's shows in the television schedule. Up until the early 1980s, there were several film-related shows on ARD and ZDF, such as ARD's *Kennen Sie Kino* (a quiz show about movies) and ZDF's *Neues von Film* (What's New in Movies). Most of those shows were dropped, and in late 1987 ARD canceled *Treffpunkt Kino* (Rendezvous at the Movies) and ZDF announced plans to shorten and change the viewing day of *ZDF Kinohit-Parade*. As the West German movie industry has seen a considerable decline in production of theatrical films, it became concerned that the chief force in that decline — television — also was cutting back on a type of program that probably attracted a fair share of the movie audience. As Klaus Dahm, head of publicity for Warner Brothers in West Germany, put it, "If the general public is to be kept informed about theatrical films it is one of the networks' *duties* [italics mine] to help in doing that."[48]

The two industries are linked in another interesting way: The Radio and Television Union and the German Union of Film Workers merged in 1968. One issue taken up by the combined union, now called the Radio-Television-Film Worker's Union, is better social security for free-lance workers in the broadcast and film media.

International Cooperation

The larger West German state stations and ZDF have been able to enter into coproduction agreements with almost every other television service in West Europe, although most often with British, French, and Italian television; they are more apt to have the money necessary to carry out the large-scale projects that typify coproduction. There also have been several smaller-scale coproductions with the Swiss and Austrian systems, where the very similar cultural heritages and the presence of a common language make such cooperation desirable, natural, and fairly easy.

West German TV services are frequent donors, as well as recipients, in Eurovision's news exchange. The state stations (working through ARD) and ZDF both have correspondents in many foreign countries, and the news budgets are large enough to afford satellite reports from them. As West Germany is a major political and economic force in West Europe, domestic coverage of events often is in demand by other European TV systems. In 1986, West German stations sent nearly six hundred items to the exchange (about one hundred more than Great Britain).[49] West German television is also heavily involved in the exchange of sports news through Eurovision.

The ARD and the ZDF services cooperate with the federal government through an agency called TRANSTEL, a nonprofit corporation founded in 1965 to place West German TV programs with foreign systems. Those systems pay fees according to the economic strength of the nation, so Third World countries get TRANSTEL-distributed programs for next to nothing. Roughly a hundred nations receive programs, which range from documentaries about Beethoven to a series of five-minute tips on soccer playing.

The New Media

Because apartment houses are quite common in West German cities, master-antenna television systems have a long history and are quite numerous there. They are used only to improve reception of existing channels, for the most part, although this sometimes includes Austrian, Swiss, French, Belgian, Dutch, and Danish TV services if their border-zone stations are close at hand. Cable TV in any of its more programmatically ambitious forms simply had not developed until the early 1980s, in part because disagreements between the states on cable policy made progress very difficult, but also in part because public-opinion surveys found relatively little enthusiasm among West German viewers for the sorts of additional services that cable could provide.[50]

There had been a proposal in Bremen for a cable-TV service in 1974; the city-state's mayor wanted to set up a three-month or so experiment, largely in one of Bremen's "new town" areas. It would relay existing programs but also would add a nightly local newscast that would not be available over Radio Bremen. The other state stations were alarmed over this proposal, since it came without warning and presented them with a challenge to their usual ways of thinking about broadcasting. The mayor dropped the plan after speaking with the West German postal minister.[51]

The federal government already had appointed an inquest commission (Commission for the Construction of a Technical Communications System, or KtK) in November 1973, simply because cable and satellite were becoming common topics of discussion all over Europe, and West Germany had a vested interest through its electronics industry in seeing what might develop and be developed. Also, there was the question of jurisdiction: Were cable and satellite *broadcast* media, in which case the states would regulate them, or were they properly part of the postal service, which was a federal government function? The KtK reported at the end of 1975 and recommended that a few experimental projects be set up in various parts of the country but also made it quite clear where authority over the new media should lie: "Objectively speaking, it is indispensable that the states, which have particular legal responsibilities in the area of broadcasting, come to a decision forthwith on the . . . question of supplying programming [for cable]. The construction of the [cable] network depends upon this decision."[52]

The federal government advanced the claim that the post office was the proper agency for the establishment and licensing of cable TV, and the KtK report did not lead it to change its mind. The states, logically enough, contested that claim, but several years were to pass before there would be sufficient compromise among them to permit agreement on a state cable policy.

Meanwhile, there were various proposals for experiments. Kassel and Cologne (the latter with the active participation and even leadership of WDR) considered experiments in the mid-1970s but did not carry them out. Finally, in 1983, four cities, with some financial assistance from the federal government, agreed to establish experimental cable projects. Ludwigshafen started in early 1983, Munich in late 1983, West Berlin and Dortmund in 1985. With the exception of West Berlin (over 300,000 cable households as of early 1988) none has been a huge success thus far, probably because none offers a great deal more than can be obtained over conventional television; some of the additional channels are services from neighboring lands (the French-Swiss-Belgian TV-5, Sky Channel from Great Britain), and ARD's Eins Plus is mostly old ARD station material, while 3SAT is made up largely of current and old ZDF material, with much smaller contributions from Swiss TV (less than 10 percent) and Austrian TV (just over 30 percent).

However, some of the satellite-delivered private services have begun to offer a bit of alternative material. The RTL Plus and SAT1 services began breakfast TV programs (6:30–8:30 A.M.) in the fall of 1987. Furthermore, some of the cable systems offer access channels. My own 1986 observations and the remarks of staff members at the Ludwigshafen system lead me to conclude that the access channel there goes unused on some days and at most has three or four programs. The channel's only office, where help and equipment are available, had been moved twice in two years, and the service was not very well publicized. The Dortmund access channel appears to be doing better.[53] Numbers of subscribers have been far below projections, although the Ludwigshafen service began to catch on in the mid-1980s and as of late 1986 had about 60,000 subscribers among the 170,000 homes or apartments passed. Berlin simply hooked up the many master antenna television (MATV) systems around the city and offered basic cable free of charge, but at least one cable-delivered private radio service there went out of business in less than a year because it got so few listeners.

Those studies conducted in the late 1970s and early 1980s, which revealed relatively low levels of public interest in cable TV, were based upon what people thought cable might offer. When the first detailed research was conducted with viewers and nonviewers of the Munich cable service in 1984 (N = 9,000 households), reactions were much more positive: A full 96 percent of the viewers wanted to continue to receive cable TV. Most people using it claimed to go to the movies less often, but to read magazines, newspapers, and books.more often, than did noncable households.[54]

The West German government launched a major project in 1983 to cable most of West Germany, particularly in order to bring service to smaller cities and to villages. The project, which was expected to cost somewhere in the hundreds of millions of marks upon its completion in the early 1990s, had passed slightly over 40 percent of the nation's households by early 1988. However, only about 15 percent of all households actually had subscribed, and there is some question as to how many households will choose to do so, given rapidly rising acquisition of VCRs. Also, cable-connection costs are very high: DM 675 (about $325 as of early 1988) per individual household, although there is a decreasing scale of fees for apartment dwellers. Monthly fees for basic cable are DM 11, or about $6.

Satellite television (DBS) in the home, as of 1988, is still a few years in the future. European launches of communications satellites have been plagued by various problems and are running behind schedule, as are their U.S. counterparts. The November 1987 launch of *Ariane 2* was a failure in the sense that one of its solar panels failed to deploy, which rendered its DBS component unusable. The huge costs associated with operating DBS services and doubts as to whether there would be all that many customers for them have discouraged investors, and the federal and state governments are not interested in subsidizing them. The Bertelsmann-Luxembourg RTL Plus service eventually may be shifted over to DBS, but the service probably would have to acquire many more subscribers than it presently has in order to make such a shift financially feasible.

Videocassette recorders have sold well in West Germany; over one household in every three has one or more VCRs as of early 1988. They are used most often to play videocassettes of movies and other prerecorded entertainment and instruction, rather than to record material from the TV services for later playback. Foreign feature films are particularly popular choices; in 1985, some of the biggest sellers were action films, followed by comedies and thrillers with horror movies, war, and pornography trailing. Concern over the ease with which young people could obtain videocassettes of pornographic and violent material led the federal government in 1985 to pass legislation making it more difficult for young people to rent cassettes.

THE GERMAN DEMOCRATIC REPUBLIC

Finance, Governance, and Decision Making

The East German broadcasting structure presents few of the complications characteristic of the West German system. There are no broadcast or administrative councils, no pressure groups with specific interests in broadcasting, and no division between states and federal government. The State Committees for Radio and for Television are in charge of day-to-day decision making and are made up of members selected by the SED (Communist) party. Those committees make annual budget requests, which are considered by the East German Parliament but which are not subjected to rigorous examination. The money itself comes from the national budget and not from license fees, although license fees of up to OM (East marks, officially at par with West German marks) 10.50 a month are assessed and then absorbed into the national budget. It is up to the government to determine how much it can afford to put into broadcasting, and to the state committees to live within those means. There is a small amount of TV advertising, usually ten minutes or less each day between 5:30 and 6:30 P.M., but the money earned from it also goes into the national budget.

The fact that the state committee members also are members of the SED takes care of many potential problems. First, it minimizes the possibility that the broadcast services will air anything that is likely to embarrass the party or the government, since the party members serving on the committees will know the latest interpretations of party and government policy, or, if they do not, will insure that broadcasting refrain from setting forth any interpretation of events until one becomes clear. Second, it insures that broadcasting will not become a political football, with arguments over whether one party or another receives more favorable treatment. Third, it means that the broadcast system will have access to the highest levels of decision making should it have points that it wishes to call to their attention; broadcasting is considered by the SED and the government — for all practical purposes one and the same — to be extremely important in the development of society, and proposals for modification and expansion to better serve society are likely to be considered seriously.

Programming

PHILOSOPHIES   The overriding purpose of East German broadcasting is to improve society and to do so through all types of programming: entertainment, education, information. Radio and TV are to provide examples of socially acceptable and socially unacceptable behavior, through items on newscasts, musical lyrics, actors in dramas, contestants on quiz shows, competitors in sports events, and so on. Socially acceptable behavior consists of such things as helping others in society, both in East Germany and abroad; working on behalf of society and not of oneself; and fighting injustice (however that might be defined).

Of course, it is not easy to realize such lofty goals when West German radio and TV programming are readily available to the vast majority of East German listeners and viewers. In order to keep them from consuming more western programming than they already do, East German programs cannot be too obviously purposeful too much of the time. Not every song that is broadcast can be in praise of socialism or against U.S. actions in Central America when East German teenagers are almost certain to be attracted to the latest hits from the West and when they can listen to them so easily. Therefore, many of the songs presented on East German radio or television (there are music videos, after a fashion) often may be about young love and its problems, social alienation, and so on. Television variety shows offer both "communist" and "noncommunist" music. And there will be TV programs imported from the West, although often they show an undesirable aspect of western society, such as greed or lust. (Whether East German viewers notice those aspects or find them undesirable is another question.)

RADIO   There are four national radio services in East Germany: DDR 1 and 2, Berliner Rundfunk, and Stimme der DDR (created from a merger of two services, Deutschlandsender and Berliner Welle, in 1971).

Stimme der DDR and Berliner Rundfunk are on twenty-four hours a day, DDR 1 for nearly twenty-one hours, and DDR 2 for fourteen hours a day. All four carry music for half or more or each broadcast day; DDR 2 offers more classical music than do the others, but all carry both classical and popular music. There is nothing resembling nonstop pop, nor even a service such as the Soviet Union's Mayak, with music and short newscasts throughout the day and night. Program blocks featuring one particular kind of music seldom last more than two hours and more often are an hour or less; furthermore, they may be intermixed with programs for children, programs about politics, and so on.

The DDR 2 service is more "serious" than the other three, carrying school broadcasts two or three times a day, readings from novels, talks on culture, and programs on the nature and history of socialism. Several radio plays are presented each week, usually original works by East German writers (and often on the theme of individuals helping others) or adaptations of novels and stage plays (often by other East European writers). A quiz show of some sort usually is available each day. News comes on the hour over most services, and on the half hour as well during the 4:00 to 7:00 A.M. period on DDR 1 and Stimme der DDR. (East Germans rise very early!) The newscasts come from a central newsroom; there is no variety between the four services in that respect, although one or two services may carry newscasts at times when the others do not. The usual news lineup starts with items about governmental and political activities in East Germany, moves to consider other East European countries, then has a few items about West Germany and other nations around the world. Almost without variation, news about the socialist world (East Germany, the USSR, and other East European countries, plus perhaps Mongolia, Cuba, Vietnam, North Korea, Kampuchea, and possibly Nicaragua) is positive. Crimes and disasters rarely are reported. News about the West is quite the opposite: strikes, disasters (particularly industrial), and crimes make up the bulk of the coverage. Tone of voice and choice of language, however, generally are neutral throughout the newscasts, giving them a somewhat disembodied sound. The Soviet policy of *glasnost* so far has had little effect on East German broadcast journalism.

Aside from specific program content, the overall schedule differs from that of West German radio in its inclusion of a great deal of programming for and by children, from preschoolers to teenagers. A number of the broadcasts feature popular music, but there are also interviews conducted by teenagers, fairy tales, music performed by children and teenagers, radio plays for children (again, usually featuring individuals or small groups working to help others, or stories of inspirational figures, such as cosmonauts), and features about things to make and do around the home. Clearly East German broadcasters believe that radio continues to be relevant for younger listeners and is not just a source of music.

The regional stations in East Germany—there are eleven of them, distributed quite evenly across the country—have periods in the morning and late afternoon when they break away from the national service and carry local and regional news. The station in Cottbus broadcasts for thirty to sixty minutes a day in Sorbisch to serve the fifty thousand or so Sorbs living in that area, and the station in Rostock, on the Baltic coast, has a special holiday service for vacationers during the summer months, with information in German, Czech, Slovak, and Polish about what to see and do in the area. There also is a special international fair service in Leipzig for the weeks in the spring and in the fall when the Leipzig Trade Fair is on. The larger stations have their own broadcast orchestras and also may produce radio plays. Regional stations also have stringers reporting from the smaller cities and towns in their areas. (During the 1950s, those stringers also were expected to report on any politically suspect behavior they observed, but such attempts made people unwilling to cooperate with them in developing news items, so the observation task was dropped.)[55]

TELEVISION   While the variety of programming on the two East German television services does not begin to match that of West German TV, it is far greater than what is available to other East European viewers (aside from the USSR and those Hungarian viewers who have cable), and it is very well produced. High production quality is in part a response to West German programming and serves to attract both East German and possibly West German viewers. The broadcast day on both channels begins shortly before 9:00 A.M. and ends around midnight, often with one to three hours blank in the early to middle afternoon on weekdays. Much of the morning-program block consists of repeats from the previous day or week, as on West German TV, and for much the same audience: shift workers and viewers in the other Germany. There also is educational programming for primary and secondary schools.

The first service carries a somewhat greater quantity of light entertainment than does the second, but both carry a few to several hours of educational broadcasting each day—for schoolchildren on the second service (chemistry, biology, geography, civics, music) and for adults on the first (English, Russian), as well as some repeats of second-service educational material. Feature films, not all that common on West German public TV, are available almost every day of the week on East German TV and range from *The Battleship Potemkin* (1925) to *The Coast of Love* (French, 1982), with films from East European nations predominating. East German TV also has access to a huge stock of German films from before 1945 and shows them often; they are great favorites among West German viewers, since few of them are available over West German TV. Newscasts are on five times a day over the first service, twice a day on the second, and bear a close resemblance to radio news in their content, with the addition of visual material from Intervision, Eurovision, and the Fernsehen DDR crews. There are few East German broadcast correspondents stationed outside the country—the cost in precious hard currencies is too great—so foreign items usually are handled through voice-overs in the studio.

There is a wide variety of material for hobbyists: gardening, pet care, photography, and other hobbies all receive frequent coverage, sometimes in weekly series. Quiz shows are few in number, but variety shows, often with lavish costumes and sets, are common. There are several travel programs as well, some to highlight various cities and nature areas of East Germany, others to present foreign lands. Because few East Germans enjoy the freedom to travel widely, these travelogues may be a substitute, but they also may remind viewers that there is a lot that they cannot see for themselves. Television plays, original and adapted, classical and contemporary, are on almost nightly. Commemorative ceremonies, such as the opening of the rebuilt German Playhouse in East Berlin in 1984, receive heavy coverage, perhaps because they give the government a chance to tout its support for culture.

As with radio, TV has a great deal of material for children, especially toward the end of the afternoon.[56] Most of the programs are produced for, but not by, children, and are full of suggestions for hobbies (pet care and gardening seem to lead the way) and for good behavior. Perhaps the most subtle of the behavior programs is the nightly *Sandmannchen* (Sandman), a ten-minute show that combines puppet and toy figures with brief film clips showing such things as model families (e.g., a father who has educated himself and who has a responsible job in a factory, but who helps his family members and neighbors, too) and model acts (e.g., obeying traffic signals, keeping the dog on a leash). They are charmingly done, and not at all heavy-handed. Many West German viewers who live within range of East German TV claim to watch them quite regularly. The weekends represent the one intrusion on the policy of "late afternoons for children," because sports events often are televised then.

East German coverage of sports is plentiful. The country's athletes have done well in international competition, and their triumphs seem to have added to the average East German's sense of self-worth. Televising the events also allows for interviews with the athletes, who often are encouraged to tell viewers how much they (the athletes) owe to East German society for having made possible the training, including workouts with neighbors and co-workers, that led to victory. But occasionally athletes in some of the more demanding sports will state that their neighbors and co-workers soon lose interest in working out with them!

During the 1970s, East German television acquired a much more relaxed character. There have been fewer and fewer instances of variety-show hosts, performers, and other entertainers reminding viewers of East German economic progress, the advantages of living in a socialist rather than a capitalist Germany, and so on. Also, there are fewer dramas stressing such themes as individuals working on behalf of society, the dangers of ideological contamination from the West, and the need to work together to achieve progress, and when those themes appear, they are presented more subtly. Spy dramas still tend to present U.S. and West German agents in very broad, stereotypical ways, but the same can be said for most U.S. TV dramas with spies from "the other side." And there are far fewer newsreel-type shows featuring developments in the other East European countries, whereas these used to be on several times a week.

Certainly the major commemorative events, such as the thirty-fifth anniversary of the founding of the German Democratic Republic (celebrated in the fall of 1984), see many references to what has been achieved over that time—a great deal, actually—and there are many short, "person-in-the-street" interviews in which people are asked what the event means to them (their replies often sound bored and formal). But all in all the use of television as an ideological transmission belt is far less obvious and rather less frequent than it was before the conclusion of the interstate treaty in 1972 and the widespread diplomatic recognition of East Germany by western nations at about the same time. West German TV certainly has had its influences on its eastern counterpart, but a greater sense of self-confidence and security within East Germany has had its effect, too.

The Audience

There were sporadic and rudimentary attempts at audience research in East Germany during the 1950s and early 1960s, but anything more permanent or better developed was hindered by the "of the people, by the people, for the people" stance of the SED, which claimed that there was no need for audience research in a society where audience and broadcaster were so closely linked. Also, it was common for leaders of the communist countries to brand survey research as a capitalist tool for the further exploitation of the masses. Hungary and Poland began to make regular use of it by the early 1960s, claiming that it could help to make known the degree to which the audience really understood and accepted the messages contained in broadcasts, whether certain programs were gaining or losing popularity and therefore might have to be modified, and so on.

East Germany established a television research department in 1964, and in 1968 it began to carry out surveys every two weeks, using questionnaires with a set of standard questions and a set of questions especially drawn up for each survey period (e.g., What constitutes a "hero" in a TV drama, and which figures do you find "heroic"?). Radio had started the same practice in 1966. In both cases, surveys are done nationwide; respondents are selected randomly, and there are a thousand for each TV survey and fifteen hundred for radio.

Results of the surveys rarely are made public. From what is known, it appears that the variety shows and travelogues are the most popular TV program genres, with foreign films close behind. Survey results do not indicate the extent of viewing of West German television, but reports of West Germans who have visited relatives in East Germany indicate that it is viewed much more heavily than is East German TV, and that its news and other informational programs are particularly popular. However, those same reports also indicate that at least some of the West German news reinforces some of the more negative images of life in a capitalist society—it is a competitive jungle, employers are heartless, the country is an armed camp, and so on.

Data on radio listening show that the popular-music programs attract the largest audiences, but also that brief newscasts are more attractive than longer ones for the majority of the listeners. As something like three-fourths of all East German teenagers have their own radio sets, the radio services are compelled to consider more carefully how to retain the young audience, since broadcasts from West Germany are easily receivable in East Germany and are very popular there—especially those like the American Forces Network station in Berlin, RIAS Berlin, the British

Forces Berlin station and a few of the West German state stations that
play large amounts of the latest hits.

East Germany does not encourage letter writing to the same extent
as does the Soviet Union, but there are occasional programs on radio
and television where audience reactions are read and replied to, and
quite a few programs where audience requests for music are honored.
Also, East German broadcast personnel are expected to get out and meet
with the public, at factories, in schools, in old peoples' homes, and even
in jails. They also are expected to return to their stations and share with
their colleagues the information gathered in those meetings, although
how much effect that has on program decision making is impossible to
discern.

Problem Areas

Because of the relatively closed nature of East Germany, there are
few major public complaints about the quality of broadcast programming. East German newspapers do print complaining letters from time
to time, but the problems seem to be rather minor ones: too many
repeats, too much sports, not enough or too much of certain kinds of
music. The one great West German obsession, television and politics,
simply does not surface as an issue in East Germany, although individual
citizens will personally express their boredom or fatigue with TV news
portrayal of one official ceremony after another; this, that, or the other
successful business enterprise, collective farm, or factory; and so on.

Even if complaints could be voiced more freely, it is possible that
there would not be all that many. West German TV is a readily available
alternative for most East German viewers, and there is a fair amount of
anecdotal evidence to show that East German viewers regularly take
advantage of it, as well as of the many radio stations broadcasting from
Western Europe in German — probably a dozen of so, including two
services from RIAS Berlin and one from Deutschlandfunk that identify
East Germans as a major target audience.

Foreign Influences on Programming

East German broadcasting has had to contend with the very powerful influence of West German programming almost from the beginning,
and that appears to have made East German TV, if not radio, the most
professional in quality of production of any of the East European television services. Aside from that influence, there are also the influences of
those other East European services. Items furnished through Intervision
appear nightly on TV newscasts and conform with and reinforce the
prevailing tendency in East German broadcast journalism to rely heavily
on politically "safe" items such as receptions, arrivals, and departures of
distinguished visitors and ceremonies marking major events and their
anniversaries. Television's manner of portraying such items varies little
among East European broadcasters, East Germany included.

Feature films, too, often come from the other East European nations.[57] Hungarian films often are very lively in theme, style of acting,
and editing, but there is little sign that they have influenced East German
producers that much. Instead, East German feature films shown on
television bear more resemblance to those made in Czechoslovakia,
Bulgaria, and Romania, in that they are a bit somber and plodding, in
acting, plot, and editing. Serial drama is not very frequent on East
German TV; about half of what there is comes from the other East
European nations or from the West, but the typical East German series
bears far more resemblance to the former than to the latter, for instance,
the popular Czech series *Hospital at the Edge of Town,* which showed
the deep humanity of two doctors with very different personalities. In
other words, thematic influence is more likely to be along the lines of
"working on behalf of society." However, there has been a greater tendency for East German TV drama to show characters with more doubts,
and in greater conflict with themselves and with others, than used to be
the case. It is quite likely that both western (especially West German) and
eastern (especially Hungarian and Polish) TV drama may be partially
responsible for this change, although it also may be one more reflection
of a more confident society.

Relations with Other Media

There is no formal question of intermedia competition in East Germany. Film, press, radio, and television are seen as complementary, and
they do not compete for advertising money or for funds from the na-

tional budget. The degree of artistic freedom is higher for film than it is for television, and the print media enjoy slightly more journalistic freedom than do their electronic cousins, but the differences are not great. The official East German wire service, Allgemeine Deutscher Nachrichten (General German News) supplies both newspapers and broadcasting, and there is great similarity of style and content in press, radio, and television presentation of the major news items of the day. East German feature films appear often on television, and some are quite recent, even though this probably has a negative effect on cinema attendance. The East German film industry is paid for the use of films on TV, but both are government operations, so there is no question of profit.

International Cooperation

East Germany has entered into coproduction agreements with each of the other East European television services at one time or another, usually on projects requiring authentic settings in more than one country. Lack of hard currency has made similar arrangements very difficult where West European TV systems are concerned, but DDR-TV has been involved in a few coproduction projects where it played a relatively minor role, for example, on surveys of the works of artists, architectural styles, and so on. East Germany receives a large amount of news material both from Intervision and from Eurovision. It also both receives and originates sports and light entertainment through Intervision and Eurovision, but it takes far more from the latter than it receives: In 1986, it supplied four programs for a total of 9 hours but took two hundred programs for a total of almost 440 hours.[58]

The New Media

East Germany has had little new-media activity. Most East Germans know about cable and satellites, and some households are on master antenna systems, but they are not high priorities in any part of East Europe, and the government could not justify the outlay of hard currency to purchase the necessary equipment from the West, which is where cable equipment would have to come from. The one exception is the southeastern section of the country, especially the region around

Dresden, where the government began to install cable in 1986 in order to provide for reception of West German programming; as noted earlier, that assuredly embarrassing move came as a result of the difficulty encountered in getting people to move to or stay in the Dresden area, since it was the one major city in East Germany where citizens could not receive West German TV.

The Soviet Union has experimented with DBS but has no immediate plans for introducing it as a consumer item. Since East Germany has no satellite launch capacity of its own, DBS is unlikely to appear there soon. Furthermore, there are limits to how much time the government wishes to see its citizens spending on leisure pursuits, which is how cable and satellite appear to be perceived in East Germany. Videocassette recorders also are few and far between, since the Soviet Union is the only East European producer of them as of 1988, and it produces very few. Certain "privileged" East Germans (usually high-ranking government officials) have them, but they are not available in the stores—even those that sell goods only for hard currencies. For the foreseeable future, East Germans will have to make do with conventional broadcast technology.

Conclusion

Even though the occupation following World War II resulted in the creation of two very different German nations, one thing seems quite clear: Radio and television have served to maintain or establish at least some traditions common to the two. The popularity of *Schwarzwaldklinik* in West Germany and *Hospital at the Edge of Town* in East Germany seem to stem from a shared taste for sentimentality, goodness, and paternalism. There have been West and East German "Sandmen" to dispense moral lessons to young viewers. Variety shows often feature comedy routines and songs familiar to German audiences on both sides of the wall. Old German movies appear regularly on the East German TV schedule (West Germany has fewer of them), and draw many older viewers in the West.

There are many sharp differences, as well, especially in informational broadcasting. East German newscasts stress positive news about the GDR and its Eastern European compatriots, and negative news about West Germany and the capitalist world in general. West German TV carries large amounts of negative news about the Federal Republic and about the capitalist world in general, and in addition carries many vigorous political discussions, which stand in marked contrast with the bland and sometimes boring political presentations (rarely are they true discussions) on East German TV. Few West Germans watch East German informational programs with any regularity, but East Germans seem to be regular watchers of West German informational programming, if my discussions with East German citizens are a reliable guide, as well as the many East German newspaper reports warning the citizenry not to be taken in by one or another West German TV report. Some of the West German concentration on negative news may make East German viewers more willing to believe their own system's newscasts in that particular respect, and more than one East German has told me that she or he saw considerable advantage to living in a society where crime was rare and where unemployment was even rarer. West Germany seemed in many respects to be a (relatively) crime ridden, frantic, uncertain society, at least as depicted on West German TV. Yet there also is envy and admiration for the greater range of material goods, freedom to travel, and the ability to express differing political opinions.[59]

Future prospects for the two Germanies could see them pulling closer together, at least in broadcast terms. If cable and satellite-delivered TV gains a solid foothold in West Germany, and if private broadcasting continues to develop there, the medium of television is quite likely to become more entertainment oriented. In that case, both East and West German public television are likely to have to work harder to hold their present audiences, either by becoming more entertainment oriented themselves or by finding ways of packaging their informational and high culture programs more attractively.

Considered as separate systems, both East and West German television have some interesting features with wider implications. East Germany's heavy emphasis on children's programming in both radio and television would seem worthy of emulation, especially in its varied approaches to inducing active participation on the part of young viewers. West Germany's broadcast councils are an unusual approach to providing for public input, in that they are drawn from designated societal groups and in that the groups themselves choose their representatives. If some of the more recent attempts (NDR, Radio Bremen) to build in some flexibility to the process of designating societal groups become the norm, that might answer one major criticism of the West German council system: that it doesn't keep up with a changing society.

There is also a question of how long West Germany can rely upon its state-based system in this era of rapid change in communications technology. A state-based system is an excellent way of preventing a central government from accumulating and exercising power over the electronic media, but it is not very efficient, and cable and satellite technology demonstrate that inefficiency clearly. It took nearly ten years for the states to agree among themselves on an overall cable-satellite policy, and even then there were the "rear guard battles" fought by Hesse and Bavaria that showed that politics would be played with these new media just as politics had been played with the old. Inefficiency usually translates into higher cost, and there may be limits to what viewers and listeners, and the states themselves, will be ready to pay to preserve states rights in broadcasting.[60]

5

The Soviet Union
Of, By, or For the People?

T HE world's largest nation has a broadcast system equally vast: Despite exceptionally difficult economic, geographic, and linguistic conditions, the USSR has managed to bring radio and television to the great majority of its population. What that population sees and hears often differs sharply from what Western European and North American audiences see and hear, because the Soviet government views broadcasting as a powerful instrument in the shaping of society. Yet it would be a mistake to think of the Soviet broadcast system as unchanging or as unresponsive to public opinion, nor are its broadcasts an unending stream of praise for the Communist way of life. Its programming often is far less ideological than that. The pressures that have led to programming changes have come from a variety of sources, some internal, some external. The basic structural form of Soviet broadcasting has not changed in over fifty years, notwithstanding which the system does possess a certain degree of dynamism.[1]

Basic Factors

GEOGRAPHIC   The vastness of the Soviet Union is difficult to grasp. To say that it occupies a sixth of the world's land area still sounds quite abstract. It becomes more concrete when one realizes what this means in terms of time zones: There are eleven of them across the USSR, which means that it will be early afternoon in Moscow or Leningrad when it is

247

very early morning of the next day in Vladivostok. Yet this huge territory has a population perhaps 13 percent larger than that of the continental United States, which is little more than one-third the size of the Soviet Union. Anyone who has traveled through the western part of the United States knows that there are long stretches of land with very few people. A traveler in Siberia experiences much the same sensation, magnified three times! Furthermore, the climate often is hostile: The USSR lies farther north than does the United States, and large portions of the country are in the grip of winter for almost half of each year.

These conditions have led to a very uneven distribution of population. Roughly three-quarters of all Soviet citizens live in the western ("European") USSR, which makes up about one-fifth of the total land area. There also has been a sharp increase in urbanization: Roughly three-fourths of the people lived in rural areas in the early 1920s, whereas only about a third are rural dwellers as of the mid-1980s. The USSR has attempted to control population distribution by limiting the issuance of work permits for positions in the more popular cities such as Moscow, Kiev, and Leningrad, and by offering inducements such as higher salaries and better housing in the less desirable areas, especially Siberia, but many individuals find ways to live in the more popular areas, anyway.

For such a large country, the Soviet Union has relatively few neighbors, in part because the Arctic Ocean forms most of the long northern border, the northern Pacific Ocean much of the eastern border, and the People's Republic of China a large part of the southern border. Furthermore, most of the larger cities are located some distance from the borders, so that, where broadcasting is concerned, there is limited spillover of signals that any substantial number of Soviet citizens could receive. (International broadcasts from more distant nations are a different matter and will be mentioned at various points in this chapter.) Yet another factor that reduces the effect of any spillover of signals is the uniqueness of the Russian language itself: There is limited similarity with Czech, Bulgarian, and Polish, and almost none with any other language used in a neighboring country. Some of the languages spoken in certain regions of the USSR, such as Estonian, bear greater similarities to languages spoken in neighboring countries (Finnish, in the case of Estonian); but there are few such instances, and none that involve more than a small fraction of the Soviet population.

DEMOGRAPHIC   A visitor to Moscow on May Day or on the anniversary
          of the October Revolution receives a graphic demonstration of the
demographic diversity of the USSR. Not only do the flags of the various

Soviet republics fly all around Red Square, but also Moscow's streets are crowded with people from all over the country, many of them brought to the capital as honored guests for outstanding service performed on behalf of society. There are reindeer herders from the far north, Mongolians, Uzbeks from central Asia, Ukrainians and many others, all of whom can speak Russian more or less well (it is the chief language of instruction for the entire educational system) but many of whom may be more comfortable speaking Tadzik, Uighur, or any of the 110 languages other than Russian that are in use somewhere or other in the country. Because Russian is spoken throughout the country, and because the languages other than Russian usually are spoken only within a particular region, broadcasting faces a difficult but not insuperable task. Russian can be used for broadcasts throughout the country, and the other languages can be employed within their particular geographical regions. In that way, the many peoples of the USSR can maintain their sense of cultural identity and at the same time be part of the entire nation.

Quite apart from its role in helping to build a sense of national unity out of what is a highly diverse mixture of cultures and nations (bear in mind that the Soviet Union was wracked by civil war, itself aided by other nations such as France, Great Britain, and the United States, for the period 1917–20), the universal employment of Russian in education and in broadcasting has another purpose: It has permitted the national government to more easily transfer to the smaller republics "greater Russians" — those living in the Russian Soviet Federated Socialist Republic, the largest of the fifteen Soviet republics — who work in government, education, and so on. That further encourages the use of Russian throughout the country, although some observers have claimed that it also is an indication of greater Russian insecurity and/or arrogance — an unwillingness to trust those who are not greater Russians to perform the really important tasks of society. There are Ukrainians, Georgians, Byelorussians, and other "non–greater Russian" national groups represented in positions of high national responsibility, but the central Asian national groups, which are the fastest growing of all in terms of population, certainly are not numerous at that level.

There is some disagreement over just how unified the Soviet Union is. There are many manifestations of cultural diversity in folk music, literature, and other art forms, and many of those manifestations are made available to the entire nation over radio and television, so that most Soviet citizens are well aware of the great variety of cultures in their country. The political histories of the various regional groups, especially those with some tradition of national independence (e.g., Latvia, the Ukraine) generally are not that well-known outside the region itself and may not be that well-known within the region. Broadcasting is far less frequently used to convey political diversity; that task, when it is fulfilled, is more likely to be the province of the schools. It may be that Soviet authorities view political diversity, even within the overall framework of communism, as less compatible with national unity than is cultural diversity.

ECONOMIC As modern industrialized nations go, the Soviet Union has a fairly high percentage of its population employed on the land: About one-fourth work in agriculture, forestry, and fishing. Farms are state-operated collectives, but increasing numbers of farmers are tending private plots in their spare time and often selling their excess produce to supplement their incomes. Business and industry, too, are state operated, but people in certain lines of work, especially anything having to do with machine repairs, sometimes find ways of moonlighting in order to supplement their incomes and frequently expect payment in 'material goods rather than in money. Private enterprise is not an official part of the economy, but it serves an important function for consumers.

Because of a rather poor transportation infrastructure and frequent harsh or uncertain climatic conditions, the Soviet economy often turns in a very uneven performance, and manufactured and agricultural goods often must be imported. Nevertheless, Soviet citizens regularly are urged to work to overcome those difficulties, even though rewards in terms of direct benefits to their lives may not be immediately apparent. When there are improvements in the lot of consumers, say in the increased construction of housing units, broadcasting and the other media are sure to feature them. Economic setbacks usually will be mentioned, but there will be an accompanying explanation of the circumstances, and an indication that things are almost certain to improve, especially if people redouble their efforts.

The Soviet Union has gone further than have most nations to link broadcasting and the major occupations. Many of the collective farms have their own radio operations, and so do a fair number of the larger factories. There are special programs on the larger stations at the national and republic levels for teachers. News and light entertainment programs regularly feature people who are engaged in some form of work and usually provide numerous details on the nature of that work, its value to the nation, and so on. Broadcasting also is used to inform citizens of the country's overall economic progress, often related in highly detailed figures and, in the case of television, with pictures of tractors in the fields, sheets of steel rolling through factories, fish hauled in by the netful, a new rail line coursing through Siberia.

CULTURAL   As already mentioned, the cultural diversity of the Soviet Union is great, and broadcasting plays a major role in displaying and promoting it. The traditions upon which that diversity rests may be religious, feudal, or any number of things that are discouraged or even forbidden by the present government, but the songs, dances, tales, costumes, and other cultural manifestations often continue with the blessing and even encouragement of that government. To be sure, they may be placed in context: Viewers of a TV program featuring old Kirghiz songs and dances are quite likely to be told of the economic subjugation, the male chauvinism, the blind devotion to religious leaders that characterized the society of those songs and dances. They also may be told how much better things are in the present-day Kirghiz Republic. But the songs and dances will occupy center stage, precisely because they so graphically display the USSR's rich cultural tradition and the concern of the government that the tradition be preserved.

There are certain aspects of cultural life that are common in other countries but rare in the Soviet Union. Where religion is concerned, the USSR is an atheist nation, so of course there is no state church. That does not mean that people do not have the freedom to worship, and there are churches, synagogues, and mosques throughout the country, with fair numbers of believers present on days of worship. But those religious institutions may not operate their own schools, may not proselytize, and may not be used to convey messages that could be considered as antigovernment. Furthermore, people willing to identify themselves as believers may find it difficult to rise to positions of major responsibility in government, industry, or education, all of which are government run. Attacks upon religion through the media are nowhere near as frequent now as they were in the Soviet Union's earlier years, but it is not that uncommon to see a television play in which a character holds notably "backward" religious views.

Certain kinds of foreign music have been discouraged by the Soviet government in the past, although that, too, is less frequent now. Jazz and rock music in particular were rare to nonexistent on the Soviet airwaves until the late 1960s, when Soviet rock and jazz groups, some of which had been functioning for years in nightclubs in some of the large cities, began to appear live and in recordings over Soviet radio and TV. Even the western groups upon which most of the Soviet groups had modeled themselves appeared occasionally on record. Jazz and rock had been regarded earlier as symbols of western decadence, but international broadcasters such as the Voice of American and the BBC found plenty of listeners, younger ones in particular, ready to hear the decadent messages of the Beatles, Elvis Presley, and the Rolling Stones. Some of the more modern forms of classical music, especially that of the twelve-tone school (Arnold Schonberg, Anton Webern) and of Igor Stravinsky and the neoclassicists, were discouraged for the same basic reason. The fact that Stravinsky had been born and raised in Russia (imperial Russia, to be sure!) and that some of the objectionable works were by Soviet composers (Prokofiev, Shostakovitsch), mattered not at all. That, too, changed in the 1960s, in part as a result of the relaxation in cultural vigilance that had followed Soviet premier Josef Stalin's death in 1953.

The country has a very rich literary and musical tradition, and broadcasting has been used from the earliest days to bring books, drama, poetry, opera, orchestral concerts, and vocal and chamber music recitals to a wider public. Some of these works are by Soviet writers and composers; others come from artists who functioned in prerevolutionary Russia. There is heavy emphasis on works written in Russian on the national radio and TV services, although works by Ukraines, Georgians, Kazahks, and other nationalities also appear in translation. The republic services frequently feature the works of native writers. The national and republic broadcast services frequently present dramatizations of novels currently being studied in secondary schools. Even the cultural broadcasts for the general public are quite apt to contain a fair amount of explanation of a major literary or musical work; the process of education does not stop with the end of formal schooling, and broadcasting is one of the most efficient ways in which to continue it. There are plenty of foreign musical and literary works, too, although sometimes they may be selected for their ideological content, such as the protest novels and poetry of U.S. black writers.

Education is a universal right, and school attendance is compulsory to age seventeen, in theory (full secondary education facilities are lacking in some rural areas). Adult education is strongly encouraged; factories, collective farms, and large businesses often make special provision for their employees to continue their formal education during their working hours. Radio and television play a major role in both of those levels of education, and primary and secondary schools, farms, and factories make considerable use of it. Many Soviet citizens also pursue self-education at home, and here, too, television and radio are important. Far less frequent use is made of broadcasting at the university level, where the audiovisual media in general receive rather short shrift.

POLITICAL   Unlike the other nations discussed in this book, the Soviet
      Union does not feature a multiparty system of government. There is
only one party—the Communist party of the Soviet Union—and voters

have the choice of voting for its candidates or leaving their ballots blank. Because of that, it is very difficult to distinguish between the government and the Party. A given individual may speak as a government official or as a Party member; the message may be the same, but remarks coming from someone claiming to represent the Party, or perceived as doing so, probably will carry even more weight than remarks made by someone speaking as a government official. That may be because there is a perception of greater collective weight behind Party statements, which often are thrashed out in high-level meetings before they are released to the public. Government officials have been known to speak off-the-cuff (and off the record), but that would be rare behavior for a Party official speaking as a member of the Party. But caution is the hallmark of both sorts of officials, and it can take hours or even days for government or Party to decide how it wishes to respond to a situation. Until there is an official response, the mass media must keep silent, even though broadcasts coming from outside the country may be covering the event in considerable detail.

Government functions at several levels in the Soviet Union: national, republic, district, and local. Its basic organization at any one level is the same throughout the country, even though the various parts of the country featured many different approaches to government before they all were consolidated in the Soviet Union. Any responsible position in government is almost certain to be filled by a member of the Communist party (only about 5 percent of the population belongs to the Party). The same is true of industry, the collective farms, and the mass media. That unity of Party and government with the economy and the media insures rapid and widespread dissemination of Party decisions, although it cannot insure that it will result in the desired actions. People with complaints about the way in which things are working, all the way from the difficulty of purchasing the right kinds of light bulbs to accusations of graft or fraud on the part of a manager of a large factory, are supposed to present them to local officials, who will decide whether they should be passed on to higher authorities or not. Again, catching the attention of a Party member generally gets faster results than does working through government officials, who probably would check with the Party before acting, anyway. Many Soviet citizens resort to the media to voice their complaints, through letters to the editor and radio and TV call-in shows, although most complaints surfacing through those channels tend to be minor ones, and they may or may not result in action. (It often helps if the newspaper printing the letter is an official organ of the Communist party.)

Both government and Party officials make heavy use of the broadcast media to communicate with the general public, although, as in most nations, the communication flows overwhelmingly in one direction: from the top down. Probably there is more of such communication in the Soviet Union than there is in most other nations: It is rare to have a day go by without several official statements carried by radio and television, most of them originally written for publication in the print media and too long, detailed, and formal to constitute effective use of broadcasting. Many nongovernmental groups that work closely with government, such as trade unions, teacher's associations, young people's organizations (e.g., the Young Pioneers), also use broadcasting quite regularly to communicate with their members and to inform nonmembers of what they are doing to aid in the progress of Soviet society. Broadcasting definitely is viewed by officials as an important part of the apparatus of governance, although whether the governed see it in a similar light is open to question.

A Brief History

In the period before the Russian Revolution of 1917, there was considerable experimentation with wireless transmission in Russia, and in fact the Soviet Union claims that a Russian, Alexander Popov, was the first individual to demonstrate wireless transmission of a signal (code, not voice). Popov did conduct a number of impressive experiments as early as 1895, but like the other father of radio, Marconi, he was not interested in developing anything resembling radio broadcasting for the general public. By the time of the First World War, Russia had wireless transmission stations and receiving stations for the army and navy.

When Lenin returned to Russia to lead what eventually would be called the Bolshevik Revolution, he already had had experience in working with newspapers. As he learned more about wireless transmission, he became excited about the prospects for a "newspaper without paper and without boundaries." He saw radio as a way to communicate with Russia's masses, many of them illiterate and unorganized. Radio could bypass illiteracy and could help to unite a nation that was made up of so many disparate parts. He encouraged transmission experiments that already were underway at a laboratory in Nizhni-Novgorod (since renamed Gorki, and about 150 miles east of Moscow). During the revolution itself, he used radio to communicate the Bolshevik call to revolution to military personnel and to foreign countries, although it is probable that the message was carried in Morse code. He even devoted a portion of the country's scarce gold reserve to furthering experiments. Concerts, talks, and readings were broadcast starting in August 1922, over a twelve-kilowatt transmitter (the largest in the world at the time) that had just been installed in Moscow; Lenin had high hopes that it would reach most of the country. He also was anxious to overcome the negative influence of noncommunist teachers by using radio to present the instruction of the few communist teachers available.[2]

Interestingly, Lenin did not establish radio broadcasting as a department of the government or as a function of the Communist party. He seemed content to let it develop along its own lines, provided that they were compatible with the overall communist philosophy. Radio amateurs were active in the Soviet Union at the time — already there were hundreds of them — and they were encouraged by the government because their experiments and their reactions to the broadcasts coming from the Nizhni-Novgorod transmitter were invaluable for the development of broadcast technology. Some of those amateurs set up their own stations. So did trade unions, collective farms, and other elements of Soviet society. The official station founded in 1924 was to be supported and administered through a joint-stock operation, with teachers and trade unions subscribing the stock. However, there were at least two other stations in Moscow as of the mid-1920s. The Party took considerable interest in the broadcasts of all of them but did not dictate their contents at first, although a series of orders and decrees from the Central Committee between 1925 and 1927 made it clear that the party wanted close coordination and supervision of agitation and propaganda broadcasting.[3] However, stations around the country remained responsible for their own programming — there was as yet no network — and the carrying out of those decrees and orders probably differed from station to station.

Lenin and the staff at the Nizhni-Novgorod laboratory realized that the manufacture of individual radio receivers would be slow to develop, partly because of the country's tight economic situation, partly because so few households were electrified. Loudspeakers placed in public squares and public buildings were one answer, and Lenin called for their manufacture and installation. A few were placed in service for special events as early as 1921. Wired radio, roughly similar to cable TV, seemed to offer a solution, too, and again Lenin took great interest in that development. The first wired radio installation was made in Moscow in 1925; within three years there were over a hundred such installations, most of them in cities in the European USSR (RSFSR). Usually they relayed the signals of broadcast stations, but occasionally they originated their own material — a practice that grew as the years passed. The stations themselves also increased in number; by 1928 there were between twenty-five and sixty-five of them (Soviet sources disagree on the exact number). Again, most of the stations were in the European part of the country and in larger cities; the rural areas and most of the Asian USSR were very poorly served by radio.

If Lenin had lived longer (he died in 1924), it is entirely possible that radio would have developed at a faster rate. He had great hopes for it and frequently saw to it that those who were developing it received special treatment in food, money, and supplies (particularly fuel, very scarce in the Soviet Union in those days). But after his death the radio technicians appeared to fall from favor, as Stalin and his closest associates seemed far less interested in the medium that Lenin had been. But the radio amateurs continued to promote it, and the newspapers gave it considerable publicity. It was used by many different groups to communicate news of their activities to their own members, and in 1926 the Central Committee of the Communist party ordered stations to broadcast *Worker's News* once a day and *Farmer's News* three or four times a week. Some stations went further: Leningrad carried news programs for children, students, soldiers, Young Pioneer, and Komsomol members. Some of these groups even developed their own radio reporters. Such practices led to a fractionalization of the broadcast day but caused more people to become more involved with radio.

In addition to the many news programs, radio also provided a great deal of music, ranging from folk and popular to classical. Lenin, Trotsky, and other Soviet leaders felt that it was necessary to bring culture to "the masses," and more than one musician or actor spent a lot of time in the early 1920s giving performances in factories and farms. Radio made it much easier to reach the masses, and phonograph records as well as live performances formed a major part of the broadcast schedule. Russian works predominated, although gradually the Ukraines, Georgians, and others began to hear their own music, drama, and poetry. Other forms of entertainment were in short supply or nonexistent. Radio was not considered an entertainment medium; it was for the enlightenment of its listeners, and often for their instruction in the rights and obligations of members of a Communist society. That was radio's *agitation* function, in the Soviet use of the term: broad cultivation of the correct ways of thinking among the masses.

Radio had another function, which the Soviets called *propaganda*. Propaganda was more sophisticated than agitation and was aimed at narrower segments of the public, especially Party workers, who were expected to take propaganda messages and adapt them in ways that would make them more palatable and more understandable to the masses. Certain broadcasts were intended for that specific purpose; although other listeners could tune in, it is doubtful that most of them would have found the subject matter very interesting, and the programs often were quite long.[4]

In 1928, the post office took over the operation of the Moscow radio station, and, through a Central Radio Committee, supervised other radio stations in the country. The Central Radio Committee was closely linked with the Central Committee of the Communist party, and in 1933 the radio system was removed from the post office and placed under the direct supervision of the Council of People's Commissars, or cabinet. Day-to-day direction of operations was carried out by the All-Union Radio Committee, the chair of which became a cabinet member, although of relatively low rank. The tightening of control over radio during the period 1925–33 hardly was surprising, since that was the customary approach taken by Stalin (Lenin's successor). While he paid lip service to the idea of semi-independent republics within the Soviet Union and semi-independent people's councils, or *soviets,* he was far more comfortable with centralization and moved to achieve it as rapidly as possible. Lenin might have done the same, although he appeared to be somewhat more tolerant and even encouraging of diversity than was Stalin, who saw the press, and by extension broadcasting, as a way of insuring that "the thread from the party, through the newspaper, extends to all worker and peasant districts without exception, so that the interaction of the party and state, on the one hand, and industrial and peasant districts, on the other, is complete." His "interaction" was a one-way street, and he did not want to see the press used to disseminate alternate viewpoints arising within the Party, lest that damage the Party's "iron discipline."[5]

Despite that centralization, radio was carrying more and more entertainment, such as sports (the first test broadcast of a soccer match came in 1929) and programs that mixed music, weather reports, responses to listener's questions, and brief news bulletins. But there was a centralization of news, through the creation in 1932 of a central editorial bureau; no longer would there be a host of largely uncoordinated news broadcasts for different segments of the audience. And now that there was a fair-sized body of communist literature, music and other cultural material, in 1932 the Central Committee created an Artist's Union of Workers for Cultural Broadcasting, to insure the use of radio for the promulgation of "socialist realism" (the dignity of labor, the rejection of individualism, etc.). Radio also began in 1928 to provide educational broadcasts for the masses, under the broad title of "the radio university," although the "courses" offered did not carry academic credit.

Radio reception remained a problem. There were fewer than 1.5 million sets in the country by 1932, and all but about 100,000 of them were wired radio receivers, which were limited to picking up whatever the 4,800 wired radio central exchanges provided (which usually was the Moscow station or a major republic station, but not both at the same time, since the service was limited to one channel in those days). Most of the exchanges and receivers were located in the European part of the country, and villages, where the bulk of the population still lived, had just under 26 percent of the receivers as of 1932. There were various calls in the five-year plans starting in 1929 for the increased construction of transmitters, studio equipment, and receivers, but progress was slow: By 1937 there were some 3.75 million receivers and over 9,000 wired radio exchanges, but only 321,000 radio sets capable of receiving a variety of signals. Such sets were especially needed in Siberia, where there were few stations or exchanges, but few Siberians had them. And the villages were slipping in terms of the percentage of receivers located there, from 25.8 percent in 1932 to 22.9 percent in 1937. In part that may have been a reflection of increasing urbanization in the Soviet Union, but there remained many thousands of villages in the country that were without radio service.

Throughout the 1930s, broadcasting was dominated by the Moscow service, which more and more assumed the function of the central station in a network. Most of the republics had their own stations by that time—Byelorussia, the Ukraine, Azerbaijan, and Kazakhstan all had them by 1927—and those stations all broadcast in the major languages of the republic, as well as Russian. But the Russian services were relays of Moscow, and the All-Union Radio Committee, working through radio committees at the republic level, insured that the medium be used properly. Most of the wired relay exchanges originated very little of their own material, and some exchanges originated nothing at all. Still, control was not completely effective, and many radio officials were criticized for their lack of emphasis on "pointed Bolshevik material" and overemphasis on "objective" or "trivial" news items.[6] A few officials were removed from stations in the Ukraine, Byelorussia, and elsewhere on charges of "nationalism" (meaning, for instance, that they overemphasized Ukrainian or Byelorussian nationalism).[7] The wired radio exchanges, too, sometimes decided for themselves whether they wanted to carry some of the material coming from Moscow, and the All-Union Radio Committee in 1935 issued a decree that had the effect of limiting the freedom of the exchanges to select programs. In fact, the majority of the exchanges were forbidden the privilege of originating any programs whatsoever.[8] And in 1939, the Radio Committee publication *Radiofront* called for "a more unified direction of radio broadcasting,"[9] which indicates that some still felt the system to be too loose.

WORLD WAR II   At the outbreak of World War II in 1939, the Soviet
Union still could afford to relax, since the country was not involved
in the war. Some predicted that it could not help but become involved
sooner or later, but almost nothing was done to prepare for that possibility. Where radio was concerned, that proved to be a costly mistake. The
country continued to rely heavily upon wired exchanges, which had the
decided advantage of keeping enemy messages from the ears of the people; no relay exchange operator was likely to pick up and relay broadcasts from the Nazis, British, or any other foreign power without explicit
permission to do so. (It had been illegal since 1924 for a listener to
record and disseminate foreign broadcasts, but it was not illegal to listen
to them.)[10] Since wired receivers outnumbered standard radio sets by
more than five to one as of 1940 (the numbers were 5,853,000 to
1,123,000), there were few people around the country who had any real
choice in what they listened to. But that advantage soon turned to disadvantage when Germany declared war on the USSR in June 1941 and
moved rapidly across Byelorussia, the Ukraine, and much of the European part of the Russian Republic, gaining control of the wired exchanges as they did so. People in many of the villages had not a single
standard set among them, so they were cut off from the rest of the
country, and the Germans, when they wished, used the exchanges to
disseminate their own messages. The Moscow station almost immediately added broadcasts in Ukraine, Byelorussian, and so on, to its
schedule, but few people were in a position to hear them.

The Soviet government decided early in the war that it would be
better not to take any chances that people in the unoccupied parts of the
country listen to foreign broadcasts, so it confiscated all standard radio
sets will in private hands. Possession of a private set and, worse yet,
listening to foreign broadcasts, were crimes punishable by special wartime laws. Soviet citizens listened through wired exchanges or in public
places, where extra loudspeakers were installed. After the war, sets were
returned to their owners.

Wartime programming continued in the same vein as before the war,
but with certain added features, such as messages from and to front-line
military personnel, instructions and morale boosters for guerrilla
fighters active in the Nazi-occupied areas, dramas and documentaries on
the acts of individual heros, and a good deal of specially composed
patriotic music. But many of the standard orchestral works continued to
be broadcast, most of them Russian or Soviet, and music took up about
a third of total airtime. Much of the music was provided by live ensembles; the Moscow station, as well as many of the republic stations, had
their own folk, popular, and classical orchestras and choruses and also

commissioned many original works. A BBC Monitoring Service Report on the Moscow Municipal Network, a wired radio service, vividly describes the nature and purposes of that service:

> With the exception of some music there is nothing which has not a direct bearing on the war. Clearly the intention is to impress upon listeners the fact that this war is a total war rather than to make them forget the horrors of the struggle and to provide relaxation.
> Considerable time is devoted to reports of military operations, descriptions of acts of bravery occupying a prominent place. Partisan activity has come increasingly to the foreground during the recent months, and the heroic spirit of the Soviet people in the present struggle is illustrated by numerous examples.[11]

It is questionable how much effect radio had on public morale during the war, simply because not many individuals had access to it under conditions where they could concentrate on its messages. Public listening areas were not conducive to concentration, and wired exchanges were not universal. Furthermore, a number of them were out of service in the early war years because of lack of spare parts. The larger cities were better off in that respect, and there radio may have had some impact, especially in Leningrad, which remained under siege for over nine hundred days, yet was able to keep its radio station in operation throughout and used it to sustain morale by passing along messages of support from the rest of the country and the free world.

FROM STALIN TO KHRUSCHEV   At the end of the war, the Soviet Union was economically devastated but probably more psychologically unified than it ever had been. The war seemed to have pulled the diverse population together in a way that no previous action by the government — collectivization of farms, purges of dissident elements — ever had done. Radio service was restored quickly to the villages and cities of the western USSR, some parts of which had been under German occupation from 1941 to 1944. The radio industry had begun to produce more equipment for the wired exchanges by the end of 1942, and in the next three years 1,800 new exchanges were established, but few standard radio sets were manufactured during the war. By 1945, the industry was able to gear up for peacetime production, and the manufacture of both wired and wireless receivers was a high priority. The government continued to place great emphasis on the former, since wired receivers were so inexpensive and since many villages still did not have exchanges, but it was clear that standard receiving sets were in high demand, too. For those with standard sets, the choice of domestic services still was very limited: the national service from Moscow and one or two republic services, in most cases.

Nor did the programming change radically following the war. The special wartime programs were dropped, of course, but examples of heroism and sacrifice were not: Listeners were reminded daily of how much the country had suffered during the war, of how much they owed to those who defended the motherland, and of the need for eternal vigilance and readiness to detect and oppose any future military threat. It was implied, and sometimes stated outright, that the country faced further sacrifices in the form of continued high expenditures for military purposes, with fewer consumer goods than people might feel entitled to now that the war was over. Programs about the war have remained a major and constant feature of Soviet broadcasting ever since, although the message about the need for continued sacrifice in the form of better standards of living is handled more subtly or even dropped completely.

Stalin's preoccupation with maintaining the "iron discipline" of the Party seemed to have increased after the war, and some of his close associates rode herd on the mass media to insure their purity. A. A. Zhdanov, a high-ranking Party member, attacked several Soviet composers in 1948 for writing music that was too formal, academic, and tuneless for the people, and radio stations not only had to purge their record libraries of "offensive" works, but also try to anticipate whether any new work might upset some high Party official. But the increased manufacture of standard sets — there were just under five hundred thousand of these at the end of the war, but over 3.6 million by 1950 — made it easier for people to listen to broadcasts from foreign countries, which no longer was illegal.

Some of those sets could receive shortwave broadcasts, since the Moscow station used shortwave as well as long- and mediumwave transmitters, and Great Britain, the United States, and a few other countries were broadcasting to the Soviet Union in Russian by the late 1940s. Those stations often carried a wider range of music than did the Soviet domestic services and began to add more and more popular music that Soviet radio would not carry because it was too "decadent" and "capitalistic." They also carried a great deal of news that was not available to Soviet listeners, either, and began to attract the attention of the Soviet government in two forms: increased arrests of people who allegedly passed along to others what they had heard over the BBC, VOA, or some other unfriendly station, and jamming of the signals of those stations. At the same time, people were warned of the dangers of listening to such stations, sometimes in highly colorful terms: "Many rusty nationalist hooks with rotting maggots have been thrown into the ether by our bitter enemies in the hope that maybe some fool will bite. And unfortunately there are those who then go and talk, and repeat all manner of lies."[12]

Foreign stations increased in number and in amount of broadcast hours in Russian, and a few began to add broadcasts in Ukraine, Byelorussian, and other major languages of the Soviet Union. Radio Liberty, a United States government-supported (Central Intelligence Agency) station based in Munich, carried as many as seventeen Soviet languages, including a twenty-four-hour-a-day service in Russian. During most of the 1950s, the Soviet Union placed heaviest emphasis on arrests, warnings, and jamming, but toward the end of the decade certain officials, including Premier Nikita Khruschev, issued calls, usually through the Communist party, for Soviet broadcasting to fight back by offering a better product — more complete and up-to-date newscasts, more interesting announcers, a wider range of music. But reforms were slow to appear, and the Party continued its criticism, as in this commentary in the Party's leading theoretical journal, *Kommunist:* "There is often little information, insufficient commentary in our newspapers and on radio to help understand current policies. In our time, when radio receivers are in almost every home, to ignore this or that event, to fail in pointing it out from the standpoint of socialist ideology means to give 'freedom of action' to the falsifications of bourgeois propagandists. . . . One must admit that bourgeois information agencies have achieved great efficiency, reacting quickly to everything occurring in the world, while we sometimes are late."[13]

The Soviet radio system had increased listener choice to some degree in 1946, when it added a second national service during the late afternoon and evening hours. It added a third service in 1947 (evening hours only), but it was not available to the entire country. But those changes added little that was new, since the second and third services simply increased the amount of "serious" material available: operas, concerts, plays, educational broadcasts. The content of the news did not change at all, and there was little growth in light programming.

Finally, in 1964, the Soviet listener got a real alternative. Mayak, or "beacon," came on the air with a twenty-four-hour-a-day schedule made up largely of brief newscasts and music, presented in a somewhat more relaxed fashion than was characteristic of the existing program service. Some of the transmissions were on frequencies used by foreign stations broadcasting to the USSR, and the late night programming furnished better competition for the foreign broadcasters, who before then had been able to take advantage of the fact that Soviet radio generally signed off at midnight.

Television had made its debut in the Soviet Union just before the war but was suspended during the conflict. It came back on the air a month or so after the end of the war in Europe, but it was many years before any substantial number of viewers had their own sets; by 1950 there were roughly twelve thousand of them. The main stations were in Moscow and Leningrad, but amateurs were constructing stations in Kharkov, Odessa, and Dniepepetrovsk, much as radio amateurs had done in expanding radio in the early to mid-1920s.[14] By 1960 there were just under 5 million, with television stations in most of the large cities, but they broadcast for only a few hours each day, and the republic stations took the bulk of their material from Moscow, translating it into the appropriate republic languages.[15]

In the early 1960s, Soviet Prime Minister Khruschev and his associates began to see television as one of the chief symbols of a more consumer-oriented policy, and encouraged its manufacture and sale, chiefly by making it possible for people to buy TV sets on the installment plan — then a rarity in the country. By 1964, the year when Khruschev was deposed by the Party leaders, there were nearly 13 million sets in Soviet households. Development of a second service in Moscow and other large cities, and third and fourth services in Moscow, continuation of installment plan purchase, the introduction of programming in color in 1967, and expansion of broadcast hours and relay transmitters, helped to bring about a doubling of that figure within the next four years.

Structurally speaking, there had been an administrative change of sorts in 1953, when the All-Union Radio Committee came under the direction of the Ministry of Culture, but that did not mark any fundamental alteration in the programming of radio and television. In 1957, the All-Union Radio Committee became the State Committee for Radio and Television Broadcasting and was made a department of the Council of Ministers (cabinet) itself. There have been some minor name changes since that time, but the basic organizational structure has remained intact.

HANDLING COMPETITION AND DIVERSITY—THE MID-1960S TO THE MID-1980S   The Soviet Union long had faced the problem of serving its rural areas. Many villages still had no electricity as of the 1950s and thus had no wired radio service. (It is possible to set up a wired radio exchange without having electrification, but at the very least that would require a power generator for the head end of the exchange.) Radio sets were becoming more and more common, and some villagers could afford them, but broadcast signals often were weak because there was no nearby relay transmitter. As for television, most villagers had heard of it by the early 1960s, but few of them had sets in their own homes, and if they had them, few were close enough to a TV relay (which has a much smaller radius than do long-, medium-, and shortwave radio transmitters) to pick up a signal.

Construction of more standard radio receivers, especially low-priced, battery-powered transistor models, increased markedly in the 1960s. Sometime around the middle of the decade, the numbers of standard sets finally exceeded the numbers of wired radio receivers, and by 1970 there were nearly 50 million standard sets in the USSR. However, there still was a good deal of emphasis on developing the wired exchanges, since they afforded villages the opportunity to include material of particular local interest. The Party Central Committee even passed a resolution in 1967 calling for the accelerated development of wired radio exchanges, especially in connection with the government's attempts to encourage settlement in Siberia, where in some areas only one out of every ten villages had exchanges.[16]

Television was a far more difficult matter, but Soviet technology found a solution in the development of an elliptical orbit satellite — one that would stay close to the ground over the Soviet Union, then go far out into space in a cigar-shaped orbit. The first test of such a satellite, dubbed the *Molniya* (lightning) series, was in 1965, and by 1967 there were seven of them in orbit, with ground receiving and relay stations at some twenty locations across the country. Many areas now began to receive television for the first time. The expansion continued in the 1970s, and in late 1975 the first geostationary orbital TV satellite, *Raduga* (rainbow) was launched.

This expansion of services helped lead to a real boom in the purchase of sets; by 1970 there were nearly 35 million of them in the country, and by 1974 over 50 million. But it also was becoming evident that many of those sets were not in use, not because of dissatisfaction with the programming (although that occurred often enough), but because the sets broke down so often. There were estimates that one in every three sets was nonfunctional at any one time. Part of the reason was poor quality standards, but part of it was also lack of competent repair personnel. Letters to newspapers began to recite tales of how set owners had to take sets to the shop (house calls almost always required a bribe of some sort, whether vodka or food) three or more times to get the same problem fixed. Some newspaper reporters even conducted their own investigations of the situation by removing a tube from a TV set in their home, taking it to a shop, and being told that the problem was very severe, would cost a lot to solve, and would take a lot of time, but perhaps not so much *if* the customer could help the process along with a small "contribution." Despite the complaints and articles, standards of production and repair have remained a problem to the present.

Broadcasts from outside the country continued to concern Party leaders and government officials, who issued frequent calls for "brighter" programs, more up-to-date news, and better standards of production. A 1967 article in *Komsomolskaya Pravda* contended that educational television was watched by very few students and had failed to identify who it should serve and how.[17] A survey conducted in Leningrad in that same year revealed that news broadcasts were among the lowest rated of all TV programs.[18] A survey in Sverdlovsk around 1970 yielded similar results. A Kazahkstan TV official offered some self-criticism in 1970: "We still have much work to do to deliver the air from dull, stereotyped broadcasts which offer little to the mind and heart, to get away from sketchiness, an illustrative nature, and a dry, informative nature, and to overcome relapses into superficiality, pomposity and declamatoriness."[19]

Improvements were slow in coming, but by the middle to late 1970s there were visible changes in the style of presentation of television news. In 1978, Soviet television added a twice-nightly news program, *Today in the World,* where the style of delivery was far less formal than on other news broadcasts, where a rotating staff of commentators had more than the usual freedom to comment on current events, and where there were live reports from overseas correspondents. The program may have been a response to remarks made by Soviet President Brezhnev in addressing the November 1978 plenary session of the Central Committee of the Communist party. Brezhnev stated that "it is high time to make reporting on international affairs prompt, more understandable and more concrete . . . not a repetition of the accepted truths but an in-depth and well-argued analysis of the facts of international life."[20]

The construction of a new television building in the late 1960s finally had made it possible for producers to mount ambitious productions in TV studios, but for the most part they were slow to take advantage of their state-of-the-art technology, and dramas, unless they were shot on location, often were stiff, featured artificial-looking settings, and were shot unimaginatively. The best writers saw little to interest them in television, preferring instead to write for film or the stage. Party and government criticisms rarely mentioned drama, and changes came more slowly, but dramatic production, too, has improved over the past several years, to the point where more prominent dramatists now are quite eager to write for TV.[21]

Choice, however, remains limited. The Muscovite has access to four or five TV channels (a UHF service began in 1984); other big-city dwellers have two or, for Leningrad, three TV channels; and rural areas may be within range of one TV signal. Anyone with a reasonably good radio set can pick up several radio stations within the country and more from outside it, especially if, as is often the case, the set can receive shortwave broadcasts. Most rural dwellers rely on the wired exchanges, which seldom carry more than one radio service. It has been a major accomplishment to supply that much broadcast service to such a huge and linguistically diversified country. Yet listeners and viewers, the latter in particular, would appreciate a greater choice. Videocassette recorders, which began to make their appearance in the early 1980s as more privileged Soviet citizens brought them back from their travels abroad, could offer a solution, but their domestic manufacture, which started in 1985, is not a high-priority item. However, video rental and sales shops are spreading quite rapidly in the largest cities. Cable TV is limited to master antenna installations to improve reception for apartments; access cable is unheard of. Television's rapid development during the 1960s and 1970s was in part a response to public demand for more and better service, but the government sees no real need, and some possible harm, in letting the medium expand to the multichannel dimensions that characterize much of Western Europe and North America.

Mikhail Gorbachev became prime minister of the USSR in early 1985. Within a few months, he began to challenge some of the practices of the Soviet media, for most of the same reasons voiced by his predecessors: dull, slow treatment of events. Unlike those predecessors, he used himself as a role model, encouraging television camera crews to cover his often informal, spontaneous behavior, and using radio and television to tell Soviet citizens that all of them had the duty to improve production methods, even if that meant challenging their supervisors. He conveyed that message in vivid terms, often visiting factories and farms and engaging workers and farmhands in discussions concerning what sorts of improvements were needed. It is still too early to tell whether Gorbachev has reformed Soviet broadcasting in any fundamental sense, but certainly it had become a great deal livelier by the late 1980s.

Financing

In comparison with other broadcast systems covered in this book, the Soviet system features a very simple mode of financing: The money is provided by the government. The State Committee for Television and

Radio Broadcasting prepares and proposes an annual budget, and the government decides how much it actually receives. Those figures are not made public, so Soviet viewers and listeners have no real sense of how much of their annual taxes go to support broadcasting.

There was a more direct form of contact between audience and broadcaster in the past. When Soviet broadcasting officially began in 1922, listeners were required to register their radio sets and pay a license fee on them; while the fee money went to the government, there was a general understanding that it helped to offset the expenses connected with broadcasting. Interestingly, not everyone paid the same fee: soldiers, sailors, those handicapped with war or work injuries, and students living on a fixed stipend all paid one ruble; workers, employees, military officers, and students not living on a fixed stipend paid three rubles, and other citizens paid ten. Clearly the government wanted to encourage listening by people with low incomes. In 1926 the government changed the fee structure to one based on type of set, although clubs, societies, groups, and periodical rooms in rural areas paid a reduced fee.[22]

When television became available to the general public just after World War II, the government assessed a separate license fee on owners of TV sets. That lasted until 1 January 1962, when license fees were abolished. At that time, license fees for radio were about three dollars per year and for TV twelve dollars. The fees did not begin to cover the costs of the services, especially television, and they were very difficult to collect in the thinly populated areas of the country. There also was some evasion of payment. The leading Soviet newspapers heralded the dropping of the fee as a "Gift to Ten Million," but some viewers wrote in to say that, given the poor quality of TV programming, it would be more accurate to describe the fee as a "Gift *from* Ten Million," since viewers were forced to give money to the government and got little in return.[23] The fees were replaced by an excise tax levied on each set at the time of purchase — much easier to collect and not easy to evade. Again, the government received the money and applied it toward the costs of providing broadcast services; the State Committee had no absolute rights to the tax proceeds. The excise tax still is in effect, but it produces uneven amounts of annual revenue, since there is fluctuation in numbers and types of sets sold each year.

Advertising was a part of early Soviet broadcasting, although apparently very few ads were carried. In 1935 the practice was forbidden and did not resume until 1947 (it seems to have been considered too capitalistic). Since that time, both Soviet radio and television have carried advertising, but not in any great quantity. Radio ads run between 7:00 and 9:00 A.M. and 5:00 and 8:00 P.M.; television ads appear in the morning on Channel One and in the evening on Channel Two, and are grouped together in clusters, so as to minimize interruption of the programs. There is no sponsorship of programs. Most ads are short and to the point, emphasizing clear and simple delineation of the product's qualities; psychological appeals of the "be more popular" or "stand out from the crowd" sort are rare.[24] Many of the ads are for food, drink, and clothing and often are used when an overstock of an item has developed. For example, if a factory making winter coats runs into production or shipping delays (quite frequent in the USSR), it and/or the stores selling the coats may place ads calling people's attention to their "unexpected availability." (They probably would sell quite well, since the tendency of most Soviet shoppers is to pick up an item they think they might eventually need, or that someone they know might need, because there might not be another chance for a while.)[25] The money generated by advertising may go to help offset the costs of broadcasting but certainly is not considered to be profit. Other sources of financial support do not amount to enough to be considered significant. Program sales abroad are rare; program exchanges are far more frequent.

Governance and Administration — Internal

It is a simple matter to describe the overall system of internal governance and administration in Soviet broadcasting. The State Committee for Television and Radio Broadcasting is in charge of governance and administration for the overall system, the head station in each republic has a republic committee, and there are similar committees for other stations. Ultimate power (internal) is in the hands of the State Committee, which does not concern itself overmuch with the operational details of the other stations. Its chairperson and other members are appointed by the cabinet; they may or may not have had experience with broadcasting, but they will be Party members of some standing. The republic committees are appointed in a similar manner by the republic cabinets and have similar backgrounds as well.

THE DECISION-MAKING STRUCTURE   Under the State Committee
and the republic committees is an organizational structure that divides activity into four main spheres — radio, TV, foreign broadcast-

ing, and material/technical — and subdivides programming into its general categories: news, children's, drama, and so on. Each main sphere has a head who is a vice-chairman of the committee and almost certainly a member of the Communist party. (The head of material/technical, since that sphere does not involve program content, might not belong to the Party). Heads of program divisions generally are Party members. There are frequent meetings within each program division to discuss program strategy and content, and heads of the divisions as well as others within them may be called upon to meet with the state or republic committee from time to time, but there is a fair amount of autonomy in day-to-day decision making. The fact that the top decision-making positions all are in the hands of the *nomenklatura,* or list of important positions to be filled by the Party, means that those decisions are in "safe" hands.

The basic rules are clearly understood, and division heads and others can ask for guidance and interpretation if they feel the need, but they also get to exercise considerable individual initiative. That initiative rarely extends to sensitive issues such as corruption by Party officials, major natural disasters, and human-made accidents, although Prime Minister Gorbachev's policy of *glasnost* (openness) has caused reporters and editors to be at least slightly quicker to publish articles on such issues. Slow Soviet media coverage of the nuclear plant explosion at Chernobyl in 1986 brought in its wake considerable criticism from high-ranking Party and government officials for giving Soviet citizens one more excuse to listen to western radio stations in order to be fully informed. That in turn caused Soviet media to treat the Chernobyl situation far more fully and frankly once they began to cover it (nearly three days after the explosion) than ordinarily had been the case with such events, where the tendency was to mention them briefly, if at all. Certainly *glasnost* has led television to cover events that it would have ignored in the past, such as the large and sometimes violent demonstrations in Armenia in late February 1988. However, as James Oberg has pointed out, there still is little tendency on the part of the Soviet media to cover most problems which seem to have no immediate solutions.[26]

The news departments are the most politically sensitive programming units, but here, too, there is some autonomy — more in the past few years because of increased emphasis on timeliness of news. There are daily editorial meetings, and disagreements surface regarding which stories should be carried and what they should contain. The official Soviet news agency, Tass, provides the bulk of the material for newscasts, but its items can be and are sometimes rewritten, and any station of any size has its own reporters who gather further items. Stations in the smaller republic and rural areas also may rely to some extent on "citizen reporters" for some of their items. Since there will be several newscasts each day on radio and on television in the larger cities, editors often cannot wait for guidance from above but must make their own decisions on the spur of the moment. Often those decisions are cautious—better to eliminate an item or to include the official version word-for-word than risk being wrong—but editors will take risks on occasion and sometimes arouse the wrath of local Party officials, especially when a story calls attention to foul-ups or corruption in management and the manager in question is a Party member of some standing. Still, there is a basic system of censorship that lies outside the broadcast services themselves, and editors rarely attempt to challenge it.

Although unions (e.g., of writers or journalists) exist within Soviet broadcasting, they do not constitute a separate and potentially opposing element in its operation, as they do in many western broadcast systems. They do not go out on strike; instead, they generally assume a cooperative role, looking for new and better ways to accomplish the goals of the system and "socializing" new union members in the ways of the organization.

Governance and Administration— External

GOVERNMENT AND PARTY   The major source of external influence over the governance and administration of Soviet broadcasting is the Communist party. Actually, since most of the middle- and high-level administrators of the broadcast system are Party members, it is difficult to separate "internal" and "external." But there are occasions when the Party clearly assumes an external role, particularly when its leaders criticize broadcasting. Occasionally the Party Central Committee or republic committee will meet with editors of newspapers and broadcast stations to discuss overall priorities, strategies, and approaches. And finally, as the Party is virtually synonymous with the government, any directive coming through the latter has the sanction of the former.

There are specific governmental departments that have a more continuous relationship with broadcasting. The most important of these is Glavlit, or the Chief Administration for the Protection of State Secrets in the Press. Such an agency had existed in czarist times and was revived by the Soviet government in 1922. During a period running from the 1930s to the 1950s, it exercised considerable direct power over broadcasting, in that it could and did judge the "acceptability" (to the government, and therefore the Party) of an enormously wide range of subjects: Military, political, economic, and cultural information all fell under its purview. Its chief duty was to see to it that no information potentially damaging to the country appeared in print or over radio, and its stamp of approval was required for most spoken and written material (which meant, of course, that spoken material had to be delivered from written texts, depriving radio broadcasts of spontaneity). In its period of greatest power, it sought to exercise authority over material that would be potentially damaging to personal morals as well.

Glavlit was not always a model of efficiency, despite the fact that it worked closely with the security police. Archives providing details on Glavlit's work were found by the German army when it captured Smolensk in World War II; the United States Army acquired them in Germany in 1945, and they have been the subject of a study by Merle Fainsod.[27] The records reveal an agency that sometimes was understaffed, had too few trained personnel, and lacked solid criteria for making judgments. It appears to have become better organized and more strict during the war and on up to the death of Stalin. Khruschev's 1956 criticism of some of the excesses of the Stalin years seemed to encourage newspaper and broadcast editors to be a bit more bold, especially after Khruschev and other Party leaders had criticized the media in the late 1950s and early 1960s for being too slow, incomplete, and dull. The agency continues to function, but the government's and Party's desire for more spontaneity in broadcasting have made it something of an anachronism for broadcasting; although there still are Glavlit personnel on duty at broadcast stations, their role in clearing acceptable material seems to have been circumscribed. They may say whether a TV newscast can show a picture of a new model of tank, but they are unlikely to tell a producer of TV drama that a certain scene is pornographic. Also, broadcast personnel themselves probably have accepted the ground rules laid down by Glavlit in past decades, so Glavlit staff would not have to apply them; self-censorship would have done the job.[28]

The Party has an organization similar to Glavlit. It was called Agit-Prop when it was developed in 1920, but since the mid-1960s it has had the less colorful title Department of Propaganda. Such a department exists in connection with the Party Central Committee and with the various republic Party committees, we well as with larger local Party committees. Each is subdivided into sectors responsible for the different media of communication. On the whole, the department plays a somewhat more positive role than does Glavlit; that is, more of its time is spent in trying to get certain messages placed in the media than in trying to keep them out. For example, it may attempt to get the television service of a republic in the Asian part of the USSR to carry more dramas, documentaries, and other programs about "modern" and "feudal" views of women in society (some of the Asian republics remain quite feudal in that respect). As television and radio programmers have to accommodate a wide variety of tastes and a large number of demands with limited amounts of money, talent, and air time, staff members of a department of propaganda may have to employ persuasion if they expect results. It is not enough to say, "The Party want/demands it," although that tactic is not unknown.

Given the nature of the practice, it is difficult to find precise documentation on censorship of the media in communist nations, but late in 1977 a Polish censor defected to Sweden, bringing with him several hundred pages of official documents on censorship. Many of the prohibitions were predictable, such as "no information written in an approving, tolerant, understanding tone about hippies in Poland may be published." Some others were amazing, such as "banned is all information about food poisoning and epidemics affecting larger groups of people."[29] The overall thrust of the prohibitions seemed to be to keep any potentially negative (that is, contradictory to the continued improvement of standards in a communist nation) information from the general public. By that token, plane crashes, train collisions, and ferry boat sinkings ordinarily would not be reported, and generally speaking they are not, although the aforementioned *glasnost* spirit is beginning to change things. The Polish system is not likely to differ very much from the Soviet system, and certainly there is a close resemblance between the categories of material not released to general audiences in the two countries. From what we know about the master list of categorical descriptions (known within the USSR as "the Talmud") of what is not to be published or broadcast, the systems in fact are very similar.[30]

The Ministry of Communications is responsible for allocating broadcast frequencies, but that power does not result in the friction that has resulted from conflicts between broadcasters and telecommunications ministries, post offices, and so on in many other countries. Military services have top call on frequencies, but broadcasting comes in a strong second, and denials of requests are rare. Legislative bodies at the various levels of government can and occasionally do debate aspects of broadcasting, and in theory could punish radio or television by cutting or threatening to cut a portion of the annual budget request, but the budget is an area in which the cabinet reigns supreme.

The Soviet legal system becomes involved with broadcasting in several ways, but little of that involvement has to do directly with the official broadcast system. There is no Fairness Doctrine in Soviet broadcast law; although any Soviet citizen can protest unfair broadcast treatment, no right of reply guarantees airtime for responses. There are laws on libel and slander, but it is not easy to invoke them against government-operated media. Most laws apply to the activities of listeners (it is illegal to pass on to others any information of an "anti-state nature") and to amateur radio operators (who must be licensed, and who cannot transmit "pornography").[31]

NONGOVERNMENTAL There are no formal structures permitting public involvement with broadcasting in the USSR. There are no broadcast councils, and no public organizations dealing specifically with broadcasting. Trade unions, youth groups, and other organizations may have "interest sections" that concern themselves with broadcasting, and they may bring pressure to bear on broadcasters to modify program content. But for the general public, the main avenues for expression of dissatisfaction are through Party officials, government officials, and letters to newspapers and to stations. From time to time, stations will encourage letter writing, and many stations offer regularly scheduled programs on which letters are read and reacted to. There are accusations that some of the letters are fabricated by stations so as to be able to appear responsive to public complaints, but the writing of letters of complaint to the mass media is a long-standing practice in the USSR, and the vast majority almost certainly are genuine. Most seem to be of the "why can't we have more (or less) of . . . ?" or "Why was _____ (program or individual) dropped?" There are between 1 and 2 million letters each year, of which only a very small number are read on the air, and of which the majority are requests for musical dedications, information, or announcements on behalf of some group or other. However, when there is a major event, such as the drafting of a new Soviet constitution in 1977, the Party urges the media to urge the public to write or telephone their reactions, and many letters are read on the air and printed.

Programming

PHILOSOPHIES   Various statements on the purpose of Soviet broadcasting indicate that it is to improve the condition of society by making its members aware of their obligations to others, of the need to remember the sacrifices of those who built and defended the Soviet Union, of the diversity and yet unity of the country, of the blessings of communism, of the overall equality of humankind (the classless society), and of the inevitable triumph of communism and just as inevitable decline of capitalism. That list of purposes does not include the need for relaxation after a hard day's work (in fact, Soviet sociologists find it very difficult to acknowledge the validity of the concept of entertainment as a mass media function and often go out of their way to describe it as something else—such as "relaxation"); the provision of information that will help someone cut through bureaucratic red tape; or the satisfying of people's desire to see and hear about morbid events (disasters and crimes). The initial list of purposes forms the backbone of the philosophy of Soviet broadcasting: Its purpose is to inform, enlighten, persuade, inspire, and guide proper behavior. But the provision of entertainment, consumer-oriented information and sensational material is a part of the broadcast schedule, too, and not all of it can be justified in the name of the Soviet broadcasting philosophy.

Like any philosophy of broadcasting, that of the Soviet Union has had to respond to realities, and two in particular: the availability of money and talent, and the ability of the audience to choose to listen and watch or not. In the early days of the system, a great deal of the programming was of the "purposeful" variety and was intended to carry out the lofty ideals just stated. But few would have been willing to listen to talks all day long, and developing more subtle means (dramas, comic skits, etc.) to express those ideals took both time and talent, not to mention money, so music became an early staple of the daily schedule. It was cheap, it was available, listeners liked it, and it could even help to illustrate the cultural diversity of the USSR, although listeners probably did not want to be lectured on that between every number. In the late 1930s, broadcasters decided to use the attractive value of music within a program that had news and features intermixed with it; thus, listeners lured by the promise of music might stick around to hear the talks and news. Increases in broadcasts to the USSR from outside the country, and seemingly popular broadcasts at that, caused Soviet broadcasters to respond with Mayak in 1964; it offered more music and less talk than Soviet listeners were accustomed to receiving, and it has become quite popular.

In short, what Soviet leaders say they would like the broadcast media to do and what the media actually do are somewhat different, at least in terms of emphasis. One can hear and see programs that illustrate one or more of the basic purposes just outlined every day of the week, and even every hour of the day, but they share the limelight with material that contains few if any "purposeful" elements and seems intended to cater to desires for relaxation, enjoyment, and satisfaction of curiosity. And it is the latter, so audience research data reveal, that attract listeners and viewers in substantial numbers, while the overtly purposeful broadcasts often draw very few and often are criticized by the audience, the press, and the Party for their dullness.

RADIO   Soviet radio functions at several levels, national, republic, district, local, and yet is subject to overall coordination by the State Committee on Television and Radio Broadcasting, which approves the schedules of all stations.[32] That coordination is made easier because stations below the national level take a share of their programming from Moscow Central. Some of that material is put on the air in its original language, Russian, because that is the national language and because many individuals throughout the country use it as their first language. Some of it is translated into local languages.

The situation in Taganrog, an industrial city in the southern part of the Russian Republic (RSFSR) with a population of somewhat over 250,000, is fairly typical of what a listener in a larger population center would have to choose from. If she or he has a good radio set, it will be possible to pick up three national services from Moscow, a service from the major regional (*oblast*) station in Rostov, and a city radio station in Taganrog itself. Other stations may be receivable but probably will be less clear. If the listener happens to work in one of the ten local factories that have in-plant radio services, that will add to the choice. On the other hand, if the listener is on the wired radio exchange, there is only one channel, which is the First Service from Moscow from 6:00 A.M. to midnight, with a two-hour-a-day interruption for the Rostov station and roughly two hours a week for the Taganrog station. Even the listener with a standard set will have less choice than it might seem, since the city station usually is on the air for just an hour a day, at 5:00 P.M. and the factory stations are confined to the factories themselves. Those stations, too, broadcast for an hour a day, at noon.[33]

As for the three national services from Moscow, Moscow 1 begins its broadcast day at 5:00 A.M. with a short newscast, press roundup (Soviet dailies) and calisthenics, then some light music. As the day progresses, there will be further newscasts and press roundups, as well as a great deal of music—folk, popular, classical. Special reports on activities of various groups (Young Pioneers, Komsomol) also are part of the schedule. There also will be educational programs intended for the use of primary and secondary schools. Toward the end of the afternoon, there will be a children's radio drama or after-school educational program, perhaps on the life of a famous writer such as Turgenev. Classical music takes up the supper hour and often is followed by a radio play, sometimes original, sometimes an adaptation of a classic (Lermontov, Jack London). Sports events sometimes are covered in the evening, and if there is a major chess match, there will be brief reports on its progress. Live transmission of theatrical productions and concerts also is fairly common in the evening. Sign-off is shortly after 1:00 A.M.

Moscow 2 (Mayak) is a twenty-four-hour-a-day service of music, news, and brief programs for and about certain groups (young people, soldiers, etc.), with music predominating. Much of the music is popular, and most of the selections are brief. Moscow 3 carries mostly classical music, educational programs for adults, and plays in its 7:00 A.M. to midnight schedule. There also is a Moscow 4, available only to listeners in the Moscow area; it specializes in classical music and broadcasts from 4:00 P.M. until midnight. Both Moscow 3 and Moscow 4 broadcast blocks of airtime in stereo.

The regional (*oblast*) and republic capital stations concentrate much more heavily on informational broadcasts; only about 20 to 25 percent of the broadcast day (variously ten to twenty hours, depending upon the size of the city and region) will be made up of music and other entertainment, and the music often has a particular local or regional character. A great deal of the informational programming is given over to material about agriculture and industry in the region and frequently includes radio portraits (a combination of interview and documentary) of model workers and citizens who have overfulfilled their production norms, helped out in old people's homes, and contributed in other ways to the betterment of society. (Whatever else they may be, the model citizens usually are not very comfortable in front of the microphone, and listeners sometimes get the impression that they are reading prepared responses to questions. However, that too is changing as *glasnost* takes hold, and Soviet broadcast reporters take to the streets to genuinely seek spontaneous expression of viewpoints.)

City and factory or collective farm radio stations broadcast little but information, although occasionally a local musical or other cultural group will get to perform on the air. Announcements of activities; orders; readings from the city, factory, or collective farm newspapers fill the hour or less that each of these stations in on the air each day (except weekends). Portable equipment and trained personnel may or may not be available to stations functioning at this level,[34] and on many of them most of the material is written out before being put on the air, then often read in a none-too-lively manner. This lack of spontaneity has drawn the criticism of Party and government officials and the listeners themselves but is a natural consequence not only of lack of equipment and trained personnel, but the need to check material over carefully and perhaps pass it by censors before it is broadcast.

Readings of material from newspapers probably are more common over Soviet radio than over any other radio system in the industrialized world. Lenin clearly saw this as one of radio's chief tasks in the early 1920s, when so many (well over half of the population) were illiterate and when newsprint was scarce. Whether it remains necessary in the USSR of the mid-1980s is another question, although it does provide listeners with the highlights of editorial opinion, which is the main thing many of them want from the papers: some indication of how to interpret the day's events. It also provides radio personnel with ready-made and approved broadcast copy.

Soviet radio makes considerable effort to act as a patron of the arts, and not only has its own orchestras and choruses (these exist not only at the national level, but also in the republic stations and in some of the larger city stations, such as Leningrad) but also commissions original musical works and radio plays. Stations frequently broadcast young people's, factory's, and collective farm orchestras and choruses as well and host music festivals centering around folk, jazz, and classical music. Young people also become directly involved in producing material for certain shows, such as the daily *Yunost* (Youth) program. And poetry, a major element in the country's culture, appears frequently on broadcast services at all levels.

Finally, radio stations at the various levels are expected to broadcast programs about (and sometimes from) the other "people's democracies" (the Eastern European countries plus Vietnam, Mongolia, North Korea, and Cuba), Third World nations, some of the other European nations, and other parts of the USSR. Music is the most common feature of such programs, but sometimes they cover the history of the country or people, talk about its landscape, or even provide weekly summaries of recent events there.

Because music forms such a major element in the various radio schedules, it is not surprising that music broadcasts draw a large share of the criticism that the stations receive.[35] Listeners may object to the broadcasting of jazz (now permitted over Soviet radio, although it was discouraged during Stalin's rule, and Khruschev claimed that it gave him "gas on the stomach") as too "jarring" or "decadent," but they also may complain about the large quantity of classical music, certainly far more prevalent over Soviet radio than over radio services in Western Europe or North America. They also may dislike the endless repetition of the same tunes in the many listener request shows; one Soviet sociologist explained the apparent reason: "As a rule the same works are presented over and over again in such concerts. This happens because over many years precisely these compositions become known to the broad circle of listeners, and naturally it is they that appear above all in listener's letters. The radio editorial board has the illusion in reading mail from listeners that they are able thus to determine listener's interests and requirements, although in reality they learn only from such letters which works they are actually playing most often in musical request programs, including on concerts composed of listener requests."[36]

In sum, there is a fair amount of variety on Soviet radio, but listener letters reveal a desire for considerably more, and surveys reveal a considerable amount of tuning to foreign stations—the BBC, VOA, Deutsche Welle, and Radio Liberty for news, those same stations and a number of the Polish, Hungarian, and Czech stations for greater variety in music, especially popular music.

Some listeners have taken matters into their own hands and have created their own stations. While amateur radio is legal in the Soviet Union, it must be licensed, and amateur operations are not to function as broadcast stations. Yet there may be a few hundred illegal amateur stations on the air at any one time, broadcasting material ranging from jazz to *samizdat* (self-published writings, usually critical of the Soviet government, and also illegal) to information on sexual assignations. Soviet law provides for fines and possibly jail terms for illegal broadcasters, which some of them have received after show trials designed to hold them up as bad examples, but which does not appear to have discouraged them. They usually operate on shortwave and over a limited radius and do not follow predictable schedules. They give themselves colorful titles, such as Lion, Dragon, or King, and usually are one-person operations. They present a sharp contrast to what is available over Soviet radio, especially in their informal style of presentation.[37]

TELEVISION Television functions under far more severe technical limitations than does radio. There is no way to transmit television signals over short- or longwave and thus compensate for the huge distances and sparse populations that characterize so much of the Soviet

Union. The advent of broadcast satellites in the mid-1960s had helped, but the satellite transmissions still have to be received by earth stations and then retransmitted. Because of this, there are large areas of the country that receive no television at all, and other areas that are served by passive relays so that there is no programming specific to their regions. The cost of television, too, has meant that many cities and towns that have their own radio services would not be permitted to set up their own television stations; that is a matter for the State Committee on Television and Radio Broadcasting to decide, although cities and towns can make requests for stations.

All of this has meant that television programming generally is far less local in character than is radio. There are about sixty television studio complexes in the Soviet Union as of 1987, all of them in republic capitals or, with a few rare exceptions, in cities with more than 100,000 people. Most of those operations originate their own programs for no more than a few hours a day, and many for an hour or less. Their main source of supply for the remainder of the schedule is Moscow. Several cities with populations in excess of 250,000 have no TV studios of their own.

Residents of the Moscow area are "television-rich" compared with most other Soviet cities, and even major centers such as Leningrad and Kiev have considerably less TV airtime: Most large cities have no more than two channels, but Leningrad has three. Moscow has four, although a fair share of broadcast time goes into repeating at different times and on different days some of the shows that originally appeared on other channels.

Channel One begins its broadcast day at 7:00 A.M. with a relatively informal, somewhat *Today*-like breakfast show containing news, interviews, weather, and some "soft" feature material, delivered quite informally from a living-room-like set. This show came on the air early in 1987, probably as part of the *glasnost* spirit; there never had been anything quite like it on Soviet TV. Much of the morning period is taken up with repeats, usually sports, films, and documentaries and a pause at about 11:15 A.M. after a brief newscast. Transmission resumes at 2:30 with a newscast, followed by a film or documentary, TV dramas (one-shot and serial), a newscast at 6:45 (*Today in the World*), concerts, ballets, operas, plays (many of them televised live or recorded at the theater or concert hall), documentaries and TV dramas, *Vremya* at 9:00 P.M., more concerts, drama or sports, and *Today in the World* at 10:55, with sign-off around 12:00. On a few days of the week there will be quiz shows and variety shows, the latter often featuring "People's Artists" who have been honored for their performing skills, whether music, acting, juggling, or some other form of artistry. Aside from feature films (some of them appearing on TV even as they are making their debuts in the cinema houses), few programs run as long as an hour, and many are thirty to forty minutes. There also are series on science and technology, ideology, and other specialized subjects, but often they are presented during the daytime and/or on weekends, when the Channel One schedule runs straight through from morning to night. Sign-off may not come until nearly midnight on Saturday, since Sunday is a day of leisure. Sports are on most nights, whether live transmissions of hockey, soccer, or some minor sport, or excerpts from sports events held earlier that day, for example, reports from championships in gymnastics being held in another country.

Channel Two's schedule bears a close resemblance to that of Channel One, with two major differences: the daytime break in the schedule does not come until 3:30 P.M., with broadcasts resuming at 6:00 with the news, and there is heavy emphasis on educational and instructional material, starting with gymnastics at 8:00 A.M. and continuing with material for adults and schoolchildren during the morning and early afternoon. Geography, government, foreign languages, Russian, botany, and many other subjects fill the screen, usually in thirty-minute blocks. Channel Three is for the Moscow area only, signs on at 7:00 P.M. and off at 11:15, and features news, sports, and information about local organizations and activities, plus occasional films and concerts. Channel 4, on the air from 4:00 P.M. until between 8:00 and 9:00 P.M., carries repeats of some of the educational programs, occasional feature films, and features about scientists, military leaders, cosmonauts, and so on, as well as model workers, farmers, schoolchildren, and others whose good examples should be an inspiration to all. The UHF channel (33) does little but repeat programming carried on the other channels.

The schedule is so arranged that, most of the time, a viewer will have a considerable range of choice, although *Vremya* is simulcast over the first three channels. Soviet TV used to be criticized for stacking the schedule in such a way that viewers had little choice among types of programs, but now there is far more diversity at any one time. For example, on 2 October 1984 a Muscovite tuning in a 7:00 P.M. would have had a choice between a documentary (*Terrorism USA*) on Channel One, a championship soccer match (*Dynamo vs. Torpedo*) on Channel Two, news and features about the Moscow area on Channel Three, and the tail end of a program about the great Russian novelist Pushkin, followed by *Health* on Channel Four. Most of the channels — Channel Three is the one exception — go to longer schedules on Saturday, increasing the range of choice to more times of the day. Channels One and Two also have longer schedules on Sunday, but Channel Four is off the air then.

There is heavy use of film in the schedule. Feature movies appear on one or more of the channels each afternoon and/or evening and range all the way from silent film classics to the latest releases. Soviet cinema attendance has dropped sharply as TV viewing has become more wide-spread, and managers of cinemas sometimes have protested that they cannot very well be expected to show strong attendance figures when television makes some of the latest movies available to their viewers. Apparently the government feels that the attractive value of the movies (which may be preceded or followed, or sometimes interrupted, by po-litical, economic, or social material) outweighs concerns about cinema attendance. Well over half of the movies shown are Soviet made, but many come from the Eastern European countries, some from Third World nations, and a few from the West. Many of the films are heavy on "prosocial" content—the sacrifices made by peasants, factory workers, military personnel, and so on to help build socialism and to oppose its enemies, but some are relatively profound studies of human nature, and there are not always happy endings.

The regular schedule frequently is interrupted by the telecasting of special events—major political addresses, the visits of important foreign dignitaries, and above all anniversaries of everything from the 1917 rev-olution to the births and deaths of distinguished leaders, but perhaps more than anything else the important events of World War II. The mass media in general, and television in particular, commemorate those events not only because the Great Patriotic War, as it is called in the USSR, was such a unifying experience for the nation, but also because it reinforces the message of the need for eternal vigilance and the sacrifices which that requires of the people. That commemoration appears in feature films, newscast items, commentaries, special interviews, quiz shows, children's programs, and just about every other program genre. A very popular program called *With All My Heart,* which bears a strong resemblance to U.S. shows of the *This is Your Life* variety, sometimes has reunions of World War II comrades who were separated in battle, lost track of each other, and may even have believed each other dead. Russians are very sentimental people, and such episodes move them on purely human grounds but also serve to highlight such values as loyalty to and sacrifice for others.

Still, while those values and others may be highlighted in most pro-gram genres, there are many hours of entertainment on Soviet television. Quiz shows, some of them featuring audience participation, contain a certain number of simple (and simple-minded) questions, just as quiz shows do all over the world. Satires often poke fun at bureaucratic red tape. Variety shows feature some of the best entertainers available, and singers are more apt to offer such time-honored favorites as *Moscow Nights* than they are odes of praise to Lenin, Marx, or (in a show at the time of a mid-1970s Communist party Congress), *My [Communist] Party Card!* Shows about nature and geography usually avoid heavy social and political issues and are very well shot and narrated.[38] And some of the messages are woven into programs very subtly, as in the long-lived series *Let's Go, Girls,* which features weekly competitions among women engaged in specific occupations, for example, hairdressers. The participants show their skills in a variety of ways but also talk about why they have chosen their line of work and what they like (and occasionally dislike) about it. That reinforces the value of the dignity of labor and the importance of everyone's contribution to society, but the message usually comes out quite naturally and takes up little airtime. Most sports shows are light on the political angle, too, although sometimes athletes are interviewed in such a way that they will be likely to say how much they owe to Soviet society for allowing them to excel.

Using humor to convey certain prosocial messages is not all that common on Soviet TV, but in recent years the Drama Department has come up with a few shows that do. One, *Apartment for Rent,* portrays everyday life in a Moscow apartment block (most Muscovites live in apartments), with plenty of emphasis on the need for mutual consideration (Soviet teenagers like their music as loud as do their counterparts elsewhere, and older people frequently complain about the racket), for the restraint of pets, and for cooperation in keeping the building clean. There also are jabs at the governmental bureaucracy for being slow to repair leaking roofs and dripping faucets and for being frequently unresponsive to people's complaints. The series has proven effective enough to cause the bureaucracy to protest to the Drama Department that it is adding to officials' workloads.[39]

Certain material rarely if ever appears on Soviet television. Criticism of communism itself is out of the question, and the Party as an institution is above reproach. If Party officials make serious mistakes or commit crimes, they may be covered on TV and may even confess their crimes and make their apologies on television, although such appearances are far more apt to feature dissidents.[40] Major officials almost certainly will not be placed on "TV trial"; instead, if they have been demoted or dropped from the Party, they simply disappear from view, become "nonpersons," and spend the rest of their days in obscurity. That also had been the fate of most of the historically important Soviet officials who had fallen out of favor, but starting in 1987 some of them,

such as Bukharin and Khruschev, began to be mentioned. The drama-
tized portrayal of Khruschev in the TV play *Risk* (fall of 1987) generally
was favorable in showing him as a "man of action" during the 1962
Cuban missile crisis.

Disasters, especially those caused (or even *possibly* caused) by human error, generally are reported only when they are so prominent that it
would be almost impossible to hide them, as was the case with the crash
of a Soviet plane at the Paris Air Show in 1973. Stories of more routine
disasters—auto accidents, fires, and so on—that are so prominent on
U.S. television simply do not appear on Soviet TV, and reports of
criminal acts are almost as rare. When the latter do appear, generally
they are presented as stories with beginnings, middles, and ends: Viewers
learn of how the criminal got started down the wrong road, what she or
he did, and how the trial came out; thus, the communist system of
justice is shown to have worked. Only in rare instances of really dangerous criminals will unsolved crimes be reported, as was the case in the
Moscow area a few years ago when a rapist-murderer was at large and
panic was rising.

Occasionally TV has televised criminal trials,[41] but for their educational value, and not to cater to any public taste for sensationalism. A
few surveys have revealed that viewers would like to see more reporting
of "sensational" events, and it is doubtful that they want this for educational purposes, but it remains a rarity. Sexual display rarely goes beyond slightly low-cut gowns, unless it is absolutely essential to a
drama—and that is a rare exception. Violence also is limited to what
appears to be dramatically essential, although it may appear in news and
other informational programs to portray antigovernment demonstrations in the capitalist world (and may be taken directly from capitalist
TV services).

Quality of production in Soviet television varies a great deal but in
general has improved markedly over the past decade or so. Up until the
early 1970s, most of the camera work was unimaginative and the staging
rather flat. In the early days of TV, most of the dramas, operas, ballets,
and other spectacles were shot in their own locales, and with relatively
little use of close-up shots; when dramas were produced in TV studios,
they sometimes featured a proscenium arch, so as to give the feeling of
being in a real theater. Now the shooting is far more typical of what
viewers in Western Europe, North America, and Japan are used to,
whether the productions take place in or out of the studio. Lighter material, such as quiz shows and satire or comedy (but there is nothing
resembling U.S. situation comedy), feature a more leisurely pace of editing than is customary in Western Europe, North America, and Japan.

Newsreaders, too, have become more relaxed, although not to the level of the chatty approach taken by many U.S. newscasters, and partly thanks to satellites, film clips and on-the-scene reports are far more common. Up until the Gorbachev era, interviews usually had been very sober affairs, especially when a high government official was being interviewed, but Foreign Minister Andrei Gromyko took the unusual step of allowing himself to be interviewed by a team of news reporters upon his return to Moscow from talks with U.S. secretary of state George Schultz in early January 1985. Later in 1985, as Gorbachev assumed leadership, Soviet viewers began to see a very different sort of political leader on TV—one who displayed and even encouraged spontaneity. (As I sat in the office of one of the vice-chairmen of the State Committee in September 1985 and watched the relay of a transmission from Siberia showing Gorbachev making spontaneous comments, mixing with the crowd, encouraging others to be frank and open, the vice-chairman told me, "I think your Mr. Reagan has met his match!")[42] Not all high-ranking Soviet officials have followed Gorbachev's lead, but clearly he hopes that more will, and he frequently appears in newscast items as the questioner, the challenger, seeking more direct involvement by officials and the broader population alike.

Viewers from Western Europe, Japan, or North America who watch Soviet television will find the newscasts on Soviet television very different from what they see in their own systems. Material about the Soviet Union takes up about two-thirds of each edition of *Vremya* and about half of *Today in the World*. That material almost invariably will feature the activities and statements of Soviet leaders, will include at least one item about increases in factory or collective farm production, and will be filled out with other positive items about the USSR and its various republics. There will probably be an item or two about some model citizen. There also may be one or two items on such social problems as industrial pollution, alcoholism, or drug abuse (the two latter issues have been brought to the fore in the Gorbachev era), but often the problem will be presented so as to show that someone either has a solution to it or is working on one. Soviet TV rarely leaves its viewers in suspense, at least regarding events and situations within the country. The foreign news items often include positive stories about the country's allies and about the developing (Third World) nations and almost always feature problems in the capitalist world: strikes, inflation, unemployment, crime waves, racial prejudice.[43]

Whether items are fresh or a few days old does not seem to matter, so long as they illustrate some important point. Items even may be held back for a few days so that their disclosure will coincide with the occurrence of a predictable event, for example, the release of an item on a defector from the North Atlantic Treaty Organization (NATO) on the day NATO begins its annual conference. Soviet journalism operates under different standards than does western journalism, by and large—standards that place a higher premium on the ideological value of information as illustrations of such tenets as the progressive nature of socialism/communism and the decline of capitalism. Not that western journalism is not ideologically based, but Soviet journalism entails a more conscious process of displaying ideology.

That extends to some entertainment programs, as well: In the course of my September 1985 visit to Moscow I saw a delightfully produced animated program (paper cutouts) for children which illustrated a poem by Marshak entitled *Mr. Twister.* It showed a rich American turning away a hungry black man, then, for whatever reason, deciding to travel abroad with his family (wife, daughter, daughter's pet monkey) *and* his car (the "Twistermobile") to Leningrad. He checks into an elegant hotel, only to discover that there is a black guest, which causes him to depart immediately. But the hotel clerk telephones other clerks and tells them about this prejudiced American who probably will come to their hotels, with the result that all of the hotels in Leningrad sprout "no vacancy" signs and the Twister family spends the night on park benches, then leaves the country the next day. The one thing that the program does not point out is that Marshak's poem was written in the late 1920s, yet much of the production gives the impression that this is a slice of contemporary America.

Regional capital and other large-city television stations take far more from Moscow than they send to it. Currently, many of them receive two services, via land line or satellite, but it is a mixture of programming from the various Moscow channels, with the exception of Channel Three. Current plans call for the transmission of two services to the entire nation by the early 1990s. But stations outside Moscow also contribute to the central operation, and several productions each week come from Kiev, Leningrad, Tashkent, Alma-Ata, and other centers, which also provide items for *Vremya* and *Today in the World.* There are series on Soviet TV each week that feature life in different parts of the country, for example, *Atlas of the Soviet Peoples.* A Soviet sociologist conducting an ethnosociological study in Moldavia in the late 1970s estimated that about 5 percent of Moldavian TV's First Program was devoted to such programs.[44]

There is also some use of regional TV to instill more "modern" values in "traditional" societies. That is seen as particularly important in the predominantly Moslem republics of central Asia, where religious customs, holidays, and practices still play important roles in many people's daily lives. Television and the other mass media have been used to replace (or to attempt to replace) religious holidays and observances with secular ones, such as Shepherd's Day.[45] In republics with a strong Russian Orthodox tradition, TV sometimes has been used to show viewers how such events as weddings should be treated. The problem here was that weddings handled by the local government (which is the way things should be done under communism) were so cheerless, bureaucratic, and even rude that many people, believers and unbelievers alike, wanted the dignity and splendor of a church wedding. By watching "proper" weddings on TV, bureaucrats might understand that they could do considerably more to give weddings meaning and beauty, and viewers in general might be more inclined to use them.[46]

There is some scattered evidence to indicate that listeners and viewers may not find much that is truly local or regional in local and regional broadcasts.[47] A few of the regional TV services take special pains to produce high-quality programming because they have some outside competition. Parts of the Ukrainian Republic adjoin Poland, much of Estonia is within reach of Finnish television, and Moldavia borders Rumania. In all three cases, some (and for Estonia nearly all) viewers can understand the other languages, and especially in the case of Estonia-Finland, will see television fare that differs from much of Soviet TV. Producers in those republics have tried to present material in a livelier style and to emphasize regional events and culture in ways that avoid the sometimes stereotypical approach of the national services. Estonian TV even developed a monthly program in the late 1960s in which government officials were confronted with questions called in by viewers, some of them quite embarrassing.[48] Polish TV had a similar program in the 1970s, but nothing like it appeared on national television in the USSR until a year of so after Gorbachev's rise to power.

The Audience

For the past several decades, most western broadcast systems have utilized survey research to assess the size, composition, and preferences of the audience; a few have been doing so since the mid-1930s. Soviet assessments have developed along somewhat different lines. For one thing, the "of the people, by the people, for the people" aspect of communism seemed to retard the development of survey-based audience research, not only in broadcasting, but in most other fields; there was little

felt need to assess audiences, since those in charge of broadcasting naturally would have the best interests of the public in mind (and often
thought themselves to be in a better position to judge what those interests should be than was the public itself). For another, Stalin and his
closest followers had little love for sociological research, perhaps because they found it too heavily influenced by bourgeois (meaning western) though and practices, perhaps because they were so autocratic that
they saw little value in asking the public's opinion on anything. At any
rate, after some promising beginnings on the development of Marxist-
Leninist-based sociological research methods in the 1920s, such research
came to an almost total halt by the early 1930s and did not resurface
until the late 1950s, following Khruschev's 1956 denunciation of many of
Stalin's more brutal and restrictive practices.[49]

Soviet broadcasters did encourage listeners to write letters, and to
this day letters are regarded as an important element in assessing audience reactions. There is nothing very systematic about that encouragement, however, and therefore no way for broadcasters to conduct analyses of trends in viewing or listening. Also, there is no way for
broadcasters to determine how representative such letters and their writers are of the more general public. So, although the 1 to 2 million letters
sent to Soviet radio and TV stations each year are subjected to more
careful analysis than they would be in most western countries, they do
leave large gaps in the overall picture.

By the late 1950s, it was clear to Soviet broadcasters that they
needed to know more about their audiences, yet even then broadcasters
seemed reluctant to establish units to conduct the necessary research. It
was obvious that western broadcasters were reaching a fair share of the
audience (precisely how much was unknown, due to the lack of survey
research), and anecdotal evidence indicated that Radio Liberty, the BBC,
and the VOA were enjoying some credibility. Yet the first survey-based
studies of the broadcast audience did not come along until the early
1960s, and even then radio and television were a small part of a larger
area of inquiry. These "time budget" surveys (how do people spend their
leisure time?)[50] almost always looked at the leisure time pursuits of urban dwellers, either en masse or as some specific occupational category
and almost never looked at the satisfaction or dissatisfaction the audience might express about programming in general or in particular. The
first few surveys showed people spending far more time with radio than
with television—not surprising, since there were not as yet all that many
TV sets in the country—but surveys taken in the late 1960s showed TV
pulling ahead of radio by a substantial margin and in fact outstripping
all other leisure-time activities. For example, a 1968–69 survey of sec-

ondary school students conducted in several cities of the Russian Republic showed that boys spent an average of 4½ hours a week viewing TV and 1¾ listening to radio, while girls averaged 5⅓ hours a week with TV and a little over an hour with radio. Television viewing topped all other leisure-time activities.[51]

Most surveys in the 1960s were conducted by sociologists from the major Soviet universities (Moscow State, Leningrad, Kiev); Soviet broadcasters took some interest in the results but rarely conducted their own survey research. However, the State Committee for Television and Radio Broadcasting carried out a major survey in 1968, with a sample size of over five thousand and at thirty locations, urban and rural, throughout the country. Furthermore, the major object of inquiry appears to have been degrees of satisfaction with various media presentations of various types of material. Newspapers were favored for foreign news, followed by radio and then TV, but there was widespread dissatisfaction with the amount of foreign news on radio and television (although collective farmers by and large felt there was enough). Broadcast media interpretation and comment on international affairs also got fairly low marks for amount and for credibility (collective farmers, Communist party members, and government workers gave the broadcast media higher marks than did other occupational and social groups.)[52]

But the most sensational survey from the 1960s was a detailed study of audience preferences for TV programs in Leningrad, conducted by University of Leningrad sociologist Boris Firsov in 1967.[53] Sample size was nearly two thousand, all of those surveyed lived and worked in Leningrad, there were roughly equal numbers of each sex, and there was representation of different educational levels. About 85 percent of them had TV sets (unusually high for the Soviet Union at that time, but Leningrad viewers already had access to three TV channels, and the city is prosperous by Soviet standards). Nearly 40 percent of those who had sets said that TV lived up to their expectations, but nearly 40 percent said that they felt "some disillusionment" with the medium, while slightly over 20 percent found it "hard to say" how they felt. When it came to specific program preferences, over 80 percent said they liked TV's coverage of sports and TV quiz shows and contests, just over 70 percent said they liked light music concerts and variety shows, about 66 percent felt that way about movies, and about 60 percent liked TV plays and broadcasts for young people.

Educational programs and broadcasts on sociopolitical themes got "hard to judge–rarely watch" responses from over half of those surveyed, and serious music and opera pulled just under 50 percent in that category. Twenty-five percent of those sampled said that they did not like serious music and opera broadcasts. Only one program type turned out to have a higher dissatisfaction figure, but it was an extremely important category: news and current affairs, where 27 percent said they did not like such broadcasts. In another section of the survey, Firsov asked viewers what it was that they found most inadequate in television information broadcasts; although about a third of the respondents said that they had no specific complaints, a fourth of them answered that they rarely watched such broadcasts (Firsov did not ask why), and just under a fifth criticized them for lack of candor and for poor on-the-spot reporting of events. A smaller-scale survey done in Sverdlovsk in 1971 showed much the same results, as did a study of rural viewers undertaken at about the same time, although the latter showed even less interest in watching informational broadcasts. They appeared to regard TV almost exclusively as an entertainment medium.[54]

In 1969, Soviet sociologist L. Kogan summarized various studies of television audiences and concluded that people tended to look to the medium for general information and for entertainment. He intimated that those in charge of TV should not expect to use the medium as a transmission belt for heavy, detailed propaganda.[55] When I visited Moscow State University's faculty of Journalism in 1970, one researcher told me that broadcasters and government officials alike were quite concerned over the various indications of public disinterest in or dissatisfaction with TV news but seemed at a loss to know what to do about it. His proposal for a study of psychological characteristics of audiences in terms of their preferences for different types of news and modes of presentation met with little response, probably because it was considered too "radical."

Further studies undertaken during the 1970s have tended to reinforce those earlier conclusions, but also have shown that Party workers and government officials had high levels of interest in the news and its interpretation.[56] A Leningrad study conducted by Firsov et al. in 1978–79, sample size thirteen hundred, showed that some 10 percent of those surveyed now had a second set, that 40 percent claimed to watch more than fifteen hours a week (a high total, given the limited amount of time that TV channels were in service), and that Party workers and social activists had a high interest in TV coverage of social and political information.[57] However, a 1979 Firsov study in Leningrad, sample size eight hundred, sought to discover whether people thought that newspapers, radio, and TV should be more active in "expressing public opinion," "informing people on work done by governmental bodies," and so on. Depending upon the specific question, between 35 percent and 53 percent of the sample thought that newspapers and radio should become more active along those lines, but the figures for TV ranged between 12 and 18 percent.[58] That seems to confirm Kogan's earlier suspicion that most viewers do not look to TV as a major source of detailed information, although it is impossible to tell from the survey data whether that is because they get plenty of it from other media, whether TV does a poor job of presenting detailed information, whether people crave relaxation so much that they resent anything that takes time away from it, or some combination of these elements.

Despite the negative findings, it is clear that Soviet citizens like a lot of what they see on television. Set sales continue to increase (and, as Firsov's 1978–79 studies show, two-set households are becoming fairly numerous) and more recent time-budget studies (Zuzanek, Mickiewicz) show average amounts of viewing time increasing. Those are average figures, and some of the studies reveal that better-educated individuals spend considerably less time (as much as a third less) watching than do others.[59] The older people are, the more they tend to watch, and men spend more time with TV than do women (probably a function of the dual role of so many Soviet women, who very often have full time jobs *and* are expected to "keep house").

There is a great deal more that one would like to know about what Soviet listeners and viewers think of broadcasting, but survey results, especially those resulting from studies undertaken by the broadcasters themselves, rarely are made public. (Most of the major republic stations by now have their own research departments and carry out a major project at least once a year, usually in door-to-door surveys.) University studies are becoming quite numerous, and some of them are reported in Soviet journals, though not always in enough detail to answer important methodological questions. But most of the studies seem to be very general, very "safe," or both. Time-budget surveys still are common and have the virtue of being as politically nonsensitive as anything can be in the Soviet Union. Very few studies follow the paths that Firsov and his associates have blazed. Firsov himself stated in a 1971 conference on public opinion and mass communication that "it would be a narrow view to consider the process of mass communication only and exclusively as a flow of information aimed at influencing the public. In the conditions of a developed socialist society the subjective side of the process is no less important: the contents of mass communication must reflect the desires, interests, opinions, etc. of the public."[60]

However, there have been few studies of audience interests, desires, and opinions. Such qualitative studies as there have been indicate pretty widespread dissatisfaction with a lot of the informational programming on Soviet TV, and Soviet broadcasters seem to accept their results as

valid. Yet there are almost no research projects employing in-depth interviews to get at more specific causes of dissatisfaction or indifference, and
almost none that test the effects of varying styles of presentation on
comprehension of programs, audience satisfaction, and other subjective
factors.

Such studies would not be out of order in Soviet society, and people
probably would respond to penetrating and critical questions quite hon-
estly, although Soviet citizens are far less accustomed to being asked
such questions by survey researchers than are Americans. As I have
already noted, there is a long-standing tradition of writing critical letters
to the media and about the media, so survey questions along the same
lines probably would not be regarded with that much suspicion, at least
by residents of the European part of the USSR. (Surveys seldom are
conducted in the Central Asian republics.)

But there still appears to be a "we know best" attitude among many
broadcasters, as there is the world over, and when that attitude is coupled with the overall "from the top down" pattern of decision making in
Soviet society in general, that does not produce an optimal climate for
meaningful and influential survey research. The *glasnost* spirit may produce changes in that climate, and in fact there were moves in the direction of learning more about audiences desires shortly before Gorbachev.[61] The State Committee for Television and Radio Broadcasting
established a full-fledged research department for broadcasting in 1984,
and the head of the department, V. P. Volkov, told me in a 1985 interview in Moscow that the department's work was receiving serious attention, both at the top of the State Committee and within the production
departments.

The real breakthrough in establishing respectability, according to
Volkov, came when the producers of a series called *Youth and the World*
realized through survey data that their program was very little watched
by its target audience: teenagers. At first the producers refused to accept
the data as valid but eventually came around and finally asked the research department to try to discover why their program was not popular.
The department's in-depth interviews showed that teenagers did not like
the "pat" interviews that characterized the program: The Soviet and
foreign interviewees seemed to be responding to formulaic questions
with formulaic answers, most of them heavy on ideology. Teenagers
wanted to know more about the everyday lives of the interviewees and
wanted to see them speak in "natural" language and in "natural" settings.
The producers made such changes and soon saw their target group ratings double and even triple. Other producers realized the value of carefully conducted surveys, and the department's workload increased to the

point where it had to schedule some surveys a year or more in the future. According to Volkov, it helped a great deal that the State Committee itself took the department's work seriously and made it clear that it expected producers to do so as well.[62]

Problem Areas

There is so much about Soviet broadcasting that is not made public that it becomes difficult to discern problem areas. In line with the overall Soviet philosophy of concentrating attention on positive aspects of Soviet society, broadcasting is not subjected to continuing critical evaluation. However, Party and government officials have made critical comments from time to time, newspaper reporters occasionally have written articles about the shortcomings of broadcasting, and newspapers as well as radio and TV have carried extracts from audience letters, some of which have featured very sharp criticism.

Probably the most often cited problem has been technical: Television sets break down too easily, and repairs are hard to arrange and often are unsatisfactory. Following that would be the issue of program choice, although viewers in Moscow and Leningrad have less to complain about on that score than do the millions of people living in rural areas and small towns (or even some fairly large cities), where there is still only one TV channel available. Even where two or more channels are available, viewers sometimes complain that there is no real choice between them, because both may be carrying the same sort of program at the same time. That particular problem appears to be less common now; schedules seem to be arranged so as to give more real choices during the same time period.

Dissatisfaction with program content probably is common enough, but there is less direct evidence on it. Audience letters on the subject do appear in newspapers and on the air, and occasional surveys refer to it as well. Certainly the sorts of surveys that ask people to express their program preferences show that a fair share of informational programs, which take up a good deal of airtime, do not appear to be appreciated by the vast majority of viewers. But those surveys do not tell us why they are not appreciated; what we know along those lines comes out of some of the letters and also is reflected in Party and governmental criticism of the broadcast media. From those comments, we gather that informational broadcasting often is seen as slow, incomplete, predictable, and dull.

As surveys from the early to mid-1980s begin to appear in Soviet journals (it usually takes two to four years for that to happen), there may be indications that informational broadcasts are reaching larger and less critical audiences. It wasn't until the late 1970s that major steps were taken to improve the quality of TV news, and a few years would have to pass before viewers would acknowledge that a real, lasting change had taken place. But some of the things that have bored the letter-writing public may be so much a part of the Soviet philosophy of broadcasting that no amount of change in presentational techniques will redeem them. One particularly prominent example of this is the model person, whether factory worker, soldier, teacher, farmer, student, or whatever else. Such figures appear over radio and television daily, most often in news items, but also in documentaries, features, interview shows, and even, as in *Let's Go, Girls!,* in game shows. They also crop up in feature films. Part of what makes their appearances boring is the very predictability of those appearances. I have known Soviet viewers to say, when watching a newscast, "It's about time for another hero to appear," and usually they are right. The "model," or hero, hardly is a Soviet invention — Russian Empress Catherine the Great issued a directive outlining a "positive hero's traits" more than two centuries ago and advocated that writers include them in their works[63] — but they are seen by Soviet authorities as especially important in reinforcing the concept of "the new Soviet man." Often, however, they are simply too good, smart, and strong to be true to life; often, too, when actual Soviet citizens are the "heroes," they sound as if they are reading lines for the interviewer, which probably has been the case on some occasions.

Yet another example of predictable, boring material is the tendency of news and other informational broadcasts to illustrate the progressive nature of socialism by showing activity on a collective farm or factory while reciting highly detailed figures on the latest reported increase in industrial or agricultural output. Viewers sometimes point out that TV uses stock footage for some of the farm and factory scenes, even when it is a matter of increases in a specific factory's or farm's output, and viewers and listeners alike find it difficult to grasp the significance of the specific percentages and other numbers that come pouring out of the loudspeaker. The predictability of the appearance of such items on newscasts matches that of items on heroes: Viewers and listeners know just about when to expect them and what they will say and show. What's worse is that viewers compare the conditions under which some model worker has fulfilled her or his quota with their own working conditions, as did a worker interviewed for a *Pravda* article in 1982: "Often when taping a program about 'model' workers the producer doesn't show that production is the hard work of many different workers. When you watch the film you hear the announcer telling about records, percentage of growth, but on the screen the workers are smiling and doing something easy. In that way we get an incorrect idea of the price of a record and the work that goes into it. When talking about socialist competition one has to look at work conditions, is there enough equipment."[64]

Soviet broadcasting will continue to feature "hero" and "progress" items, despite any indications of audience lack of interest, because they are so basic to communist philosophy. What is surprising about this is that there is so little apparent attempt to make the items fresher, livelier, and less predictable. It may be a matter of those in the highest level of authority not really understanding such a need, and those lower in command understanding it but not daring to take corrective measures. Most broadcast systems are slow to change their basic modes of presentation, and the Soviet system is no exception to the rule. Certain departments, the Youth Department in particular, are making some breaks with that tradition; the Youth Department series *Twelfth Floor* (the department's location), a live studio show that encourages young people to pose sharp questions to administrators and other in power, is quite bold by the standards of Soviet TV. However, maintaining the interest of younger viewers is a top priority for Soviet TV—there are concerns that those viewers will be indifferent to the medium because they do not see it as terribly relevant to their own lives—so experimentation may be more acceptable in this area.[65]

Yet another problem may be basic comprehension of broadcasts. Soviet reporters and writers, much like their counterparts in most broadcast systems, have a tendency to write and speak in terms that *they* understand. When there is a long-standing tradition of discouraging the rewriting of political statements (most of which sound terribly formal), the results may leave some audience members wondering just what the message was. Soviet surveys reported by Mickiewicz seem to indicate as much:

> In the Taganrog survey, respondents were asked to define fifty words commonly used in newspaper articles in foreign affairs. About a quarter of the respondents had absolutely no understanding of the word "colonialism" and about two fifths had no understanding of "dictatorship." Almost half were unable to say what "imperialism" meant. . . . In a survey on television programs, 93 per cent of the rural Russians with up to a fourth grade education could not understand programs on socio-political topics. . . . Nonetheless, even though lack of audience comprehension was more widespread than had been expected, Soviet theorists still widely held that this differentiation, attributable to lack of formal education, would not be permanent.[66]

Foreign Influences on Programming

Aside from recorded music, Soviet radio uses very little imported program material. Soviet television, on the other hand, makes rather heavy use of broadcasts originating in other countries, especially those from the socialist nations of Eastern Europe. Some of the programs are prepared especially for Soviet TV by East German, Hungarian, and other broadcast systems, but more come in the form of news items and sports coverage exchanged through the Intervision system. It is a rare night when at least one such news item does not appear on *Vremya* or *Today in the World,* and a rare week when there aren't two or three sports events (usually highlights, but sometimes complete coverage) from East Berlin, Warsaw, Sofia, or elsewhere in Eastern Europe, usually received through the Eastern European Intervision TV Exchange system. Feature films from those same nations often appear on Soviet TV, as well.

Broadcast systems in the Third World (developing nations) occasionally place material with Soviet television, although such material is most apt to be feature films, which may or may not have been made for TV in the first place. When news items originate in such countries, usually they are produced by Soviet broadcast reporters or are picked up from news services such as Visnews or UPITN, then given voice-overs in the studio.

Entertainment programs originating in western television systems rarely appear on Soviet screens, although BBC's television adaptation of John Galsworthy's *The Forsythe Saga* was carried in the early 1970s and seemed to be quite popular. (The description of it in the Soviet TV guide highlighted the class structure of British society portrayed in the series and stated that present-day British society still showed many of those same features.) Documentaries appear somewhat more often, but most of them are critical of some feature of capitalist society. Feature films from western nations are shown on Soviet TV every now and again; they, too, are apt to portray the negative aspects of life in those nations.

Intervision and Eurovision regularly exchange material, and the Soviet Union receives news items and sports coverage from Western Europe (and occasionally the United States) through this channel. In fact, Soviet TV officials are fond of pointing out that they receive from the West far more than the West takes from them. The figures seem to bear them out: The average yearly ratio is between four and five to one, and the lion's share of imports from the East are sports programs, not news items.[67] A Polish TV news director mentioned to me in the course of a 1978 visit to the Polish broadcasting facilities that Polish TV itself rarely took news items offered by Soviet TV through Intervision "because they were so boring." But that, too, appears to be changing as a result of *glasnost,* and the more conservative Czech and East German administrations now at times refuse items from Soviet TV because they are too "radical."

Whether any of the imported programming has had any effect on Soviet TV production and programming practices is questionable. Most of it is chosen for ideological reasons, and not for whatever entertainment value it might have. But some of it may have had its effect on viewers: Even shows featuring crime, police brutality, greed, and so forth may portray fascinating or attractive settings. The fashions, house furnishings, automobiles, and many other things that western viewers would take for granted often catch the attention of Soviet viewers. Whether they believe what they see is another matter, and if they do believe it, they may feel that the price to be paid for it — slums, crime, unemployment, which usually are prominent in such programming — isn't worth it.

Relations with Other Media

The Soviet press regularly carries information on broadcast schedules, but most newspapers do not feature a daily column of criticism and evaluation of broadcasting, as do many western European newspapers. Party and government comments about broadcasting are published, and often those comments are highly critical. Yet the press does not often take it upon itself to rake television or radio over the coals. When it does, the criticism probably is inspired by comments made by a Party or government official. For example, on 13 December 1982, *Pravda* (the paper of the Central Committee of the Communist party) carried a long article by Candidate of Historical Sciences D. Lyubosvetov, entitled "Announced by Radio . . . " Much of the article was a review of changes in the presentation of radio news, and much of that review was favorable. But coverage of economic news received low marks:

> The economy is invariably the focus of public attention, but analysis of it on radio programs often suffers from dryness and narrowness of theme. "Fulfilled," "overfulfilled," "competing to fulfill," "brought into operation," "commissioned" — phrases like those and figures are constantly heard in bulletins and often provide no impression of the scale of successes or the way they were achieved. Of course, it is not easy to do without weighty figures. But all the same, the impact on the listener is more effec-

tive when a vivid comparison is made or a story about people and their destinies is told.[68]

The Soviet central news agency, Tass, supplies a daily service to all Soviet broadcast stations, but its style is more suitable for newspapers than for broadcasting, since it is full of precise figures and other details that may be difficult to grasp in oral presentations. Just the same, Tass output is regarded as the backbone of newscasts, and much of its copy is read on the air verbatim, making many newscasts sound very much like "oral newspapers," which was one of Lenin's original purposes for radio.

There is considerable cooperation between broadcasting and the Soviet film industry. Soviet television makes some of its own short films, but most feature films come from the Soviet film studios. Many are made for distribution through both the cinema and television and often are released through the two outlets almost simultaneously. A few are made specifically for television. Television pays for this service, but as both media are operated by the state, there is no profit involved. Soviet cinema operators often complain about the negative effect that TV has had on cinema attendance, especially because of the policy of showing brand-new films on television, but the complaints fall on deaf ears: By now, the public is far too accustomed to seeing new films on television to tolerate their disappearance.

International Cooperation

In addition to its exchange of materials through Intervision and Eurovision, Soviet television sometimes is involved in coproductions with TV systems in other countries. Some recent examples include *The Raids of Captain Grant* with Bulgarian TV and *Toilers of the Sea* (a Victor Hugo novel) with French Pathé. *Peter the Great,* a four-part 1986 miniseries about the seventeenth-century Russian emperor, involved the joint efforts of the U.S. NBC network and the Soviet Gorki Film Studios, plus several other European television systems.[69]

The USSR has held an annual TV program convention since the mid-1960s, mainly for the purpose of encouraging program sales to nations that do not belong to Intervision. Intervision members display their wares to interested buyers from two to four dozen other countries, usually including several from Western Europe and many from the Third World, such as Iran and Argentina. Entertainment programs attract the most attention, especially children's programs (a category in which many of the Eastern European nations and the USSR excel — they are imaginatively produced and push well-nigh universal messages such as "be kind to others," "respect your parents," etc.) and TV productions of classical drama such as Chekov's *The Sea Gull*. Documentaries on cultural subjects and on nature also attract buyers.[70]

The New Media

Although the Soviet Union has developed a very ambitious system for delivering TV signals to most of the country through communications satellites, in most other respects it lags behind Western Europe, North America, and Japan in working with the new media. There are several million TV sets in large cities that are served through master antenna systems, but none of those systems has the capacity for program origination. Aside from that, cable television does not exist, although many Soviet citizens know about it, and a few academics, such as Boris Firsov,[71] have advocated experiments with cable. Soviet authorities announced early in 1987 that fiber-optic cable would be laid throughout Moscow over the next two years, in order to improve reception: Most Soviet citizens, and those in Moscow in particular, live in medium- to high-rise concrete and steel apartment houses, and reception sometimes is poor.[72]

Direct broadcasting through satellites (DBS) also has been discussed in the USSR, and Soviet satellite technology is sufficiently advanced to make it feasible there. Furthermore, it would help to extend service to the most remote corners of the nation. It would be especially handy in Siberia, where many small villages receive little if any TV at present, and the authorities show some awareness that the availability of TV can help to get people to remain in remote areas.[73] But it does not appear to be a high-priority area for the time being, and one high-ranking State Committee official with whom I spoke in 1985 speculated that it might not become available for another decade or more. A Soviet telecommunications official stated in mid-1986 that the first scheduled launch of a DBS-capable satellite was to take place "before the end of the decade" but said nothing about whether individual households would be equipped to receive it.[74]

Videotape recorders have been available for some years, but they are expensive (about twenty-five hundred dollars) and there is little prerecorded material for them. Videocassette recorders have been available in special stores that allow purchases only in "hard" currencies (dollars,

Swiss francs, etc., but *not* rubles) for the past few years, at about thirty-five hundred to forty-five hundred dollars for Japanese-made machines, and there is a black market in used western machines, which may cost as much as twenty-five hundred to three thousand dollars. Soviet citizens fortunate enough to travel abroad often bring back recorders, which can be converted quite easily to fit Soviet standards. There was little prerecorded material available for VCRs earlier in the decade, but again the black market provided some western cassettes, and in 1982 the government announced new laws that required customs officials to check any cassettes brought into the country and to confiscate any that "could harm the country's political or economic interests, state security, public order or the population's health or morals." Notwithstanding that sweeping prohibition, there are black-market rings and illegal clubs where enthusiasts can view and purchase movies from the West. There also are growing numbers of home-video makers, who produce and exchange cassettes among themselves.[75]

In 1984, the Soviet Union began to produce its own VCRs, basing them on Japanese technology, but an author writing in *Literaturnyi Gazeta* (Literary Gazette) early in 1984 said that the software (prerecorded programs) simply was not available; the Soviet broadcasting and film industries had not taken steps to record cassettes of the most popular Soviet TV shows and films, much less make any special material for distribution through VCR.[76] Within a year, such cassettes did begin to appear, in part because of the black market in western cassettes, especially feature films. A few video rental shops were in business by the end of 1985, and they have continued to grow; almost all of what they distribute is Soviet-made material. Much of that material is of excellent quality, with top-level performers (the Bolshoi Ballet and Opera, for example), but TV administrators and performers do not appear to have come to grips with some of the more difficult issues, such as performers' rights to extra compensation, if my conversations with State Committee officials in September 1985 are any guide.[77]

There seem to be two major reasons for the slow development of the new media in the Soviet Union. One is the identification of many of those media with the West and with "mindless entertainment." The other is the complex structure of COMECON, the economic community set up to coordinate the production of the USSR and the socialist states of Eastern Europe. By mutual agreement, the various members of COMECON are supposed to determine who gets to produce what. Some tentative decisions have been reached regarding production of the new media, but no nation seems ready to move ahead in a major way. This may be part of an overall reluctance to set in motion a type of activity that would give the public a much freer and greater choice in what they receive and that might even encourage a measure of decentralization in business and industry. According to Rex Malik,[78] "Far from the Soviet Bloc catching up, the consensus seems to be that it is falling further behind. The snag with a philosophy of copying our [the West's] successes is that by the time they have been copied we have already moved on." While Malik's remarks dealt mainly with computers and the transfer of data, they seem equally relevant for the new media in the USSR. Computer education in the grade and high schools dates from the mid-1980s and is spreading slowly through the education system, but it is far ahead of the development of VCRs or interactive cable.

Conclusion

Clearly Soviet broadcasting is not immune to change. Stalin would not recognize much of what he might see or hear on Soviet TV or radio in the late 1980s, and he probably wouldn't approve of much of it, either. Even Leonid Brezhnev, who died in 1983, would be astonished to see such programs as *Twelfth Floor* or unrehearsed, unstaged press conferences, or coverage of the war in Afghanistan in which Soviet citizens could actually see their nation's soldiers wounded and dead. Until late in 1984, the war was presented very abstractly, but at that time the newspapers, followed later by broadcasting, began to single out heroes who had died in combat and began to show actual combat footage.[79] Gorbachev's support for *glasnost,* plus his own enthusiastic television personality,[80] have touched off a minor revolution in broadcasting, where presentational styles and topics seem to be warmer and more self-critical than they have ever been in the past.

There could be reversals, of course, particularly if Gorbachev falls from power. Prime Minister Khrushchev also pushed the mass media to become more personal, more self-critical, speedier in reporting events, but some of those changes disappeared when he was deposed. Yet some of them remained (especially *Mayak*), and it is very likely that some of the changes encouraged by Gorbachev would remain even if he himself died or were deposed within a few years of taking office. Broadcasts from outside the country remain quite popular, especially when rumors spread and people want to check up on them, (on Afghanistan, for instance, where a 1985 Radio Liberty survey of Soviet citizens' sources of information on the war there showed foreign radio and Soviet radio named almost equally, while both were several percentage points ahead of Soviet television).[81] Videocassettes are spreading, and they also appear to be spreading western cultural material.

In short, despite certain geographical and technological advantages that enabled the country to shut out unwanted messages from abroad with reasonable success for some period of time, the broadcast system has had to adjust to hang onto its audiences, especially young people. There was genuine concern among the State Committee staff with whom I spoke in 1985 as to whether the present young generation could really understand the sacrifices of World War II, whether they would be ready to make the same sacrifices themselves, and whether TV could find ways to keep that sacrificial spirit alive in them.

In early 1986 Gorbachev stated that "only ideologically motivated literature could educate people to shoulder the burden of their time."[82] The trick will be to humanize that literature, whether radio news or TV drama, so that listeners and viewers will welcome it. In an increasingly diversified media environment, viewers and listeners do have other choices, and it wouldn't be easy to eliminate those choices. Whether Soviet officials like the idea or not, their media world increasingly is driven by one powerful market force: competition. Not every viewer or listener necessarily welcomes change—media accounts of official wrongdoing, poor hospital care, and so on have caused some citizens to write letters containing observations such as "even an avowed enemy of the USSR would think twice before saying this about our motherland."[83] It is clear that there is no one audience in the Soviet Union, any more than there is one audience anywhere else. But will those in charge of the electronic media be able to discern the differences between audiences, and will they be able to adapt their messages accordingly when it is obviously much easier to think in terms of "one audience, one message"?

6

Japan

From Kabuki to Crime Drama

LTHOUGH Japan is a nonwestern nation, its broadcast system has borrowed from and has been influenced by the experiences of several of the western nations, Great Britain, (Nazi) Germany, and the United States in particular. Still, many of the features of that system surprise and impress observers from other parts of the world. Its achievements in helping to preserve traditional culture, to promote educational development, and to inform the audience with some of the most detailed and comprehensive newscasts available anywhere are stunning. Yet there is another side of the system, with violence, sex, and inanity as some of its chief ingredients. Taken as a whole, then, Japanese broadcasting may seem internally contradictory— or it may seem to offer an extremely wide range of choice for almost all tastes.[1]

Basic Factors

GEOGRAPHIC Japan comprises four large islands and hundreds of smaller ones, and has a total surface area of just over 370,000 square kilometers, which makes it just slightly smaller than California. Yet its population as of 1985 was approximately 120 million, giving it one of the highest population density figures in the world: about 320 inhabitants to the square kilometer. Even that figure is deceptively low, because about 80 percent of Japan's landscape is hilly or mountainous. As a result, most Japanese live in cities, ten of which have populations of over a million; Tokyo, the capital, has over 8 million inhabitants within the city proper, and 14 million in the greater metropolitan area. Fewer and fewer people choose to live in rural areas, which themselves are being eroded by city growth.

The mountainous landscape has made it difficult to develop broadcasting that would reach all corners of the nation, although there have been huge investments in relay transmitters in order to bring clear radio and TV signals to everyone. It also has resulted in a certain feeling of isolation from the cultural mainstream on the part of those who live in the more remote areas, although broadcasting itself, coming as it does primarily from the largest cities, may have served to decrease that feeling.

Japan enjoys another sort of isolation thanks to geography. The four main islands all are separated from Japan's neighbors by distances of twenty-five (the extreme tips of two Soviet islands) to a few hundred miles. South Korea and the USSR are the country's nearest neighbors, but both are far enough away that TV reception from them is difficult, and radio reception, except at night, not all that easy. Nor is either country all that close to major centers of population in Japan. Thus, there is very limited spillover of signals. Furthermore, the Japanese language does not have that much in common with Korean, and virtually nothing in common with Russian. Those Japanese who wish to pursue their studies of foreign languages by listening to broadcasts must purchase shortwave receivers.

DEMOGRAPHIC Japan is a remarkably homogeneous nation. Even in recent years, when the European nations have seen their nonnative populations swell through the influx of guest workers, the Japanese have maintained what almost amounts to a purely Japanese population. The closest any group comes to being a significant minority is the Koreans (both South and North), who number some six hundred thousand, or less than 0.5 percent of the total population. There are some tens of thousands of Chinese, and some thousands of Western Europeans and North Americans. Most of those minority groups live in the large cities; very little is done to reach them through broadcasting, but there are several small circulation newspapers in their languages. There also is an ancient Japanese people called the *ainu,* most of whom live in the northern island of

Hokkaido. There may be twenty thousand or so *ainu,* all of whom are considered to be Japanese and who speak Japanese.

National unity has not been a problem for Japan for the past several centuries. There have been wars within the country at various times, but they did not involve struggles between states or regions. The country's relative isolation from the outside world, vigorously enforced by governmental policies that kept outsiders from entering the country or, for a time, restricting them to the use of one small island in the port of Nagasaki, probably helped to maintain that sense of national unity. Even after the visit to Japan by United States commodore Matthew Calbraith Perry in 1853 and the subsequent opening of trade with the outside world, followed by the Meiji Restoration (1868) and its more western-oriented policies, the country preserved its sense of nationhood. Foreign visitors and foreign ideas were welcome, but the Japanese themselves decided how to utilize them. That sense of readiness to receive but then to adapt to national conditions continues to hold today, not least of all, as you will see, where television programming is concerned.

ECONOMIC   A century or so ago, Japan was still a heavily agrarian nation. As it moved into the twentieth century, industrialization gained in importance, until now Japan is recognized as one of the leading industrial nations in the world. The nation still grows enough rice to feed itself, but much produce has to be imported, and fewer and fewer people gain their livelihood through agriculture: less than 10 percent of the population as of the early 1980s, and declining steadily. Fishing is extremely important to the national economy, but less than 1 percent of the population is engaged in it.

Manufacturing, on the other hand, engages nearly 25 percent of the population, construction nearly 10 percent, wholesale and retail trade about 23 percent, and services a bit over 18 percent. Services and wholesale and retail trade are growing rapidly, too, just as is the case in the United States and in several of the Western European nations. While the average Japanese is not wealthy—per capita national income was about eight thousand dollars as of the mid-1980s—the gap between Japan and Western Europe in this regard is steadily narrowing and is virtually closed where France and Britain are concerned. The average Japanese household can afford a car, take an annual vacation (usually within the country), and own a color TV set and several radio sets.

Broadcasting takes account of some of those economic characteristics by making available various program services for certain sectors of the economy, especially agricultural and fisheries. There are even some radio stations that cater specifically to those whose occupations require them to work late at night, especially truck drivers. Stock market reports are regular features of some stations, and the country's one domestic shortwave radio service specializes part of the time in economic news.

CULTURAL   Japan is not rich in cultural diversity. There are folk festivals and traditions, regional and local dialects, and costumes specific to certain areas but no particularly strong sense of regional or local literary, music, or dramatic traditions. Western dress is replacing traditional Japanese dress in the larger cities and even smaller towns, although home life still often features the wearing of robes and sandals. The education system — compulsory through age fifteen, with most Japanese continuing on through high school and some 20 percent beyond that — probably has helped to create a certain degree of homogenization. Although local boards of education exist throughout the country, the national Ministry of Education still has "guidance and advice" functions, and national exams determine who goes on to college, where, and in which fields. Thus, there is a strong degree of centralization, and little encouragement of localism.

Religion is a fairly powerful influence in Japanese life, but not in ways that would be readily recognizable to westerners. Buddhism, imported from China, has many Japanese followers, but they are apt to blend it with *Shinto,* a belief system that accords an especially prominent place to reverence for one's ancestors. There are many shrines and temples throughout Japan, but the Japanese do not visit them weekly for formal services of worship. The broadcast of prayers that opens and closes the broadcast day for some U.S. stations would strike the Japanese as quite odd, since prayers are not a public act there. But religious festivals certainly will be broadcast, and not only for the country's major religions: Christianity, Judaism, Islam, and others also find their major holy days mentioned, if not often highlighted, in Japanese broadcasting. Japanese society is very tolerant with respect to religion, although broadcasters occasionally satirize aspects of Christianity.

Quite aside from the national culture, which may appear in broadcasting through *noh* and *Kabuki* drama, *sumo* wrestling, performances on the *koto* and other Japanese musical instruments, visits to cultural monuments, and so on, there is the presence of western culture. Some of that culture had begun to appear in the latter part of the nineteenth century, while other cultural artifacts that look like western imports on the surface, such as pornographic material, have been a part of Japanese culture for centuries. But Japanese radio, and later TV, have helped to enlarge the western cultural presence enormously since World War II. The western popular culture of detective shows, game and quiz shows, cartoons featuring monsters and child heroes, all had counterparts in Japanese broadcasting, many of which emerged in Japan as an amalgam of U.S. and Japanese traditions. Television ads sometimes feature western models, product users, and even backgrounds. Western high culture, especially classical music, receives considerable airtime. Television program formats on the commercial stations often seem to be borrowed directly from the United States, even to the occasional inclusion of laugh tracks.

Three aspects of traditional Japanese culture — respect for family (and especially for older family members) and for one's "social superiors," identification with the group rather than assertion of individuality, and male dominance — remain powerful today but are being challenged by some of the younger Japanese, particularly those who have received higher education in the West. Western and western-inspired popular music, television programs, and movies probably have made their contribution to this unrest, as well, although they also frequently serve to reinforce and perpetuate traditional ways.

POLITICAL   In the late nineteenth century, Japan moved in the direction of becoming a parliamentary democracy, and the 1889 constitution was modeled after the French and Prussian constitutions. Political parties and popular elections followed. In the process, the Japanese Parliament acquired more power. Nevertheless, the emperor and his closest advisors retained and wielded the predominant share of political power. By 1925, when broadcast stations first were licensed, there was a fairly even balance between the major political parties, grouped into liberal and conservative factions. However, by the early 1930s, conservative and even fascist parties had achieved predominance, and Japanese government became more and more of a dictatorship. The militaristic, expansionist policies of the government brought about invasions of Manchuria, China, and, by the early 1940s, much of southeast Asia and the Pacific. They also brought Japan into World War II, at which time political parties ceased to exist. Initially, Japanese military forces were highly successful, but by late 1942 the "Greater East Asia Coprosperity Sphere," as the Japanese government called its expanding empire, was beginning to erode. By the end of the war in August 1945, Japan had little but its four main home islands and a few smaller outlying islands left, and the country came under foreign military occupation for the first time in its history.

The military occupation, with the United States as chief occupying force, saw the restoration of parliamentary democracy and the abolition of the emperor's power, although he remained symbolic head of state. Political parties regained their former prominence. Because there are several parties (usually between five and seven) represented in the Diet, or Parliament, coalitions of parties often are necessary in order to form governments. With the exception of a brief period just after the end of the war, when the Socialists held power, the Liberal Democrats (conservatives) and their associates have been in control of government throughout Japan's postwar history. That government generally has been supportive of private industry, and that has included broadcasting.

Outside observers often have noted a "clubby" atmosphere that interlinks those who occupy positions of power in government and in private industry, including the mass media. Many of the Japanese power elite have attended the same few prestigious Japanese universities, and many move in the same social circles. When this is coupled with traditional Japanese respect for authority and reluctance to utter criticism in public, the overall effect is not conducive to investigative reporting by the media. However, in recent years Japanese reporters have been behaving a bit more like their Western European and North American counterparts, and Japanese politicians have been the target of sharper and more persistent questioning.

A Brief History

Conditions attending the birth of Japanese broadcasting were much the same as in Europe in the early 1920s: Tens of thousands of radio amateurs were anxious to have stations to receive over their frequently homemade sets, and manufacturers of parts and sets were anxious to increase their sales. Also, major Japanese newspapers put on public demonstrations of radio transmission and reception, in large part because they helped to publicize the newspapers themselves. By 1924, the Ministry of Communications, having conducted its own experiments with radio and having visited other countries to obtain a clearer picture of the possibilities, was ready to license radio services. The government did not wish to operate a radio service itself, partly because it did not feel that it could justify the expenditure,[2] but it did not want the technical chaos of the U.S. system, either. The geographical conditions of Japan, coupled with its high population density and strong national unity, favored a centralized, monopolistic approach to the licensing of radio.

Initially, the ministry opted for a "one station per area" plan and called on interested parties to submit joint bids, much as the British Post Office had done in 1922 and for some of the same reasons: to avoid having to choose among applicants, and to stress the public service character of radio, as opposed to its profit-making character. The service would receive its financial support through license fees paid by individual set owners. If profits exceeded 10 percent, the excess would be used to reduce those license fees. There would be no advertising.

The ministry decided to authorize station in three major urban centers — Tokyo, Osaka, and Nagoya — to begin with. One applicant from Osaka proposed that he be allowed to create a nationwide network, but the ministry decided against this for the time being. The various applicants came primarily from among radio manufacturers and dealers and the press; they merged themselves into corporate bodies in each city, although only after considerable infighting in Osaka, and the Tokyo station came on the air in March 1925, followed by Osaka in June and Nagoya in July. There were some 5,000 licensed sets at that time; set owners were responsible for notifying the station in the local reception area that they had sets and wished to enter into contracts with the station so as to be legally entitled to receive the signal, and many set owners either did not understand the licensing system or chose to ignore it. But increased publicity for the system, combined with threats of legal reprisals by the government, soon brought about greater complicity, and by early 1926 there were over 250,000 licensed sets in the country, each set owner eventually paying one yen a month. The broadcasters themselves were allowed to collect the fee; this represented quite a departure from the practices of other countries, where the post office or government usually collected the fee and skimmed off some of it to cover expenses or fatten the national treasury. Japanese broadcasters received all of the proceeds, and that system exists to this day.

At first, the three stations were on the air for portions of the day, rather than continuously, and programmed a mixture of news, music, drama, talks, weather, and stock market reports. They were under severe restrictions regarding broadcast content, especially for anything connected with politics. The Japanese Home Ministry, which often found itself in conflict with the Ministry of Communications over broadcast policy, wanted tight content controls and was able to exercise them quite effectively under the 1925 Law for Maintenance of the Public Peace, "a severely suppressive law aimed at those who would form societies aimed at changing the national polity or denying private property, as well as at scholars and cultured people who were deemed as being in sympathy with such ideas."[3] The Ministry of Communications had full power of review over each station's financial affairs; daily program schedules and summaries of program content were to be reported to the ministry's Bureau of Communications one day in advance; the bureau could request the stations to carry "items of public benefit"; and the government could take control of or purchase the stations "for the public benefit."

It is not surprising that the quasi–private enterprise broadcasting system lasted for less than eighteen months. The government had been somewhat uneasy about the regional, individualistic nature of the stations from the beginning, and the operators of the stations did not find the arrangement particularly comfortable, either. The Ministry of Communications released a document in January 1926 in which it argued the case for a unified national broadcast system, which it saw as the most efficient way to bring high-quality broadcasting to the entire country. Meetings held between the ministry and the three stations later that year finally produced agreement for a merger of the stations, and in August 1926, articles of incorporation were drafted and approved, although not without some opposition: The Ministry of Communications itself claimed the power to appoint general managers for the various stations in the new system, which caused some Japanese newspapers to warn of actual government operation of the system, and the Tokyo station even broadcast a statement critical of the action. Nevertheless, opposition was not strong enough to change the conditions of the merger, and it was approved late in August. Henceforth, Japanese broadcasting would be handled by a single public service corporation, the Nippon Hoso Kyokai (NHK, or Japan Broadcasting Corporation), but a corporation with a strong degree of government involvement in determining the nature of that public service.

THE NHK: EXPANSION AND CONTROL (1926–45)   In its first few years, NHK was slow to develop. By 1930 the number of license-fee payers had more than doubled and the total NHK staff had more than quadrupled, but the number of stations had expanded only from three to seven. The Great Depression of 1929 had its impact in Japan, but that was not the only factor. The government itself seemed uncertain of the roles that broadcasting should play, although it was certain that broadcasting should not become a vehicle for dissemination of "radical" (Marxist, certainly, but probably socialist as well) ideas, and the Home Ministry continued to push the Ministry of Communications to preview broadcast content. The latter ministry itself had placed high priority on developing a broadcast service capable of reaching the entire nation within five years, but such expansion was proving very costly, given the mountainous nature of the country. Also, most broadcast equipment had to be imported—a far cry from the situation today.

Japanese government officials began to discuss possible revisions to the articles governing NHK in 1930. One aspect of the system that particularly bothered some of them was the relative autonomy of the NHK stations around the country. The Tokyo station already was supplying a good deal of program material to the branch stations, but the latter enjoyed a considerable degree of freedom in programming, and through a complicated administrative setup, even had a fair amount of influence over NHK Tokyo. Such a system was difficult to supervise, and the Japanese government was becoming more and more centrist, anyway, and in the process seeking to impose more control over all of the mass media. The Ministry of Communications presented a draft plan for reorganization in 1934; it proposed centralization of NHK through the Tokyo station. As it was presented, one ministry official declared that the new system should insure that "not only those broadcasts with contents preferred by listeners *but also those that will lead the public towards consolidation of the national spirit* [italics mine] shall be included."[4]

The NHK already had begun to move in that direction, particularly in connection with Japan's successful invasion of Manchuria in 1931. Radio gave heavy attention to the Japanese campaign and victory, which also served to boost the popularity of radio and cause more people to buy sets and take out licenses. The number of license holders reached 1 million by 1931 and doubled again by 1934. However, since the government was anxious to increase the numbers of radio listeners as rapidly as possible, it cut the license fee in 1931 and in 1935, so revenues did not increase all that dramatically. Still, there was enough economic strength to permit further construction of stations (twelve by late 1930, twenty-seven by 1935), and even to permit the introduction in 1931 of a second radio service, largely for educational and cultural broadcasts. The introduction of that service caused a bit of interministerial friction, since the Ministry of Education thought that it, rather than the Ministry of Communications, should be responsible for supervising the programming of the new service, but the latter agreed to consult regularly with the former.

The new articles of incorporation were approved in 1934, and a more centralized NHK played a larger and larger role in the development of national unity. In 1935 it invested some of its capital in the newly created Domei News Agency, itself designed to disseminate the "correct" interpretation of events in Japan to the Japanese and to the outside world. (This also brought an end to a several-year period of tension between the Japanese press and broadcasting, somewhat reminiscent of the U.S. Press-Radio War of the early 1930s.) The Ministry of Foreign Affairs had proposed the creation of such an agency, and now NHK agreed to use only Domei's news items. In 1936, an Information Committee was created and placed under direct control of the cabinet. The committee directly supervised Domei and gave directives to NHK through the Ministry of Communications. By late 1940, the government concluded that the system of media supervision had to be even more direct, so the committee became a bureau, staffed by civilian and military personnel, and with control over media content. In theory, the Ministry of Communications remained responsible for the actual task of previewing NHK programs. In practice, the bureau exercised its control through ministry personnel who were assigned to the bureau.

Japanese friends of mine who were children in the 1930s have spoken of the mobilizing role played by radio even in educational broadcasts. Not only did the broadcasts glorify the emperor and stress that Japan was far superior to other nations, but also it promoted the idea of readiness to sacrifice oneself in the national interest and even programmed calisthenics for students, who would gather in the schoolyard and exercise so that they would be more fit to serve their emperor and country. Nazi broadcast policies probably helped to shape NHK policy, and there were numerous meetings between Japanese and Nazi broadcast officials during the 1930s. The Japanese banned certain types of "decadent" western music (jazz in particular), even as had the Nazis, and also outlawed the private possession of shortwave receivers shortly before World War II.

Once World War II started for Japan in December 1941, controls over both the transmission and reception of broadcasting became even tighter, with more thorough previewing of program content and encouragement of group listening to programs with political themes. Military marches preceded programs containing news from the fighting front, reminiscent of Nazi Germany's "Special Announcements." However, Japanese authorities were wise enough to mix in a large amount of light entertainment such as popular music and variety shows. Western music (but not jazz) still could be played, but British or U.S. music was outlawed. Poster campaigns promoted the idea of listening to radio as a patriotic act. Throughout the war, the government gave high priority to maintaining broadcast services. The total number of stations grew from just under eighty to over ninety during the war itself, and only ten of them were heavily damaged by air raids, with all but the Hiroshima station (completely destroyed, as was virtually everything else in the center of that city) being returned to service quickly. Radio sets were a greater problem: Over 3 million Japanese homes were destroyed during the war, and few radio sets were saved from them. Also, it became more and more difficult to get sets repaired. By early 1944 there were well over 7 million licensed sets in the country, but by the war's end between 2 and 3 million of them were destroyed or no longer functional.

RADIO UNDER MILITARY OCCUPATION (1945–50)   When the Pacific phase of World War II ended in August 1945, the Japanese broadcasting system faced an uncertain future. The stations themselves largely were intact, sets were fewer in number but still quite widespread, and most broadcast staff still were available for service. Still, as Japan never had been occupied, no one knew what to expect of the Allied Command that would govern the country for the indefinite future. Many Japanese assumed that, since the United States would be the major actor in determining occupation policies, there might be a new broadcast system for Japan that would include private, advertiser-supported radio. Some thought that the NHK might be abolished altogether, on the grounds that it was too closely associated with "thought control" on the part of the fascist government. The existing Japanese government even proposed the creation of a commercial broadcasting system, to exist alongside and secondary to the NHK, in a plan drafted for the General Headquarters for the Allied Powers (GHQ) only a few weeks after the end of the war.[5]

The GHQ praised the plan and stated that it would respond soon. In fact, nearly five years passed before a broadcast law emerged and Japan acquired the dual (public service–commercial service) system it has to this day. The period between was marked by uncertainty (particularly on the part of the GHQ), by unease over the possible reemergence of a politically dominated, centralized broadcast system (many GHQ personnel and Japanese officials, especially those from smaller political parties, shared this fear), and by intensive lobbying campaigns for the introduction of commercial broadcasting (particularly by the Japanese press, ostensibly in the name of democracy, but also because they saw themselves as likely investors in what could become a very lucrative business).

The GHQ's uncertainty seems to have stemmed from various internal disagreements regarding postwar broadcast policy. Unlike Germany, Japan was not divided into zones of occupation, but the four allied powers, Great Britain, the USSR, China, and the United States, did have to come to agreement on that policy. Great Britain and the USSR particularly favored a monopoly broadcast system, since it corresponded with their own practices. China agreed. The U.S. view was not clear, but a December 1945 memo on broadcasting drafted by an American made a point of not mentioning the introduction of commercial broadcasting, and its drafter, a Colonel Hanner, remarked when submitting it that "it is GHQ's intention not to consider the introduction of private broadcasting."[6] All of the occupation authorities seemed to agree that a monopoly broadcast system was easier to supervise than a dual system would be.

The NHK itself continued to operate much as it had during the war, with much the same equipment and staff (few broadcast personnel were placed on trial for war crimes, in contrast with the situation in postwar Germany), and with supervision of scripts, as well, but now under the eye of GHQ rather than the Bureau of Information. The GHQ insisted upon the introduction of programs that would give the Japanese people a clear idea of the sins of the fascist government and of the tremendous responsibility borne by both government and people for the crimes committed during the previous fifteen years. But some GHQ officials also promoted new entertainment formats for Japanese radio, such as quiz shows (which became very popular, and which remain popular today), "person in the street" interviews, audience participation shows, election campaign broadcasts, and so on. Perhaps the greatest lasting legacy of the GHQ where broadcasting is concerned was its insistence that NHK achieve closer contact with its listeners—an insistence that also led to the creation of an ongoing audience research unit in NHK in 1946. As NHK's *The History of Broadcasting in Japan* puts it, "Changes that were unthinkable in prewar days were introduced into NHK's broadcasting both in content and form."[7] Transmitters were repaired, new ones added, more stations came on the air for the second radio service (which had been suspended during the war), and by 1948 there were over 8 million licensed households in the country, surpassing the highest wartime total by several hundred thousand.

Meanwhile, the occupation authorities and the Japanese government went back and forth over the eventual fate of the broadcast system. Campaigns for commercial broadcasting conducted by the Japanese press were having some impact upon the public's perception of the situation, and formal and informal surveys indicated an increasing desire for, or at least willingness to accept, a commercial alternative to the NHK. The U.S. dominated GHQ was not unmindful of public opinion, and in October 1947 it released a memorandum on the drafting of a new broadcast law in which "provision shall be made contributing to possible development of private commercial broadcasting when the economic conditions should permit."[8] One possible cause of this more favorable attitude toward commercial broadcasting probably was the deterioration of relations between the USSR and the United States. The USSR had strongly favored a monopoly for Japanese broadcasting, which may have caused the United States to favor the addition of commercial broadcasting in part because such an act would be "anticommunist." The Japanese press also stressed the point that a monopoly broadcast system was not particularly democratic.

The Ministry of Communications immediately set to work drafting a broadcast act. Short legislative sessions, a national election, objections raised by GHQ officials to some provisions of the draft, and reluctance on the part of the Diet (Parliament) to accept all of the changes that GHQ wanted delayed consideration of what ultimately became the Broadcast Act until late December 1949. The relevant bills (there were three of them) received several amendments and finally were passed by the lower house of the Diet on 2 May 1950 and became law on 1 June.

There were several points of disagreement between the Japanese government and the GHQ, but the two most important issues were the separation of the NHK from the government and the creation of an independent administrative agency to license new stations. Officials of the GHQ were anxious to see NHK become a true public service operation and to that end already had insisted upon the creation of an administrative oversight board which, although appointed by the government, would be independent of it. As the final bills were under consideration, the GHQ continued to push for as much financial autonomy for the NHK as possible. General Headquarters officials also wanted to see the creation of an FCC-like administrative agency, even though the Japanese system of government had no tradition of such regulatory agencies. Because the GHQ had what amounted to veto power over legislation, it was in a position to insist that those conditions be met in the broadcast bills. Thus, the NHK became a more independent organization than would have been the case had the government had its way; the road was open for the creation of commercial broadcasting; and Japan acquired a Radio Regulatory Commission for the licensing of new stations. But with the signing of a peace treaty in 1952, the occupation came to an end, and one of the first acts of the government was to absorb the Radio Regulatory Commission into the Ministry of Posts and Telecommunications: The RRC was the one major "graft" of the GHQ broadcast policy that didn't 'take' where the Japanese approach to regulation was concerned.

RADIO FLOURISHES, TELEVISION LIMPS (1950–58) Would-be commercial broadcasters had been lining up with applications in hand ever since September 1946, when it looked as if the Japanese government were ready and able to authorize private radio stations. It was no wonder, then, that passage of legislation in 1950 that permitted such stations would find a flood of applications. There were twenty-three of them in 1949; the number grew to seventy by the end of 1950. The Radio Regulatory Commission needed several months and a five-day public hearing to determine its licensing standards. The standards were made public in December and included not only the need to provide a well-rounded service of benefit to the public, but also the physical limitation of just one commercial station per city (two for Tokyo). That limitation stemmed from the supposed scarcity of available frequencies, but it also served to prod some of the would-be broadcasters into applying for licenses jointly (in other words, merging their applications, much as had been done back in 1925) and also applying for them in some of the smaller cities that might have been bypassed if there had been plenty of licenses available in the larger cities.

Many of the applicants were newspaper companies – not surprising, since they had campaigned for commercial stations – and advertising agencies. The largest Japanese newspaper companies, including Asahi, Mainichi, and Yomiuri, were especially active, but were unable to form networks in the U.S. sense of that term because they could own only one station and could not require the exclusive affiliation of any other station. Nevertheless, as commercial radio developed, disc and tape exchanges became more and more common, and stations in Tokyo and Osaka began to take on the aura of network "head-end" operations. The commission licensed sixteen applicants in April 1951; by September, two of them were on the air, by the end of the year there were four more, and in 1952 the commercial broadcasters formed their own National Association of Commercial Broadcasters (NAB). It was hard for them to make headway against NHK at first, since the latter had been the only form of domestic broadcasting that the Japanese had ever know, save for the 1925–26 period; also, NHK reacted to the birth of commercial radio by reexamining its own schedule and initiating some programs that had tremendous mass appeal, especially a long-running "sad love story" entitled *What's Your Name?* The commercial stations borrowed some of NHK's most popular formats, too, especially quiz shows and amateur singing contests; few commercial stations were without at least one. Certain commercial stations began to specialize, as well, offering popular music every evening.

Luckily for the commercial stations, the Korean War had brought relative economic prosperity to Japan, and more and more Japanese were purchasing radio receivers. There were about 9 million license contracts as of 1950, and more than 12.5 million in 1954. That same prosperity led more and more Japanese businesses to advertise over radio.

The licensing of commercial stations continued, aided by a reallocation of frequencies in 1953, until by 1958 there were about one hundred of them, and polls and surveys indicated that they were attracting large numbers of listeners. Some of the techniques that used to increase listenership should sound familiar to a U.S. reader, since they included quiz show prizes of as much as a million yen, music-by-request broadcasts, and purposely brief newscasts. Some of the commercial stations did offer classical music concerts, educational broadcasts, and other elements of high culture at first, but these became less and less numerous as competition rose.

Television, NHK and commercial alike, got off to a slow start. The lower house of the Diet passed a resolution in May 1951 calling for the early establishment of TV, but there were few Japanese manufacturers ready to make TV sets, and most commercial broadcasters and the NHK wondered whether financial conditions permitted the development of such an expensive medium. Both groups were compelled to reconsider their reluctance when Matsutaro Shoriki, former president of the Yomiuri newspaper company, announced in September 1951 that, acting upon a suggestion made by United States Senator Carl Mundt, he planned to establish the Nippon Television Network.[9] There would be American assistance in the form of technological aid and facilities. The advantage to the United States would be Japanese use of U.S. equipment, broadcasting on U.S. standards, which—irony of ironies, given the present source of most TV sets—would lead to a market for U.S.-manufactured sets, parts, and transmission equipment. The Radio Regulatory Commission received NTV's application in October 1951; it was followed quickly by applications from NHK (which already was conducting experimental transmission and even had conducted a few before the Second World War) and from four commercial radio operations.

The commission's hearings on the license applications turned out to be difficult and even acrimonious, since the commission itself and NTV favored a six-megahertz band for TV broadcasts (the U.S. standard), while NHK and the Japanese communications equipment manufacturers wanted a seven-megahertz band, which they felt would be more compatible with eventual color TV transmissions. The commission finally approved the six-megahertz standard, and, on 31 July 1952—the last day of its existence (its functions were taken over by the Ministry of Posts and Telecommunications)—it awarded a preliminary license to NTV. The commission deferred action on NHK's proposal on the grounds that the Diet would have to approve the necessary reallocation of the NHK budget to permit an ongoing TV service. Applications from the other commercial operations either were denied or continued over.

The NHK quickly sought and received Diet approval to introduce a TV service, sent a staff member to the United States to bring a U.S. TV producer to Japan, and otherwise prepared itself for the initiation of a regular TV service as soon as possible. It carried out experimental remote telecasts of baseball games and of a sumo wrestling tournament, refitted a radio studio for TV, and on 1 February 1953 began regularly scheduled TV broadcasts. The NTV network followed about seven months later. At first TV broadcasts were limited to the Tokyo area, but the Ministry of Posts and Telecommunications had authorized TV stations in the Osaka and Nagoya regions in December 1952, and the NHK set up a microwave link with experimental TV stations it had developed in those two cities, so all three cities broadcast the opening transmission. There were not many viewers, however: Aside from the sets in dealer's shops, there were less than a thousand license-fee-paying TV households in the country, and a year later only sixteen thousand. The financial burdens for NHK and NTV alike were enormous, but especially for the latter; since NTV's final plan of operation differed considerably from what Shoriki initially had discussed with Mundt and other Americans, most of the offers of U.S. loans and assistance fell through. Shoriki, using his old newspaper connections, eventually secured investments from Japan's three largest newspaper companies (Asahi, Mainichi, and Yomiuri) and from assorted businesses.

Early TV productions featured several formats that had been popular on radio: quiz shows, amateur talent contests, and sports. But stations also attempted to display some of television's unique characteristics, especially through remote telecasts of important events such as the departure of the crown prince by ocean liner to attend the coronation of Queen Elizabeth in 1953. The NTV network worked hard to popularize TV viewing by installing hundreds of sets in outdoor locations, and restaurants and tea- and coffeehouses found that the sets helped to bring them additional business. But set sales lagged, chiefly because even the least expensive ones cost considerably more than the average person's annual wage. Then, in a policy move that has become very familiar to foreign business competitors ever since, the Ministry of International Trade and Industry decided to extend assistance to Japanese TV manufacturers and to restrict TV set imports. Domestic set manufacture boomed, the price of sets fell rapidly, and individual set ownership began to climb. Still, the number of licensed TV receivers did not reach a million until early in 1957, and advertisers continued to consider radio as a better buy. The NHK continued to expand its microwave network and to put new stations on the air, while other commercial stations came into operation, as well, but by 1957 there were still only eighteen of the former and five of the latter. One of the commercial stations, (JOKR, Tokyo), seeking financial support wherever it might exist, hit upon the novel idea of having the leading character in a detective show (*Mr. Busy Rushes Out*) drink a vitamin preparation made by a sponsoring pharmaceutical firm![10] Both the license fee and rates for ads remained low; it was not possible to justify fees or rates that would begin to pay the costs of television when relatively few people had sets. Nevertheless, NHK continued to add stations to its network, commercial TV stations also increased in number, albeit more slowly, and by 1959 there were forty-four of the former and twenty-seven of the latter. Critics now began to speak of the "television era."

TELEVISION COMES TO THE FORE (1959–72) Two events in 1959 showed that television had made the transition to become a truly mass medium: Advertising revenues for TV first topped those for radio in that year, and Japanese newspapers began to list TV programs above, rather than below, radio. Receiving licenses passed the 5 million mark, meaning that nearly 30 percent of all Japanese households had sets. Over the next five years, that figure rose to over 80 percent, as licensed sets topped 17 million by 1964.

But with that increase in popularity came an increase in notoriety. Various public interest groups, especially parents and teachers, became concerned over the portrayal of violence and the stimulation of what Japanese call the "gambling" instinct: playing games for money. The NHK TV programs largely were untouched by those criticisms, since portrayal of violence on them was rare and since NHK quiz and game shows were not high-stakes affairs. In the increasingly competitive atmosphere of commercial television, however, contest formats offered two advantages: They were inexpensive to produce, and they seemed to be immensely popular. As a result, few evenings went by where there weren't several of them available, with higher and higher stakes to attract and hold a potentially jaded audience. United States TV quiz shows appeared to be a powerful model for their Japanese counterparts. As for violence, that seems to have developed from the importation of U.S. programs in the mid-1950s, but it was enhanced by the creation of a number of Japanese-produced crime shows, usually with big-city settings, in the late 1950s. Also, TV dramas featuring samurai warriors became increasingly popular in the late 1950s. The NHK showed them on occasion but tried to observe as faithfully as possible the original stories of centuries earlier in which the samurai played a role, which in turn meant that fighting was a minor part of the whole. Commercial TV usually used the original story as a basis for productions in which fighting became the dominant element; thanks again to the competitive situation, those fights became rougher and more spectacular as the years passed. (However, oversaturation in this genre by commercial broadcasters led to its virtual disappearance by the late 1980s.) The NHK did import and show some of the more violent U.S. series as well, but that practice pretty much ceased by the early 1960s.

Radio was not immune to those criticisms, either, although in that case it was most likely to be the allegedly immoral content of some of the popular songs that were played over and over again by many of the commercial stations. As the transistor revolution was beginning to make its mark in Japan, more and more teenagers were able to purchase their own radio sets, and radio, which only recently had been a family medium, was beginning to fractionate and specialize, just as was happening in the United States and Canada at that time. As of 1955, an average of 40 percent of all Japanese households listened during the "Golden Hour" (Japan's designation for the prime-time period), but by 1962 that figure had dropped to around 10 percent. So the protests — which usually took the form of letters to newspapers or visits to stations with petitions for moderation in, or elimination of, "objectionable" programs — generally were directed against television.

The Broadcast Act of 1950 was amended in 1959 to include the provision that all stations, NHK and commercial alike, must have a broadcast consultative committee to advise them on their programming practices. Public discontent played some role in the passage of that amendment and in the establishment by the NHK and commercial broadcasters of detailed program standards (also now required by the law). Those moves in turn may have caused NHK to reconsider its policy of direct competition with the commercial TV stations; at least some of the more violent imported shows began to disappear from NHK's schedule. But the practices of the commercial stations remained largely unaltered; with four commercial TV stations in Tokyo and two to four in other large cities throughout Japan, most of them linked with one or another Tokyo or Osaka station, competition overrode any very substantive concession to public discontent. United States shows continued to be prominent in the "Golden Hour" schedules of the commercial stations, but they were increasingly the subject of criticism, and some of it began to appear through surveys conducted by such groups as the Japan Teacher's Council for Better Television Programs or under commission from the United States Information Agency. Those surveys revealed that, although there were many U.S. programs (the *Andy Williams Show, Bewitched, Lassie,* several westerns) that many Japanese liked and thought of as conveying a positive image of the United States, a good many others were considered harmful to children and even to a better understanding of the United States (e.g., *Batman, Popeye,* several crime and detective shows).[11]

During most of the 1950s, television newscasts were slow to develop. Expense of production was one reason, lack of apparent public interest another. By the late 1950s, NHK was utilizing its extensive worldwide correspondent network for increasing numbers of television reports, and the public was becoming increasingly TV news conscious. By 1965, that consciousness had developed into a minor mania, as NHK's Studio 102, a 7:35 to 8:15 A.M. national and international news and feature program, began to get ratings (not shares of audience) of over 25 percent at times. The commercial stations had their own morning offerings; they featured "wide" shows, multiple-topic combinations of news and hard and soft features, presented in an entertaining manner. In other words, they weren't too much unlike the NBC *Today Show.* One of the commercial stations hired a popular NHK announcer, Norio Kijima, to act as host of the *Norio Kijima Morning Show,* which obtained ratings around 15 percent. (*Very* few staff from commercial broadcasting have come over to NHK, however; while it pays less, NHK considers itself quite superior to the commercial stations.)

Whatever specific criticism may have been directed against television—and one Japanese academic claimed that it was turning the country into a "nation of a hundred million imbeciles"—it did not seem to discourage the vast majority of viewers from spending more and more of their time with the medium, and placing more and more trust in its messages. The NHK conducted surveys in 1960 and in 1965 in which selected samples of over 154,000 viewers were asked how much time they spent on "primary" and on "secondary" ("split concentration") TV viewing. The 1960 figures were just under an hour for primary and less than fifteen minutes for secondary; the respective 1965 figures were almost three hours and about one hour and fifteen minutes.[12] Some of that increase was due to the growth in average broadcast hours per day; most stations were running sixteen to eighteen hours of programming by the mid-1960s. But the credibility of television probably helped to stimulate viewership, as well: In 1963 the NHK conducted a survey ($N = 2,000$) in which respondents were asked which medium they most likely would believe if the mass media presented different versions of a given event. Forty-three percent chose TV, 32 percent newspapers—results remarkably similar to those obtained by the Roper Organization in the United States. An NHK follow-up survey in 1975 saw 58 percent choosing TV and 28 percent newspapers.[13]

Commercial radio stations in the 1960s continued to specialize in certain formats that appealed to specific audiences. Some began to venture into the early morning hours, where many of their listeners would be truck drivers, students, and insomniacs; for those listeners, such stations presented soothing music and soothing (some claimed "sexy") female announcers. Other stations moved into "talk" radio and attempted to interest listeners in calling the station with their questions or comments — a device that worked quite easily in the United States but was a bit more difficult to achieve in Japan thanks to a combination of fewer telephones and a greater reluctance, especially on the part of Japanese women, to call strangers and engage in conversation. All-news stations were nonexistent, but there were a few classical music stations. The NHK's two radio services continued to offer a wide variety of broadcast fare, and in 1965 NHK completed an eight-year project for the development of a separate FM network to serve the entire nation. The network remained experimental until 1969, by which time several million Japanese households had FM receivers, many of them stereo. The NHK switched many of its FM programs into stereo, but also sought to take advantage of FM's capacity for providing a highly localized signal by setting up a system whereby each prefecture (county) could broadcast news edited for its particular region.

The first commercial FM stations came on the air in late 1969 and early 1970 and featured little but music, most of it movie music and foreign and Japanese pop. While radio stations weren't exactly prospering, they at least were stabilizing, in part because the Ministry of Posts and Telecommunications was not issuing any new licenses: By 1960 there were 111 stations (including repeaters) and 44 radio companies; by 1965 there were 144 stations and 46 radio companies. Growth was almost entirely limited to repeaters, most of which were low power. That also served to keep out further competition, much to the pleasure of the companies holding licenses already.

Commercial television continued to draw public criticism for its alleged emphasis on sex and violence throughout the 1960s. The Japan Broadcasting Federation, a voluntary group which includes the NHK, the Federation of Commercial Broadcasters, and Nippon Telephone and Telegraph, established a Broadcasting Program Improvement Committee in December 1964. The government released a "White Paper on Young People" in mid-1965 and in it stressed the need for closer surveillance and tighter standards on violent and sexual programs but felt that voluntary regulation was the best way to achieve this. A bill to revise the Broadcast Law was introduced in the Diet and 1965 and carried over into the 1966 spring session; one provision in it would have underscored the

"obligation . . . to prevent the undesirable influence of vulgar programmes on young people,"[14] but the revisions were set aside and never
acted upon. In 1970 the minister of posts and telecommunications
threatened to establish a monitoring system for television programs,
which was greeted with dismay by the mass media in general, because
they saw it as an infringement of freedom of expression. The threat
never materialized. Then in 1971, the lower house of the Diet set up a
subcommittee on broadcasting and held four sessions to examine
"vulgar" programming and advertising practices (the Japanese Fair
Trade Commission had ordered several commercials off the air in the late
1960s on the grounds that they were deceptive). There was widespread
agreement that much of TV was "vulgar" — indeed, in 1972 the Tokyo
Metropolitan Police Department began to tape late-night shows in order
to see whether they were violating public decency laws[15] — but there were
no visible changes in the Broadcast Law or in mechanisms for the governance of broadcasting. Commercial broadcasters advanced the claim
that they themselves were unhappy about the quality of much broadcast
fare, but that, like the devil, competitive pressures "made them do it."

By this time, almost all television programs were made in Japan,
although some U.S. children's cartoons and a few U.S. comedy and
drama series continued to enjoy some popularity on the commercial
channels. The vast majority of programs came from the key stations in
Tokyo and Osaka, although formal networks continued to be illegal
under the Broadcast Law. Color TV, which dated back to 1960, was
widespread within a decade: Most stations were broadcasting several
hours a day in color, and color sets sales, slow until the late 1960s, began
to climb rapidly. Satellites were coming into use for international transmission and reception (the 1964 Olympic Games, held in and around
Tokyo, were the first to be transmitted by satellite). On the other hand,
the development of cable TV was slow, perhaps because so many Japanese viewers had access to anywhere from four to seven channels,
perhaps because there were few independent sources of programming
that could have added to what already was available.

THE NEW TECHNOLOGIES AND THE OLD COHABIT (1972–88) Despite the slow progress of cable TV, the Diet in 1972 passed a law for
the regulation of cable. Already there had been experiments with cable,
and some commercial businesses had developed community and master
antenna systems for residents in the largest cities as early as 1968; there,
skyscrapers were making clear reception, especially in color, increasingly
difficult. However, the new law did not specifically encourage the devel-

opment of supplementary services on cable — in fact, it was labeled the Cable Television *Broadcast* Law, and a supplementary provision of it stated that the law would not apply to two-way communication.[16]

Even as the law passed, however, the Ministry of Posts and Telecommunications was preparing for a demonstration experiment with two-way cable. It selected the "new town" of Tama, just outside Tokyo, for the project and started transmissions in January 1976. People could volunteer to receive the service, and it was free of charge. Several hundred households participated, but no single household received all ten of the services provided, which included rebroadcast of existing signals, provision of a local TV service, pay TV, facsimile newspaper, question-and-response (something like Warner's interactive TV service, QUBE), and still-picture request. Once the experiment was over (December 1977), households were asked to indicate which services they found useful and which not: The response service and a "flash information" service (indication on the screen to turn to the local channel for some important information) were considered valuable by most people who had used them, while the pay TV services and the still-picture request service were thought "rather" or "totally" useless by their users.[17] The service had not been reinstated or tried elsewhere as of the late 1980s, but a roughly similar project using fiber-optic technology started test transmissions in Higashi-Ikoma, another new town, in 1978. The project, called HI-OVIS (Highly Interactive Optical-Visual Information System), was developed by the Ministry of International Trade and Industry; slightly over 150 households participated in the experiment.[18]

In addition to those two experiments, some 10 percent of the two hundred or so larger (fifty-household or more) cable TV services in Japan as of the mid-1970s were offering a local TV service as a part of their cable package, but few viewers seemed interested in it. And, although the cable law required cable operators to lease their unused channels to any firm that might wish to use them, there were few customers. In short, cable posed little threat to broadcast television and might even have been of some help to it.

Satellites, too, became more and more prominent in the 1970s, and there was considerable discussion of direct broadcasting from them — not, however, with the idea of increasing and diversifying program choice. Instead, DBS was seen as an excellent way to bring clear broadcast signals to remote parts of the country where, despite the best efforts of the NHK and commercial broadcasters (efforts that cost huge sums, especially when calculated on a per-viewer basis), there were still pockets of poor reception. There was very little consideration of the development of new TV services for transmission through DBS, in large part because the quasi-monopoly character of Japanese broadcasting did not encourage independent program producers.

The NHK and the commercial television stations continued to enjoy the fruits of an expanding audience. Almost all Japanese households had at least one TV set by the mid-1970s, and about a fourth of the households had more than one set. First used for regular transmissions in 1967, UHF television afforded some new applicants the opportunity to establish TV stations, and they spread rapidly: Over forty UHF TV companies were on the air by late 1975. Both NHK and Japanese Nielsen research data showed that the average Japanese household spent more time watching TV each day than did the average U.S. household, and thanks to the tremendous popularity of the morning shows (among them a daily fifteen-minute soap opera on NHK), the morning viewing figures rose to peaks of 50 percent or more of the possible audience. Commercial broadcasters were finding ways to jam more and more commercials into the programs, even going so far as to superimpose commercial messages in characters running across the bottom of the screen during various programs. Five-second commercial messages also proliferated; their frequent and mindless music (most were jingles) often drove viewers to distraction—I recall watching them while waiting for a plane at Osaka airport in 1976 and still can remember the music of one especially annoying ad for soy sauce—but many advertisers loved them because they were cheap and effective. In 1975 the Japanese NAB revised its standards on permissible amounts of TV commercial time and outlawed superimposed commercials except in cases of coverage of extended events without natural breaks (sports in particular), but there was no notable decrease in amounts of time given over to commercials.

The controversy over violence on television continued throughout the 1970s, fueled by TV coverage of the Vietnam War, the dangers of environmental pollution, and other factual violence. While some viewers praised television for bringing the attention of the public to such things, others thought that there was too much emphasis on the more gory details. Neither the commercial stations nor the NHK at that time went to the sensationalizing lengths exhibited by U.S. TV news operations, but competition among the commercial stations sometimes did drive them to provide particularly thorough, well-nigh obsessive coverage of disasters.

While local and regional broadcasting had developed rather nicely in radio, television remained essentially a national medium until the mid-1970s, when the NHK and some of the commercial stations (especially those that found themselves facing increased competition in the early 1970s' wave of UHF licensing, which brought a fifth commercial station to Tokyo) began to add and/or expand local newscasts and public affairs shows. Even as of the mid-1980s, however, NHK's General TV Service offered an average of only about 1½ hours of local programming out of an average 17½-hour day. Commercial TV stations were averaging something over 10 percent of the broadcast day in local programming, although some stations fell below that mark.

As the NHK and the commercial stations headed into the 1980s, they could look back upon more than two decades of rapid growth in television and the decline and recovery of radio: Almost every household had a TV set, nearly two-thirds had two or more, and one or another household member watched TV daily, while radio listening climbed from an average daily figure of 21 percent in 1970 to 26 percent in 1980. Commercial revenue figures grew nicely during that decade, as well, and for both radio and TV. For NHK, however, the fact that almost all Japanese households had TV sets meant that there would be practically no further expansion in license-fee revenues unless the fees themselves were raised—an unpopular move, but one that became necessary in 1976, when the color TV fee was increased about 50 percent and the black and white fee about 33 percent. Even at that, NHK ran a deficit during much of the 1970s and continued to do so into the 1980s. It economized on administrative staff but attempted to keep the same over-all quantity and quality of production. As of the mid-1980s, it still was able to compete successfully with individual commercial TV stations, but collectively the latter usually had higher ratings, especially in the "Golden Hour." In turn, that led some Japanese households to grumble about paying license fees at all, let alone higher ones, since, as some of them claimed, they themselves never watched NHK and therefore did not see why they should pay for it. But NHK programmers remained determined to produce high-quality news, documentaries, special events coverage, educational material, and traditional as well as contemporary drama. Commercial broadcasters had become more and more active in developing newscasts and special events coverage, but both they and NHK seemed to feel that the latter probably still was best equipped to handle certain types of programs. Thus, the Japanese viewer continues to enjoy the benefits of a system with some very clear programming choices.

Financing

Broadcasting in Japan is financed by two means: annual license fees for NHK and advertising for the commercial stations. Program sales abroad constitute a negligible source of income for either sector. License fees are proposed by NHK when it submits its budget to the Diet each year; in some years, NHK does not propose an increase, in some years it proposes one and the proposal is rejected by the Diet, and in some years the two parties agree, although not often does the Diet approve the full increase requested by NHK. Increases often have come in spurts: The inflationary years immediately following World War II saw several increases, as did the period from the mid-1970s to the mid-1980s, during which time production costs rose rapidly. In 1968, licenses for radio sets only were abolished and higher fees for color TV were introduced. Over the next several years, color TV set ownership increased rapidly, and NHK was able to do without license fee increases. However, by the mid-1970s most households had color sets, and revenue increases leveled off. As costs of providing service continued to climb, NHK felt compelled to propose a sharp increase in 1976. It took the precautionary step of convening a council made of up twenty-three prominent citizens to study the proposed increase and evaluate it.[19] The council's report was supportive, but there was considerable public criticism of the proposal, in part on the grounds that some viewers claimed to watch only commercial TV. The increase passed, but subsequent increases also have met with opposition of much the same nature, and NHK has operated at a deficit for over a decade.

Commercial broadcasting had to convince business and industry that broadcast advertising would be useful to them — no easy task in a nation where mass media advertising had been pretty much limited to the press. As listenership and viewership for commercial radio and television increased, so did advertising expenditure on them. TV trailed radio until 1958, but then moved ahead rapidly. As of 1985, advertising expenditures on television took up about 35 percent of the overall Japanese media advertising budget, while newspapers accounted for 29 percent and radio about 5 percent. Competition among the radio and TV companies has been severe, but no commercial company has gone out of business, although one radio station supported by a religious group failed in the mid-1950s and a commercial educational TV station in Tokyo founded by the Japan Science Foundation was allowed to convert itself into a general broadcaster in the early 1970s after having failed to operate profitably.

The Japanese National Association of Commercial Broadcasters has established time standards for commercials, which stood at six minutes per hour for radio and for TV as of 1985. Total TV ad time was not to exceed 18 percent of total broadcast time. But five-minute programs could carry one minute of advertising, and in theory an hour made up of twelve five-minute programs could carry twelve minutes of ads. No such broadcast hour exists, but there are some five- and ten-minute programs that appear to have been developed especially to maximize ad time. As with U.S. broadcasting, there is sponsorship, participating sponsorship, and spot advertising. Japanese viewers sometimes complain about frequency of interruptions of programming for ads, as well as the timing of interruptions (often at the crucial moment of a drama), but surveys have indicated that most Japanese think of ads as a small price to pay and often consider them highly useful in daily living. Some even consider the musical jingles — a common feature of Japanese broadcast advertising — to be a good way to develop a musical sense in children![20]

There are relatively few restrictions on the content of advertising. The NAB's Code of Broadcasting Standards forbids ads "questionable for public morals and [for] sexual apparatus [sic], ads encouraging belief in superstitions, promoting the services of private investigators or for the sole purpose of publicizing an individual." The standards also discourage use of superlatives in ads, and caution against carrying ads that "overly excite or influence children's desire to obtain advertised article or object."[21] Most of those restrictions allow considerable latitude of interpretation. Rare among broadcast organizations around the world, political advertising is legal on Japanese commercial broadcasting, so long as all candidates competing for the same office are allowed to purchase time. Subtitle ads (characters superimposed and run across the bottom of the screen during a production) are allowable only if the program is of a continuous nature, with no natural breaks (e.g., sports events). Most ads run ten to thirty seconds; about 75 percent of them run fifteen seconds. Five-second ads were common until the mid-1960s but largely disappeared then because of expressions of intense public dissatisfaction. Foreign (and especially U.S.) faces appear frequently on Japanese TV ads for luxury products,[22] partly because of the implication that people buying the products are "worldly," partly because use of foreigners shows that the advertiser is sound enough financially to hire them.[23] It is not unusual to see shaving lotions or other "glamour" products advertised in such incongruous (for Japan) surroundings as fox hunts, complete with Japanese actors decked out in appropriate hunting livery and surrounded by hounds!

The largely unregulated nature of broadcast advertising has led to calls from some consumer groups for tighter controls, but so far the advertising industry and the commercial broadcasters have convinced the Diet that self-regulation works perfectly well. One aspect of broadcast advertising that has caused problems in other countries, advertising directed at children, has been handled in Japan by the simple expedient of the NAB's banning such advertising. Many products that children are likely to buy, candy in particular, are advertised on radio and TV, but ostensibly the ads are pitched at adult viewers and listeners.

Governance and Administration — Internal

In U.S. business circles, Japan has become known for an approach to decision making that places great emphasis on collective mediation, discussion, and final decisions. Such an approach also characterizes broadcasting, both NHK and commercial, but only in certain situations. Long-range program planning and consideration of broader financial matters are handled in that manner, but day-to-day program decision making is not. The collective approach takes time, and most Japanese programs are made within the same time constraints as are programs in most parts of the world. Thus, heads of programming departments, producers, and others involved in the production process have considerable autonomy. There may be more collective consideration of how to shoot a given scene or whether to modify a certain line of script than there is in U.S. broadcasting, as I have witnessed in my visits to NHK TV studios, but decisions are not reached in a leisurely manner.

The president of NHK (appointed by the NHK Board of Governors) works with the board of managing directors, itself composed of the president and vice president of NHK, the director general of engineering, and the NHK general managing directors and managing directors, to consider broad policy and administrative and financial issues. The board deliberates overall program policy but seldom concerns itself with specific programs. Up until the late 1970s, it had been established practice to appoint the president from outside the NHK, but in the late 1970s the board chose an NHK senior administrative official for the post, partly in reaction to the resignation of NHK President Kichiro Ono in 1975 for his "lack of political neutrality." (He had paid a house call on Prime Minister Kakeui Tanaka when the latter was under indictment for his role in the Lockheed bribery scandal.)

The Broadcast Act of 1950 requires NHK and the commercial broadcasters to appoint broadcast consultative committees, but it is up to the broadcasters themselves to decide who shall be invited to join. The act specifies that no more than one-third of the committee membership shall be broadcast staff. Committees meet as often as the broadcaster wishes to convene them, but usually for one-day sessions and four to six times a year. Most people consider it an honor to be appointed to such a committee, and the committee membership seldom engages in anything resembling a vigorous critical review of programs.

The Broadcast Act also specifies a board of governors to supervise NHK. Its twelve members are appointed by the prime minister with the advice and consent of both houses of the Diet. Eight of the members are to come from the country's eight administrative districts, while the remaining four are chosen at large. No member is supposed to think of her- or himself as representing a district or any particular occupational or other constituency; instead, each is to evaluate NHK in terms of how well it fulfills its broad public-service mandate. Appointees usually come from a wide field of occupations: industry, labor, education, science, religion, and so on. The board approves financial plans made by NHK, examines past, present, and projected programming, and has several other powers that in theory are quite broad. But the board and NHK management generally present a united front in any public statements, partly because of the Japanese fondness for a "consensus management" style, partly because NHK management usually is able to convince the board that management knows what it is doing. As board members rarely have much experience with or prior knowledge of broadcasting, and as the board meets only once a month and usually for less than a day each time, it is a bit difficult for a board member to take issue with an NHK administrator.

The commercial stations have their industry-wide self-regulatory body, the National Association of Commercial Broadcasters. Membership is voluntary, but every commercial station belongs to the NAB, which administers the aforementioned code. There are no penalties for violation of code provisions — just the strong moral pressure of other broadcasters to keep in line, so as to avoid the admittedly remote possibility of increased government regulation. The NAB itself does not inform the public of alleged violations of the code, but there is a Council for Better Programming, established jointly by NHK and the commercial broadcasters, which is made up of seven persons of high public standing (appointed by the broadcasters), and which meets several times a year to discuss programs and to pass along the results of its deliberations to the broadcasters. It has access to reports from one thousand observers throughout Japan, and some of those reports as well as the council's deliberations occasionally receive media attention, particularly if the council testifies before the Diet. Still, broadcasters are not required to pass the results of those deliberations along to the public, and given the strong ties that link the major newspapers and the leading commercial broadcasters, adverse publicity regarding the latter is not likely to be published by the former.

Local stations throughout Japan, both NHK and commercial, originate relatively little programming and have little to say regarding what comes to them from the major program sources in Tokyo and Osaka. It is legally possible for local stations to reject the offerings of the major sources, but such a move would risk incurring the wrath of local viewers and would make it necessary for the local station to fill the gap with its own resources. Most local stations have modest production budgets and little production capability other than for informational and educational programs; nor is there much syndicated material available.

There are unions of broadcast personnel in Japan, and every now and again they protest employment practices and conditions of employment. However, although there have been major strikes in various Japanese industries, and even occasional general strikes, these have had little effect upon broadcasting, and broadcast unions have not put stations off the air even temporarily.

Governance and Administration – External

NATIONAL GOVERNMENT The Broadcast Act of 1950 was passed by the Diet, which also has the power to amend it and has done so on several occasions, generally to clarify responsibility for programming decisions. The Diet also on occasion holds hearings on various aspects of broadcast policy, especially program policy; while some criticism may emerge in the course of those hearings, it is rare for them to lead to changes in the law or to any sort of penalty for the broadcasters. The Diet also reviews NHK's annual expenditures and proposed budget and approves changes in the license fee. That review provides the closest thing to periodic government review of broadcasting, but it covers only NHK, and it usually does not probe program practices all that deeply. The Diet also passed the Radio Law of 1950; that law deals with the technical aspects of broadcast communication.

The Ministry of Posts and Telecommunications is responsible for licensing stations, and no station may broadcast without a license from the ministry. Presuming that there are frequencies available—and the crowded nature of much of Japan means that often they are not—an applicant should be of good character, have ties with the community to be served by the station, have no more than one other station of the same kind (FM radio, UHF-TV, etc.), and own no other media outlet in the same community. Licensing of NHK stations differs from licensing of commercial stations in several respects: It is understood that NHK stations will be part of a network and will be subordinate to the central station in Tokyo, whereas commercial stations may not form networks based on central stations to which others are subordinate; NHK stations generally will be given priority in licensing, since they form part of a national public service for which the general public pays; and NHK stations are not subject to ownership limitations, since in effect they are "owned" by the public.

The ministry grants licenses for periods of up to three years. Public hearings precede the issuance of the initial license, but thereafter renewals are pro forma and do not involve public hearings unless there is a challenger to the present licensee (there have been none in the history of Japanese broadcasting) or unless specific complaints have been lodged against the station (exceedingly rare). If there are complaints, the ministry's Radio Regulatory Commission investigates them and issues recommendations for the minister of posts. Such investigations are publicly announced, and any interested party may participate; however, commission investigations are rare. The commission also may hear station complaints against ministerial decisions. The minister may take away a station's license, which never has occurred, but there is no penalty short of this, such as fines. A station dissatisfied with its treatment at that level may take its case to the Tokyo High Court, but none ever has.

In short, the governmental system does not exert much pressure on broadcasting. It seems to be assumed that those entrusted with the responsibility will broadcast in the public interest and do not need continual supervision or threat of legal action to be induced to do so. It also helps that the "power elite" of Japanese society includes a number of station administrators, and it would be a most unusual move if the government were to bring ultimate disgrace to a station owner by revoking her or his license (almost certainly "his" in male-dominated Japan). Too, the interlinking structure that knits newspapers and commercial stations together has power of its own, and any individual politician or government minister considering punishment of a station might run the risk of adverse media publicity. Such a politician or minister would be far more likely to talk things out with the station.

The Ministry of Posts and Telecommunications takes a cautious approach to the issuance of licenses for commercial stations, allocating only a few in any given market. Tokyo has three NHK radio stations, four AM and one FM commercial stations, and six commercial and two NHK TV stations, while Osaka, Nagoya, and most of the other "million plus" cities have only slightly less; but many other Japanese cities have only one or two commercial radio and commercial TV stations. Smaller towns and cities, even some with populations in excess of one hundred thousand, may have no stations of their own, although they will be served by NHK and commercial station relay transmitters. Competition, then, is more severely circumscribed than is the case in many countries with commercial broadcast systems. In part this is caused by a lack of enough mutually exclusive frequencies in this crowded country, but in part it seems due to a deliberate attempt on the ministry's part not to allow too many stations on the air so that those that are licensed will not have to sacrifice program standards in the name of economic survival.

Individual citizens wishing to complain about the content of a specific broadcast are encouraged to direct their complaints to a station's consultative committee, which all stations must have. If the complaints involve allegedly untrue broadcasts, and provided that the complaints are lodged within two weeks of the broadcast, the station's consultative committee must investigate. Complaints also may be brought to the Radio Regulatory Commission and to the courts but very rarely are.

There is no significant involvement of either prefecture or local governments in broadcasting, although municipal governments have shown some interest in working closely with cable operations.

NONGOVERNMENTAL   In some respects, Japanese broadcasting is organized to take into account several manifestations of citizen reaction to radio and television. However, most of this is done on the broadcaster's initiative or is prescribed by law but with power of appointment to the advisory councils in the hands of the broadcaster. The NHK, for example, has several means of keeping in touch with the public, including audience advisory councils (required by law); audience and program forums (not required, but used by NHK to allow members of the public at large to attend meetings and ask questions directly of NHK staff); a Long-range Vision Council appointed by, and advisory to, the NHK president and made up of "prominent members of society"; broadcast utilization groups (an NHK-developed system for getting comments from people who view and listen to NHK cultural and educational broadcasts); as well as the more common modes of survey research, visits to broadcast stations, and audience mail. Those means combined produce millions of audience-broadcaster contacts, and no one requires audience members to initiate them, so they doubtless serve to reflect some aspects of public opinion. The commercial stations have a far less elaborate system of audience feedback, but it, too, results in millions of contacts.

Citizens wishing to express their discontent with broadcasting may do so through the system just outlined, but some feel that their reactions either will fall on deaf ears or will be lost in the bureaucratic maze, so a few groups, especially parents and educators, have organized their own forums and have attempted to work through the Diet and/or through the print media (much of which, as already mentioned, is linked financially to commercial broadcasting) to achieve reform. They have met with little success, although some group members have become fairly prominent as protest figures. There is no absolute right of access to the media themselves, for these groups or for any other outsiders, and the sorts of "access TV" programs that have become fairly common in U.S. and some Western European broadcast systems are extremely rare on Japanese television.

Programming

PHILOSOPHIES   There is a vast difference between a typical broadcast day on an NHK radio or television station and on a commercial station. Because NHK derives its financial support from license fees, it considers itself to have a responsibility to serve both the general public and as many specific segments of it as possible. Its domestic program standards[24] also make it clear that NHK sees itself as upholder of traditional Japanese moral values and even linguistic standards. The commercial stations, too, have sets of program standards and present themselves as public servants, but competition and financial need combine to create a far more mass-oriented approach to programming than that displayed by NHK. There is no coordination of program schedules between the two entities, but they have jointly established, and are advised by, a Broadcaster's Council for Better Programming (seven prominent individuals, appointed by the entities) and the two and other groups also have created the Broadcast Programming Center of Japan, to aid commercial broadcasters in producing and airing educational broadcasts.

The NHK and commercial broadcasters have roughly similar philosophies in presenting informational material, but quite different philosophies when dealing with cultural programs. Several provisions of the Broadcast Act of 1950 (Articles 1, 50, and 52) speak to a requirement of impartiality, freedom of expression, and the presentation of diverse points of view on controversial issues, and Article 52 specifically requires that, if one candidate for public office is allowed broadcast time, whether paid or unpaid, all other candidates are to be allowed equal time on equal conditions. The NHK has invested more time, money, and effort in the presentation of informational material than have the commercial stations: Its General TV Service devotes over 50 percent of its total airtime to informational programs, while the most information-oriented commercial station, the Tokyo Broadcasting Station (TBS), offers about 27 percent.[25] The NHK may not editorialize; private stations are allowed to, but very few do so.

There is a fairly large amount of political broadcasting on both NHK and the commercial stations. Most stations provide time for political discussions and interviews, the NHK more than the commercial sector. No station may endorse candidates, but all must provide time for candidates during election periods. Article 150 of the Election Law states that broadcasters may not censor candidate broadcasts, but Article 250 of the same law states that candidates may not say things that are harmful to the public welfare. The NHK did prevent one candidate from airing his message on those grounds (he made what were felt to be slurs against the handicapped), and when challenged, finally won the case in Tokyo High Court in 1986.[26]

Both broadcasters seem to take the requirements of the Broadcast Law seriously where information is concerned and provide reasonably complete and impartial treatment of news and public affairs, although neither does much along the lines of investigative reporting. Nor does either appear to go out of its way to cover controversial issues, although TBS broadcast the anti–South Vietnamese/United States views of one of its reporters, Hideo Den, at the height of the Vietnam War (and shortly after was pressured by unspecified sources, but probably within the pro–United States Japanese government, to "accept the resignation" of Den).[27]

Cultural broadcasts differ in part because the NHK generally has taken upon itself the obligation to preserve traditional elements of Japanese culture and to promote living culture. If NHK broadcasts a fifteenth-century tale, it will make the production as authentic as possible, in setting, costuming, and staging. If it broadcasts an original drama for television, it will employ the same care and will enlist the cooperation of the author in making the production as true to her or his vision as possible. Commercial broadcasters are far more apt to treat traditional or contemporary drama as pegs on which to hang action, feeling that this is the key to attracting larger audiences. Commercial broadcasters also are more likely to imitate already successful entertainment shows and to emphasize the colorful, loud, and comedic aspects of shows than is the NHK; again, the attraction of large audiences seems to be the main reason for the difference in approaches.

RADIO   The NHK has two AM radio services and one FM service. The First Service on AM (5:00 A.M. to 12:00 midnight) carries frequent and often highly detailed newscasts throughout the day and evening, a great deal of Japanese and some western popular music, and many talk and discussion programs for particular segments of the audience: farmers, homemakers, fishermen, and so on. Some of the shows involve audience participation, either through telephone or in person. Much of the content of the Second AM Service (5:30 A.M. to midnight) is directed to schools and to people studying on their own, and both this radio service and the NHK Educational Television Service broadcast many programs for the NHK Correspondence High School, a continuing education project that has existed since 1963 and that combines broadcasts, correspondence, and classroom sessions to allow students who dropped out of high school to complete their education.[28] The FM service (6:00 A.M. to midnight) is very music oriented and broadcasts both western classical and Japanese classical and traditional music in stereo during most of the day and evening. It also occasionally presents radio dramas, both Japanese and foreign. The NHK's local and regional stations usually provide an hour or two per day of regional and local news, reports on cultural activities, and for some stations, educational broadcasts.

Commercial radio is a much simpler mix of program elements. Most companies have only one radio service, and almost all of them provide little besides four commodities: news (usually of a wire services supplied "rip and read" variety or from a central station in Tokyo) and weather; sports (baseball); quiz shows and other contests; and most of all music (popular and a mixture of Japanese and western, which sometimes are barely distinguishable). There are ads, too, of course, sometimes for as much as twelve minutes in the hour. A few commercial stations in the largest cities broadcast Japanese and western classical music. A number of commercial stations broadcast twenty-four hours a day. Two of the commercial networks began to strengthen their news operations late in the 1970s, and one of them, Bunka-Hoso, became the first western station to obtain an interview with the students who were holding American hostages at the U.S. embassy in Iran.

TELEVISION   The two NHK television services, the general and the educational, are as different as their names imply. The General Service (6:00 A.M. to 12:00 midnight) provides a wide variety of programming: news and public affairs; quiz shows; soap operas; traditional and modern drama, both domestic and foreign; documentaries; discussion and panel shows, often for specialized audiences; concerts of traditional and modern Japanese and western music; series about nature; and, to a very small extent, sports. The Educational Service (6:00 A.M. to 12:00 midnight) is far less balanced in output, devoting almost two-thirds of its airtime to specifically educational material for children and adults, in and out of school. The University of the Air, which began broadcasting in 1984, is an especially impressive example of the government's interest in opening higher education to those previously unable to afford the time or the money for it. It is modeled after the British Open University, which the Japanese studied for several years before mounting their own version of it. The remaining airtime goes into cultural programs, the majority of them factual presentations about architecture, history, science and technology, the theater, cinema, literature, and the visual arts. The commercial stations offer programs in most of the genres presented by the two NHK services, but entertainment series and game shows generally account for over 50 percent of their output, and cultural programs (factual programs about or exhibiting culture) account for well under 10 percent of their broadcast days. Most of them broadcast very little educational material.[29]

Unlike many European television systems, Japanese TV stations are on continuously from morning until night, and there are periods in the morning, afternoon, and evening when both NHK and the commercial broadcasters assume that there are large audiences available to watch. It is the only television system in the world where weekday morning and afternoon audiences reach mass proportions. This is due in large measure to a seemingly insatiable Japanese appetite for news, and almost every station (NHK's Educational Service is the major exception) provides a block of news somewhere between 8:00 and 10:00 A.M. and again around the noon hour, while one commercial channel, TV 10 Asahi, brings in the U.S. Cable News Network service (in English) after

1:00 A.M., mixing it with Japanese news and often using female anchors. The morning and noontime news programs usually are combined with light feature material and a fifteen-minute soap opera. NHK has broadcast fifteen-minute soap operas in the morning since the 1950s, and some have become tremendously popular. *Oshin,* which ran for a year from 1983 to 1984, and which presented the hard and sometimes tragic life of a fictional female who achieved success in her older age but who had "paid her dues" in attaining that success, quite regularly pulled ratings of 50 percent and led politicians and other prominent figures to invoke the image of the "Oshin spirit" in their public remarks.[30]

Much of the morning and afternoon periods on the commercial channels is given over to quiz shows, interview shows, and other low-budget offerings (some of which look as if they have been shot with no more than two cameras, and relatively immobile cameras, at that). Weekends often mean baseball on the commercial channels, and one sometimes finds as many as four baseball games on the six commercial channels in the Tokyo area. The NHK sports broadcasts are more likely to feature unusual contests (fencing, for example) or amateur contestants. Late afternoons on weekdays are cartoon time for children on commercial TV. Quiz shows, variety programs, and dramas fill the evening hours on NHK's General Service and on the commercial channels, but documentaries, especially on foreign countries and on nature, also are fairly common on both types of broadcast service. Few U.S. dramas appear on Japanese television, and when they do, they are usually relegated to something other than a "Golden Hour" time slot — usually after 12:00 midnight (most commercial channels stay on until 1:00 A.M. or later, and a few of them in the larger cities may not sign off until after 3:00 A.M. on weekends). Certain U.S. dramas that have become very popular in other parts of the world, notably *Dallas,* have not done at all well in Japan,[31] apparently because they are too slow moving, and are centered on moral issues (e.g., extramarital sex) that many Japanese find uninteresting. *Miami Vice* got a somewhat warmer reception. Japanese feature-length movies, most of them made for exhibition in cinemas, appear fairly often during the "Golden Hour."

The late-night broadcasts on the commercial channels probably have earned the nation's (commercial) broadcast system more notoriety than has any single block of program material anywhere else in the world. Late-night game and interview shows feature nudity (usually female, but occasionally male), very risqué jokes and skits, "frank" discussion of sexual problems and situations, and so on. One game show, which ran for years, was a TV version of strip poker, with two men playing rounds of a game and two women removing their garments. The game never concluded with either woman forced to divest everything, because the contestants always would "run out of time," as the losing woman was begging not to suffer the ultimate humiliation. There are late night Johnny-Carson-like shows in which "experimental" filmmakers display what amounts to "blue" movies, but which are passed off as "high art," usually because they feature unusual cutting techniques, lenses, visual angles, and so on. Daytime shows aren't quite so bold (by western standards — most Japanese viewers don't appear to be offended by them), but for years there have been "amateur stripper" and "breast size" contests on some commercial stations during the early afternoon hours.[32] There have been some complaints from feminist groups, parent, and teachers about these and other shows centering on sex, but no serious attempts on the part of the government to prohibit them.

The typical Japanese TV schedule would seem quite familiar to an American viewer, aside from the specific content of many of the late-night programs. So would many of the situations portrayed in the dramas. For example, a drama presented on (commercial) NTV in February 1987, *Onna Keiji* (Detective Woman), had the following plot outline: "Special police detective Reiko's best friend commits suicide after having an affair with an assistant professor. When he also commits suicide, Reiko suspects murder. The prime suspects are the professor's wife and lover, as well as the father of Reiko's friend."[33]

Big-city settings and crime, usually committed by amateurs, are common attributes of drama on Japanese commercial television. Situation comedies are rare; when they appear, they are quite apt to feature school settings. Satire is even more rare, although one commercial channel, TV Tokyo, has produced a parody of TV news called *The Television*. United States movies, too, show up once or twice a week during the "Golden Hour" on the Japanese commercial channels. Contests featuring amateur performers, popular since they were introduced on radio just after World War II, are available on one or another channel most nights of the week.

Where program popularity is concerned, the morning news shows and soap operas, especially that on NHK, the "Golden Hour" game and variety shows and amateur talent contests, and several of the crime and samurai dramas, appear to be the leading choices. Given the highly competitive situation prevailing in the Tokyo (or Kanto) and Osaka-Kyoto (or Kansai) areas — where there are five to six commercial stations and two NHK stations and, in effect, five commercial and two NHK networks — program ratings above the 20 percent range are not that common. Percentage ratings in the high teens, which would have been considered marginal in the U.S. system before the mid-1980s, long have been acceptable in Japan.

Although NHK still is regarded as the leading purveyor of broadcast journalism, the commercial networks have increased the quantity and raised the quality of their efforts in that domain since the late 1970s. Most of them carry news programs three times a day, and a few have four or five newscasts daily. A few of the newscasts last no more than four or five minutes, but some take up nearly an hour and often feature reports from the station's own overseas correspondents. The NHK and commercial station reporters and correspondents provide very thorough coverage of events but very seldom indulge in anything resembling investigative reporting. There probably are several reasons for this, but one surely is the "clubby" atmosphere in which Japanese reporters seek to interview important governmental and nongovernmental news sources. Reporters, print and broadcast alike, are assigned to certain beats, and often the reporters who cover a given organization or ministry will function as a group, operating through what are called *kisha* (reporter) clubs; the clubs themselves may have office space and even clerical help provided by the organizations they cover. Reporters are expected to conduct group interviews; individual interviews are a rarity.[34]

In another respect, however, Japanese reporters appear to behave in a way that would be immediately recognizable to a U.S. observer of the media. Once certain major cases involving alleged criminal behavior have been made public (often through revelation by some small circulation magazine), reporters have gathered outside the homes of suspects, "keeping watch . . . from morning to night so that members of the families could not even go out shopping and were confined indoors literally holding their breath."[35] The right to privacy is not clearly defined in Japanese law, and despite protests over such behavior by reporters, that behavior continues.

Documentaries often appear in the "Golden Hour," and usually are beautifully produced. The Chinese Television–NHK 1980 twelve-episode documentary on the "Silk Road" that served as a trade link between East and West centuries ago was shot at a cost of over 10 million dollars but managed to achieve ratings of nearly 20 percent against stiff commercial competition during the "Golden Hour." *The Yellow River,* an NHK–Chinese Television multipart documentary aired in 1987, did nearly as well. The commercial Tokyo Broadcasting System has produced many documentaries about Japanese history and has broadcast them during the "Golden Hour," at times with ratings in the midteens. Documentaries dealing with history and with problems and situations in other countries are most common, but there are productions by both NHK and some of the commercial stations on contemporary problems in Japan, too: Teenage suicides (alarmingly high, and due in large measure to the intense pressures of the Japanese educational system), industrial pollution, Japan's self-defense policy, AIDS, and so on. As with the news, those productions are thorough, but accusing fingers are pointed far less often than is the case in U.S. or British television. Perhaps this stems from a reluctance in the Japanese character to confront other individuals directly, perhaps the "club" system of reporting has its influence, perhaps the interlinked nature of the "movers and shakers" segment of Japanese society mutes direct criticism. Whatever the reasons, Japanese broadcast journalism appears to be far stronger in its capacity as reporter than in its capacity as interpreter or critic.

The Audience

Few broadcast organizations anywhere in the world can rival the Japanese in conducting audience research. Commercial broadcasters restrict themselves largely to quantitative data gathering (research firms operate much as do their counterparts in the United States, and A. C. Nielsen has a Japanese affiliate), while NHK operates a Public Opinion Research Institute which gathers both quantitative and qualitative data.

Quantitative research studies reveal that the average Japanese individual spends approximately forty-five minutes a day listening to the radio and approximately three hours and ten minutes a day watching television. As mentioned earlier, news and public-affairs programs often achieve very high ratings, especially on TV. Fictional series and game and quiz shows do likewise. Cultural and educational programs, though many in number and high in quality of production, usually are watched by less than 5 percent of the available audience.

The NHK's Public Opinion Research Institute conducted a survey in 1971 in which Japanese viewers were asked why they watched TV drama. The two leading reasons, offered by 40 and 35 percent of the sample (N = 2,712) respectively, were "just to enjoy" and "to relax," but the next three (32, 31, and 29 percent) had to do with "thinking about the way in which various people live," "gaining help in leading their own lives," and "satisfying interest in customs, manners, eras, and places shown in the dramas."[36]

Late in 1982, NHK conducted a survey (N = 2,737) in which respondents were asked to take a retrospective look at television, now that it had been around for roughly thirty years. Thirty-eight percent said that they now watched television for less time than they used to, and 28 percent stated that they were less interested in television than they once had been. However, when respondents were asked whether they though that it was necessary to have NHK TV and commercial TV, 89 percent said yes to NHK and 88 percent to commercial TV. Younger viewers, especially those in their twenties, were most apt to like to watch TV commercials (73 percent of male and 75 percent of female viewers in their twenties said they did). Many viewers claimed to have been inspired to do certain things after watching TV: Of the women, 53 percent interviewed said that they had cooked dishes according to TV recipes, and 35 percent said that they had exercised while watching TV gymnastics. Looking to the future, there was especially high interest (35 percent or above) on the part of viewers in having special news or information appear on the TV screen on command, in having specialized TV stations (all sports, etc.), and in having access to first-run movies, international sports events, and so on. Respondents claimed that they would willingly pay for such services.[37]

Reactions to TV by Japanese viewers are not all that different from reactions of U.S. viewers. As I mentioned earlier in the chapter, the relative credibility of TV in Japan is about the same as it is in the United States. The amount of time spent on TV viewing in Japan is even higher than it is in the United States, and the size of TV audiences in the weekday morning and noon hours would make U.S. TV executives envious, but viewer likes and dislikes are quite similar. And, just as in the United States and in some Western European nations, there are a few signs of disenchantment or weariness with television. In 1969 and again in 1979, NHK asked survey respondents to evaluate the "pleasure of television viewing" on a five-point scale. The fourth ("watching TV is more fun than doing nothing, but it is nonetheless little more than a way to help pass the time") and fifth ("cannot enjoy watching contemporary TV") positions on the scale showed respective figures of 18 percent and 1 percent in 1969, and 24 percent and 3 percent in 1979. However, there was no overall pattern of decline in terms of hours spent watching television, so it may be that viewers were more dissatisfied and yet watching just as much as ever.[38]

Broadcasters rely on other evidence when attempting to determine audience preferences and objections, of course, and NHK in particular, as I have indicated, diligently elicits audience feedback through a variety of mechanisms. But the audience appears to be a passive one: A 1980 NHK survey ($N = 4,048$) asked respondents whether they would like to convey their views or have their wishes reflected in TV programs; 4

percent said they "would like actively to do so" and another 36 percent said that they would like to do so "if the opportunity presents itself," while 45 percent said that they were "not particularly interested in doing so" and another 14 percent claimed "absolutely no interest whatsoever in such things."[39] As former NHK executive Tadao Nomura has pointed out, "access" broadcasting has no specific legal status in Japan, although Haiman indicates that broadcasters *are* obligated to broadcast corrections or withdrawals of false statements; however, there is no provision that requires stations to allow the injured party to reply on her or his own behalf.[40] Also, few Japanese appear to think of themselves as active participants in broadcasting. More and more Japanese households are acquiring video cameras along with their VCRs, but that does not appear to have led to increasing demands for access to the airwaves.

Problem Areas

In view of what I have just said, it might be especially advisable in considering problems within Japanese broadcasting to remind ourselves that those problems are likely to appear far larger and more serious to the small band of TV critics (professional and amateur) and introspective broadcasters than they are to the viewing nations as a whole. Although there are no precise measurements to support this statement, it is my impression that the problems of television receive far less media and public attention in Japan than they do in the United States, Great Britain, West Germany, and other large industrial nations in the West. It could be that Japanese broadcasting is more problem free than it is in other countries, but the passivity apparent in the 1980 survey just cited probably plays a role here, too. Recall also that the Japanese press is a major source of financial support for commercial broadcasting, which may have the effect of muting broadcast criticism in the newspapers.

That small band of critics has been quite consistent over time in its observations of the shortcomings of Japanese broadcasting. Heading the list would be "inanity": A number of critics have repeatedly decried the mindless nature of so much Japanese television and radio, especially the commercial variety. The aforementioned claim that TV was turning Japan into "a nation of a hundred million imbeciles" has been repeated many times. It does not appear to have deterred the viewing public from watching those programs, and every year the "Golden Hour" is certain to include many action-filled comedies and adventure shows, most of them repetitions of formulas that have been around since the early days of TV.

The daytime shows, usually cheaply produced, repeat the same formulas year after year, adding occasional bits of novelty, as in the "talk and amateur variety" show *Waratte-iitomo* (Go Ahead and Laugh), which uses "telephone shocking": A person in the studio audience calls a total stranger and asks all sorts of very direct and personal questions. The stranger is invited to come to the studio the next day and do the same to someone else, and so on. The average audience for the show is about 20 million.[41] Japanese commercial broadcasters have told me that they feel ashamed to exhibit most of their entertainment programs to non-Japanese, because *gaijin* (foreigners) will get the idea that Japanese are rude, boisterous, silly people, and some of the broadcasters have said that they prefer that their children not watch those programs. But the highly competitive nature of Japanese television and the apparent continuing popularity of the old formulas have meant that the status quo has prevailed, even extending to apparent rudeness to foreigners: One commercial station produced a documentary featuring two nomadic herders from Kenya, brought to Tokyo by the station. As they expressed dumbfounded amazement at such things as telephones and roller coasters, they were teased and mocked. The Kenyan ambassador to Japan protested, and Kenyan President Daniel Arap Moi warned the nation's people not to be tricked into similar episodes.[42] Still, commercial broadcasters, if not critics, always can excuse themselves by noting that NHK provides a clear alternative, if viewers want one.

Whether that alternative is sufficiently creative is another issue that sometimes concerns media observers. Few critics expect the commercial stations to exhibit much originality and seem to be quite amazed when they do. Critics give NHK high marks for quality of production in terms of careful lighting, staging, editing, and so on but sometimes fault it for lacking boldness. In the mid-1970s, NHK developed a Special Projects Department, mainly for the purpose of getting individuals from various program production divisions together to share ideas and to make documentaries cooperatively. While there remain some questions as to whether the best production staff will be encouraged or even allowed by their divisional directors to divert some of their efforts in this direction, the system appears to be working to produce innovative material.[43]

A third concern of critics is investigative reporting. As I have already noted, that is a problem for all of the media, not just broadcasting. Furthermore, there is some question as to whether the vast majority of Japanese expect or desire investigative reporting by the media. Even Tadao Nomura, otherwise quite outspoken in criticizing broadcasting, observed that "it *may be* [italics mine] the responsibility of the mass media in a democratic society to strip away the veil of secrecy hanging over the exclusive elite groups and expose corruption and its true nature before the public."[44] There is a reluctance in Japanese society to criticize those who hold positions of honor, at least until they have shown themselves to be unworthy of that honor. But how is the public to learn of dishonor? Media reporters, including those in broadcasting, may be increasingly interested in investigative reporting, but the systemic constraints of broadcast journalism described earlier will not make this an easy objective to achieve.

A fourth problem takes the form of political influence, which usually manifests itself through members of the government administration or Diet calling broadcasters to express their personal concerns over one or another program. Broadcasters are expected to take their cues from such personal expressions and mend their ways. The NHK, which has its annual budget approved by the Diet, may receive personal threats of budget cuts, as it did in the mid-1970s when it covered the Tanaka-Lockheed scandal. (It stuck to its reporting, and the budget was not cut.)[45]

A fifth concern is the role of women in television. Beginning in the mid-1970s, a few women who had been utilized as coanchorpersons on TV newscasts publicly complained of two things: first, relegation to a supporting role status, which is some instances meant that the women coanchors were restricted to making brief observations, such as "Yes," or "Is that so?" on items read by their male counterparts; if they got to report stories at all, it would be those with a clearly feminine angle. Second, women who were perceived by their male supervisors as aging (most female coanchors were, and still are, young and attractive) were taken off the air; one of them, Setsuko Murikami, challenged her demotion at Nippon Television in court and won. By the end of the 1970s, most stations had added women to the news teams, but roles changed slowly. In 1979, Nippon Television installed Yoshiko Sakurai as a full-fledged newscaster of the 11:00 P.M. news show and almost immediately enjoyed a surge in ratings, which touched off a small flurry of imitations on other stations.[46] Women are being used increasingly as reporters of something other than female stereotype stories (e.g., covering fashion shows), but two newsroom staff executives at Asahi TV told me in September 1985 that only 5 percent or so of their reporters were women, and expressed the opinion that the general public "was not yet ready" to see women interviewing politicians or business leaders, because women "lacked sufficient authority" to make such interviews credible.[47]

A sixth problem arises from the highly competitive nature of Japanese TV and takes the form of sensationalism in covering domestic events. This sensationalism attracted considerable public criticism in the mid-1980s thanks to three specific events: the deaths of over five-hundred passengers in the crash of a Japan Airlines Boeing 747 in August 1985 and the subsequent tendency of TV camera crews to dwell on the agony of relatives and of the few survivors themselves; the murder of an alleged criminal in his home, which reporters actually filmed in progress after they had surrounded his house in hopes of getting a story from him — no reporters called the police or tried to stop the killing; and the staging by an Asahi TV director of an attack by two unemployed teenagers on five schoolgirls for an Asahi TV "documentary" program entitled *Violent Shots: Total Confessions of Sexual Torture,* broadcast in November 1985.[48] (Having seen some of the coverage of the Japanese Airlines story in a visit to Japan in September 1985, I would have to agree that treatment of survivors and of relatives of victims was unusually sensational: Cameras and microphones were shoved in front of grieving individuals, most of whom tried to fend off the TV crews; even NHK, where news treatments generally are more restrained than is the case with commercial TV, was guilty of such behavior.) A number of articles in newspapers and some discussion shows on radio and TV took up the issue of why the media behaved in that fashion, to which the most common answer was "because all of the media do it." Japanese journalists may function as groups and may hold certain ethical standards in common, but competition can be an even more powerful force on occasion.

Foreign Influences on Programming

Japan has been described by some Japanese observes, such as Robert S. Ozaki and Mitsuyuki Masatsugu,[49] as a society ready to embrace wholeheartedly the latest fashion, especially if it comes from the West. During the 1950s, Japanese television certainly exhibited that trait, although part of the reason might have been the sheer inexpensiveness of imported (mostly U.S.) programs, which was especially attractive to commercial TV stations. Imports assumed a less and less prominent place as television hit its stride in the late 1950s to early 1960s, and by the mid-1980s there was little imported material left. No quota system was necessary to achieve this; the Japanese simply discovered that they could make most of what they needed, and that advertising and license fees could cover the costs.

However, much of what the stations made bore a close resemblance to U.S. television, which may or may not mean that it was consciously modeled after the U.S. example. Certainly many Japanese TV producers and directors visited the United States in the 1950s and early 1960s, and some U.S. producers and directors came to Japan to direct or participate in training programs for Japanese. Too, the U.S. shows often featured universal formulas of love, death, power, and so on, with many variations played on the same basic theme. If there was anything at all unusual in the process of influence, it was the great popularity of crime shows. Japanese society has its share of crime, but studies over time reveal that it trails the United States by a considerable margin in the extent of almost every category of criminal activity. There is a fair-sized body of crime-oriented literature (such as detective novels) in Japan, and there is considerable public fascination with criminal life, especially the activities of the Japanese mafia. But neither of those factors would fully explain why *U.S.* crime shows should have become so popular among Japanese viewers in the 1950s. However, that success soon led the commercial stations and NHK to try their hands at this genre, to the point where, at present, there are a few to several such dramas on TV during each day's "Golden Hour."

Japanese television shows a fascination with things American in a number of other ways. In 1977, Nippon Television began to broadcast a series featuring a six-year-old American (not Japanese-American) girl in a Japanese setting. The girl spoke fluent Japanese, which apparently intrigued viewers, but her outspoken manner was even more exotic: Japanese children are supposed to be seen but not heard. The series was a great success.[50] But stranger and even more popular was the *Trans-America Ultra Quiz,* a show that first came on the air in 1977 and at times reached 40 million viewers. Contestants were tested on their "knowledge" of the United States (mostly trivia questions), and the winners were flown to the United States to be subjected to further questions, the losers there being required to do peculiar stunts such as make and then row a paper boat on Lake Powell. Apparently the show is perceived by the Japanese as the portrayal of a country in which anything can happen, including making their fellow citizens perform uninhibited acts that never would be performed in Japan.[51]

Other influences are more conjectural. For example, it may be that Japanese reporters have learned the technique of staking out a news source from practices of western journalists. It may be that certain Japanese quiz shows continue to be based on U.S. models. It may be that Japanese situation comedies with high school settings have been inspired by similar U.S. shows. Most Japanese broadcasters with whom I have spoken are well aware of current program practices in the United States, although none of them has stated that there was direct U.S. influence on their offerings. (A few, however, expressed some regret that Japan had nothing quite like CBS's *Sixty Minutes* or ABC's *Twenty-Twenty.*) The commercial networks and NHK do have news item exchange agreements with a number of U.S. and Western European TV broadcasters, but those agreements do not appear to have influenced the Japanese manner of presenting TV newscasts.

Influences from other countries seem minimal; although the administrative structure of NHK bears some resemblance to that of the BBC, few British programs have appeared over Japanese television. *Monty Python's Flying Circus,* a zany and often satirical BBC humor review, appeared on a Japanese commercial station in the mid-1970s, but every episode required explanation as to why certain things, such as Robin Hood stealing from the poor and giving to the rich, were funny, and some sections, such as the "Ministry of Silly Walks," were cut, apparently because they were felt to be incomprehensible, at least to the Japanese.[52] There may have been some latent influence from *Monty Python,* because another commercial station began in the mid-1980s to broadcast a roughly similar show, *Oretachi hyohkaizoku* (We are playing the fool). Japanese TV documentary producers of nature and travel shows claim to have been inspired by British examples. A number of journalists, especially within NHK, have worked with BBC domestic and external services newsrooms through an exchange program and feel that the exposure to another system has led them to change their own practices.

Relations with Other Media

As previously discussed, the Japanese newspaper industry and Japanese commercial broadcasting are economically intertwined. Each of the five major Japanese newspapers based in Tokyo has a large investment in one of the "head-end" stations for the commercial networks, as follows: *Asahi Shimbun,* (Asahi National Broadcasting), *Yomiuri Shimbun* (Nippon Television), *Mainichi Shimbun* (Tokyo Broadcasting System), *Nihon Keizai Shimbun* (Channel 12 Tokyo), and *Sankei Shimbun* (Fuji TV). The first three stations dominate the commercial market. The broadcast stations function under separate management, but there is no real difference in editorial policy between each station and its newspaper owner. Other investors in Japanese commercial broadcasting include large manufacturers (candy, beer, etc.) and financial institutions.

The relationship between the press and broadcasters probably does little to promote journalistic competition between the press and broad-casting, although scoops by commercial broadcasters certainly are not unknown. That relationship may have more harmful effects where criti-cism is concerned, in that press criticism of the performance of broad-casting tends to be quite mild in Japan, especially in comparison with Great Britain, West Germany, and the United States. Also, some Japa-nese critics have expressed concern over the media monopoly situation in terms of the way in which it may protect both the press and broadcasting from regulation. As the critics see it, politicians and government officials would be loathe to risk angering the monopolies by suggesting restrictive legislation for any single element in the monopoly arrangement, since the entire force of the monopoly could be directed against the politician or official.

The existence of the monopolies has interesting implications for advertising, as well. The stronger a monopoly is, the better able it is to work out collective deals with advertisers, and the more difficult it will be for a nonmonopoly media enterprise to compete with it. Also, the largest newspapers own some of the most popular baseball clubs, which locks the televising of most baseball games into the present commercial broadcasting structure and makes it almost impossible for any commer-cial competitor to develop a baseball network. Dentsu, Japan's largest advertising agency, enjoys close working relations with the "Big Five" and their broadcasting colleagues, to the extent where no other ad agency in Japan can come close to competing with it for most of the large accounts. Dentsu also has helped arrange financing for some large-scale TV productions. As a further twist on cross-ownership, the major Japanese news agency, Kyodo, is part owner (about 25 percent) of Dentsu.

The film industry, once a world leader, has fallen on hard times since television's rise to popularity. Some film companies, those spe-cializing in animation in particular, have grown in business volume be-cause of their association with television (late weekday afternoons and Saturday mornings are dominated by children's cartoon shows, most of them exceptionally violent and quite crude in terms of animation tech-niques). The feature film industry, however, has suffered greatly, and is a shadow of its former self. Certain art films by noted Japanese directors continue to be produced, but mass audience films, to the extent that they are produced at all, most often are produced for television. Akiro Kuro-sawa, easily the best known of all Japanese film directors, has produced very little for television. According to Donald Richie, the leading west-ern expert on Japanese film, Kurosawa would like to do more, but his painstaking production methods are too slow and costly for Japanese television, where tight schedules and low budgets are the general order of the day.[53] There are large independent production companies such as Totsu that are active in both film and television production, but very few of the smaller independent producers one finds in Great Britain and the United States. One large production company, Tokohushinsha, was one of the major forces involved in negotiations for a pay-cable movie channel in the mid-1980s.[54]

As of the late 1980s, the major TV stations and some of the film companies were undertaking a number of joint productions, primarily for theatrical release. Some of these had further financial support from department stores, ad agencies, and electronics manufacturers. One of the great advantages to such an arrangement is the tremendous publicity that TV can provide: Fuji TV produced the film *Antarctica* in 1984, publicized it with broadcast trailers at all times of the day and night, carried specials on it, and had staff announcers mention it often. *Antarctica* subsequently became one of the all-time top-grossing Japanese films.[55]

The sorts of cross-ownership exhibited in and around Japanese broadcasting evoke few of the fears of media monopolies that have characterized U.S. broadcast regulation in the 1970s and 1980s. Whereas the FCC and the Department of Justice have succeeded in dissolving most of the one-city, one-broadcaster, one-newspaper partnerships on the grounds that they contributed to a monopoly on information, the Japanese see nothing wrong with cross-ownership among related media. Such cross-ownership fits the Japanese business practice of *keiratsu,* where several corporations have close financial relationships and to some extent coordinate planning, although they also compete.

International Cooperation

Japanese broadcast institutions belong to or are associate members of several international broadcasting organizations but are most active in the Asian Broadcasting Union (ABU). They have taken a role of leadership in ABU, frequently hosting its annual conferences, assisting other ABU members financially and with expert advice, and promoting interchange of programs, especially through the ABU's Asiavision satellite news exchange system, where the NHK serves as coordinator for the eastern sector of Asiavision and also contributes financially to the enterprise.[56] The NHK and the commercial stations also have supplied programming on tape to every nation with the ABU at one time or another, and certain foreign broadcasters, Hong Kong in particular, are regular customers.

However, the bulk of Japan's video trade comes in the form of animation, most often children's cartoons. An NHK survey of Japanese programs exported in 1980 showed that animation accounted for 56 percent of all export material in Japanese and dubbed into other languages. Where dubbed programming alone was concerned, animation accounted for 75 percent of the total.[57] Much of that animated fare was violent, but it was inexpensive to produce, and thus attractive on the world market. In some countries, notably Italy, Taiwan, Switzerland, South Korea, and several Latin American nations, animation accounted for 90 percent or more of the material imported from Japan.

Japanese broadcasters also attempt to support Japanese-speaking communities overseas, particularly in Brazil and in the United States (especially Hawaii), and export a wide range of programs to them at very low cost. The NHK makes a special effort to place its documentaries and some of its educational programs with other nations and has some of its greatest success in that regard in Western Europe and the United States. Again, the programs are very inexpensive, especially in relation to their original production costs. Occasionally NHK or one of the commercial stations will arrange for coproductions, usually of documentaries, with one or more foreign systems.

All of the major Japanese broadcasters are making increased efforts to sell certain types of programs abroad and are meeting with some success. Still, the volume is small when compared with the volume of TV program export from the United States or Great Britain. Aside from animated cartoons, where the characters often are drawn in such a way as to make them look almost exaggeratedly western (especially the round eyes), most Japanese programs look "too Japanese, too different" to most program buyers to have attracted much of a market outside of East Asia. Documentaries are exceptions to that rule, but they must be priced low in order to compete at all, and they usually become subsidized exports of Japanese culture.

Coproductions with other nations also are not that common, although NHK, as I have already noted, has had excellent success with its coproduced *The Silk Road* and *The Yellow River*. The NHK entered into some twenty coproductions during the 1979–84 period, including *Connaissez-vous Bigot?* (Do You Know Bigot?), which involved shooting in both France and Japan and used French and Japanese actors. Although commercial stations are less active, NTV and BBC teamed up to produce *The Shogun Inheritance* in the early 1980s.[58]

The New Media

Japan has been associated with technological development of broadcasting for so long that it surprises many western visitors to learn how slow the growth of cable television or the use of direct broadcast satellites has been. Canada, the United States, and several Western European countries have a considerable lead over Japan in their use of one or both of those distribution systems. Cable television was available in Japan in the 1960s, but mostly as a means of overcoming poor reception due to mountains or skyscrapers; only a handful of the cable systems included provision for local origination of material at that time, and only just over one hundred out of thirty-six thousand cable systems in Japan had local origination as of 1984. Nor were independent producers clamoring to be allowed to lease unused channel space on the cable systems, partly because there were and are few independent TV production firms in Japan. And, while large numbers of Japanese who have been surveyed about their desires for additional forms of TV have indicated that they would like to see all-movie or all-sports channels, few firms other than those already involved in commercial broadcasting appear to have the desire or the ability to establish such services. The large media monopolies have tended to discourage such ventures, although they were beginning to show some interest in cable by the late 1980s.

The experimentation with cable noted earlier (p. 324) resulted in greater public awareness of the possibilities of cable but did little to hasten its commercial development. The Cable Law of 1972 had banned two-way communication over cable, although the aforementioned experiments in the late 1970s and early 1980s were allowed exemptions. Then, in 1983, the Ministry of Posts and Telecommunications eased that ban (which had been intended to protect the interests of the Nippon Telephone and Telegraph monopoly) and soon received thirty applications for Community Antenna Television (CATV) licenses. In November 1983, the ministry granted a license to the International Cable Network (ICN) for the establishment of a multipurpose CATV system in the Tokyo suburb of Machida. It went on the air in April 1985, carrying the already available NHK and commercial TV channels, four channels of news and information, and two additional fee services, an all-movie channel and a package of four FM music channels (many TV sets in Japan are equipped for stereo). Two-way services were to be offered later and again would be on an additional fee basis. A small scale survey (*N* = 550) conducted in Machida just prior to the introduction of ICN revealed that 40 percent of the respondents were interested in having cable TV, but only 7 percent felt they could afford the two-hundred-dollar initial subscription fee and the eight- to twelve-dollar monthly service charge.[59] By September 1985, ICN had several thousand subscribers but was far from making a profit.

On 1 January 1984, the Dentsu advertising agency began to provide the Japan Cable Network (a loose distribution system feeding a few dozen CATV outlets around the country) with movies, variety shows, and other original programming as a test of the efficacy of cable as an advertising medium. Dentsu had several corporate sponsors for the project, including food processing, electronics, and manufacturing companies. At the end of the year, Dentsu evaluated the project and pronounced it a success. Meanwhile, it also had established a consultancy service for CATV, as had another ad agency, Hakuhodo Japan Cable Television, a thirty-thousand subscriber English-language cable service largely for hotels, which also had contracted with Ted Turner's Cable News Network in Atlanta to bring in the twenty-four-hour-a-day CNN service starting in April 1984. Observers predicted a rapid expansion of CATV, which had some 4 million subscribers as of 1987. Many large corporations, especially rail companies (which control many cable rights of way) and newspapers, are becoming more interested in cable. However, the use of satellites for distribution of program material, which aided the rapid development of cable in the United States, is out of the question in Japan at least until 1991, when there are plans for the deployment of an advanced satellite that might be used in part for such a purpose.

There was a launch of a satellite with direct broadcast capability in 1984. The BS-2a, financed jointly by NHK and the Japanese government, should have had three-channel capability, but two of the channels failed. A backup satellite was to be launched in mid-1985 but had to be delayed until 1986. These satellites have been used for limited tests of direct household reception and have brought NHK signals to remote islands and valleys where formerly viewers received programs on tape, but they are not available to commercial users. In July 1987, NHK began to use the satellite for two special services, the first an amalgam of NHK's two existing channels, the second a news service drawn from the U.S. Cable News Network and ABC network, BBC and other foreign and Japanese sources, plus domestic and foreign sports and entertainment.[60]

A more powerful satellite, BS-3, is to be launched in 1990 or 1991, and it will include provision for a commercial channel. Commercial firms were allowed to apply for use of the channel, and when the application period closed on 30 September 1983, fourteen companies had submitted bids. Large business firms, commercial TV stations, and newspapers dominated the list. The bidders eventually came together as a consortium (a commonly employed Japanese way of avoiding the need for making choices, which also insures that no interested party will come away empty-handed.)[61] The mass-media-related companies had nearly 40 percent of the shares, but others (manufacturers, universities, retail stores, etc.) had the remaining 60 percent. Commercial broadcasters had sought 51 percent of the shares, based on their contributions to and experience in broadcasting, but received only 19 percent. Still, the consortium, called Japan Satellite Broadcasting, Incorporated, is not likely to create and distribute program material that differs markedly from what television carries at present.[62]

Videocassette recorders were available in nearly 40 percent of all Japanese households as of mid-1987. Their growth in the late 1970s was slow, but the early 1980s saw the same sort of VCR boom that hit much of Western Europe and North America. Feature films were especially attractive VCR fare, and there was a certain amount of time shifting, but many Japanese also began to purchase video cameras, especially as these became more compact and less expensive, and VCRs often are used as outlets for home movies. So far, there is little sign that they are seriously eroding NHK or commercial station shares of audience, but their continued growth (some project that VCRs will be in half of all Japanese households by 1990) is almost certain to have some eroding effect sooner or later. That growth already has had an impact on cinema attendance: Low rental costs of recordings of feature films (one hundred yen, or about seventy-five U.S. cents for overnight rentals) allegedly will have caused cinema attendance to decline by about 15 percent in 1987.[63]

Conclusion

The Japanese broadcast system offers a great range of choice for viewers, largely because the public-service element in that system is reasonably well-financed (although NHK continues to operate at a deficit) and because it chooses to emphasize the distinctions between itself and the commercial sector. The NHK did not always do so: During the 1950s, there was considerable direct competition between it and both commercial radio and TV. Nor did all commercial stations always choose to imitate one another in the quest for the highest ratings, although those stations that chose to follow a separate path generally failed to sustain themselves and eventually fell into line with their mass-oriented colleagues.

Government regulation had nothing to do with this division of labor. In fact, Japanese broadcasting probably is the least regulated system in the industrialized world, at least where program content is concerned. (Allocation of licenses is another matter, and the Japanese power elite tend to be well protected by the regulatory structure.) Nor did public pressure bring it about, since public pressure traditionally has had little impact on overall decision making by broadcasters. If there is a single explanation for this well-balanced dual system, probably it lies in the conviction on the part of most senior NHK officials that a public broadcast service should attempt to satisfy as many tastes as possible and as well as possible. The statement is a simple one, but underlying it is the determination to win the public's confidence through diversity and quality of programming, to maintain contact with that public through various means, and to attempt to parlay public confidence into justification for license-fee increases sufficient to maintain that quality and diversity.

However, license-fee increases have become more and more of a struggle (although the struggle probably is not as severe as that experienced by the BBC), and some Japanese are beginning to express the sentiment that, with so many other sources of television (the commercial networks, VCRs, and though still minor, cable TV), they could live without NHK, especially if that would free them from the obligation to pay the license fee. It is not likely that NHK will disappear anytime soon, but already it has begun to lay plans for separate services through cable TV and/or DBS, and it has stepped up its attempts to sell its programs abroad. The government appears ready to continue to support NHK for the foreseeable future, partly because it is considered to be important to the sustenance of Japanese culture.

Where the problem areas are concerned, the coming years well may see more female newsreaders, but programming as a whole is likely to continue to be male oriented and male dominated. There may be changes in broadcast journalism's investigative role, as well, but those are likely to come slowly. And violence in various forms probably will continue to proliferate, however loud the protests; it has proven audience appeal, and competition among the commercial stations probably is stronger than it is in any other country. The Japanese system may be ready for a "new era," especially in the form of cable TV and DBS, but it is unlikely that program content will change appreciably.

Finally, as has been the case in the past, accommodation will continue to play a dominant role in the shape of Japanese broadcasting. Consortia of various types will insure that no single party's financial or other interests are irreparably damaged, while the country's interlocking power elite structure probably will rule out any radical changes in some of the more objectionable types of programming.

7

What's Comparable, What Isn't, and What It Means

WHILE the six broadcast systems covered in the previous chapters represent differing national circumstances, and thus differing approaches, there are several respects in which direct comparisons are both possible and meaningful. Admittedly, those respects must be treated rather broadly; still, they do illustrate not only how it is possible to compare broadcast systems in general, but also why such comparisons are important in understanding the interactions between broadcasting and society. They even may help us to predict the likely future development of broadcast systems, although admittedly the rapid development of new broadcast technologies makes prediction rather difficult.

The broad respects in which comparisons seem most fruitful are, by and large, the traditional ones emphasized in comparative studies by Paulu, Kuhn, Howell, Burke, Smith, Head, Emery, and others.[1] They come down to one common denominator: the interactions of broadcast institutions and broadcasters with society. Society may include governments, public interest groups, labor unions, technologists, members of a linguistic subculture, and so on, but the fact remains that broadcasting is first and foremost a social institution. Throughout this book, I have attempted to emphasize that aspect, which means that I have largely ignored the specific role played by technological innovation in the overall development of broadcasting. However, the adoption or nonadoption of a given technological development at a given moment, and the reasons for that decision, well may be an important part of broadcasting and its relationship to the larger society, and you have seen examples of that. I have said little about the internal financial administration of broadcast systems, either. Aside from the fact that it is quite difficult to get broadcast administrators to disclose how such decisions come about, there is my personal impression that better knowledge of such decision making would throw less light upon the relationship between broadcasting and society than do the aspects I have chosen to develop here.

For the sake of organizational convenience, I have grouped my comparisons under several broad headings: relationships between government and broadcast systems; internal relationships of broadcast system program decision makers and program makers; relationships between the various publics and broadcast systems; relationships among the mass media, including the so-called "new" media; regulation, communications policy, and the new media; paying for broadcasting; and programming practices. I begin, however, as I have begun each previous chapter: with a consideration of basic factors.

Basic Factors

Now that we have considered five basic factors that influence all broadcast systems, and now that we have seen how they have affected the development of several specific systems, are there any conclusions we can reach as to the relative importance of those factors?

First, it seems evident that geography is somewhat less important than it was when broadcasting began, especially for large or exceptionally mountainous nations. The coming of communication satellites has made it possible (if expensive) to conceive of bringing broadcast services to every corner of a nation. That same development has implications in terms of broadcast spillover, and as a result it has taken a crowded area such as Western Europe far longer to work out and implement a plan for satellite usage than it has such large and relatively isolated nations as the Soviet Union, Canada, and the United States.

Second, it is exceptionally difficult to consider the four remaining factors in isolation. The development of more efficient means of communication itself has meant that nations have become increasingly interdependent, so issues of culture, economy, politics, and demography have more and more supranational ramifications. The flow of goods between countries has increased; so has the flow of the labor force. Speakers of minority languages are becoming more and more aware of each other's experiences with the mass media around the world, particularly as technology makes it imaginable for them to have their own radio and even television services.

Even if it were not for the "internationalization" of those factors, there appears to be a growing interdependence of them on a national level. For example, if societies within nations are becoming increasingly pluralistic (probably with the help of the mass media), any decision taken to augment the level of broadcast service to those societies will have political implications (politicians usually are elected by small to medium-sized factions) and economic implications (added services cost money, and who will pay? — but added services also may bring more jobs and stimulate the economy), as well as the very obvious demographic and cultural implications. And if certain groups seem to be getting more favorable treatment than others, or if certain groups seem to use the added services to separate themselves from the larger society, the implications for national unity are considerable.

But the political factor seems the most crucial. So many major changes in broadcast systems have come about because of changes in political power, for instance, privatization in France and in West Germany, while lack of change in political power seems to have been accompanied by lack of notable change in broadcasting, as in Gaullist France, in Japan under the Liberal Democrats from 1950 to the present, and in East Germany and the Soviet Union before Gorbachev. The economic factor often runs in tandem with the political factor, as the more conservative parties look upon broadcast technology (fiber-optic cable, satellites) and on the licensing of commercial stations as "engines" to drive the economy.

Governments and Broadcasting

As the studies in the book indicate, no government ever has been willing to give broadcasting a totally free hand. I stated in the first chapter that there are good technological reasons for this, chief among them the need to keep broadcast signals within the country and between countries reasonably interference free; nevertheless, no government ever has permitted total freedom of speech in broadcasting. There are differences in the degree of freedom of speech permitted. Sometimes those differences become very evident when we measure broadcast systems against one another, but sometimes the degree of freedom changes over time, almost imperceptibly, within a system.

The ability and desire of governmental administrations (the ruling party or parties) to limit the degree of freedom of speech for broadcasting usually is thought of in what might be called traditional political terms: limits on criticism of the political party in power at a given moment, which usually extend to limits on criticism of the individuals exercising that power. Because administrations often have influence over how much money a broadcast system receives, because administrations sometimes appoint the chief administrators of broadcast systems and/or regulatory agencies that license and supervise broadcasting, and because there is almost universal acceptance of the need for administrations to address the public by means of broadcasting, it follows that they have numerous ways of imposing limits on what broadcasters can say about them, and of replying to criticisms if and when broadcast systems carry any. Those same limits can be imposed on other less obviously political forms of broadcasting, as well: More than one administration (e.g., the USSR, France, East Germany, Nazi Germany) has imposed its moral standards on radio and/or television, both to reinforce certain "desirable" (to the administration, at any rate) forms of moral behavior and to eliminate "undesirable" forms.

Certainly the most fundamental reason for administrations to be concerned over freedom of speech for broadcasting is the assumption, usually unquestioned, that broadcasting has a powerful influence on its listeners and viewers. That assumption not only has led certain administrations (Nazi, Soviet) to prevent and/or to encourage the broadcast of certain types of material, but also to intervene in a technological sense: encouraging the manufacture and distribution of certain types of receivers to insure that the largest possible audience could be reached, but discouraging the ownership of other types of receivers that could pick up broadcasts from outside the country. The white South African government may have had the same objective in mind when it developed its Radio Bantu service for black South Africans on FM, since FM receivers could not pick up most broadcasts coming from outside the country. Such a policy may lead to short-term success, but it appears to be hard to sustain over the long haul.

That assumption concerning the power of broadcasting to influence society may need to be questioned as broadcast systems themselves offer a wider and wider range of choice. Very few nations nowadays have just one radio service, and many nations, certainly in the industrially developed world, but sometimes in the developing world as well, have two or more television services. As soon as a choice is offered, it becomes possible for audience members to avoid what they consider uninteresting or threatening without turning off the set. That in turn may mean that audience members have fewer and fewer programs that most of them have seen and that most of them can discuss among themselves or with the guidance of a discussion leader. Also, as broadcast systems expand the numbers of radio or television services, often they fill the increased airtime with imported material: records in the case of radio, entertainment programs in the case of television, and international news services (Associated Press, Visnews) in the case of both. If that occurs, audience members have the opportunity to measure the products of domestic broadcasting against the imported material, and the former may suffer by comparison, especially if the administration has considerable influence over the nature and form of domestic broadcasts. And if those audience members have ready access to and can understand broadcasts from neighboring countries, the problem may be compounded. Most administrations seem to have little skill in preparing messages so that they will be understandable, let alone interesting, to the mass audience.

But administrations often *are* skilled in preparing messages that *broadcasters* will understand. Theodore Roosevelt once noted that the presidency gave its occupant a "bully pulpit" from which to address the nation, but the pulpit needs an outlet, and the outlet usually is the mass media. If a national leader should consider any one of the mass media to be in need of a lecture itself, for whatever real or imagined offense, such a lecture also can be delivered through the mass media. Even if the offending medium itself or some member of it should refuse to carry the lecture, the other media usually will do so. President Nixon, through the agency of Vice President Spiro Agnew, berated the U.S. commercial networks for their alleged liberalism in 1969 and after; various Soviet Communist party leaders and presidents have criticized Soviet broadcasting for its alleged dullness; Prime Minister Helmut Schmidt of West Germany called for a television-free day in a 1982 speech. In each of those instances, both the print and broadcast media gave the messages widespread coverage. And if a medium or one of its members should refuse to provide the desired coverage, there are still other means available to bring (or to attempt to bring) it into line, as President Reagan's press secretary did in the summer of 1986 when he told the Mutual Broadcasting System radio network that he was withholding the cooperation of the White House Press Office in retaliation for Mutual's decision to make use in advance of material contained in the president's 16 August Saturday morning radio address.[2]

Administrations also appoint review or study committees in many nations, and this, too, becomes a means of bringing governmental influence to bear upon broadcasting, since administrations tend to appoint committee members who agree with a given government's political philosophy. Rarely is there much attempt to appoint a bi- or multipartisan committee, even though that probably would enhance the credibility of the committee's report. Also, administrations have a great capacity for ignoring those parts of a committee's report that they do not like, as Mitterand's Socialist administration in France did with the Moinot Report in 1985 and as Thatcher's Conservative administration did with much of the Peacock Report on the financing of the broadcast media in 1986.

Legislatures, as we have seen, also can be a powerful source of influence on broadcasting, if there are two or more reasonably independent political parties, and presuming that the leading party does not enjoy too top-heavy a majority. The French experiences of the 1960s and 1970s have shown us that there are circumstances in which those challenges have little effect, but the United States Congress's success in preventing the Reagan administration from cutting annual budgetary appropriations for public broadcasting back to almost nothing in the 1980s tell us that checks and balances can work.

Legislative bodies often end up deciding how broadcast systems are to be financed and in some cases decide how much money they will receive. We have seen several instances of how that power may be used or misused, once again with examples of both in France over the years. With the coming of the costly "new technologies" and the push for the privatization of broadcasting in many Western European nations in the 1980s, the use of financial power took a slightly different turn: Some legislatures (e.g., the Netherlands, certain West German *Länder,* Great Britain) held down license-fee increases while at the same time permitting and even sometimes encouraging private enterprise to enter the broadcasting field.

There are differing interpretations of why legislatures have acted in those ways; the usual explanation is that people (meaning the voters) are tired of paying higher and higher license fees, and legislators do not wish to incur their wrath. Yet another explanation is that some legislators and some political parties believe that broadcasting should allow for a wide diversity of presentational styles, program types, viewpoints, and so on, and that privatization will accomplish this, and accomplish it more economically than will license-fee-based broadcasting. (That was a prominent argument from some British Conservative party politicians in the 1980s, and it also arose in the aforementioned Peacock Committee report of 1986.) And still another explanation is that some legislators, especially those of a more conservative bent, often feel that license-fee-based or annual appropriation-supported broadcast systems tend to favor a liberal or even leftist point of view; reducing or not increasing appropriations or fees may warn such systems to mend their ways, and encouraging private enterprise to establish stations may better insure expression of the conservative point of view. (The latter sometimes has been offered by West German media observers as a major reason why the Christian Democrats opened up broadcasting to private enterprise in the mid-1980s.)

Most legislators, acting individually or collectively, are able to call upon broadcasters to account for their specific programming decisions. Certain individuals become quite famous as broadcast critics. Winston Churchill (grandson of the famous British prime minister) got a fair share of media attention in the mid-1980s by attacking the BBC for its broadcast of "pornographic" material. United States Senator Thomas Dodd became quite well-known as a critic of television violence in the 1960s. French Senator André Diligent became a prominent advocate of broadcast reform in the 1960s. However, such individuals seem to have little lasting impact on the medium.

Should a number of legislators become involved, matters can be more serious, as CBS television learned in the 1960s and early 1970s when it had to spend considerable time and money defending its documentary programs, such as *Harvest of Shame, The Selling of the Pentagon,* from attacks by various members of the United States Congress. Those attacks probably led CBS to schedule fewer documentaries, and perhaps to tone down those it did carry, although the network continued to attract congressional criticism into the 1980s, most notably with *The Uncounted Enemy—A Vietnam Deception.* Many members of the British Parliament attacked the BBC in 1983 for its alleged "even-handedness" in covering the Falklands War, when some of those members wanted a more partisan account. But generally speaking, such instances of legislator disapproval do not result in fundamental changes in broadcast law. Legislators seem content to rely on their expressions of disapproval to get the broadcasters to think twice before acting in a similar fashion in the future, because they are aware that broadcasters do not wish to spend large amounts of time and money in legislative hearings, which also may generate a good deal of unfavorable publicity for broadcasting. (The press in many countries seems to delight in exposing the woes of its fellow mass medium, even though broadcasting rarely returns the favor.)

Legislative bodies in many countries also appoint commissions to study broadcasting from time to time, usually in reaction to a crisis or problem. As the French experience shows, such commissions probably will have little impact upon broadcasting unless the political party in power wishes them to. The 1977 report of the Annan Committee in Great Britain, which contained a number of quite thoughtful and very interesting recommendations for the future of British broadcasting, had a limited impact on the system because the committee reported while the Labor government was in office, but the Parliament that finally acted on the report a few years later was dominated by the Conservative party.

There is another connection between legislators and broadcasters that should be mentioned, if only for its comparative singularity. Critics of U.S. broadcasting are fond of pointing out that broadcast stations and legislators have an interesting symbiotic relationship: The legislators depend upon the broadcasters to publicize their activities, while the broadcasters depend upon the legislators to keep government regulation from becoming too onerous. According to some critics, that prevents either group from being terribly critical of the other, to the general public's loss. There may be some truth to that argument, although it is a rare year when there aren't at least a few congressional committee investigations of one or another aspect of broadcasting.

However, such an accusation is rare in most other industrially developed nations, in part because few of them permit political advertising of any sort, in part because many systems provide blocks of airtime for the use of political parties, which accept full responsibility for whatever their membership chooses to put on the air. Also, many systems devote some airtime to political discussions in which politicians can be challenged by other politicians and/or by broadcast and press reporters. In those other systems, then, politicians are far less free to present their points of view and their personalities without challenge than they are in the United States (with the sometime exception of U.S. public broadcasting). Therefore, politicians are far less likely to curry favor with broadcasters in hopes of receiving more favorable treatment. The Soviet, East German, and French systems are obvious exceptions, but then, politicians in those nations do not appear to worry about currying favor, at least if they are from the dominant or sole political party.

If you are familiar with the role played by the judiciary in influencing U.S. broadcasting, you may have been surprised to see so little indication of judicial influence in the national systems covered in previous chapters. There are several possible explanations. For one thing, the United States probably is a more litigious society than are most others, so there is a greater likelihood that there will be legal cases involving stations. For another, there are large numbers of independent broadcast stations in the United States, which itself increases the possibilities for legal cases. And for a third, the presence of a regulatory commission in charge of both licensing stations and supervising their output (admittedly in a very loose manner) is almost guaranteed to produce conflicts that must be resolved by the judicial system. The FCC is not a court of last resort, and communication lawyers and their clients are well aware of that. It is probably a combination of those three elements that produces the degree of judicial involvement with broadcasting that exists in the United States, since other countries have large numbers of independent stations (Italy, France, Belgium, Australia, Canada, Japan, and some of the Latin American nations), a few are quite litigious (India, Mexico), and some have regulatory commissions (Canada, France, Australia).

When the judiciary does become involved in broadcasting in most countries, it is likely to be over a relatively limited range of issues: whether the government (usually the administration, but sometimes Parliament) has the right to do something to or about broadcasting, as has happened in West Germany; or whether a station should or should not have carried a specific program, often on a broad political or societal issue (e.g., the Holocaust, news about a national election campaign). Questions of whether a specific station or would-be station should or should not be permitted to operate rarely arise, perhaps because so many broadcast systems operate on the assumption that, once a station is licensed or otherwise authorized, it will stay on the air forever (or at least as long as there is financial support for it). Demands from members of special-interest groups for airtime to reply to broadcasts with which they disagree are about as rare. That may be because right of reply is built into the broadcast systems themselves, as it is in the Netherlands, or because there is a quasi-judicial body to handle such complaints, such as the Broadcast Complaints Commission in Great Britain. There also seems to be less of a presumption in other countries than in the United States that the courts can and should serve as a means of publicizing one's cause, by which token courts in other countries rarely if ever handle cases involving broadcast advertising opposed by ecological groups (e.g., the 1971 case involving Friends of the Earth and the FCC) or demands for airtime to oppose government policy (e.g., the 1973 Businessmen against the War in Vietnam vs. CBS case).[3]

Regulatory agency involvement in broadcasting may have seemed as rare as judicial involvement in the systems we have considered, but there are signs that it is on the rise: As some of the Western European nations begin to permit private broadcasting on a large scale, there may be more regulatory commissions. However, many nations seem uncertain as to the mandate of a regulatory commission, how its members should be chosen, who should supervise the commission, and so on. Lacking their own precedents, countries either establish a commission, give it a very loose mandate (and often a small budget), and hope that it will work, or they turn to the few examples they can find in other countries and model their commissions on those experiences.

Those few concrete examples themselves offer conflicting evidence of how a regulatory commission might be structured, but they seem to agree in certain respects: Such a commission should have a fairly sizable full-time staff that is *not* subject to political appointment and should be headed by a small group of commissioners which *is,* but which cannot contain more than a bare majority of commissioners associated with a given political party. A commission should have an annual governmental appropriation, although those using its services may be asked to pay fees to help offset some of its costs. Its decisions must be a matter of public record and must be challengable in courts of law. The licenses it awards are to be for specified periods and on specified terms and may be renewed. It determines its own procedures but is subject to the limitations of the law establishing it, which may be amended by the appropriate legislative body.

Thereafter, regulatory commissions part company. The Canadian Radio-Television and Telecommunications Commission (CRTC) holds hearings for the initial licensing and subsequent license renewals in the community where the station is to be licensed; the Australian Broadcasting Tribunal follows much the same practice. The U.S. FCC and the French CNCL hold almost all such hearings in their respective national capitals. The FCC pays, or at least claims to pay, some attention to broadcast content as a criterion for determining whether a station's license should be granted or renewed; the French CNCL pays little attention to programming practices, although it gives some lip service to the notion of "French program content." The FCC attempts to promote diversity of ownership in the media by refusing to grant a broadcast license to a corporation that owns a newspaper in the same city; the Australian Broadcast Tribunal has renewed the licenses of many "same-city-newspaper-owned" stations, although as of mid-1987 the government was moving to change the broadcast law to prohibit this in the future (present license holders would be protected under a "grandfather clause"). The CRTC and the Australian Broadcasting Tribunal both have requirements that promote the placement of Australian- and Canadian-produced programs on the stations they license, and the CNCL is developing such requirements, but the FCC has no comparable requirement.

Those differences may be a reflection of cultural philosophies: Canada and Australia, for example, do not wish to be flooded by U.S. programs, which they fear will weaken their indigenous cultures. France has very strong feelings about promoting French culture. Differences also may stem from socioeconomic philosophy: The FCC and the United States Department of Justice believe that diversity of expression may be hampered if newspapers also operate the broadcast stations in their cities, while newspapers are the dominant investors in private stations in West Germany, Australia, and Japan, including many stations in the newspapers' own communities. Broadcast regulators in those nations seem to feel that it is logical for the publishing industry to protect itself by investing in a potentially competitive medium, and besides, the publishing industry probably has a better notion than do most potential investors of how to manage a communications outlet successfully.

But some of the differences are difficult to explain in any rational way: Australia and Canada both are large nations, as is the United States, and yet the regulatory commissions in the first two manage to conduct hearings in the cities where the stations operate, whereas the U.S. FCC does not. If the airwaves are considered to be the public's property — the usual philosophical basis upon which governmental regulation of broadcasting rests — why not give the public the opportunity to comment on how well they think they will be served or are being served by a station and give them that opportunity in a fashion that makes it easy for them to comment? The answer may be that the process of licensing and renewal can be handled more efficiently if it all takes place in one location, and the taxpaying public saves money when a governmental agency can increase its efficiency, but that is not the answer given by the FCC. To the extent that there has been an answer, it has been that the public did not seem all that interested in making its views known when the FCC conducted renewal hearings in Omaha and in Chicago in the early 1960s. As it takes some time for the public to become familiar with any new process (and perhaps to learn that its time will be well spent in using that process), it may not be surprising that public interest was low.

Finally, if a nation has a very uncomplicated broadcast system (e.g., a single broadcast corporation financed by annual appropriation, as in East Germany and the Soviet Union), or if it chooses to operate a broadcast system in a paternalistic manner, with the government deciding what is best for viewers and listeners, a regulatory commission makes very little sense. It makes better sense in a situation where there is more than one major component to the system, and where those components differ in some substantial way, say in manner of financing. If there are many independent private stations in the system, and especially if those stations are licensed periodically, a regulatory commission makes even better sense. A ministry of posts and telecommunications or a ministry of information is unlikely to wish to employ the body of experts necessary to regulate a more complex system, and even if it does, there is likely to be the suspicion that the government of the day will have more influence over the system than it should. That is not likely to be of concern to a totalitarian administration, but a democratic (nominally, at least) administration should give some thought to that point.

There are some fairly complex systems of broadcasting that do not feature regulatory commissions, but which are in democratic nations. Of those we have considered in previous chapters, Japan and the Netherlands are good examples. The Dutch system does reflect societal interests in its very structure, and there are not all that many individual stations, so the absence of a regulatory commission may not be all that surprising. (Whether the new Commissariat for the Media will undertake such a role is yet to be seen.) But Japan has a dual system, the private sector contains a fair number of independent stations, and there is periodic relicensing. Yet the U.S. occupation authorities' introduction of an independent regulatory commission failed to take hold, and there has never been one since. Various Japanese broadcasters and critics of broadcasting have told me that the concept of such a commission is alien to the Japanese, which begs the question. A few of those broadcasters and critics have gone on to say that it is alien because the Japanese are an authority-loving (or at least authority-respecting) people and do not sense the need for a commission that, ideally at least, would be relatively free of influence from the government and the broadcasters and at the same time open to public input. As the Japanese system does not appear to be notably less democratic than other systems where a commission exists (except that investment in private stations is dominated by publishers, and except that politicians seem to be treated more respectfully and less critically than in some other systems), perhaps it proves that a regulatory commission is not absolutely necessary, but it also simply may prove that Japan is a singular case.

Internal Relationships

The systems covered in this book have shown that the internal structures of broadcast systems are two-layered for the making and transmission of programs, and the administration of the enterprise. Theoretically, one could dispense with administrators, at least those at the top, on the grounds that they do not contribute directly to the program production and transmission process, which after all is the essential business of broadcasting. Some small stations take a step in this direction by not having any full-time senior administrators: Any individual who has administrative responsibilities also will have production or engineering duties. That is possible as long as the station not only is small but also has an uncomplicated program structure (an all-music station is an excellent example) and an uncomplicated financial support base. Many stations possess the former, but few the latter; except for radio stations financed by club or association members who themselves operate the station, virtually every type of financial support base requires accountability, whether to advertisers, the public, the legislative body, or whatever else. And as soon as accountability enters the picture, top-level administrators seem to become indispensable, if only to provide that accountability and to keep the money flowing into the station so that the producers and engineers can function.

However, many of those administrators also have first-hand experience with broadcasting and use that experience when working with program makers. And if they do not have that experience, as often is the case with administrators appointed by governments, they soon begin to feel that they should take a more active role in the process of program production, if only to show that they mean to run "a tight ship" and to "keep on top of things." Such an approach may be necessary if they are to explain to the government officials who have appointed them, to the advertisers who support the operating costs, or to the public that listens and watches that they really know why programs look and sound as they do. In other words, many top administrators have a public-relations function, although not only with the general public, and it is a function that demands some degree of working knowledge of the programming process as well as a display of the ability to influence that process.

It would be difficult to discover whether one specific approach to the development and maintenance of a "good" internal relationship has been better than any other. "Good" for whom? Administrators? Producers? The financiers of the system? The audience? And might there not be some potential merit in having a "bad" internal relationship, on the assumption that such a relationship would cause all involved to keep on their toes, always watchful, so that any misdeeds by one partner in the relationship surely would be exposed by the others?

It seems more profitable to ask what the end product of the internal relationship should be, although even here it all depends upon one's perspective: Autocratic governments want strong and even absolute control from the top down, while democratic governments at least profess that they want (relative) freedom of expression for diverse opinions, cultures, and so on. But most individuals connected in one way or another with broadcasting do seem to agree on the need for broadcast systems to operate with reasonable fiscal efficiency, to be responsive in some fashion to the wishes of listeners and viewers, to present programs with some degree of professionalism, especially in appearance, and to present them in an interesting manner.

That list looks almost too obvious to merit examination, but in fact the systems covered earlier and many more not mentioned in this book have had problems in one or more of these areas. "Fiscal efficiency" was a major issue for French broadcasting in the 1970s, and it has been a major justification for the appointment of certain committees to examine the BBC in the 1970s and 1980s. In contrast, I have heard many European broadcasters praise U.S. commercial and noncommercial broadcasting for fiscal efficiency, especially when compared with their own experiences. Responsiveness to audiences certainly takes many forms, and no one system seems to follow precisely the same approach taken by any other in that regard, but French public broadcasting seems to get low marks from critics for its responsiveness, while Japanese public broadcasting tends to get high marks. As for professionalism of appearance of broadcast material, most systems exhibit high quality, but some, such as the Soviet system, seem to have taken longer to reach that level than have others. And while "interesting" programs, much like beauty, are in the eye of the beholder, there seems to have been more criticism of the Soviet and French informational and U.S. educational programs in this regard than there has been of similar British or West German programs.

Are there differences in the internal relationships within the systems themselves that seem to promote greater satisfaction with the end product, at least on the part of the viewing and listening public? Leaving aside the question of whether we have fully adequate measures of public satisfaction, and confining ourselves to such partial measures as public-opinion surveys that explore public satisfaction with broadcasting; amounts and types of critical mail received by broadcasters, other media, and those who supervise broadcasting from outside; degree of compliance with license-fee payments where they exist; criticisms of broadcasting raised by the print media; and criticisms of broadcasting by legislative bodies and by governmental administrations, does any one system seem to come out on top?

The Japanese public system (NHK) seems to achieve the highest overall levels of public satisfaction by the above measures, although that in part may be a function of the allegedly traditional Japanese reluctance to criticize. It also may be because the NHK employs so many different approaches for assessing public satisfaction. It may or may not have much to do with internal relationships. The NHK appears to have much the same sort of internal structure as do other broadcast systems, although unlike certain other systems (notably those in communist countries and, much of the time, the French system), politics is but one of several factors in the selection of most administrators. Nor are there any particularly strong unions within NHK, which might promote a more cooperative atmosphere. And finally, there is the legendary Japanese mode of group decision making, which certainly is not followed as rigidly in broadcasting as it is in various industries, but which does stress the importance of cooperation.

If part of the Japanese experience stems from a cultural characteristic that probably will not exist in most other countries, part of it may be more universally applicable. The way in which administrators come to hold their positions seems to be an important factor in promoting greater trust and cooperation within the system and between the system and the press, the audience, the legislature, and so on. Broadcast administrators in the BBC seem to enjoy a fairly high degree of trust on the part of program producers, critics in the print media, and political figures (although the last named have ripped the BBC often enough for its alleged political imbalance). That may be because most of them rise through the ranks and usually have held several different positions in production and administration by the time they arrive at or near the top of the administrative pyramid. Thus, if a high-level BBC administrator makes an observation about program production, there is a fair likelihood that she or he arrived at the observation through practical experience. French production staff would not expect a high-level administrator to know one end of the camera from the other and resent attempts by administrators to tell them how to produce programs.

The diversity of modes for assessment of public satisfaction that the NHK displays nearly are matched by the BBC, and West German broadcasting is not far behind. But what really matters in assessing the relationship between the internal organization of the system and public satisfaction with its product is how the system uses those modes. The NHK and the BBC both publish at least some results from their audience research studies, and both organizations hold a number of public meetings each year at which audience members are invited to express their opinions about broadcasting. The public then may believe that those results and opinions must play some role in the program decision-making process, and broadcast administrators occasionally make public statements to that effect. Still, the "reality" of program decision making, insofar as I have been able to examine it, does not show that programmers attach much importance to those opinions and results.

And finally, the success or failure of any given form of internal administration is affected heavily by available resources—not just budget (although that is of supreme importance), but also of top-quality personnel. If the government or other forms of private industry manage to siphon off the best talent for their own purposes as soon as it has exhibited its quality in broadcasting, the quality of broadcast output is bound to suffer. This happens with some frequency in Third World broadcast systems, where the best talent in broadcasting often is drawn into other branches of private industry or into government, sometimes because of money, but sometimes because of the insistence of top-level government officials that their needs come first. A promising program director soon may find her- or himself heading a branch of the Ministry of Agriculture.

Relationships between Publics and Broadcast Systems

It should be clear by now that there is no single public for broadcasting, nor probably ever has been. However, there have been systems in the past and there are systems at present where broadcast administrators and program staff seem to think of a monolithic public for at least some of their program output, especially for news broadcasts. And in most systems of broadcasting, a monolithic pubic ends up paying for the services it receives, even if not everyone pays the same amount. For those reasons, broadcasters may feel perfectly justified when they speak of "the public" as a whole, and sometimes for those same reasons broadcast systems have included certain structural provisions in their organizational makeup that at the least allow for some sort of general public input and which on occasion even strongly encourage it. You have seen examples of the former in the USSR's inclusion of "letters from the audience" programs in its broadcast schedule, and of the latter in NHK's coupling of annual license-fee collection with a brief questionnaire on audience satisfaction with the NHK broadcast services. Several systems include general broadcast advisory councils, which are supposed to represent a broad spectrum of public opinion and reaction, although there is little that is specifically representative about them.

But most broadcasters realize that much of the energy they spend in dealing with the public in fact will be spent in dealing with specific interest groups or with individuals who think of themselves in group terms. Again, the systems covered in this book exhibit a number of ways of treating this situation. In some, the broadcasters take the initiative and appoint advisory councils or committees of experts that will consult with the broadcasters on the most correct and/or best ways of preparing programs on religion, education, or whatever the subject area might be. In others, the citizenry itself will take the initiative and will attempt to bring pressure to bear on the system in order to prompt more suitable (to the group in question, at any rate) programming.

Whether their efforts will be successful or not probably will depend upon how well organized they are and whether they can obtain coverage of their activities by other mass media, but it also may depend upon how impervious the system is to public criticism of that sort. In Japan, for example, the many protest campaigns launched by parents and teachers against "immoral" programming on Japanese commercial television by and large have failed, perhaps in part because the commercial system felt that it could ignore such pressures. That feeling probably has stemmed from the fact that commercial broadcasters had many "friends" in the Japanese Diet and from the fact that there is a very close link between the press and commercial broadcasting, making the former less likely to carry criticism of the latter. In France, the close linkage between the governmental administration and broadcasting seems to have had the same effect, and in Australia the financial ties between the press and commercial broadcasting also appear to have made it difficult for groups unhappy with one or another sort of programming to obtain coverage.

I mentioned in the previous section of this chapter that a few broadcast systems or parts of systems had managed to achieve fairly high levels of public satisfaction with their performance. We can take another perspective on that issue if we look at it from the standpoint of how the public, but especially individual members of the public and specific interest groups, have sought to express their *dis*satisfaction with broadcasting, and how successful their efforts have been. I think it is fair enough to conclude that the vast majority of the audience in most countries does not even think of expressing dissatisfaction with broadcasting most of the time; it sits back and takes what it gets, sometimes with a bit of grumbling, seldom with anything worse. The most popular form of public expression of feelings throughout the world seems to be the letter, and the many broadcasters with whom I have discussed audience mail and the studies of its content that I have seen cause me to conclude that little of that mail expresses dissatisfaction. The head of the Audience Research Division of Soviet Radio and TV told me in September 1985 that the system receives a few million letters a year, most of them with requests for more information about "stars," about how certain aspects of broadcasting work, and for revivals of formerly broadcast programs and series. Both BBC and U.S. commercial network research division staff have confirmed to me that the pattern is roughly the same for their operations. And when critical comments do appear in letters, often they are so generally stated (e.g., "There's far too much sex/violence/sports/advertising on TV") that it is almost impossible to draw any firm conclusions from them.

As I have just noted, there are other ways of expressing dissatisfaction, especially through groups. Some groups have proven to be quite adept at presenting their grievances. Certainly the National Viewer's and Listener's Association in Great Britain has attracted a good deal of print media (and some broadcaster) attention for its allegations of explicit sexual content on TV and has found allies in the British Parliament to express those concerns in that body. Certain religious organizations, especially in the United States and in West Germany, have had similar success through similar channels, and some of those organizations also have their own publications through which they can work. Some of the "fringe" political parties or groups within larger political parties have carried out their protests in a similar fashion, and in some countries, especially West Germany and to a lesser extent the Netherlands, also have managed with some success to place members within broadcast organizations, which at least has the potential for insuring that the group's points of view will find their way into programming. Certain social interest groups, for example, gay rights groups, occasionally have employed the last-named tactic in the United States, but also have worked through production houses such as Norman Lear's Tandem Productions to sensitize producers to their concerns.

All of those approaches can work some of the time. The major problem with them is that they take a lot of effort, they need money, and they need continuity: Jefferson's dictum about eternal vigilance being the watchword of liberty can apply just as well to groups seeking to combat what they see as unfavorable or improper broadcast programming. In almost all instances, the money has to be raised by the groups themselves, although grants from various U.S. foundations helped to keep several citizens' groups alive in the 1970s, and there even was a proposal (never enacted) that the Federal Communications Commission cover certain legal costs associated with citizen group versus broadcaster cases brought before them.[4] Furthermore, the legal system of any given country may not encourage court cases from such groups, and even if it does, the legal assistance necessary in presenting a case itself is expensive. A few countries have provided something a bit less formidable and certainly less expensive for the presentation of such grievances, for example, Great Britain's Broadcast Complaints Commission. But often such mechanisms have no true legal standing themselves, so that the broadcaster suffers the ignominy of bad publicity, but nothing else. Regulatory commissions such as the CRTC, the Australian Broadcasting Tribunal, and the FCC may be a bit less daunting and expensive than the courts, but not much.

There remains the type of broadcasting council that is not appointed by the broadcaster and that has some real power over the broadcasting organization, but there are few examples of this: West Germany and some of the Dutch broadcast organizations, and to a lesser extent certain of the Scandinavian broadcast councils, make up the list. Even here, as we have seen in the case of West Germany, groups on the fringes of society—guest workers, feminist organizations, the elderly—may lack formal representation. Also, such councils meet infrequently—four to six times a year is typical—so a group seeking to work through such a council may find that the specific grievance it is expressing will be a few to several weeks old by the time the council next meets.

It is not surprising that some groups dissatisfied with broadcasting have taken matters into their own hands and set up their own stations. French and Italian radio in the late 1970s and early 1980s probably furnish the largest number of examples, but most of the industrialized nations in the western world have had at least occasional instances of such operations. Sometimes they're legal, sometimes they're not. Always they take some time, money, and effort. Some of the earlier efforts along those lines did not last more than a few months, often because they had little or no support from the larger group of which they were a part.

The experience of certain French pirate radio stations operating on behalf of the workers in the late 1970s is instructive: Their staffs found that union officials often were suspicious of such efforts and preferred to work through the "tried and true" channels with which officials felt comfortable (meaning those that they could control).[5] Most of the Italian worker-oriented stations that operated in the late 1970s had disappeared by the early 1980s, bought out by commercial radio interests or devoid of sufficient financial support. The call of the British government's Home Office for applications for community radio services in the spring of 1986 brought forth nothing from labor unions, even though some union figures (notably Arthur Scargill, head of the Coal Miners' Union) frequently criticized the BBC and IBA for "antiunion bias." Certain individuals deeply involved with community radio in Great Britain told me in September 1986 that that did not surprise them, since union officials seemed to have little interest in expressing themselves through their own stations, or at least over stations that would operate more or less permanently.[6] However, the Coal Miners' Union and the Printers' Union each operated pirate stations during strikes in the mid-1980s.

Some ethnic groups, notably blacks in Great Britain and the United States, Arabs in France, and some linguistic groups, notably Spanish in the United States, have had more success in organizing themselves and in getting stations on the air, but that seems to have been largely because they constituted numerically viable groups as targets for advertising. Religious groups have enjoyed similar success in a number of countries: In the Netherlands, as you have seen, some of the broadcast societies are linked with religious organizations, and there are many such stations in the United States and in various Latin American, African, and Asian nations. But only the larger organizations, or at least wealthier ones, ordinarily can afford the cost of such a venture. A rather different situation confronts political groups; very few countries allow such groups to operate their own stations, while many countries make some provision for political party airtime on radio and TV. However, such arrangements usually exist only for the mainline political parties, and smaller parties rarely gain access.

The Scandinavian *närradio* services noted in the opening chapter seem to have achieved the most satisfactory method for permitting a wide range of religious, political, ethnic, and cultural groups to broadcast, since a group does not have to be especially wealthy to support its broadcast efforts, and since there are very few restrictions on what a group can say or do over radio. But it *is* radio, with all of the attendant restrictions on audience size and on types of programming that can be presented. Access programs on TV are few and far between, when they exist at all, and a *närtelevision* operation would cost each group a lot more than does *närradio*. The Dutch Migranttelevision service is severely handicapped by lack of financial support. Cable radio offers similar possibilities and limitations and has been utilized by few groups thus far: Surinamese in the Netherlands, blacks in the United States.

Certainly the capacity of any broadcast system to accommodate all points of view as frequently as those holding those points of view would like is limited. Large and wealthy nations such as the United States clearly have faced such limitations, so it is not surprising that smaller, less wealthy nations, especially if they have great sociocultural diversity and lots of geographic neighbors, may face even greater limitations. It is also quite clear that many groups in many countries do not want the fulltime responsibility of running a station. Again, however, the *närradio* concept, at least as it is practiced in Sweden, allows groups to have their own broadcast outlets on very modest terms — as little as fifteen minutes a week, if that is all they want. The one thing that *närradio* cannot accommodate is a group that does not want to broadcast on any regular schedule but might wish to have access to airtime on an occasional basis, especially to reply to a broadcast it considers damaging to itself. No system anywhere guarantees that form of access, although the Netherlands comes fairly close with its quite liberal provision for airtime on the spur of the moment.

Relationships among the Mass Media

In most of the nations examined in this book, and in the vast majority of others, as well, there is at least some degree of adversarial relationship between the press and broadcasting. It may be because the press has been around longer and feels that it knows better, it may be because there is competition for advertising revenue, it may be because broadcasting is enormously popular and newspapers can count on some reader interest in it, especially if stories contain a hint of scandal. Even in countries where the press is a major investor in broadcasting—Australia and Japan, certainly—newspapers do not hesitate to criticize broadcasting, although a given newspaper may not do so for its particular station or network. Some broadcast systems are set up so that they do not compete with newspapers for advertising, some feature restrictions on that competition, and some engage in head-on competition, but the press seems equally adversarial in all three conditions.

Perhaps that is just as well, since most broadcast systems do not feature much by way of self-criticism. The BBC, the IBA, the ZDF, and several other Western European systems have had occasional televised meetings with one or another segment of the public, and some of those meetings have been forums for some rather sharp criticism of various program practices. Such broadcasts are not a regular occurrence in most systems, however, and when they are, they are usually made over radio, which draws much less public attention. Great Britain's Channel Four does have a weekly program featuring viewer observations on television. *Right to Reply* is edited from comments recorded by individuals in "video boxes" located in London, Manchester, and Glasgow. (My visits to them in September 1986 showed low rates of usage—three or four a day—and mostly general comments.) But viewers and listeners cannot demand meetings or broadcasts, since they are not required by law.

However, press criticism of broadcasting often *is* a regular feature in many Western European and some Eastern European countries, where the majority of the nationally distributed newspapers carry critical columns daily. Not all such columns actually criticize broadcasting, or at least not all of the time; many devote much of their space to describing upcoming programs, giving profiles of actors and directors, and so on. Still, there is enough criticism that it appears to inspire the public to write letters to newspapers on the subject of broadcasting rather more frequently than is the case in the United States.

Whether this adversarial (some would claim healthily adversarial) stance on the part of the press will continue as broadcast program outlets expand and as the press itself gains more opportunities to invest financially in stations, cable, and satellite services is another question. The fact that most of the industrialized nations have had relatively few broadcast services until quite recently has made it easier for the press to speak about broadcasting, since most readers would be interested in and familiar with the programs, policies, and personalities it was covering. That broad public familiarity is not so easy to assume any longer. And if the press becomes a colleague rather than an adversary, it probably will mean that at least some broadcast services—chiefly those owned by the papers and magazines—will be treated kindly, as so often happens in Japan and in Australia. Furthermore, press treatment of major legislation affecting broadcasting possibly could be influenced by press ownership in the medium.

If parts of some broadcast systems are being "invaded" by the print media, those systems themselves are becoming more and more important in the life of the motion-picture industry, although not without complications (note France and West Germany). Most of the industrially developed nations do not have large cinema industries, and television has had much the same effect on them as it has had on cinema in the United States: The industry keeps itself alive in large part by making films for TV, and in some cases (e.g., Italy) making a given film in versions for TV and for the cinema.[7] We may assume that many of those made-for-TV films are not the sort of work that filmmakers would undertake for the cinema, both in subject matter and in types of visual effects. However, it has been possible for certain film directors and writers to create works of unquestioned artistic merit for television, as with Ingmar Bergman's *Fanny and Alexander* (much longer as shown on Swedish TV than the cinema version, and richer and probably more comprehensible in its story line, too) and Rainer Fassbinder's *Berlin Alexanderplatz.*

There is no reason why broadcast systems could not treat filmmaking as they have treated classical music for so many decades. Most of the major European systems, as well as Canada's CBC, Japan's NHK, and Australia's ABC, have commissioned composers to write music of all sorts—chamber music, choral music, jazz, symphonies, and so on. Furthermore, most of those systems have recorded that music and made it available to the record-buying public. Composers have had the creative freedom to write pretty much what they wish, and there is adequate rehearsal time to allow their works to have the benefit of first-class performances. Some broadcast systems have commissioned films and have accorded their makers the same creative freedom, but that has not yet become as frequent a practice as it has for music. However, the Dutch system, as noted, has taken a few steps in that direction.

There also are broadcast systems in which the broadcasters sign contracts with the film industry that establish both rental costs and conditions of usage, often including the provision that the film will be broadcast as it was shot and will not be edited to the point where it becomes almost unrecognizable.[8] Some also set aside a sum of money that will be used to assist various filmmaking projects. We have seen such an arrangement in West Germany, and it gives filmmakers the opportunity to make films that might offend most TV watchers and probably never will appear on that medium. (However, in 1987 the West German government did withdraw subsidies from two feature films on the grounds that they made fun of religious feelings.) There also has been pan-European consideration of a film and TV production fund financed through the European Economic Community, although as of early 1987 it lacked the support of three EEC members—Great Britain, the Netherlands, and West Germany—which doubted that it would be effective.[9]

The coming of pay-TV systems to some countries also may provide a financial shot in the arm for some domestic cinema industries. France's Canal Plus shows little but feature-length movies and is obligated to use large quantities of French-made films; that stipulation already has resulted in an increase in the annual production of French feature films. Whether such films will be of uniformly high quality is doubtful, but that at least insures a large quantity of domestic material, which should help to quell the fears of those who see a pay-TV service as an invitation to a "cultural invasion" from the United States. Not every country is as large as France or enjoys the level of potential sales to other French-speaking nations. Still, pay TV is likely to spread across Europe fairly rapidly (Great Britain, France, the Netherlands, and to a very small extent, West Germany, all have it as of 1988), and other nations might consider how pay TV and the domestic cinema industry might assist each other (and presumably benefit the nation as a whole).

Regulation, Communications Policy, and the "Media Explosion"

One of the greatest changes that has come over most of the broadcast systems in the industrialized world during the 1980s has been the need to take a fresh look at regulation in the light of the "media explosion." By the late 1970s, there already was widespread discussion of cable TV, direct broadcasting from satellites and, in nations that had not considered them before, commercial broadcasting and local broadcasting. Often the press took a lively role in that debate, in part because the press was eager to invest in broadcasting. By the early 1980s, many of those services were reality or much closer to it, and nations now moved to make some sense out of the numerous requests for licenses that were pouring in. Choices had to be made where no one had thought about choices before.

The regulatory bodies that emerged often have been ill equipped to deal with the plethora of services and applications that have characterized the media explosion. Poorly financed and subject to political pressures (witness France's Haute Autorité), lacking a body of case law and experience to serve as a point of reference (the U.S. FCC had many years to "learn the ropes," first with radio, then television, then cable TV, whereas the Haute Autorité had to learn everything all at once), and with little by way of overall communications policy to guide them, it is little wonder that some of those bodies are off to a rocky start. Furthermore, participants in the new licensing game often are well connected politically and have ample money to press their suits, so regulatory bodies may find themselves making perfectly sensible licensing decisions, which then have to be unmade because some powerful entity is not happy with those decisions.

Finally, no regulatory body, whether new or old, will be able to affect the development of a well-integrated system unless there is the national will, chiefly as expressed by the national government, to formulate a communications policy that will bring about such a system. But long-range, all-embracing communications policies are rare items among the industrialized nations. If such policies could be developed (and Sweden at least appears to be working to achieve that goal), a regulatory body could do a great deal to make them become a reality. However, some nations (Great Britain, West Germany to some extent) are heading in a different direction and setting up separate regulatory bodies. Great Britain has an authority for private commercial radio and television (the Independent Broadcasting Authority), another for cable (the Cable

Authority), and probably will have a new Radio Authority (to include IBA-licensed radio) by early 1989. The BBC stands apart from any of those bodies. Such diffusion of responsibility is almost certain to make coordination of any sort of communications policy (if one exists, which seems doubtful in view of what has just been described) difficult if not impossible.

Paying for Broadcasting

As I indicated in the opening chapter, broadcasting has been financed in a wide variety of ways, ranging from the highly personal (one individual supporting one station) to the broadly national (license fees, annual appropriations) to the commercial (advertising). Three of those methods predominate: fees, appropriations, and advertising. Traditionally, broadcast systems were supported by one or another of those methods, but usually each component part of the system was financed by a single method. For example, public and private broadcasting in Japan, Great Britain, and Australia always have been supported through mutually exclusive means: the public sector through license fees or annual appropriations, the private sector through advertising. In countries where broadcasting is or has been a monopoly, such as the Soviet Union, financing often comes in one form only, although a few monopolies, (the Netherlands in 1967, France in 1968) moved from a single or dual financial source to a multiple-source system, usually adding advertising to license-fee revenues.

Recent years have brought increasing financial pressures on broadcasting, and especially on systems with a single financial source or with one major source and one quite minor source. Most of those problems have arisen in cases where the single source or the major source are provided or authorized by the national government—in other words, annual appropriations and license fees. There can be any (or all) of three reasons for such a situation: First, governments like to show the electorate that they try not to burden people with "added" expenses, in this case money to operate broadcasting. Consequently, governments are reluctant to increase license fees or to vote larger annual appropriations for broadcasting, perhaps in part because the print media are almost certain to make the public aware of any increases. As costs for broadcasting often have risen more rapidly than has the annual rate of inflation, this has produced tensions between some broadcast systems and their governments. Second, some governments, and particularly those of a more conservative economic outlook, feel that broadcasting should be open to more participants both because that will give more businesses a chance to make money and to stimulate the economy and because it will cause "old-line" broadcast organizations to become more fiscally responsible. Since a number of conservative governments came to power in Western Europe in the late 1970s and during the 1980s, pressures of that nature have increased. And third, artists (writers, producers, performers, etc.) and politicians (usually from the parties in opposition) have seen some real or potential danger in broadcasting relying too heavily on one source of income, since that might make broadcasting artistically smug and narrow or might lead to greater political influence by the government of the day.

Those factors, acting singly or in combination, have led to changes in the ways in which broadcasting receives its financial support in several European countries. We have seen those changes in the Netherlands, France, West Germany, and to a lesser extent Japan, as private radio, private television, cable TV, and pay cable have come to one or another of them in recent years. Sweden, Norway, Finland, Iceland, Denmark, Italy — indeed, most Western Europe nations — have experienced similar changes starting in the middle to late 1970s. Usually it has been the advent of the "new media" or the introduction of private broadcasting that has brought about the changes. Governments do not want to raise license fees or to increase annual appropriations to pay for those media. If investors are to become involved, then they want to be sure that there will be a decent financial return on their investments. User fees are one approach, but since many nations already have a user-fee system in the form of license fees, often the new media must consider advertising as a major, if not sole, means of support.

That in turn forces governments to reconsider their attitudes toward advertising, and particularly toward permissible amounts and types of it. Many governments (the Netherlands and West Germany are good examples) have protected the press by not allowing broadcast advertising, by permitting only small quantities, and by allowing ads for nationally marketed products and services only. But now those preexisting broadcast organizations may be asked to think the unthinkable: to institute broadcast advertising in a service that never has done such a thing and probably never thought it would or should! Some of the BBC's replies to the Peacock Committee's recommendations on advertising over BBC Radio 1 and Radio 2 were more like cries of outraged honor. Organizations that already carried limited amounts of advertising may be asked to increase that total, as were Dutch broadcasters in 1985. Governments often seem to reason that, if a new media service is to live or die on the basis of its ad revenue, then surely the preexisting services will not suffer unduly if their audiences, too, must now receive their daily dose of commercials, or a larger dose than before. After all, that helps to keep the license fees or annual appropriations lower, and it may even help to stimulate the economy.

The private broadcasters, cable operators, and other competitors with the preexisting services usually have not welcomed such an approach, since it would be very much to their advantage if those services were not competing for ad revenue. But conservative governments often take the attitude that enterprises should "compete on a level playing field," as U.S. President Ronald Reagan was fond of saying. Sometimes that philosophy has meant that governments have encouraged the old-line services to consider development of separate pay TV services, DBS services, videocassette distribution, and so on. All of this has meant that broadcasting is becoming more and more competitive in more and more nations, with private and public stations alike vying for ad revenue, sales of programs abroad, subscriber fees for special services (videotext, pay TV), and so on.

It will be interesting to see whether that competition drives the individual broadcast organizations within a given nation to become more and more alike. To the extent that those services compete for the same sorts of audiences, it would appear inevitable that there will be a greater degree of homogeneity than we now have. Some of the older duopolies (e.g., Canada, Australia, Japan, and Great Britain) continue to display a fairly high degree of programmatic differentiation between public and private broadcasting, although various British critics (Milton Schulman, Chris Dunkley) claim to see more "popularization" and "sensationalism" in the BBC's output as a result of the IBA's presence. Once those duopolies become triopolies or quatropolies, will that differentiation continue? And if that competitive situation extends beyond national borders, so that cable systems offer channels from systems in other nations, and videocassettes are available from many parts of the world, how will national systems respond? With more of the same, but better produced, more indigenous (e.g., a British or French *Dallas*) programming?

That could be a very strong temptation, so long as programs were not *too* indigenous, because it would enable those national systems to compete in foreign markets themselves. That approach was encouraged in the European Economic Community's 1984 report, *Television without Frontiers*.[10] That report urges European broadcasters and their respective governments to open national boundaries to trade in broadcast programming and advertising, just as nations in the Community are supposed to have opened their borders to trade in produce such as apples and sheep. Still, apples and sheep feed the body, whereas broadcasting feeds the mind, and the Council of Europe—a larger group than the European Economic Community, and more politically/culturally minded than economically inclined—on several occasions has discussed the potential danger to national cultures if programs are allowed and encouraged to flow *too* freely between nations.

How much the hopes and fears expressed through the Community and the Council will be realized depends to a large extent upon how broadcasting and the new media are supported financially. As of the late 1980s, that picture as yet is not very clear. Cable is off to a slow start in the larger European nations and in Japan, and is almost nonexistent elsewhere save in North America and in a few of the smaller European nations. True DBS services (from satellite to individual household) have yet to establish a foothold anywhere on the globe. Videocassette recorders are becoming important in the overall media mixes of some nations, but they are largely a matter of personal investment, whereas the establishment of cable and DBS services involves large sums of money and, on the user's end, continuing support through subscriber fees. As many nations already have annual license fees, it may be that viewers will not care to pay yet again for a further set of broadcast services. They may decide that the range of choice available through the long-standing broadcast services, perhaps supplemented by VCRs, are about as much as they want and/or are willing to pay for.

Perhaps the greatest expression of concern over future patterns of financing centers on the simple question of who pays for what. If advertising becomes the dominant form of financial support, are the advertisers simply buying numbers of viewers—the more, the better? And if license fees or annual appropriations remain the dominant form of support, will governments be willing to raise either of them enough to allow broadcast organizations to provide the public with the increased range of broadcast services the public may wish, so long as it does not have to pay too much more for the privilege? Put another way, if advertising dominates, will programming become almost entirely mass oriented and as cheaply made or obtained as possible? If fees or appropriations dominate, will broadcasting be able to change with the times? Would an ad-dominated system inevitably lead to heavy reliance on U.S. programming? Would a fee- or appropriations-dominated system inevitably lead to a preservation of the national culture?

As we have seen in the cases of the systems covered earlier, there is nothing inevitable in either scenario. License fees have not made Dutch broadcasting a model of cultural preservation, and advertising has not kept the Japanese commercial broadcasting system from producing most of its own material. Size of population and relative prosperity of the economy are important factors, of course, but so may be the high costs of the top-heavy administrations that seem to characterize so many of the appropriations- or fee-supported systems. And there are cases where ad-supported systems do produce a great deal of their own programming, and where a fair share of that programming clearly is not made for a mass audience. Great Britain's IBA is perhaps the best example of that. But the IBA also rests on a foundation of governmental commitment to the idea of public-service broadcasting. France's various private broadcast services appear to lack such a foundation, and as a result (and with the exception of certain interest-group-operated radio stations) feature little but mass-oriented programming.

We may find in the future that many of the fee- or appropriations-supported systems will place greater emphasis on alternate means of financing, and especially on means other than advertising. (Most BBC and NHK staff seem to regard advertising as a form of prostitution, and ARD and ZDF hold it at arm's length.) There is increased interest in selling various broadcast-related products, and not only programming: The BBC opened a retail store in London late in 1986, and it deals exclusively in BBC publications and other retail products such as T-shirts and coffee mugs. Symbolic of the importance attached to the selling of BBC products was the hiring in 1986 of a director of BBC Enterprises (the sales arm of the BBC) for a salary very close to that of the BBC director general. A few public broadcasting services in the United States draw some 5-10 percent of their annual revenues from sales of retail products, and most public broadcasters throughout the world probably would rather sell themselves in that manner than through the sale of airtime.

Programming Practices

It should be self-evident that the ultimate purpose of broadcasting is to distribute programming, but it is quite easy to lose sight of that purpose in the thicket of structural considerations that surrounds broadcast systems. It also may be easy to assume that, generically speaking, the program product will not vary a great deal from one country to another. If genres are defined with sufficient breadth, that is quite true: Every broadcast system (although not every broadcast service *within* a system) provides news and other informational programming and also provides entertainment. One can go a step further and state that every system provides national and international news, "serious" and "light" entertainment, programming intended particularly for adults, particularly for children, and so on. Every system also forbids certain sorts of program content: hard-core pornography, incitement to riot, promotion of violent overthrow of the national government. And there are some overall similarities in scheduling, especially in the placement of major newscasts and most of the more expensive entertainment programs in the evening hours, which may begin as early as 6:00 P.M. in some nations or time zones.

But there are some quite striking differences, as well, even among the systems covered in previous chapters. Some, and most notably the USSR, sign off on TV before or at midnight during the work week, while others, notably Japan, have extended their TV schedules to almost twenty-four hours a day. Financial resources play a role here, but so do political-sociological factors: It isn't good to have workers up too late at night! Although no broadcast system in any industrialized nation save Iceland (which has no public TV service on Thursdays) fails to broadcast seven days a week, certain political figures, such as former West German Chancellor Helmut Schmidt, have advocated "TV-free" days for the sake of social cohesion, and Iceland's public broadcasting system, RUV, had a "TV-free" month in August of each year until 1987, presumably because people would be on vacation then (but also because it allowed the small RUV staff to go on vacation as well). And the broadcasting of TV programs for the general public during the morning hours has come to most of Western Europe only during the 1980s. Again, this was due in part to limited finances, but also to a feeling on the part of some broadcasters and of some government officials that the public should not become too television-dependent.

Also, while various studies[11] indicate that percentages of time devoted to overall categories of programming do not differ that much from country to country, there are some quite clear differences in relative popularity of various program categories and in the sorts of story lines, whether fictional or factual, that are prominent. West German viewers seem to favor quiz shows and crime dramas; French viewers lean toward variety shows; the Japanese prize newscasts and variety shows; Soviet audiences place nature and geography shows at or near the top of the list. In some of those cases it may be because many of the favored shows are among the best-produced material the system has to offer. High-culture programs — symphony orchestras, operas, transcriptions of classical literature — rarely finish in any nation's top ten programs for a given week, and many of those programs end up in the bottom ten, notwithstanding which they may reach far more people than would see them in a theater or a concert hall over a period of many years. They are part of a public-service commitment that many broadcast systems seek to fulfill, and in which many systems become actively involved, as commissioning agents for contemporary drama, music, ballet, and other fine arts.

The content of similar program categories also can differ sharply from nation to nation. Most larger national broadcast systems broadcast at least a few crime dramas, but presentations of law-enforcement officials, criminals, victims, and so on shows considerable variation. West German *krimis* usually feature compassionate, rather slow-moving detectives, and we learn a fair amount about their private lives. Their Japanese counterparts tend to be fast-moving, methodical, and somewhat impersonal. Their French equivalents often are highly individualistic and a bit quirky. Overt violence is minimal on Soviet crime shows, high on Japanese. Quiz shows look at first to be cut from the same cloth, but closer examination reveals that monetary prizes are nonexistent on Soviet TV, modest in the Netherlands. Japanese commercial TV's quiz shows are even noisier and more physically active than are those in the United States, and participants engage in "zany" stunts that their opposite numbers in the United States might be ashamed to undertake (some of the stunts are downright cruel). Situation comedies, which seem to be increasing in popularity as a program genre in the western world, pick rather different targets as the objects of humor: the problems of divorced mothers raising their children and holding down jobs (West Germany), a grocer striving to function in an increasingly multiracial neighborhood (Great Britain), apartment dwellers trying to manage the everyday vexations of living in close proximity (the USSR).

While most systems do not go to the lengths of the Soviet system when it comes to modeling, all systems seem to be promoting at least some "socializing" messages through their factual and fictional programming. Ethnic minorities appearing in TV situation comedies and dramas rarely are the downtrodden or the rebellious; instead, they are either criminals (with little if any indication of what brought them to that state) or successful doctors, lawyers, judges, and so on. Women often are portrayed in traditional roles, as nurses, teachers, secretaries, homemakers, although increasingly there are professional roles for them, as doctors, lawyers, and government officials (but usually not as the characters around whom the plots revolve). Law-enforcement officials seldom come across as incompetent or venal. Most drama and comedy programs have big-city settings, with city life depicted as enjoyable *if* one keeps one's eyes open for possible deception (or worse). A small-town or rural setting for a comedy or drama almost guarantees a celebration of the values of the simple, trusting, cooperative life, just as it almost guarantees at least a few quaint characters. But there is one quite distinct difference between U.S. TV comedy and drama and its Western European counterparts: The Soviet Union frequently is featured as the enemy in U.S. shows, but that is a rarity in Western European TV fiction, and it is not all that common to see the United States depicted as the enemy on Soviet fictional TV (news programs and documentaries are something else again).

Factual programs also show some interesting similarities and differences. Most radio and TV newscasts feature rather brief (ten to ninety seconds) items, and newscasts from national services usually contain a mixture of national and international news. There even is some similarity in the nature of news coverage among western stations: more emphasis on "negative" than on "positive" items, more depiction of problems than solutions, failures than successes. The Soviet system displays a higher percentage of domestic successes and capitalist world failures than do systems in the western world, although domestic coverage began to be more self-critical under Prime Minister Gorbachev's policy of *glasnost* (openness) in the mid-1980s. United States television news seems to include more items centering on individuals than do newscasts in other industrialized nations, but some of the European systems, and especially Great Britain's, appear to be including "personality" items more and more frequently, and many of the European systems (including the USSR's) are placing increased emphasis on the personalities of the news presenters, more and more of whom are women.

Just why those similarities and differences exist is not easy to say. Some of the resemblance between newscasts can be attributed to the dominance of a few major wire services (AP, UPI, Reuters, AFP, Tass) and a few major telefilm suppliers (Visnews, UPITN). Physical similarities between quiz shows in many countries is not always coincidental: Some of the popular quiz show formats are marketed throughout the world by companies mainly in the United States and Canada. Certain situation comedies, for example, the BBC's *Till Death Us Do Part,* have been seen by producers in other nations, who have borrowed the overall plot line – in this case the U.S. *All in the Family* and the West German *One Heart, One Soul.* French TV producers bought the rights to make a French version of the U.S. situation comedy *Maude.* Also, international markets in television programs have resulted in more foreign programs appearing on screens in a number of nations, especially following a major expansion of hours of broadcasting over a given service or the expansion of stations or cable outlets available. Occasionally, some of the more successful imports spawn domestic imitations. Coproductions also have some impact upon the similar look of television from nation to nation.

As for differences, they may be a result of ideology (Soviet television's frequent depiction of World War II so that people will not forget its horrible lessons), of legislation (bans in some nations on the depiction of what authorities consider pornographic or overly violent), or of quotas set so as to keep imported programming to a minimum, which may have the dual advantage of promoting the national culture and of providing employment. However, those quotas cannot insure that programs produced within the nation will not bear some resemblance to programs produced abroad, nor do the attempts of a few nations to reward quality productions (France and Australia both have devised such schemes) insure the development of a truly national language of broadcasting, either.

But there probably are differences in national tastes, as well. British audiences seem to have a greater appreciation for satire than do their American cousins. West Germans will watch political discussions with far greater avidity than will French viewers. Soviet viewers have a love of the sentimental that goes far beyond anything I have seen in western systems. "Tastes" are not always synonymous with "popularity"; as noted earlier, West German television's presentations of political discussions do not receive high ratings when compared with quiz shows or *krimis*. They *do* result in high figures on appreciation index ratings. Perhaps a careful analysis of those ratings would reveal some interesting demographic differences, to the point where certain programs would appeal particularly to the tastes of German men, British women, French teenagers, and so on.

Although the major national radio services throughout the industrialized world are becoming more and more homogeneous — almost every industrialized nation has at least one twenty-four-hour-a-day service of pop music and brief newscasts — there still is quite a range of difference with this older medium, too. Most of the major European systems continue to program radio plays, some transcription and some original, as they have done for decades. Some still broadcast quiz shows: Several of those carried by the BBC are decidedly intellectual in content and have small but highly devoted audiences. A few have schedules that differ little from what they were before television came on the scene, with variety shows, serial dramas, and soap operas. Whether such "old-fashioned" services reflect national tastes is another question; my own feeling is that many of them are created by aging heads of service and producers for an aging audience, and that most listeners in their forties or younger pay little if any attention to them. All of this may mean that, as services, they could face extinction within the next few decades, although certain elements (e.g., original radio drama) may survive longer.

Finally, when one considers broadcasting as a whole, it is clear that there is increasing "particularization" of programming, through local and regional radio in many nations, through cable television in a few. Languages that were almost extinct or were beginning to fade from use—Occitan, Frisian, certain of the German *Mundart* (dialects)—have enjoyed something of a revival, as have elements of regional and local cultures (folk music, storytelling). Local government officials and the people they serve are beginning to think of broadcasting as a medium through which they can exchange views, seek answers, and ask questions, although often the process is slow to develop. However, for those nations where local broadcasting is a recent development, the local stations seem to be regarded more seriously by listeners than are their counterparts in North America, where the development of network television caused most local radio stations to turn to the least expensive form of programming: prerecorded music, sometimes delivered by prerecorded disk jockeys.

Toward an "Ideal" Broadcast System

If one were to combine the best features of the broadcast systems covered in this book (perhaps extended to include the oft-noted British, Canadian, U.S., and Australian systems), would it be possible to develop an ideal system of broadcasting? Given the highly public, mass-oriented nature of the medium, and given the diversity of tastes likely to be exhibited by even one public in just one nation, it probably is not. But I believe that it *is* possible to look at the factors in broadcast systems described earlier in this chapter and to extract from them some idea of what would be the most desirable goals for systems in general. It also will be helpful to consider why those goals are desirable, because that should serve to sharpen discussion of broadcasting's role in society.

GOVERNMENTS AND BROADCASTING   Governments inevitably will be involved with broadcasting, if only because news and other informational broadcasts do and should cover governmental affairs. But because broadcasting offers such tremendous advantages (and therefore temptations) to government officials—its immediacy, its mass coverage, perhaps its authoritativeness—I contend that it is necessary to keep an arm's-length relationship between broadcasting and government. Broadcasters should be able to function both as reporters of fact and as analysts and critics—roles that audiences in most nations have come to expect them to play. Governments should be able to challenge what they see as misinterpretations or errors, but preferably under conditions where the reporter, critic, or analyst and a government official would confront one another directly, so that the audience can have the opportunity to reach its own conclusions on the truth. Few broadcast systems engage in such a practice, and none that I know of has it as an ongoing function. If the government operates the broadcast system, such a practice is unlikely to be established, and if the system is supported entirely by advertising, it could only be established by law: It would be costly and time-consuming, it probably would not do all that well in the ratings, and it certainly would be controversial. Commercial broadcasters surely would balk at it for any or all of those reasons.

Governments also are likely to be supersensitive to what they perceive as public moods, and broadcasters need to have some protection on that front, as well. Sex and violence in broadcasting have become hot topics every now and again in several countries, and it would be very tempting for a government to respond to public criticism by forcing the broadcaster to drop such shows. Although broadcasters certainly should be sensitive to public criticism, whether expressed through governmental bodies or by any other means, it does not follow that every breath of criticism deserves a programmatic response. Yet dropping a program would be the most visible way for a government to show that it listens to the people.

If we assume that broadcasting must be accountable to government on the grounds that it uses a public resource and that licensing of stations is necessary to insure that that resource be used in an orderly manner, we admit the need for some sort of regulatory body to see to it, at least, that stations stay on their assigned frequencies, and at their power limits. All industrially developed nations also seem to agree on the need for governments to concern themselves with certain programmatic issues: incitement to riot, libel, hard-core pornography, positive portrayals of child abuse, and other forms of criminal behavior. Self-regulation often covers such issues, but no nation relies entirely upon self-regulation to determine whether stations have violated norms, largely because those norms cover far more than broadcasting and often are embodied in the law of the land. The courts can handle such cases; is there any need to create a specialized regulatory agency to do so, or to concern itself with other aspects of broadcasting?

As broadcasting and broadcast-related activities (cable, VCR, DBS) expand throughout the industrialized world, the resultant volume of activity seems to justify the creation of a regulatory agency. Decisions must be made as to who among a number of competing applicants should be licensed and whether a licensee should continue to hold a license. To those ends, licensees must propose *and maintain* certain programmatic standards. A specialized regulatory agency can make those decisions on the basis of a body of accumulated and expert knowledge and practice. The trick is to create an agency that will stand at the center of a triangle: broadcasters, government, and the public. The agency must be open to input from each of the three, but not under the primary influence of any one of them.

An initial sticking point is budget. If an agency is funded through annual government appropriation, the government may "lean" on the agency by threatening to reduce its budget, as the United States Congress did with the Federal Trade Commission in the late 1970s. But a regulatory commission could be paid for by a combination of license-filing fee and frequency spectrum use fee, as the U.S. FCC has been in part through the former.

A second problem is legislative authorization for such an agency. If a legislature chooses to circumscribe or otherwise influence the agency, it need only amend existing law or pass new ones. If the experience of most industrialized nations is any guide, bi- or multipartisan politics generally will insure that the law does not get bent out of shape. If there are no second or third political parties, and/or if a government is determined to have its way, the law will not provide much defense, anyway.

A third problem is avoiding undue political influence through the appointment process. Regulatory agencies usually are headed by a small body of commissioners, and it is usually governments that appoint them. Appointments to the U.S. FCC are made with the assumption that partisan politics will play a role. It is stated in the Communications Act of 1934 (as amended) that no more than three of the five FCC commissioners will be affiliated with a given political party. But such assumptions need not govern appointments, and they seldom do for the BBC or NHK boards of governors, where nonpartisanship is likely to be predominant. If the appointments were to be made for limited, nonrenewable terms, say seven years, and if commissioners were to be removable only for gross moral violations or criminal behavior, that would make their positions more secure at times of political change. It would be especially helpful if commissioners could be chosen on the basis of distinguished public service, which itself would serve as an indication of the importance of broadcast regulation.

A fourth problem is avoiding undue broadcast industry influence. Broadcasters sometimes are able to manipulate regulatory bodies because politicians and broadcasters find it in their mutual interest to have a "cozy" relationship, but also because broadcasters are in a good financial position to hire lawyers who understand the complexities of communications law and to hire regulatory body staff who understand the inner workings of the organization. If influence by politicians can be kept in line by the measures noted above, that would minimize the ability of broadcasters to use them to influence the regulatory body. Higher pay should help to alleviate the second difficulty, as would the clearer writing of communications law, but that is part of a much larger problem regarding legal language.

A fifth problem is hearing the voice of the public. If the regulatory body sits in the capital city and does not venture forth from there, if communications law is complex, and if the public does not know much about what the body does and how the public best might interact with it, then the body will not be of much use to the public. The Canadian CRTC and the Australian Broadcasting Tribunal show that regulatory bodies can get out to the public; the U.S. FCC for a brief period in the 1970s developed booklets and an information hot line that helped the public understand, in clear and simple terms, how to present its concerns to the commission. If the regulatory body also was responsible for conducting research (quantitative and qualitative) on broadcasting, as does the CRTC, that would give it increased public visibility and also a means of measuring the accuracy of broadcaster's claims of public service.

To sum up, the regulatory body would have to have a fair measure of independence from the government of the day, which probably would mean that its top officials should be selected through a bipartisan, multipartisan, or nonpartisan process, albeit not through popular elections (broadcast regulation isn't *that* important or vital as a public concern). They should have a demonstrated interest in broadcasting, although that interest need not be highly sophisticated. They should be paid well enough and provided with enough staff support that private industry would not seem all that much more attractive after two or three years on the job. And they should be required to interact with the public in various ways: through licensing hearings (in situ wherever possible); through public meetings where general topics, such as violence on television, can be discussed; through commission and publication of research on public attitudes toward broadcasting; and through preparation and dissemination of publications that outline public rights with respect to broadcasting, cable, and so on. The airwaves *are* public property, and the public has certain rights over the manner in which they are used. A regulatory body with the properties just listed, especially if it is a *single* regulatory body, should make it easier for those public rights to be upheld.

INTERNAL RELATIONSHIPS   Systems that draw their administrators largely from the ranks of staff members who have some knowledge of the production process, whether as actors, writers, producers, directors, or whatever, seem on the whole more likely to uphold high standards of production than systems that do not. The West German and the Japanese NHK experiences show at one and the same time a willingness to innovate and a resistance to immediately pick up on every trend that may appear elsewhere. The French experience, where nonbroadcasters frequently are appointed to top administrative posts for political reasons, shows an overall lack of innovation and an all-too-common openness to political influence. The U.S. experience, where top administrative staff more and more frequently come from the business world, shows a concentration on the "bottom line" (profitability) that makes a near fetish of high ratings and that imposes severe restraints on such unprofitable genres as nonserial/original prime-time drama, documentary, and even news.

There is a danger of overreliance on production staff as administrators. They may become careless about budgeting for production, finding it hard to deny to others the financial resources they were accustomed to (or at least would like to have been accustomed to!). They may be particularly reluctant to impose limits on choice and presentation of subject matter, not wishing to interfere with the creativity of others any more than they would have wanted others to interfere with their creativity. And they may have become so accustomed to viewing the production process from a particular perspective that it is difficult for them to evaluate and accept fresh ideas, especially if they come from outside the system.

There are ways of dealing with all of those potential problems. Periodical examination of data gathered on production costs within the system and from other systems, especially if it is presented to an advisory council as well as to the supervisory board of the operation, can serve as a reminder of careful budgetary practices. Some overall limits governing taste in programming can be developed by supervisory boards and advisory councils working together with producers, as the BBC has done in reviewing the treatment of violence on television. A system can impose time allotment patterns that provide the opportunity for producers working outside that system to display their wares. The Dutch system achieves this through its provision of airtime for some very small groups, and the U.S. public broadcasting system has an annual program selection process that operates through the Station Programming Cooperative and that allows at least a few independent producers to gain access to the broadcast schedule, although not necessarily on terms that encourage creativity.[12] The Independent Broadcasting Authority's (U.K.) Channel Four provides considerable airtime for independent producers, in part through a Channel Four–managed production grants program.[13] The Canadian CBC has a roughly similar arrangement.[14] And in 1987 the Conservative party in Great Britain pressured the BBC and IBA to agree to obtain 25 percent of their domestic television production from independent producers.

If production staff make the most desirable administrators, it does not follow that they will automatically possess the needed administrative skills, or that they will see administration as a worthwhile pursuit. Ideally, some in-house training — both classroom and on-the-job — would precede an administrative appointment. Also, it would contribute tremendously to the attractiveness of an administrative post if producers were able to maintain some direct involvement in production once they held it. That would help to insure that the administrator would retain some sense of the "real world" for which she or he was administratively responsible, and it would ease the transition back to production, should the administrator wish to return. If there is a relevant model here, it would be academic administration, where many professors-turned-administrators maintain their contact with teaching and research.

There also is the matter of union involvement with broadcasting. There are unions of broadcasting staff in most industrialized nations, although they appear to be less and less effective with the passage of time. However, they have been an important element in some broadcast systems in terms of their ability to win reasonable working conditions for staff who might be particularly open to exploitation. They have also been successful in a few instances in calling the public's attention to government censorship of the news, especially in France. But broadcast unions may have a hard time surviving in an increasingly fractionalizing climate: With more and more private stations, community stations, and cable operations being created in western European nations, those unions, which have become quite accustomed to dealing with one or two national organizations, are going to find it difficult to work with dozens of stations, many of them small and with modest economic resources. The overall free enterprise climate prevailing in Europe in the 1980s is not very helpful to unions, either. They definitely have a place in the "ideal" broadcast system, but they will have to discover different negotiation tactics and exhibit greater flexibility in bargaining if they are to survive.

RELATIONSHIPS BETWEEN PUBLICS AND BROADCAST SYSTEMS   I noted earlier in the chapter that the Japanese NHK probably has the highest level of audience satisfaction with its broadcast output. The NHK knows that because it asks the public regularly and in many different ways, and the act of asking itself seems to promote public confidence in the NHK as public servant. Frequent and scientifically sound qualitative and quantitative research is an absolute necessity here, and it does not seem to matter whether the research operation itself is housed within the broadcast system (as it is in the NHK, in the Netherlands' NOS, and in the Soviet and East German systems) or whether it stands outside that system (as it does in part in West Germany and Great Britain). If the research is scientifically sound and is conducted with some frequency and regularity, it will stand up to inspection.

Advisory and externally appointed supervisory councils with "public" membership appear to play a moderately important role in providing a measure of public input. "Public" may not be a very accurate descriptive term, however, as most individuals who serve on such councils come from the middle- and upper-income ranges, have high school or university educations, and tend to be active in community affairs. Those with lower incomes, of more modest educational attainments, and with relative lack of community involvement do not appear very often in council membership lists. Whether they should appear there is another question. Certainly they listen to radio and watch television, and certainly there are a good many of them. But identifying them is not always easy, and getting them to participate may be very difficult indeed. If an individual does not feel that her or his participation is going to have any effect on what is seen and heard, it is not likely that she or he will step forward in the first place.

If stations were to publicize the existence of the councils, present some of their deliberations (or at least condensations of them), and note specific broadcaster reactions to those deliberations and actions taken as a result of them, that might help to develop greater public confidence in the importance of councils. Few systems with councils do much to publicize them, especially through broadcasts, and some actually try to conceal the identities of council members from the general public, on the grounds that they do not want council members to be "pestered" by members of the general public who might wish to voice their opinions about broadcasting. The VARA and VPRO broadcasting associations in the Dutch system seem to come closest to promoting public involvement, although mainly on the part of their own members, and even they say little about council recommendations in their broadcasts. It should not be all that difficult for producers to make attractive program material out of council deliberations and recommendations and broadcaster replies.

How council members might best be selected is not a simple issue. The West German system, where councils are made up on the basis of lists of groups and organizations, appears to be a bit too rigid; it is hard to change council makeup as society changes. However, the idea of having groups choose their own representatives has much to commend it, since it removes the possibility of selection bias on the part of the broadcaster. A council that is composed of representatives from more broadly defined groups, such as education, religion, the arts, the sciences, would avoid the fractionation of the West German system and the consequent large numbers of council members. Eight to ten such members should be enough. They then could form a screening committee to select a further five to seven members to be chosen on an at-large basis, from applications that individuals would submit to the council and in which they would indicate their backgrounds and their reasons for wishing to serve on the council. Again drawing upon the West German model, an administrative committee could be chosen from within the council, leaving the council free to concentrate on programming issues (which obviously are of most concern to the general public), while the administrative committee concerns itself with budgetary and structural issues. Such a council system may not be well-suited to a broadcast system where there are dozens of stations, cable operations, and so on within one community, but in many of those situations, there are city or state associations of broadcasters; one council operating at that level probably would be sufficient. Again, the key to success would be the publicizing of council activities.

Quite aside from whatever councils may or may not do, there is another field of citizen activity in broadcasting, as I have noted earlier in this chapter and elsewhere in the book: citizen operation of broadcast facilities, whether over a shared transmitting facility, as with the Scandinavian *närradio;* cable radio, as in the Netherlands; quasi-legal stations, as in Belgium; and so on. Decreasing costs of equipment, a (belated) willingness to reevaluate spectrum use, and an increasing degree of group activism starting in the late 1960s, all have contributed to this development. Not every operation has been successful, even if "success" means nothing more than being able to stay on the air, but many of those new stations have given broadcast voices to groups that previously suffered neglect or misrepresentation over the broadcast media. Homosexuals, feminists, old people, all have found outlets, as have immigrant communities, guest workers, and members of minor (and major) political parties. It seems reasonable to expect that any industrially developed nation should be able to authorize some form of direct citizen participation in broadcasting, whether on cable, on a shared frequency, at low power, or whatever circumstances prevail. Technical limitations no longer can serve as an excuse for not doing so, nor can financial reasons. Some nations, of course, may fear such a development in terms of its potentially disruptive effects upon society, as did Great Britain until the late 1980s and as do the communist nations. That fear is not baseless: Stations have been involved in allegedly instigating riots, for example, two Spanish-language radio stations in Miami, Florida, in 1965.[15] The greater fear might be that, with such stations on the air, the largest, most powerful, most influential of the old-line stations will feel safe in neglecting the interests of minority communities. But it would seem worth that risk to develop more diversity in broadcasting.

PROGRAMMING PRACTICES The ideal broadcast system should be capable of giving viewers and listeners what they want when they want it, but no system ever could be expected to manage such an enormous and costly task, even if there were some way of knowing what audiences *really* want or would want if they knew what was available or could be made available. Large as the task seems, however, many nations are far closer to meeting it than most observers would have thought possible a decade or so ago. The expansion of cable and VCR, satellite delivery, and the opening up of hitherto unused (for broadcasting) portions of the frequency spectrum have made a wide range of choices available to audiences in many industrialized nations.

Some of those added choices have borne price tags that the audiences have had to pay in a very visible way: monthly charges for cable service, rental costs for videocassettes; other have not, although there are costs in the form of general income taxes or whatever advertising adds to the cost of a product or service. And certain sophisticated computer programs have made it possible for viewers to pay only for what they view on certain services. It is also possible to set up a computer program that can obtain a specific videotape from a collection, send the tape to a machine, and start the machine. Theoretically, then, audiences could order specific programs at the time they wanted to see them. In practice, lack of multiple copies of programs keeps this from being feasible, at least for home viewing. (It could be quite practical for an educational institution; the Japanese University of the Air developed such a system in the mid-1980s.)

But even if such a system were feasible, would it be in the audience's interests to have it? At the risk of sounding paternalistic, I would say not. If one can accept the argument that society needs certain linkages, certain ties that bind it together, certain traditions in common, then there is something to be said for a broadcast system in which most of the people are receiving the same message at certain times. The idea of a shared experience receives attention each time a major event occurs: an assassination, a moon walk, a royal wedding. But shared experiences occur far more commonly than that, although they may occur among tens or hundreds of thousands rather than among tens or hundreds of millions. United States sociologist Harold Mendelsohn has spoken of the "social lubrication" factor in the mass media, and television in particular displays it quite strikingly. A character with a particular vocal mannerism appears in film or on TV and spawns instant imitation by millions. A politician notes the attraction a certain character has for "the masses" and works that shared experience into her or his speeches, as with U.S. President Reagan's evocation of Rambo or Japanese Prime Minister Nakasone's reference to the "Oshin" spirit. We share in our recognition of certain plots, characters, events, and that knowledge serves as lubrication to our conversation. Our opinions may differ, but they are unlikely to emerge unless we sense that we do have a shared recognition. As ZDF's controller of international affairs, Hans Kimmel, observed in a 1982 paper, "It is important to have workers in the early morning busses or secretaries in coffee breaks share experiences of yesterday night's programming, and to have newspapers comment on it. There is a structurising effect of network programmes which cannot be achieved through local programmes or by selling subscription movies or videodiscs."[16]

Quite aside from the uses of social lubrication, there is also the matter of exposure to the unknown. If audiences were able to call up exactly what they wanted when they wanted it on radio or television, would they be likely to expose themselves to subjects that might be troubling or even downright provocative? Would they seek out programs that expose them to some completely unfamiliar subject? In 1984, Great Britain's BBC broadcast a very vivid and even shocking drama entitled *Threads*. It dealt with the aftereffects of a nuclear attack, and it made the U.S. ABC network's *The Day After* (1983) look mild by comparison.[17] But it touched off further discussion in Great Britain about nuclear warfare, and that discussion carried through to Parliament. If viewers had had a wealth of viewing opportunities on the evening in

which *Threads* appeared, instead of four channels of television, would
the program have achieved the impact that it did, given the large audience that had it as a common denominator and the large audience that
did not see it but that heard about it from friends or that read about it in
newspapers and magazines? On a less serious note, many hobbies and
sports have received tremendous boosts in popularity after appearing on
"the tube." Championship snooker on British television led to a considerable expansion of snooker playing around the country, and championship darts on TV helped to revitalize an old pub sport.

How "good" any of this is for society is another question, but there
should be little question about the need to achieve better understanding
among groups within a given society and between societies and nations.
Most industrialized nations, and many industrializing ones, either are
multilingual and multiethnic or are headed in that direction. Guest
workers in many Western European nations and in some of the oil-rich
nations of the Arab world; immigrants from southeast Asia, Africa, and
the Caribbean in most noncommunist industrialized nations; staff connected with multinational corporations, all have added to the cultural
mix of those nations. However, that does not mean that they have *contributed* to that mix. They may or may not have been recognized by the
mass media in those nations; they may or may not have had the opportunity to establish media outlets of their own. To the extent that they could
achieve the latter, they at least might be able to talk to themselves; to the
extent that they could achieve the former, they might be understood and
even accepted by the indigenous population.

Much the same can be said about minority groups within the indigenous society: Welsh, Breton, and Frisian broadcasting have a relatively
brief history, even though the audiences for them have been around for
hundreds of years. But do most British, French, or Dutch listeners and
viewers understand the traditions and aspirations of those groups? If
most do not, which seems quite probable, then how much more difficult
would it be if the very limited coverage of those groups over the major
broadcasting services were dropped because the groups now had their
own outlets, and no matter that most of those outlets did not achieve
anything like nationwide coverage. The Soviet broadcast system has one
of the best records in that regard: Many minorities (rarely religious, and
certainly not political) have airtime on national radio and television
quite regularly, so that at least Soviet viewers and listeners have the
opportunity to learn more about them.

Yet another dimension of this same question is programming by and
for other audiences that may not be thought of as minorities but that
certainly can be considered as such where broadcasting is concerned.

While all industrialized nations have experienced a major shift of population from rural to urban areas in the twentieth century, there still are
sizable numbers of people living in rural areas, although many are not
connected with the rural economy. As communication channels proliferate, we would do well to bear in mind that they do not automatically
become available to everyone – quite a difference from past assumptions
made in many nations, where a national broadcasting system was to be
just that and was to provide service to everyone, with programming of
specific interest to just about every segment of the population. But cable
TV poses problems: It is not financially feasible to extend it to rural
areas, especially in large nations with very uneven population distribution, such as Canada, the USSR, Australia, and the United States. Yet
with cable available in urban areas and serving the majority of the population, there may be an increased tendency to prepare and distribute
programs for that audience, and a converse tendency to neglect the tastes
and interests of the rural audience, to the extent that they differ from
those of the urban audience. The very same set of arguments can be used
with respect to the urban poor.

An ideal broadcast system should see to it that such audiences are
not neglected, at least from the standpoint of programs about them and
of special interest to them. Such programs are part of the aforementioned fabric of society and thus form part of a nation's social cohesive-
ness. But an ideal broadcast system might well go one step further and
make some of the new media services available to audiences that would
find it prohibitively expensive to pay for their true costs. Most broadcast
systems in medium-sized large nations long have accepted the principle
of subsidization of technical services in order to bring programming to
everyone. If the new media turn out to have special value to society as
purveyors of information that "old-line" broadcast services are unlikely
to produce and transmit, perhaps subsidization is appropriate. That may
be easier to do in a license fee or annual appropriations financed system
than it is in an ad-supported one, since the cost of subsidization can be
spread out through a relatively small per capita increase in fees or taxes,
but it is not unknown in private enterprise. Certainly it would be consonant with a *public* service philosophy.

There is one more possibly unserved audience worth noting, and at
first it may seem an inappropriate nominee: young people. Certainly
much radio broadcasting seems aimed at that audience, since very few
industrialized nations fail to have at least one eighteen- to twenty-four-
hour-a-day pop music service, and many have such services by the
dozens or hundreds. Television in most industrialized nations provides at
least a few hours daily of entertainment (often mixed with a bit of

instruction or a dose of the culture's dominant moral values) for children. But consider that the former is for teenagers, but not ordinarily for young children, while the latter rarely is aimed at teens. An ideal broadcast system should try to address both of those omissions, but perhaps the latter in particular, since the range of programming for teenagers seems even more limited than it does for young children. Some broadcasters have attempted to develop teen-oriented TV programs that are more than visual top-forty hits, and one Australian Broadcasting Corporation weekly TV program called *Beatbox* employed teenagers as researchers and production personnel, set up the production unit in a "rough" Sydney suburb (Parramatta), and covered some tough issues, such as race relations. It was expensive and controversial, but ABC continued to produce it anyway and was rewarded with a quite substantial increase in audience, although after two years ABC dropped it and turned to a somewhat different youth program.[18]

In visiting the broadcast systems of many countries, I have had the strong impression that the teenage audience is terra incognita for most broadcast staff and for advertisers. An executive with the Dentsu advertising agency in Japan with whom I spoke in September 1985 felt that values to which young people would respond in TV commercials were unlikely to be very different from those of their parents and grandparents, despite the evidence of various surveys that the outlooks and aspirations of the two groups were quite different. I have heard the same observation made with respect to programming in general from TV producers and executives in most industrialized nations that I have visited, while other producers have told me that use of the music video style (rapid cuts, unusual camera angles, bizarre costumes, etc.) will be enough to get the message across. As the teenage audience is one of the smaller collective audiences in most industrialized nations (the situation is quite different in the Third World), it may be easy to ignore. Certainly it is not all that easy to understand, but programs such as *Beatbox* seem to show that the effort is worthwhile.

Where programming for *any* audience is concerned, there is the need to maintain and even increase creativity in both content and style. The expansion of media outlets throughout much of the industrialized world carries with it the possibility that the cost of making or acquiring programs will become more and more important as competition between those outlets increases. That could carry with it the pressure not to spend much on programs that are costly to make and that do not attract large audiences. Program funds for the film industry of the sort described in the chapters on West Germany and France can help to counteract such pressures. The second Carnegie Commission on U.S. Public Broadcasting proposed to safeguard creativity from various sorts of financial and political pressures by setting aside a budget for the Program Services Endowment that would dispense production grants to individuals and groups making proposals.[19] The commission recommended entrusting such budgetary decisions to a committee made up of individuals who had had some experience with creativity in television, radical as such a recommendation might seem! (It never did materialize, although a specific fund for the encouragement of "creative" programming was started in 1986.)

Creativity also could be aided through more emphasis on coproduction. Technological developments have made it relatively simple and inexpensive for broadcast systems to share programs, and financial pressures (and perhaps some creative impulses) have encouraged some systems to agree to coproduce. Some of the fruits of those collaborations have been mentioned earlier. They are not always easy to arrange, although it seems less difficult for European systems to do so among themselves than between themselves and the United States.[20] If systems can arrive at compromises that will allow them to retain a fair degree of cultural integrity while opening themselves to the cultural visions of other systems, that should help to stimulate creativity and to advance the cause of international understanding.

In the final analysis, the ideal national system would involve having one's cake and eating it. There is a need both for national services, with their capacity for binding societies and possibly even nations together, and for highly particularized services, to promote and exhibit the cultural diversity of nations in its multifaceted glory. As Jean Voge, directeur delegué for International Relations of the French Direction generale des Telecommunications put it in a 1982 speech, "Any complex system's economy requires a balanced and fair distribution of *autonomy* (selection and differentiation) and *solidarity* (nucleation of subsystems) among its various organizational levels. . . . Challenging the political penchant for overcentralization, microsocieties are springing up all around us. Undoubtedly, as the sociologist Daniel Bell noted, this is because 'the Nation-State has grown too big to handle life's little problems.' "[21]

Paying for the "Ideal" System

Clearly it will take money, and a great deal of it, to make an ideal system become reality. That money probably cannot and should not come from one source. A mix of advertising, governmental appropriations, and various forms of voluntary contribution by individuals, corporations, and so on should form the backbone of the system, with add-on services (e.g., movie channels on cable) paid for by the user. A mix of systems should help to guarantee that no one financial source becomes too powerful in dictating program content. It will be especially important, as I have suggested earlier in this chapter, that certain vital services be furnished to people who otherwise could not afford them: literacy lessons through radio or TV; programs featuring assistance to people who encounter problems in dealing with bureaucracies, whether governmental, educational, commercial or whatever; certain ethnic minority broadcasts, especially in minority languages. Those are examples of services that clearly are not just pure entertainment and that probably would not attract advertising or even very much voluntary support because of the relative poverty of the particular audience.

Such a financing system, and for that matter the rest of what I have offered as part of the ideal system, rests on the overall assumption that broadcasting does have a role to play as public service, that no one system of financing will prove adequate if it is to play that role for all of society, and that such a role is of great importance to the development of society. There is a multitude of examples to demonstrate that it can play an important role in the political, cultural, and social life of the nation, but there also is a multitude of examples to demonstrate that radio and television can be used in negative ways. The decentralization and diversification of broadcasting that seems to be well under way in a few industrialized nations and at least moving in that direction in many others can help to minimize the negative uses of broadcasting, but it will require some reconsideration of the structure and financing of broadcasting if nations are to draw maximum benefit from the media.

As that decentralization and diversification proceeds, there is another potential financial pitfall that awaits the ideal system. There has been widespread reexamination of telecommunications structures and policies over the past decade, and often broadcasting has been lumped in with telephony, data transfer, and other nonbroadcast communications services in the course of that reexamination. That has led some telecommunications advisors and officials to think of broadcasting in terms of pricing structures and competition-enhancing regulation or deregulation, at least more so than they had in the past. By that token, broadcasting is quite apt to be evaluated in quantitative rather than qualitative terms, and "social benefit" may matter very little. Certain elements in the aforementioned Peacock Report tended in that direction. If telecommunications policy-making treats broadcasting as a "user service" to be paid for by users, there is a real possibility that its contributions to the broader political, social, and cultural life of the nation will diminish.

Toward the Year 2000

It is quite evident that broadcast systems throughout the industrialized world have entered a period of rapid organizational, economic, and programmatic change. Privatization, cable, DBS, VCRs and the development of low-cost equipment all have helped to break the monopolies once held by broadcast organizations in many nations. Yet it would be a mistake to view this as predominantly a technological change, although technology certainly has been a driving force. What matters far more in terms of the impact of broadcasting on society and vice versa is the programming choices that will be available, and, from among those choices, which will find the greatest favor in the eyes and ears of the audience.

There seems little doubt that the sheer quantity of broadcast material will increase considerably for most audience members, although it will take longer in the Soviet Union and in Eastern Europe than it will in most other parts of the industrialized world. (However, such increases already are taking place, with the slow spread of VCRs in the USSR and some of the Eastern European nations, while Hungary began to permit the development of local cable TV operations in the mid-1980s, and now allows the importation of such Western satellite services as Sky Channel.)

There also seems little doubt that a substantial portion of that material will be "made in the U.S.A." Already, U.S.-made feature films dominate the videocassette market throughout most of the world. Sky Channel, the most widely distributed satellite-to-cable service in Western Europe (over ten million households as of the late 1980s), relies heavily upon old syndicated material from U.S. commercial television. The Turner Broadcasting Company's Cable News Network (CNN) is finding its way onto more and more Western European and Japanese screens, thanks to satellite distribution.

But does all of this betoken the death of the public-service tradition of broadcasting, swept away by a tidal wave of inexpensive programming from the United States? Does it mean a move toward inexpensively operated, largely private, broadcast and cable operations on the part of what appear to be increasingly private-enterprise-oriented national governments? Probably not, although that tradition is almost certain to undergo change, particularly in the direction of public-service operations as suppliers of programming for various outlets: conventional broadcasting, specialized cable services, videocassette recordings.

The most worrisome aspect of such a change is that some segments of the public, especially the poor or those living in physically remote areas, could be deprived of material to which they have had access in the past, which they would continue to enjoy, and which even might be "good" for them (*pace* the BBC's Sir John Reith and his paternalistic views on the "mission" of broadcasting to improve the tastes of society!). I have suggested earlier in this chapter that some subsidization of broadcast services for "deprived" audiences might be part of an ideal system, although I am not very sanguine that most private-enterprise-oriented governments would be ready to support such a move.

The "American tide" of programming is a different sort of concern. Several nations have had quota systems designed to minimize its presence in their broadcast schedules, but such systems will become anachronistic when 50 percent or more of all households have VCRs and/or cable, as already is the case in several North American and Western European nations. Yet there are some interesting indications of how the VCR and cable public regards the greater availability of U.S. material. Feature films from the United States do very well in competition with videocassettes from elsewhere when it comes to sales and rentals of cassettes, but most European households make far heavier use of their VCRs for time-shifting of domestically available broadcasting than for playing rented or purchased cassettes. And the satellite-to-cable services featuring the largest amount of U.S. material—Sky Channel, Music Television (MTV)—have low regular viewership so far. They appear to be most attractive to young and/or unemployed or underemployed viewers.

As I have pointed out in several of the preceding chapters, U.S. programming has influenced programming in other broadcast systems in a variety of ways. It will continue to do so, for good or for ill. It simply is too large, inexpensive, and popular a body of material not to do so. Furthermore, program makers in other nations will be influenced in their own creative decision making by the presence of that material, both as competition within their own countries and regions and as competition within the U.S. market itself, where cable operations and independent television stations are proving to be increasingly interested in procuring foreign-made programming. The 1988 conference of the U.S. National Association of Television Programming Executives included a panel discussion of this two-way trade, and there was consensus that prospects for an increase in both directions were good.[22]

Still, despite the increasing availability of U.S. programming, the top ten or even top twenty ratings lists of programs in all of the major industrialized nations and in several of the smaller ones show a clear predominance of the "home-grown" product, whether quiz shows, situation comedy, newscasts and current affairs, sports, or, less often, "serious" drama. Presuming that governments do not become too economy-minded where financial support for broadcasting is concerned, that state of affairs should persist.

Finally, there are many things yet to be resolved before the new media take their places as coequals with conventional broadcasting throughout much of the industrialized world. Copyright problems impede the flow of programming across the borders of Western European nations, and the mere presence of direct broadcast satellites (presuming that they can be launched and deployed successfully, which hasn't proven all that simple thus far) will not make those problems disappear, even if it makes distribution easier. Nor have such sticky problems as right of reply to a broadcast made in one nation but readily viewable in another been addressed. And will people invest in the necessary equipment to receive DBS signals? The British Satellite Broadcasting consortium (BSB) plans to launch its system late in 1989, but the projected price tag of $340 for receiving antenna and translator, plus monthly fees in the $15–20 range,[23] may not be all that appealing to British viewers, especially if much of the program material turns out to be old British or U.S. television fare.

But public service broadcast systems will have to change in certain respects if they are to continue to play major roles in the world of broadcasting. They will have to learn how to operate more economically, first and foremost. The presence of competition is beginning to highlight just how expensive production is in many of those systems. Yet the example of a Channel Four in Great Britain shows that it *is* possible to achieve high quality and originality on a smaller production budget. Public-service systems also may have to find more ways to allow the public to feel that it has a more specific influence on program decision making than is the case at present. A public with a greater sense of involvement in a broadcast system is more likely to invest its time in listening to and watching that system's product rather than the product of a competitor. And such a public is less likely to resent increases in the annual license fee or in government appropriations for broadcasting.

Perhaps the hardest thing to realize for an individual who knows only the U.S. broadcast system is that systems in most of the larger industrialized nations traditionally have given their listeners and viewers a wider range of choice of programs than is the case in the United States. Those viewers and listeners also have been accustomed to paying directly for what they receive, in the form of the annual license fee. And if viewers wish to broaden their range of choice, the VCR provides a handy alternative. The slow acceptance of cable in most parts of Western Europe should not have been surprising under those circumstances: Why pay more when the additional material doesn't appear to be that much of an alternative? If the range of DBS and/or satellite-to-cable services does increase in the years to come, the new media may prove somewhat more attractive, but the prospects for such an expansion depend heavily upon the continued economic prosperity of the industrialized world.

A Final Word on Behalf of History . . .

Much of this book has treated broadcasting in a historical light. Given the turbulence of the world of broadcasting in the mid-eighties, it would have been easy to confine this study to the past few years, since they have been so diverse and rich in examples of how the art is practiced. But history does offer lessons that may be useful to us, if only we take the time and effort to note them. We have seen how some governments, those of Nazi Germany and militaristic Japan in particular, managed to mobilize radio and turn it to their purposes, which was all the easier because the systems already were centralized and monolithic (probably a good argument against a monolithic system). We have seen how other governments sought with varying degrees of success to prevent broadcasting from providing reasonably balanced coverage of some controversial issues, as with France and the strikes of 1968, and how many broadcast journalists refused to go along with the government, paid for their resistance with their jobs, but ultimately helped to create a less pressure-prone system. We have seen how some systems have decided to give high priority to displaying their own cultural heritages by imposing quotas on imported programming and subsidizing and/or commissioning the production of original films, radio plays, ballets, operas, jazz, and classical music. We have also seen how nations have attempted in various ways to cope with the dilemma of how to finance broadcasting, and how many of them are turning increasingly to one or another form of commercialization.

All of those issues and more are bound to recur. Solutions to them may proceed along different lines than were followed in the experiences covered here. However, history does have a way of repeating itself, and a fuller knowledge of how and why problems arose and how they were resolved (and, if we can discover the answers, how well) can only help us to approach such problems in the future with greater wisdom.

The history of broadcasting shows us something else that I feel is worth remembering as we consider its lessons: the uneven but never altogether absent conviction on the part of many broadcast staff, critics, and, though less often, public officials that broadcasting should do more than simply entertain. It has been rarer to find individuals who could see how education, information, and entertainment could be presented through broadcasting in ways that were unique, but again, there always have been some of them. Both groups appear to see themselves as fighting a rear-guard action today, defending a tradition of public service, a tradition of media artistry, a tradition of responsible journalism (this last-named often hard won).

The philosophy of "broadcast media as telecommunications commodity" noted just above threatens those traditions. Not every tradition deserves to continue, of course. But every tradition deserves to be considered in light of what it has meant to society, and then reexamined to determine whether its diminution or disappearance would leave society the poorer. We can hope that those in charge of determining the future of broadcasting will understand what they are working with in light of what it has been. We can help them to understand by reminding them of its history.

Notes

CHAPTER 1

1. For a detailed, if controversial, study of how British television portrayed union activities, especially in the course of union-management confrontations, see the following three books: *Glasgow Media Group, Bad News, More Bad News,* and *Really Bad News,* the first two published by London: Routledge and Kegan Paul, 1976 and 1980, and the third by London: Writers and Readers, 1982.

2. Donald R. Browne, "Alternatives for Local and Regional Radio: Three Nordic Solutions," *Journal of Communication* 34, 1 (Spring 1984): 36–55.

3. William J. Howell, "Britain's Fourth Television Channel and the Welsh Language Controversy," *Journal of Broadcasting* 25, no. 2 (Spring 1981): 123–37.

4. George Codding, Jr., and Anthony Rutkowski, *The International Telecommunications Union in a Changing World* (Dedham, Mass.: Artech House, 1982).

5. Fred Siebert et al., *Four Theories of the Press* (Urbana: Univ. of Illinois Press, 1963). See William A. Hachten, *The World News Prism,* rev. ed. (Ames: Iowa State Univ. Press, 1987), chap. 5, for an interesting alternative view on press theories.

6. Erwin Krasnow et al., *The Politics of Broadcast Regulation,* 3d ed. (New York: St. Martin's Press, 1982), chap. 5.

7. Hans Ehrmann, "The Media in Marxist Chile," *Performance,* no. 3 (July-August 1972): 80–85; author's field observations, Santiago and Valdivia, Chile, January 1977. Even the "mild social responsibility" Frei government sometimes put stations off the air for "antigovernment" offenses, just as previous governments had done. Some lessons are hard to unlearn!

8. Meyer Weinberg, *TV in America: The Morality of Hard Cash* (New York: Ballantine, 1962).

9. See Frank Peers, *The Public Eye: Television and the Politics of Canadian Broadcasting, 1952–1968* (Toronto: Univ. of Toronto Press, 1979); Clement Semmler, *The ABC — Aunt Sally and Sacred Cow* (Melbourne, Australia: Melbourne Univ. Press, 1981), chap. 6; and Ellis Blain, *Life with Aunty: Forty Years with the ABC* (Sydney: Methuen of Australia, 1977), chap. 8. See also Thomas Whiteside, "Annals of Television: Shaking the Tree," *The New Yorker,* 17 March 1975, 41–91, on the Nixon administration's budgetary threats to U.S. public broadcasting.

10. Les Brown, *Television: The Business Behind the Box* (New York: Harcourt Brace Jovanovich, 1971), chap. 14.

11. Don R. LeDuc, "Direct Broadcast Satellites," *Journal of Broadcasting* 27, no. 2 (Spring 1983): esp. 106–7.

12. Sydney Head and Christopher Sterling, *Broadcasting in America,* 5th ed. (Boston: Houghton Mifflin, 1987), 470.

13. Frank Peers, *The Politics of Canadian Broadcasting, 1920–1951* (Toronto: Univ. of Toronto Press, 1969), esp. 64–76.

14. "How Australia Fought for Mandatory Children's Programing . . . and Won," *re:act* [Action for Children's Television newsmagazine] 13, no. 1 (1984): 8.

15. Willard D. Rowland, Jr., *The Illusion of Fulfillment: The Broadcast Reform Movement,* Journalism Monographs, no. 79 (Lexington, Ky.: Association for Education in Journalism and Mass Communication, December 1982) provides a good if somewhat pessimistic overview of citizens' group activities in the United States.

16. Barry Cole and Mal Oettinger, *Reluctant Regulators,* rev. ed. (Reading, Mass.: Addison-Wesley, 1978), 74–76.

17. Mark Armstrong, member Australian Broadcasting Tribunal, conversation with author, Berlin, West Germany, 22 September 1984. Mr. Armstrong indicated that the ABT now has far more public participation than it did several years ago. I was able to confirm that observation when in Australia in August and September 1987.

18. Krasnow et al., *Politics,* chap. 1.

19. See "Communications Policies in (Ireland, Hungary, etc.)," Paris: UNESCO, various dates in the 1970s.

20. M. S. Gore, "The SITE Experience," Reports and Papers on Mass Communication, no. 91 (Paris: UNESCO, 1983); Alfian and Godwin Chu, eds., *Satellite Television in Indonesia* (Honolulu: Communications Institute, East-West Center, 1981).

21. There is an excellent account of the dynamics of the decision-making process concerning this issue in Krasnow et al., chap. 6.

22. I once asked a researcher for the East German broadcast service what would happen if a broadcast series that was considered by the government to be important was revealed through research to have very few listeners or viewers, and even their numbers were dwindling. She replied, "Somewhere this bargaining with the audience must stop!" which seemed tantamount to saying that certain shows *must* and *will* go on, whether there are spectators or not!

23. Patrick Hughes, *British Broadcasting: Programmes and Power* (Bromley, Kent: Chartwell-Bratt, 1981), 72–75.

24. Kaarle Nordenstreng and Tapio Varis, *Television Traffic—A One-way Street?* Reports and Papers on Mass Communication, no. 70 (Paris: UNESCO, 1974).

25. Thomas Guback and Tapio Varis, *Transnational Communication and Cultural Industries,* Reports and Papers on Mass Communication, no. 92 (Paris: UNESCO, 1982).

26. Tapio Varis, *International Flow of Television Programs,* Reports and Papers on Mass Communication, no. 100 (Paris: UNESCO, 1985).

27. Graham Chapman et al., *International Television Flow in Western Europe* (Cambridge, U.K.: Development Policy, 1986).

28. See Herbert Schiller, *Communication and Cultural Domination* (White Plains, N.Y.: M. E. Sharpe, 1976); Alan Wells, *Picture Tube Imperialism?* (Maryknoll, N.Y.: Orbis, 1972); and Kaarle Nordenstreng and Herbert Schiller, eds., *National Sovereignty and International Communication* (Norwood, N.J.: Ablex, 1979).

29. See *Social Education Through Television,* Reports and Papers on Mass Communication, no. 38 (Paris: UNESCO, 1961).

30. Douglas Boyd, Joseph Straubhaar and John Lent, *The Videocassette Revolution* (New York: Longmans, 1989); Gladys Ganley and Oswald Ganley, *Global Political Fallout: The VCR's First Decade* (Norwood, N.J.: Ablex, 1987).

CHAPTER 2

1. There are many books that provide a reasonably comprehensive picture of French government and society, among them Henry Ehrmann, *Politics in France,* 4th ed. (Boston: Little, Brown, 1982); Michel Crozier, *Strategies for Change: The Future of French Society* (Cambridge, Mass.: Massachusetts Institute of Technology Press, 1982); François Gougel and Alfred Grosser, *La politique en France,* Nouvelle ed. (Paris: A. Colin, 1984); and Gordon Wright, *France in Modern Times,* 3d ed. (New York: Norton,

1981). Ruth Thomas, *Broadcasting and Democracy in France* (Bradford, U.K.: Bradford Univ. Press, 1976) is the only near-comprehensive treatment in English of the French broadcasting system. There are excellent chapters on French broadcasting in Anthony Smith, ed., *Television and Political Life* (New York: St. Martin's Press, 1979) (the chapter by Antoine de Tarlé) and in Raymond Kuhn, ed., *The Politics of Broadcasting* (New York: St. Martin's Press, 1985) (the chapter by Kuhn). René Duval, *L'Histoire de la Radio en France* (Paris: Alain Moreau, 1979) is the one truly thorough, scholarly French-language work on French broadcasting, although there are dozens of personal opinion and/or experience books available in French, some of them cited in this chapter.

2. Roger Louis and Joseph Rovan, *Television and Teleclubs in Rural Communities,* Reports and Papers on Mass Communication, no. 16 (Paris: UNESCO, 1955).

3. Thomas, *Broadcasting,* 2.

4. Walter Emery, *National and International Systems of Broadcasting* (East Lansing: Michigan State Univ. Press, 1969), 242.

5. Thomas, *Broadcasting,* 3; Duval, *L'Histoire,* 309–10.

6. John Swift, *Adventures in Vision* (London: John Lehman, 1950), 113–16.

7. Duval, *L'Histoire,* chap. 5.

8. Thomas, *Broadcasting,* 8–9.

9. Etienne Lalou, *Regards neufs sur la télévision* (Paris: Editions du Seuil, 1957), 162.

10. Henri Spade, *Histoire d'amour de la télévision francaise* (Paris: Editions France-Empire, 1968), 127–28.

11. F. O. Giesbert, *François Mitterand* (Paris: Le Seuil, 1977), 103.

12. Pierre Descaves and A. V. J. Martin, *Un Siecle de Radio et de Télévision* (Paris: Les Productions de Paris, 1965), 92. My translation.

13. Roland Dhordain, *Le Roman de la Radio* (Paris: La Table Ronde, 1983), chap. 10.

14. Cited in Antoine de Tarlé, "France: The Monopoly That Won't Divide," in *Television and Political Life,* ed. Anthony Smith, (New York: Saint Martin's Press, 1979), 51. See also Thomas, *Broadcasting,* 13.

15. Thomas, *Broadcasting,* 13.

16. Peyrefitte cited in Thierry Bombled, *Devine qui va parler ce soir?* (Paris: Syros, 1981), 28.

17. Phillip M. Williams, *The French Parliament, 1958–1967* (London: George Allen and Unwin, 1968), 91–93.

18. "Le Debat, C'est Moi," *The Economist,* 29 February 1964, 77–78.

19. Genet, "Letter from Paris," *The New Yorker,* 1 June 1968, 105–6.

20. Thomas, *Broadcasting,* 20.

21. Genet, "Letter from Paris," *The New Yorker,* 11 March 1967, 151–52; see also Thomas, *Broadcasting,* 21.

22. "Rapport fait en conclusion des travaux de la Commission de Controle" [Diligent Report], *Journal Officiel,* Documents Senat no. 118, 13 April 1968.

23. Thomas, *Broadcasting,* 26.

24. "Un referendum de Télé-7-Jours," *Le Monde,* 31 July 1968, 9.

25. "M. Conte S'Adresse aux Personnels de l'Office," *Le Monde,* 27 July 1972, 6.

26. Jean Paul Aymon, "Arthur Conte joue son va-tout," *L'Express,* 1–7 October 1972, 36.

27. "La Crise de l'ORTF," *Le Monde,* 19 October 1973, 27; see also Nan Robertson, "Two Ousted in Paris on Radio-TV Issue," *The New York Times,* 24 October 1973, 5.

28. Arthur Conte, *Hommes Libres* (Paris: Plon, 1973).

29. "TV Talk by a Critic of Pompidou Barred," *The New York Times,* 28 November 1973, 6.

30. Thomas, *Broadcasting,* 99–101.

31. Jean Diwo, *Si Vous Avez Manqué le Debut* (Paris: Albin Michel, 1976), 264–65, cited in de Tarlé 61–62.

32. de Tarlé, 67.

33. Ibid., 64.

34. Francis Balle, "The French Broadcasting System: Public Service and Competition," *Studies in Broadcasting* [NHK Japan], no. 16 (1980): 102–3.

35. Bombled, *Devine,* esp. chap. 5; Claude Collin, *Écoutez la vraie difference!* (Claix: la pensée sauvage, 1979); François Cazenave, *Les Radios Libres* (Paris: Presses Universitaires de France, 1980). Cazenave notes (p. 47) that there may have been a student-operated pirate station (Radio Campus) in or near Lille in 1969. Jean-Emmanuel Ray and Muriel Ray, *Corsaires des Ondes* (Paris: Les Editions du Cerf, 1978), 56, mention a Radio Halles that came on the air in Paris sometime in 1976, but they furnish no details on it.

36. Caroline Pfaff, "Giscard Lowers Hammer on Pirate Socialist Station," *Advertising Age,* 10 September 1979, 86.

37. "Hunt Is on for the 'Witches' of French TV," *London Sunday Telegraph,* 21 June 1981, 11.

38. "France: New Broadcasting Law," *InterMedia,* 10 (May 1982), 7–8.

39. Adelbert de Segonzac, "French Want to See 'Dallas' and 'Kojak,' Not Socialist Sermons," *Minneapolis Tribune,* 2 May 1982.

40. Brian Moynihan, "Paris Radios Rebel," *Times of London,* 16 December 1984, 22.

41. Udayan Gupta, "French Socialist Government Shifts Telecommunications Policy," *Advertising Age,* 3 November 1983, 17.

42. Anne-Elizabeth Moutet, "Commercial Break for French TV," *The London Sunday Times,* 20 January 1985, 59.

43. "Channel 80," *The Economist,* 26 January 1985, 57.

44. *L'empire agite de la radio-télé,* Les Dossiers du Canard, no. 8 (*Le Canard Enchaînée,* September 1983), 61. Gougel and Grosser, *La politique,* 151, note a statement made by the newly appointed president of TF1 in September 1983: "I have the advantage of being fairly close to the President of the Republic [Mitterand], and for that reason no one is going to impose anything, no matter what, on me."

45. Brian Moynihan, "French 'BBC' Plan Misfires as Politics Makes a Comeback," *Times of London,* 7 October 1984, 20.

46. Jean Bélot, "La côte de Cotta," *Télérama,* 12 September 1984, 40–41. The Haute Autorité also became involved in the controversy surrounding a 1985 documentary made for A2 about the World War II activities and present status of some French Communist party members who were fighters during the Resistance (to Nazi rule of France). The Communist party objected to the documentary, the director general of A2 asked the HA to screen it before it was aired (and also asked a group of Resistance fighters to look at it) and then pulled it from the schedule. It was put back on the schedule several weeks later, but with a Communist party attack immediately preceding it and a debate following it. See Jane Kramer, "Letter From Europe," *The New Yorker,* 5 August 1985, 52–57; for a more critical appraisal, see Marcel Ophuls, "Mitterand's Red Scare," *American Film,* December 1985, 34–37.

47. Georges Ridoux, "Private Television—the Brédin Report Proposals," *EBU Review* 36, no. 4 (July 1985): 61–63.

48. Michael Dobbs, "French Government Awards Its First Private TV Network,"

Minneapolis Star and Tribune, 21 November 1985, 14A.

49. Jack Monet, "New French Government Puts TV in Spotlight," *Variety,* 8 April 1986, 10.

50. Philippe Belingard, "A New Legal Framework for Audiovisual Communication in France," *EBU Review* 37, no. 6 (November 1986), 23–27.

51. "TF 1 Looks to Hachette," *TV World,* March/April, 1987, 6; see also Paul Michaud, "The Two-Horse Race To Buy TF 1," same issue, pp. 16–17.

52. Neil Watson, "Pluralism Underlies TF 1 Decision," *The Hollywood Reporter,* 7 April 1987, I-1; "Surprise Winner for TF 1 Network," *TV World,* May 1987, 8.

53. Neil Watson, "Bouygues-Maxwell Group Gets 50 Percent TF 1," *The Hollywood Reporter,* 6 April 1987, 1, 8.

54. "France's CNCL Center of New Controversy," *Variety,* 2 November 1987, 8; Frank Eskenazi, "Radio Courtoisie a attrapé la bande par les cheveux," *Libération,* 2 November 1987, 5; Georges Bonopera, "Les anomalies des radios 'muettes' de la bande FM," *Le Matin,* 2 November 1987, 2; Bruce Alderman, *French Broadcasting Watchdog CNCL Fighting for its Political Life, Variety,* 16 December 1987, 27.

55. Ted Clark, "Disclose Setup on How Quality Affects Coin for French TV-AM," *Variety,* 21 July 1976, 40.

56. *L'empire agite,* 39.

57. Frank J. Prial, "The World's Most Popular Book Show," *The New York Times Book Review,* 29 September 1985, 3.

58. In my October 1986 visit, some station staff at Radio France Melun and Radio France Côte d'Azur did express concern that the Conservatives would cut back on funding for regional and local radio, partly because Conservatives allegedly were not all that "local-minded," partly because a few influential deputy ministers were hostile toward Radio France and saw local private broadcasting as sufficient to address local needs.

59. *L'empire agite,* 29–34; Sophie Jouve, "French Video Market Anxieties," *TV World,* December 1983/January 1984, 46.

60. Franklyn S. Haiman, *Citizen Access To The Media: A Cross-Cultural Analysis of Four Democratic Societies,* Institute for Modern Communications Research Monographs, no. 1 (Evanston, Ill. Northwestern Univ., 1987), 17, indicates that there were only three instances of the use of right of response during all of 1985 for the three public networks.

61. Diana Geddes, "Setback to Eiffel Tower TV Role," *Times of London,* 14 December 1985, 6; Michael Field, "Dubbed Films Feared as France Gets 'ITV,' " *Daily Telegraph,* 25 January 1986, 5; Paul Michaud, "Five's Rocky Road to Reception," *TV World,* February 1986, 38.

62. Bruce Alderman, "CLT Discussing TV-6's Takeover," *The Hollywood Reporter,* 10 February 1987, I-3.

63. Georges Ridoux, "Audiovisual Communications in France," *EBU Review* 33, no. 6 (November 1982): 6–13.

64. Pierre Braillard, "From TV to Video and Videotex" (Paper delivered at the Annual Conference of the International Institute of Communications, Tokyo, Japan, September 1985), 9.

65. Bruce Alderman, "1986 Radically Alters French TV," *The Hollywood Reporter,* 20 January 1987, I-8.

66. Claudine Helmlinger, interview with author, Paris, September 1972.

67. George Ross, "French Labor and Economic Change," in *France in the Troubled World Economy,* ed. Stephen S. Cohen and Peter A. Gourevitch (Boston: Butterworth Scientific, 1982), 172.

68. Bruce Alderman, "France Sets New Rule on La Cinq TV," *The Hollywood Reporter,* 3 February 1987, I-6.

69. Bill Grantham, "French Broadcasters Reacting Hot, Cool to Government Probe," *Variety,* 21 January 1987, 16.

70. Richard Bernstein, "TV Station at Center of Paris Storm," *The New York Times,* 22 June 1986, sec. 1, p. 3.

71. Joshua Jampol, "Ax Falls on TF 1 Talk Show Host," *The Hollywood Reporter,* 6 October 1987, I-1.

72. Dhordain, *Le Roman,* 204, 210.

73. Radio France, *Radio France en Aquitaine* (Paris: Société Nationale de Radiodiffusion [September 1984?]); "Micro en Périgord," *Le Monde Aujourd'hui,* 19–20 August 1984, sec. 12.

74. Marilyn August, "French Tunes Coming Back in Homeland," *The Hollywood Reporter,* 30 December 1986; author's personal visit to Radio Montmartre, Paris, 8 October 1986. Radio Montmartre features 100 percent French popular music and hosts "tea dances" (*tée dansant*) for its largely over-fifty-five audience. Its average listenership of 3 percent for the Paris metropolitan area places it among the top two or three local stations there.

75. "Le partage des ondes juives," *Libération,* 6 October 1986, 10; author's personal visit to Radio Communauté Juif, Paris, 9 October 1986.

76. "France," *Review of International Broadcasting* 68 (September 1982): 11–13; author's visits to and listening to local stations in Normandy, Brittany, Périgord, Burgundy, Provence and Côte d'Azur, 1983, 1984, and 1986.

77. *L'empire agite,* 64.

78. Figures furnished to me by SOFIRAD, Paris, September 1984.

79. Marie-Castille Mention, "Stars, Producers Defect from TF-1," *The Hollywood Reporter,* 27 April 1987, 4, 13.

80. Joshua Jampol, "TV Journalists Quit French Net," *The Hollywood Reporter,* 13 October 1987, I-1.

81. Mary Alice Kellogg, "The Scandal of Being Too Nice," *TV Guide,* 15 June 1985, 36–37.

82. "TV: L'Information Chez les Autres," *L'Express,* 25 February–3 March 1974, 34–35.

83. Claude-Jean Bértrand, *A Critique of French Media,* unpublished paper, March 1985, 12–15.

84. Bill Grantham, "French Shareholders Will Be Offered a Chunk of TF-1 Web," *Variety,* 8 May 1987, 18.

85. Ray and Ray, *Corsaires,* 109–110.

86. Paul Michaud, "Ratings in from the Cold," *TV World,* February 1986, 35.

87. Joshua Jampol, "French Stations' Battle Heats Up," *The Hollywood Reporter,* 15 September 1987, I-4; Claire Wilson, "Ratings Firms Vie in France," *Electronic Media,* 8 December 1986, 38; Bruce Alderman, "Nielsen Files Suit Vs. AGB to Block Peoplemeter Plans," *Variety,* 29 December 1987, 6.

88. Haiman, *Citizen Access,* 26–27. Haiman, 16–35, provides a concise account of procedures governing party political broadcasts and notes various allegations of abusive practices.

89. Bill Grantham, "Sale of Funds from TF-1 Pledged to Program Production," *Variety,* 6 February 1987, 16.

90. Raymond Kùhn, "France: The End of the Government Monopoly," in *The Politics of Broadcasting,* ed. Raymond Kuhn (New York: St. Martin's Press, 1985), 76.

91. Paul Michaud, "The Midas Touch," *TV World,* May 1987, 103.

92. Ted Clark, "Private TV Development Greenlight Sparks French Small-Screen Scene," *Variety,* 17 January 1986, 32, 56.

93. "French Feevee Net Can't Get Film Biz to OK Releases," *Variety,* 20 July 1983, 89, 104.

94. Clark, "Private," 56.

95. "FR 3—Dedicated to Quality Films," *Variety,* 28 March 1979, 52, 64.

96. Lenny Borger, "French Exhibs Forge Plan To Stem Pic B.O. Erosion," *Variety,* 4 November 1987, 8.

97. Ted Clark, "World Horizons of TV Markets Beckon France," *Variety,* 28 March 1979, 1, 66.

98. Ted Clark, "French Government Buys $500,000 Stake in Telefrance USA, Cable Feeder," *Variety,* 7 June 1978, 52, 68.

99. Bruce Alderman, "Int'l Co-productions Vital to France's SFP," *The Hollywood Reporter,* 13 January 1987, 1-2.

100. Neil Watson, "TV Facing Final Frontiers as Twenty-third MIP Market Wraps," *The Hollywood Reporter,* 28 April 1987, 1-4.

101. *EBU Review* 38, no. 3 (May 1987), 34.

102. Ray and Ray, *Corsaires,* 66–68.

103. Douglas Boyd and John Benzies, "SOFIRAD: France's International Commercial Media Empire," *Journal of Communication* 33, no. 2 (Spring 1983), 56–69; author's interviews with SOFIRAD staff, Paris, 18 September 1984.

104. Thomas, *Broadcasting,* 105.

105. Dhordain, *Le Roman,* 223–26.

106. Author's interviews with SOFIRAD staff, Paris, 18 September 1984.

107. Ray and Ray, *Corsaires,* 20–22.

108. Ross, 172.

109. "The Biarritz Network," *InterMedia* 13, nos. 4/5 (July-September 1985): 51.

110. Bill Grantham, "France Halts Plans for Hi-Tech Cable," *Variety,* 15 January 1987, 1.

111. "Gallic DBS Alliance Adds German TV Exec to Roster," *Variety,* 13 March 1986, 18.

112. Bill Grantham, "France's DBS Project Runs into Unexpected Roadblock," *Variety,* 4 February 1987, 16; "Gov't of Luxembourg Zeroes in on CLT Satellite Plans," *Variety,* 27 January 1987, 14.

113. Bill Grantham, "France Attempts to Halt Blurbs on TV Webs," *Variety,* 7 July 1987, 1.

114. Donald Le Duc, "French and German New Media Policies," *Journal of Broadcasting and Electronic Media* 31, no. 4 (Fall 1987): 427–47, contains a number of interesting points on the difficulties faced by French policymakers.

115. Antoine de Tarlé, "Le paysage audio-visuel français: ombres et lumineres," *Études,* July-August 1987, 39–46 contains a good summary of the rapidly changing audiovisual policies of French governments in the mid-1980s. The author is quite pessimistic about the ability of the newer private operations to generate French-produced material of much quality, especially in the form of serious drama.

CHAPTER 3

1. For general background information, see Arend Lijphart, *The Politics of Accommodation: Pluralism and Democracy in the Netherlands* (Berkeley: Univ. of California Press, 1968), and Gerald Newton, *The Netherlands: A Historical and Cultural Survey,*

1795–1977 (London: Ernest Benn, 1978). Kees van¯der Haak, *Broadcasting in the Netherlands* (London and Boston: Routledge and Kegan Paul, 1977) and Herman Wigbold, "The Shaky Pillars of Hilversum," in *Television and Political Life,* ed. Anthony Smith (New York: St. Martin's Press, 1979) offer the best accounts in English on Dutch broadcasting.

2. Lijphart, *Politics,* 16–23, and Newton, *Netherlands,* 210–14, offer good explanations of societal tensions and of the idea of "pillars."

3. van der Haak, *Broadcasting,* 7–8; P. Doorn and Y. Bommelje, *Ontkerke-lijking en verzuiling: een onderzoek naar de invloed van kerken op publieke middelen in Nederland* (Utrecht: Humanistisch Verbond, 1987).

4. N. Tj. Swiestra, "The Birth of Broadcasting," *EBU Review* 114B (March 1969): 10–15.

5. J. H. J. van der Heuvel, *Nationaal of Verzuild, de strijd om het Nederlandse omroepbestel in de periode 1923–1947* (Baarn: Ambo, 1976).

6. J. de Boer, *Omroep en publik in Nederland tot 1940* (Leiden: Sijthoff, 1946), 184.

7. Wigbold, "Shaky," 196.

8. Newton, *Netherlands,* 121.

9. See Dick Verkijk, *Radio Hilversum, 1940–1945* (Amsterdam: B. V. Uitgeverij Arbeiderpers, 1974) and Michael Crone, *Hilversum unter dem Hakenkreuz* (Munich: Saur, 1983) for detailed accounts of Dutch broadcasting under the Nazis.

10. See Wigbold, "Shaky," 197, for some interesting reflections on what a national system might have meant.

11. Lijphart, *Politics,* 183.

12. See Karol Remes, "Prevention of Broadcasts Transmitted from Artificial Islands," *EBU Review* 90B (March 1965): 47–52, for a detailed description of the complex legal maneuvers needed to authorize the invasion of TV Noordzee.

13. See Lijphart, *Politics,* 59–67, for a detailed presentation of the direct links that existed at that time between the governing councils of the broadcasting organizations and the Dutch Parliament.

14. See Wigbold, "Shaky," 203–15, for a detailed account of controversies over programming practices.

15. "Cable Television Pirates," *Broadcasting News from the Netherlands,* 1981, Issue 3, 5.

16. "U.S. Firms Irked by Dutch Pirates," *Wall Street Journal,* 21 September 1981.

17. Netherlands Scientific Council for Government Policy, *A Coherent Media Policy,* (The Hague: Netherlands Scientific Council for Government Policy, 1982).

18. Bill Third, "Progress towards a More Liberated System," *TV World,* September 1981, 8.

19. van der Haak, *Broadcasting,* 47–48.

20. Harrie Bos, Documentation and Library Department, The Netherlands Broadcasting Foundation, [NOS], Hilversum, letter to author, 4 December 1987.

21. From author's personal observation of annual meeting of the VARA board and membership, Hilversum, the Netherlands, 16 September 1972.

22. "The Battles of Brinkman," *TV World,* February 1987, 44.

23. Harry Manders and James Stappers, "Experiments in Local Broadcasting in the Netherlands" (Paper presented at the annual conference of International Association for Mass Communications Research [IAMCR], Paris, France, September 1982).

24. From author's visits to Radio Fryslan, Leeuwarden, and to STAD Radio Amsterdam, October 1986.

25. Various staff members of Radio Fryslan, Leeuwarden, conversations with author, 5 October 1986.

26. Wigbold, "Shaky," 223.

27. "NCRV. Television: A Quality Product," in *Broadcasting News from the Netherlands,* 1985, Issue 1, 5.

28. Wigbold, "Shaky," 207.

29. From author's visits to STAD Radio Amsterdam and to Radio Unique, Amsterdam, October 1986.

30. Dave Smith, "Old Friends and New Formulas," *TV World,* October 1979, 16–17.

31. Tom H. A. van der Voort, "Radio and Television in the Dutch Open School — Not Such a Good Idea After All?" and Drs Henk Jurgens, "The Open School — Present and Future; a More Optimistic View," *EBU Review* 33, no. 6 (November 1982), 25–29.

32. Manders and Stappers, "Experiments."

33. "NOS Audience Research," *Broadcasting News from the Netherlands,* 1983, Issue 1, 2.

34. "De gemiddelde kijk- en waarderingscijfers '86–'87," *De Journalist,* 20 July 1987, 14.

35. Harrie Bos, Documentation and Library Department, The Netherlands Broadcasting Foundation, Hilversum, letter to author citing NOS Research Department study on relative credibility of the mass media, [NOS], 4 September 1984, 9.

36. Statistics from *Het nui van wederwoord op radio en televisie* (Hilversum: Netherlands Broadcasting Foundation [NOS]/KIO, 1984), 29–31.

37. "Women in Dutch Broadcasting Seek to Contact Colleagues from Abroad," *Broadcasting News from the Netherlands,* 1984, Issue 2, 4.

38. Gerard Reteig, Chief Editor of Migranttelevision, transcript of press conference, Amsterdam, 29 August 1986.

39. "The Factory," *Broadcasting News from the Netherlands,* 1982, Issue 4, 8.

40. G. Cleveland Wilhoit and Harold de Bock, " 'All in the Family' in Holland," *Journal of Communications* 26, no. 4 (Winter 1976): 75–84.

41. "Briefly," *EBU Review* 37, no. 5 (September 1986): 22.

42. "Broadcasting and Culture in the Netherlands," *Broadcasting News from the Netherlands,* 1982, Issue 4, 2–3.

43. "Statistics of Eurovision Programmes and News Exchanges," *EBU Review* 38, no. 3 (May 1987): 34–35.

44. Piet te Nuyl, "Sowing the Seeds of Pay TV," *InterMedia* 12, no. 1 (January 1984), 9–11.

45. James Fallon, "Netherlands Begins Project Testing Interactive Cable," *Multichannel News,* 8 December 1986, 28.

46. Wim Bekkers, "The Dutch Public Broadcasting Services in a Multichannel Landscape," *EBU Review* 38, no. 6 (November 1987), 34.

47. Bos, 4 December 1987, 10.

48. "Filmnet Entangled," *Cable and Satellite Europe,* September 1986, 24.

49. Ministry of Welfare, Health and Cultural Affairs, *Policy Document on the Media* (The Hague: Ministry of Welfare, Health and Cultural Affairs, 1984), 20, cited in Thomas Heuterman and Toon Rennen, "Culture versus Technology: Mass Media Policy of the Netherlands Attempts a Balance" (Paper presented at annual convention of the Broadcast Education Association, Dallas, Tex., April 1987), 14.

50. "Deregulation: The Name of the Game in Europe," *The Hollywood Reporter,* 17 April 1987, S-14; "The Battles of Brinkman," *TV World,* February 1987, 44.

CHAPTER 4

1. General material on the two Germanies has been drawn largely from Gordon Craig, *Germany 1866–1945* (New York: Oxford Univ. Press, 1978); Golo Mann, *History of Germany Since 1789* (New York: Praeger, 1968); Walter Z. Laqueur, *Weimar: A Cultural History 1918–1933* (New York: Putnam, 1974); and Henry Kirsch, *The German Democratic Republic: The Search for Identity* (Boulder, Colo.: Westview Press, 1985).

2. The most comprehensive coverage for German broadcasting during the period 1919–45 is provided by Winfried Lerg, *Die Entstehung des Rundfunks in Deutschland* (Frankfurt: Knecht, 1965); Winfried Lerg, *Rundfunk im Weimarer Republik* (Munich: Deutscher Taschenbuchverlag, 1980); Ansgar Diller, *Rundfunk im Dritten Reich* (Munich: Deutscher Taschenbuchverlag, 1980); Heinz Pohle, *Der Rundfunk als Instrument der Politik* (Hamburg: Hans Bredow Institut, 1955). The period 1945–79 is covered thoroughly in Hans Bausch, *Rundfunkpolitik nach 1945,* 2 vols. (Munich: Deutscher Taschenbuchverlag, 1980). There is no comprehensive source in English; the most useful book on informational policies from the end of World War II to the mid-1970s is Arthur Williams, *Broadcasting and Democracy in West Germany* (Bradford, U.K.: Bradford Univ. Press, 1976). Williams's "West Germany: The Search for the Way Forward," in *The Politics of Broadcasting,* ed. Raymond Kuhn (New York: St. Martin's Press, 1985), chap. 3, updates his 1976 book to 1983. John Sandford, *The Mass Media of the German-speaking Countries* (London: Oswald Wolff, 1976) also is quite helpful. Hans Brack, *German Radio and Television: Organization and Economic Basis,* EBU Monograph, no. 6 (Geneva: European Broadcasting Union, 1972) covers the structural changes in German broadcasting for the period 1945–71. Burton Paulu, *Radio and Television Broadcasting in Eastern Europe* (Minneapolis: Univ. of Minnesota, 1974) provides a chapter on East German broadcasting. Gerhard Walther, *Der Rundfunk in der Sowjetischen Besatzsungszone Deutschlands* (Bonn: Deutscher Bundes-Verlag, 1961) gives a detailed if somewhat biased account of the early years of East German broadcasting, and the East German broadcast service has published a dozen or so chronicles for various years in the history of East German broadcasting in its quarterly journal *Beiträge zur Geschichte des Rundfunks* (Berlin, German Democratic Republik: Staatliches Kommittee für Rundfunk und Fernsehen).

3. Lerg, *Die Entstenung,* 197–201.

4. Pohle, *Der Rundfunk,* 140.

5. Eugen Hadamovsky, *Dein Rundfunk* (Munich, 1934), 22.

6. Tangye Lean, *Voices in the Darkness* (London: Secker and Warburg, 1943), 20, quoting an unidentified source.

7. *Rundfunk in der Region* (Köln: Verlag W. Kohlhammer, 1984), 211–16, 267–76, offers some interesting accounts of regional radio in the Nazi era.

8. Henry Delfiner, *Vienna Broadcasts to Slovakia,* East European Monographs, no. 7 (Boulder, Colo.: East European Quarterly, 1974).

9. Hugh Trevor-Roper, ed., *Final Entries, 1945: The Diaries of Josef Goebbels* (New York: Putnam, 1978). There is an excellent example of Goebbels's dual behavior in the entry for 3 April 1945, where he expresses his dismay over the worsening situation but clearly feels that propaganda, here in the form of a "pep talk" by Hitler, could help save the day (p. 305).

10. Sandford, *Mass Media,* 204.

11. Gerard Braunthal, "Federalism in Germany—The Broadcasting Controversy," *Journal of Politics* 24, no. 3 (August 1962): 545–61.

12. Ibid., 557–58.

13. Williams, *Broadcasting,* 99–135, passim.

14. Peter Grothe, *To Win the Minds of Men* (Palo Alto: Pacific Books, 1958), 111–13.

15. As RIAS is an international radio station, supported jointly by the U.S. and West German governments and broadcasting from West Berlin primarily for listeners in East Germany, its activities are not covered here. See Donald R. Browne, *International Radio Broadcasting* (New York: Praeger, 1982) for details on RIAS, Deutsche Welle, Deutschlandfunk, Radio Berlin International, and on Germany's World War II international broadcasting. See also Donald R. Browne, "RIAS Berlin," in *Broadcasting over the Iron Curtain,* ed. K. R. M. Short (London: Croome-Helm, 1986), chap. 10.

16. *Contrast* (Autumn 1963), 40.

17. Fred Casmir, "Two Unusual East German Radio Stations," *Journal of Broadcasting* 12, no. 4 (Fall 1968): 323–26; Douglas Boyd, "Broadcasting between the Two Germanies," *Journalism Quarterly* 60, no. 2 (Summer 1983): 232–39.

18. Walter Mahle and Rolf Richter, *Communication Policies in the Federal Republic of Germany* (Paris: UNESCO, 1974), 65–71; Bausch, *Rundfunkpolitik,* 2:817–19.

19. Williams, *Broadcasting,* 113–19; Bausch, *Rundfunkpolitik* 1:630–37.

20. Bausch, *Rundfunkpolitik* 2:951–65; Helmut Druck, "The End of an Era for German Broadcasting," *InterMedia,* 8, no. 3 (May 1980), 13–17; Klaus Berg, "The 'Fourth Broadcasting Judgement' of the Federal Constitutional Court," *EBU Review,* 38, no. 3 (May 1987): 37–43.

21. Hans Bismark, *Neue Medientechnologien und grundsetzliche Kommunikationsverfassung* (Berlin: Duncker and Humblot, 1982); Michael Schmidbauer and Paul Lohn, *Die Kabelprojekte in der Bundesrepublik Deutschland: Ein Handbuch* (Munich: K. G. Saur, 1983); and Schmidbauer, *Kabelfernsehen in der Bundesrepublik Deutschland: Die Interesse von Wirtschaft, Politik und Publikum* (Munich: K. G. Saur, 1982).

22. "Ein altes unternehmen auf neuen wegen," *Media Perspektiven* (March 1984), 188–91.

23. Joachim Kotelmann and Lothar Mikos, *Frühjahrsputz und Südseezauber* (Baden-Baden: E. Baur Verlag, 1981), 59–77. See also Elke Baur, . . . *und Frauen kommen vor* (Baden-Baden: E. Baur Verlag, 1980).

24. Manfred Jenke, then Press Officer of the NDR, interview with author, Hamburg, September 1972.

25. Fritz Ossenbuhl, *Rechtsprobleme der freien Mitarbeit ins Rundfunk* (Frankfurt: Metzner [Beiträge zum Rundfunkrecht Heft 17], 1978), deals with legal protection for free-lancers. A Federal Constitutional Court 1982 decision gave employers somewhat more freedom to decide whether to hire, retain, and fire free-lancers; see "Rundfunkfreiheit umfasst auch freie Auswahl der Programmarbeiter," *Media Perspektiven,* April 1982, 293–99.

26. One major problem purportedly was finding a suitable frequency: West Germany had very few broadcast frequencies available until 1986, both because ARD stations took up so many frequencies and also because it took West German (and most other European) engineers quite a while to reconsider spectrum use. Staff members of Radio 4 in Ludwigshafen told me that they felt that some of their requests for frequencies were handled slowly, for the reasons cited in the text (interviews with author, Ludwigshafen, 23 October 1986).

27. John Vinocur, "Television in West Germany Becomes Hot Political Issue," *New York Times,* 15 October 1979.

28. Bausch, *Rundfunkpolitik* 2: 934–40.

29. Mahle and Richter, *Communication,* 64.

30. These estimates are based upon my personal observations of West German televi-

sion during the period 18–25 October 1986, my examination of television schedules for the same period, and data contained in Udo Michael Kruger, "Zwischen Anpassung und funktioneller Differenzierung," *Media Perspektiven,* August 1986, 485–506, and in Horst Roper, "Ende offen," *Media Perspektiven,* March 1987, 117–86.

31. From author's visit to Radio 4, Ludwigshafen, 23 October 1986 and listening to the station during the period 20–24 October 1986; Gerd Bucerius, "Radio, wie es die Hörer wunschen," *Die Zeit,* 10 October 1986, 22; Walter Klinger and Elfriedy Walendy, "Radio 4: kommerzielle Hörfunkkonkurrenz im Rheinland-Pfalz," *Media Perspektiven,* July 1986, 444–55; Hansjörg Bessler, "Lokaler Rundfunk – grosse Hoffnung, schlechte Aussichten," *Media Perspectiven,* November 1987, 725–32.

32. Klaus Berg and Marie-Luise Kiefer, eds., *Massenkommunikation II: Eine Langzeitstudie zur Mediennutzung und Medienbewertung 1964–1980* (Frankfurt: Metzner, 1982), 20; "Briefly," *EBU Review* 38, no. 5 (November 1987): 17.

33. Christof Busch, *Was sie immer schön über Freie Radios wissen wollten, aber nie zu fragen wagten!* (Frankfurt: Zweitausendeins Versand, 1981), 185–91.

34. Karl H. Karst, "Regionalsprache im Massenmedium," in *Rundfunk in der Region* (Köln: Verlag W. Kohlhammer, 1984), 251–324.

35. Ottfried Jarren and Manfred Knoche, "Mit dem Horfunk ins Lokale," *Media Perspektiven,* March 1981, 188–203; Ottfried Jarren and Peter Widlok, eds., *Lokalradio* (Berlin: VISTAS Verlag, 1985); author's personal visits to Kurpfalz Radio, Heidelberg, and Radio 4, Ludwigshafen, October 1986.

36. Georg Feil, *Zeitgeschichte im Deutschen Fernsehen* (Osnabruck: Fromm, 1974).

37. Guido Knapp, "Contemporary History on Zweites Deutsches Fernsehen," *EBU Review* 38, no. 2 (March 1987): 22–26; James Markham, "West German TV Specials Spark Debate on Reconciliation with Nazi Era," *The New York Times,* 24 April 1985, sec. 3, p. 17. In December 1987, Werner Hofer, who had been the host of the longest-running interview show on West German TV, was forced to resign because of disclosures that he had been an active Nazi propagandist (National Public Radio, Washington, D.C., *All Things Considered,* correspondent report, 23 December 1987).

38. A comprehensive description of the history and organization of broadcast research in West Germany is provided by Hansjorg Bessler, *Hörer- und Zuschauerforschung* (Munich: Deutscher Taschenbuchverlag, 1980).

39. Ibid., 270–76; F. Bockelmann et al., *Werbefernsehkinder* (Berlin: Speiss, 1979); Otto Kelmer and Arnd Stein, *Fernsehen: Aggressionsschule der nation? Die Entlärvung eines Mythos* (Bochum: Brockmeyer, 1975); Hertha Sturm et al., *Emotionale Wirkungen des Fernsehens – Jugendliche als Rezipienten* (Munich: Verlag Dokumentation, 1978).

40. Bessler, *Hörer-,* 314–20; Karsten Renckstorf and Lutz Roland, *Nachrichtensendungen in Fernsehen* (Berlin: Volker Spiess, 1980); Wilfried Sharf, *Nachrichten in Fernsehen der Bundesrepublik und der DDR* (Freiburg im Breisgau: Verlag Karl Alber, 1976).

41. Michel Darkow, "Musik in Fernsehen," in *ZDF Jahrbuch 80* (Mainz: Zweites Deutsches Fernsehen, 1981), 197–204.

42. Sandford, *Mass Media,* 81; Bausch, *Rundfunkpolitik* 2, 637–40.

43. Williams, *Broadcasting,* 131–33.

44. Alfred Grosser, "West Germany: From Democratic Showcase to Party Domination," in *Television and Political Life,* ed. Anthony Smith (New York: Saint Martin's Press, 1979).

45. "International Ratings," *TV World,* February 1988, 49.

46. *TV Horen und Sehen,* 1–7 November 1986, 76.

47. *Mass Media in the Federal Republic of Germany* (Bonn: InterNationes, 1974), 28–30; Bausch, *Rundfunkpolitik* 2: 566–77.

48. Billy Kocian, "Axing of Film Shows in Germany Rapped," *The Hollywood Reporter,* 10 November 1987, 1-6.

49. "Statistics of Eurovision Programmes and News Exchanges . . . ," *EBU Review* 38, no. 3 (May 1987): 34–35.

50. Jan Tonnemaker, "The New Media in West Germany," *InterMedia* 10, no. 2 (March 1982): 18–26.

51. Bausch, *Rundfunkpolitik* 2, 874.

52. KtK Report cited in Bausch, *Roundfunkpolitik* 2, 878 (my translation).

53. Norbert Bohmer, "Private Burger machen ihr Programm," *Media Perspektiven,* March 1987, 81–89.

54. "Viewers Choose to Keep Cable," *TV World,* August 1986, 22.

55. Grothe, *To Win,* 97–98.

56. Hans-Dieter Kubler et al., *Kinderfernsehsendungen in der Bundesrepublik und in der DDR: eine vergleichende analyse* (Tubingen: Niemeyer, 1981).

57. Klaus Preisigke, "On the Role of the International Exchange of Culture and Information in the Programming of the G.D.R. Television Service" (Paper presented at annual conference of the International Association for Mass Communication Research, Warsaw, Poland, 1978).

58. "Statistics of Eurovision," 34–45.

59. Similar observations emerge in an interview-based study of the viewing habits of refugees from East Germany, based on their recollections of their viewing of West German TV while they still were citizens of the GDR. See Kurt Rolfe Hesse, "Nutzung und Image des 'Westfernsehens' bei DDR-Übersiedlern," *Media Perspektiven,* April 1986, 265–72.

60. Donald Le Duc, "French and German New Media Policies," *Journal of Broadcasting and Electronic Media,* 31, no. 4 (Fall 1987), 427–47.

CHAPTER 5

1. For general background on the Soviet Union, see Frederick Barghoorn and Thomas Remington, *Politics in the USSR,* 2d ed. (Boston: Little, Brown, 1986); David Shipler, *Russia: Broken Idols, Solemn Dreams* (New York: Times Books, 1983); David MacKenzie and Michael Curran, *A History of Russia and the Soviet Union* (Homewood, Ill.: Dorsey Press, 1982. For coverage of the mass media, see Ellen Propper Mickiewicz, *Media and the Russian Public* (New York: Praeger, 1981); Burton Paulu, *Radio and Television;* and Mark Hopkins, *The Mass Media in the Soviet Union* (New York: Pegasus, 1970). Ellen Propper Mickiewicz's *Split Signals,* a major study of Soviet broadcasting, is to appear as an Oxford University Press (New York) publication in mid-1988.

2. Thomas Guback and Stephen Hill, *The Beginnings of Soviet Broadcasting and the Role of V. I. Lenin,* Journalism Monographs, no. 26 (Lexington, Ky.: Association for Education in Journalism and Mass Communication, December 1972). See also Peter Kenez, *The Birth of the Propaganda State: Soviet Methods of Mass Mobilization, 1917–1929* (Cambridge and New York: Cambridge Univ. Press, 1985), chap. 7, for a thorough description of various literacy training campaigns conducted in the USSR in this early period. Unfortunately, Kenez does not discuss the role of radio in such campaigns, but he makes it clear that Soviet authorities injected specific political messages into the literacy lessons.

3. Paul Roth, "Der sowjetische Rundfunk, 1918–1945," *Rundfunk und Fernsehen,* no. 2 (1974), 205.

4. Gayle Durham Hannah, *Soviet Information Networks* (Washington, D.C.:

Georgetown Univ. Center for Strategic and International Studies, 1977), 35–36, provides a more detailed account of the distinction between agitation and propaganda.

5. Hopkins, *Mass Media,* 74–75.

6. Alex Inkeles, *Public Opinion in Soviet Russia* (Cambridge: Harvard Univ. Press, 1950), 264–66.

7. *Govorit SSSR,* cited in *The Soviet Broadcasting System* (Washington, D.C.: FCC/Foreign Broadcast Information Service, 1944), 2.

8. Inkeles, *Public Opinion,* 272–73.

9. *Govorit SSSR,* 2.

10. Vsevelod Skorodumov, "On the History and Development of Broadcasting in the Soviet Union" (Munich: Radio Liberty Dispatch, September 1973), 7.

11. *Monitoring Service Report of Soviet Home Broadcasts – 15 June 1942* (Reading, U.K.: BBC Monitoring Service). Filed with BBC Written Archives Centre under E1/1264 Countries: USSR. Broadcasting in the USSR, A-Z, 1936–1952.

12. Skorodumov, "On the History," 10.

13. Hopkins, *Mass Media,* 263.

14. P.M. Box, *Radio and Television in the USSR* (Reading, U.K.: BBC Monitoring Service, 1 November 1951). Filed with BBC Written Archives Centre under E1/1274 Countries: Russia [*sic*] Radio Centre Moscow, File 1-2, 1945–1953.

15. Walter Z. Lacquer, "What the Russians See on TV," *The Reporter,* 29 October 1959, 25–26, has a good description of Soviet TV programming in the late 1950s.

16. Hannah, *Soviet Information,* 28.

17. "Educational Television," *Komsomolskaya Pravda,* 11 April 1967.

18. Boris Firsov, "There Is No Average Viewer" (Radio Liberty Research Report, [1969?]).

19. Cited in David Powell, "Television in the USSR," *Public Opinion Quarterly* 39, no. 3 (Fall 1975): 295. Robert J. Kaiser, in his book *Russia* (New York: Atheneum, 1976), 240, notes having seen a Soviet marshal read a text on the "Exposure of False Stories of the Great Patriotic War" for forty-five minutes, only occasionally looking up at the camera.

20. Dan Fisher, "Soviet TV," *Los Angeles Times,* 16 January 1979.

21. Konstantin Kusakov, Head of the Drama Department (Television), State Committee for Television and Radio Broadcasting, interview with author, Moscow, 3 September 1985.

22. Skorodumov, "On the History," 8.

23. Paulu, *Radio,* 56.

24. Lyman Ostlund, "Russian Advertising: A New Concept," *Journal of Advertising Research* 13, no. 1 (February 1973): 13–14; Jeffrey Trachtenberg "TV Advertising Russian Style," *Forbes,* 7 September 1987, 107–8.

25. Hedrick Smith, *The Russians* (New York: Ballantine Books, 1976), 80–81.

26. Paul Lendvai, *The Bureaucracy of Truth* (Boulder, Colo.: Westview Press, 1981). Chapters 2 and 3 contain an interesting, if tendentious, account of limits placed on media reporting in various communist nations. Information on Soviet TV coverage of Chernobyl was obtained by watching *Channel 3 Moscow,* a monthly program produced by KTCA-TV Minneapolis–St. Paul, which included several excerpts of such coverage, and from a lecture entitled "*Glasnost* in the Soviet Union," delivered by Jonathan Saunders, assistant director of the W. Averill Hariman Institute for the Study of the Soviet Union, Columbia University, at the University of Minnesota on 24 April 1987. See also James Oberg, *Uncovering Soviet Disasters* (New York: Random House, 1988).

27. Merle Fainsod, *Smolensk under Soviet Rule* (New York: Vintage Books, 1963) contains a detailed description of Glavlit activities.

28. Hopkins, *Mass Media,* 123–28; Hannah, *Soviet Information,* 60–62; and Ellen Propper Mickiewicz, "Policy Issues in the Soviet Media System," in *The Soviet Union in the 1980s,* ed. Erik P. Hoffmann (New York: Academy of Political Science, 1984), 120–21 all provide descriptions of internal and external decision-making processes in the Soviet media.

29. Lendvai, *Bureaucracy,* 113–19. The major share of what the censor brought with him is included in Jane L. Curry, ed. and trans., *The Black Book of Polish Censorship* (New York: Viking Books, 1984).

30. Leonard Finkelstein, "The System of Formal Censorship," in *The Soviet Censorship,* ed. Martin Dewhirst and Robert Farrell (Metuchen, N.J.: Scarecrow Press, 1973), 55–56.

31. Hopkins, *Mass Media,* 129–33.

32. B. A. Grushin and L. A. Onikov, eds., "The Media in a Soviet Industrial City, Part 5," *Soviet Sociology* 21, no. 2 (Fall 1982): 31.

33. Grushin and Onikov, "Media," 31–32.

34. Professor Artemij Panfilov of the Faculty of Journalism at Moscow State University told me that he had gotten his start in radio by working at a collective farm station in the southern part of the RSFSR (Russian Republic) in the 1940s. He had a hand-cranked telephone and worked in a studio that could hold himself, the interviewee, and the engineer—if everyone stood up! He noted that facilities in remote areas have improved greatly since then in most, but not all, locations. Interview with author, Moscow, 5 September 1985.

35. Paulu, *Radio,* 164–66.

36. E. Ia. Tarshis, in "The Media in a Soviet Industrial City, Part 6," ed. B. A. Grushin and L. A. Onikov, *Soviet Sociology* 22, no. 3 (Winter 1983–84): 29.

37. Donald Shanor, *The Private War against Soviet Censorship* (New York: Saint Martin's Press, 1985) describes a number of unofficial (and generally illicit) media activities in the Soviet Union. See also Skorodumov, "On the History," 11–13, and Paulu, *Radio,* 48–49.

38. Vassily Aksyonov, "Selling Ideology—Not Beer," *Panorama,* May 1981, 74.

39. Kusakov, interview; Boris Kaplan, Deputy Head of Drama, interview with author, Moscow, 3 September 1985.

40. "Soviet Dissident Recants on TV," *Minneapolis Tribune,* 8 April 1982, 13A.

41. Anatoli Daryalov, "Only a Sensation?" *Zhurnalist,* no. 8, 1987, translated and published by Radio Liberty (Munich), undated but probably 1969.

42. Henrikas Yushkiavitshus, Vice-Chairman, State Committee for Radio and Television Broadcasting, interview with author Moscow, 4 September 1985.

43. Ellen Mickiewicz, "Soviet Viewers Are Seeing More, Including News of the U.S.," *New York Times,* 22 February 1987, sec. 2, p. 29.

44. Iu. V. Arutiunian, "A Preliminary Ethnosociological Study of a Way of Life," *Soviet Sociology* 22, no. 4 (Spring 1984): 47.

45. A. Karasev, "What's Coming on 'Screen'?" *Sovetskaya Kultura,* 2 November 1982, describes a TV movie entitled *White Shaman,* which portrays the conflict between a hunter who favors the new (communist) government and a rich shaman (religious figure) who represents the "decadent old order." See also Yaacov Ro'i, "The Task of Creating the New Soviet Man: Atheistic Propaganda in the Soviet Muslim Areas," *Soviet Studies* 36, no. 1 (January 1984): 26–44.

46. Leo Gruliow, "Russians Looking for Better Wedding Ceremony," *Minneapolis Tribune,* 10 June 1973, 22E.

47. Mickiewicz, *Media,* 48–49.

48. Kendall E. Bailes, "Soviet TV Comes of Age," Radio Liberty Research Paper no. 24, 1968, 4.

49. Elizabeth Ann Weinberg, *The Development of Sociology in the Soviet Union* (London: Routledge and Kegan Paul, 1974), chaps. 1 and 2.

50. Jiri Zuzanek, *Work and Leisure in the Soviet Union: A Time-Budget Analysis* (New York: Praeger, 1980).

51. Zuzanek, *Work,* 370.

52. Paulu, *Radio,* 118.

53. Firsov, "There Is No Average."

54. David Powell, *The Soviet Television Audience: Viewing Patterns and Problems, Report R-16-75* (Washington, D.C.: U.S. Information Agency, 21 November 1975), 9.

55. Zuzanek, *Work,* 95.

56. Mickiewicz, *Media,* esp. chaps. 2 and 8.

57. B. K. Alekseev, B. Z. Doktorov, and B. M. Firsov, "The Study of Public Opinion: Experiences and Problems," *Soviet Sociology* 18, no. 4 (Spring 1980): 38–54.

58. Alekseev et al., "Study," 49.

59. Zuzanek, *Work,* 320; Mickiewicz, *Media,* 25, 33.

60. Cited in Andras Czefku, ed., *Public Opinion and Mass Communication, Working Conference Budapest, 1971* (Budapest: Hungarian Radio and Television, Mass Communications Research Center, 1972), 105.

61. See esp. Mickiewicz, "Policy Issues."

62. V. P. Volkov, Head, Department of Research, State Committee for Television and Radio Broadcasting, interview with author, Moscow, 6 September 1985. See also "Soviet Advances," *TV World,* March/April 1987, 22. Saunders, April 1987, also mentioned changes of like nature. See also Mickiewicz, "Soviet Viewers."

63. Anthony Adamovich, remarks contained in "What is the Soviet Censorship?" in *The Soviet Censorship,* ed. Martin Dewhirst and Robert Farrell (Metuchen, N.J.: Scarecrow Press, 1973), 19.

64. G. Shevelev, "Workers Grade," *Pravda,* 11 February 1982, 2. A 1985 survey conducted in Krasnoyarsk, Novosibirsk, and Kemerovo showed that "Workers and their families" criticized *Vremya* reporters for too often overlooking the human element in stories (from an article in the *Soviet Radio and TV Guide* by V. P. Volkov, translated by the BBC Monitoring Service, and condensed as "Make It Better with a Letter," *TV World,* May 1986, 132).

65. Kusakov, interview; Kaplin, interview; "Soviet Advances."

66. Ellen Mickiewicz, "Feedback, Surveys and Soviet Communication Theory," *Journal of Communication* 33, no. 2 (Spring 1983): 106.

67. Figures compiled by examination of annual figures over the period 1976–85 in *Radio Television* (The periodical of the Organization for International Radio and Television published in Prague, Czechoslovakia).

68. D. Lyubosvetov, "Announced by Radio . . . ," *Pravda,* 13 December 1982.

69. Serge Schmemann, "Back to the Russia of Peter the Great," *The New York Times,* 25 November 1985, sec. 2, p. 1.

70. T. Degtrioreva, "Intervision Convention," *Sovetskaya Kultura,* 7 October 1982.

71. Boris Firsov, ed., *Massoviaia kommunikatsiia v usloviiakh nauchnote khnicheskikh revoliutsii* (Leningrad: Nauka, 1981).

72. "Soviet Advances," 22.

73. "TV Now and in the Future," *Televidenie Radio Vechany [TV Guide], Moscow,* 1 January 1985, 7.

74. Yushkiavitshus, interview; "Eastern Promise," *Cable and Satellite Europe,* September 1986, 31.

75. Sally Laird, "Videos, Pirates and the Underground: Soviet Union," *Index on Censorship* 3 (March 1986), 19–20; Douglas Boyd, "The Video Cassette Recorder and the Dissemination of Western Cultural and Political Information in the U.S.S.R. and Soviet-Bloc Countries," paper presented at annual convention of the International Communication Association Portland, Oregon, May 1988.

76. Andrew Rosenthal, "Soviets Reverse Field on Evils of Video," *Minneapolis Star and Tribune,* 18 April 1984, 12C.

77. Yushkiavitshus, interview; Kusakov, interview; Kaplan, interview.

78. Rex Malik, "Can the Soviet Union Survive Information Technology?" *InterMedia* 12, no. 3 (May 1984): 23.

79. Celestine Bohlen, "The Soviets Are Seeing the War at Home," *Washington Post National Weekly Edition,* 11 November 1985, 16–17.

80. Gary Lee, "Gorbachev in Prime Time," *Washington Post National Weekly Edition,* 11 November 1985, 16.

81. "The Soviet Public and the War in Afghanistan," Munich: Radio Liberty Research Report AR 4-85 (June 1985), 21.

82. Peter Fraenkel (Controller of European Services, BBC), "In Spite of Babel," *The Linguist* 25, no. 3 (Summer 1986): 133.

83. Bill Keller, "A Steady Diet of Criticism Frazzles Nerves in Russia," *The New York Times,* 8 March 1987, sec. 4, p. 3.

CHAPTER 6

1. Some of the more useful sources in English on politics and culture in Japan are Bradley Richardson and Taizo Ueda, eds., *Business and Society in Japan* (New York: Praeger, 1981); J. A. A. Stockwin, *Japan: Divided Politics in a Growth Economy,* 2d ed. (London: Weidenfeld and Nicolson, 1982); Bradley Richardson and Scott Flanagan, *Politics in Japan,* (Boston: Little, Brown, 1984); and Jon Woronoff, *Japan: The Coming Social Crisis,* 8th ed. (Tokyo: Lotus Press, 1985). The only English-language general description of broadcasting in Japan is Masami Ito's *Broadcasting in Japan* (Boston: Routledge and Kegan Paul, 1978).

2. NHK [Japan Broadcasting Corporation], *The History of Broadcasting in Japan* (Tokyo: NHK, 1967), 18.

3. Ibid., 27.

4. Ibid., 52. Gregory J. Kasza, *The State and the Mass Media in Japan, 1918–1945* (Berkeley: Univ. of California Press, 1988), is an excellent source of information on the increased "militarization" of radio and other mass media in pre–World War II Japan; see especially Ch. 6.

5. Yoshimi Uchikawa, "Process of Establishment of the New System of Broadcasting in Post-War Japan," *Studies of Broadcasting* [NHK], no. 2 (1964): 57.

6. Ibid., 58–59.

7. NHK, *History,* 173.

8. Uchikawa, "Process," 67–68.

9. NHK [Japan Broadcasting Corporation], *Fifty Years of Broadcasting in Japan,* (Tokyo: NHK, 1976), 215.

10. Ibid., 232.

11. "Japanese Issue," *The Viewer* [National Audience Board] 11, no. 4 [1968?]; *The Impact of American Commercial Television in Japan,* Washington, D.C.: Research and Reference Service, United States Information Agency, Report R-152-62(R), November 1962.

12. NHK, *Fifty Years,* 254–56.

13. Ibid., 256.

14. Ibid., 260.

15. Ibid., 348.

16. Izumi Tadokoro, "New Towns and an Advanced Cable TV System," *Studies of Broadcasting,* no. 14 (1978): 99.

17. Tadokoro, "New Towns," 107.

18. Masahiro Kawahata, "Hi-OVIS Project," *Studies of Broadcasting* 20 (1980): 115–58.

19. NHK, *Fifty Years,* 364–65.

20. Ibid., 275.

21. National Association of Commercial Broadcasters, *NAB Broadcasting Standards* (Tokyo: National Association of Commercial Broadcasters [1985]), 7–9.

22. Julie Talen, "And Now a Word from Our . . . American Star," *Passages* [Northwest Airlines in-flight magazine], November 1984, 77–80.

23. Terry Trucco, "In Tokyo the Ads Are Occidental," *The New York Times,* 18 April 1982, sec. 3, pp. 4–5.

24. NHK, *Fifty Years,* 390–93.

25. UNESCO, *Three Weeks of Television* (Paris: UNESCO, 1981), 74–75.

26. Franklyn S. Haiman, *Citizen Access to the Media: A Cross-cultural Analysis of Four Democratic Societies,* Institute for Modern Communications Research Monographs, no. 1 (Evanston, Ill.: Northwestern Univ., 1987), 8–9.

27. NHK, *Fifty Years,* 316–17; Judith Geller, *Japanese Public Broadcasting: A Promise Fulfilled* (New York: Aspen Institute for Humanistic Studies, 1979), 27.

28. Jose Maria de Vera, *Educational Television in Japan* (Rutland, Vt.: Charles Tuttle, 1967), 36–39, outlines the origins of this service.

29. Statistics in this paragraph are taken from UNESCO, *Three Weeks,* pp. 74–75, and the author's own examination of Japanese TV schedules.

30. Clyde Haberman, "In Japan, 'Oshin' Means It's Time for a Good Cry," *The New York Times,* 11 March 1984, sec. 4, p. 25.

31. Mike Edelhart, "Dallas Bombs in Tokyo," *Psychology Today,* 17, no. 4, (April 1983): 22–23.

32. Robert Whymant, "Here Are the Lunchtime Nudes," *Times of London,* 2 February 1975, 10.

33. Program listing in *The Japan Times,* 6 February 1987, 14.

34. Masayoshi Kanabayashi, "Japanese Reporters Aren't Often Alone with a News Source," *The Wall Street Journal,* 20 July 1979; Hiroshi Takano, senior commentator, NHK [Japan Broadcasting Corporation], interview with author, Tokyo, 11 September 1985.

35. Tadao Nomura, "Freedom of Expression and Social Responsibility in Broadcasting," in *Symposium 2 on Public Role and Systems of Broadcasting, Summary Report* (Tokyo: Hoso-Bunka Foundation, 1981), 106.

36. Tetsuo Makita, "Television Drama and Japanese Culture," *Studies of Broadcasting* [NHK], no. 10 (1974): 57–76.

37. Jun Yoshida, "Development of Television and Changes in TV Viewing Habits in Japan," *Studies of Broadcasting,* no. 22 (1986): 127–54; no. 3 (1983): 1–2.

38. Jun Yoshida, "Japanese TV Audiences as Seen from Surveys," *Studies of Broadcasting* [NHK], no. 18 (1982): 136.

39. Yoshida, "Japanese TV Audiences," 147.

40. Nomura, "Freedom," 110–11; Haiman, *Citizen,* 5. Haiman has several interesting observations on "access"; see pp. 5–11.

41. Dave Spector, "Comic-Kaze TV: At High Noon Japan Cracks Up," *TV Guide,* 10 August 1985, 35–38.

42. Kazungu Katana, "Kenyans Upset by TV Tokyo 'Documentary,' " *BME's World Broadcast News* 8, no. 1 (January 1985): 8–9.

43. Geller, *Japanese,* 52–53.

44. Nomura, "Freedom," 111.

45. Geller, *Japanese,* 50–51.

46. "Women Anchors on TV in Japan Go Unwatched," *The New York Times,* 19 June 1979, sec. 3, p. 10; John Burton, "First Woman of TV News," *Advertising Age,* 12 March 1984, M 11.

47. See also Ruriko Hatano, "Japanese Women in Media," *Media Asia,* 14, no. 4 (1987), 216–17.

48. Ian de Staines, "Abusing the News?" *TV World* 8, no. 10 (November 1985) 12–13; "Seeing No Evil," *Time,* 1 July 1985, 35; David Watts, "Director Arrested in TV Assault Scandal," *Times of London,* 21 October 1985, 8.

49. Robert S. Ozaki, *The Japanese* (Rutland, Vt.: Charles Tuttle, 1978); Mitsuyuki Masatsugu, *The Modern Samurai Society* (New York: AMACOM, 1982).

50. Robert Trumbull, "American Pixy a Hit on Japanese TV," *The New York Times,* 5 September 1979, sec. 3, p. 21.

51. Joanmarie Kalter, "The Loser Gets to Be a Human Windshield Wiper," *TV Guide,* 11 February 1984, 44–46.

52. William Horsley, "Monty Python's Japanese Circus," *The Listener,* 29 July 1976, 109.

53. Donald Richie, "Kurosawa" (Lecture delivered at the Univ. of Minnesota, Minneapolis, Minn., May 1986).

54. Graham Wade, "Cable Gets Moving," *TV World* 9, no. 2 (February 1986): 16.

55. Bill Hersey and Tsukasa Shiga, "Japan: Business Investment and New Indie Theaters," *The Hollywood Reporter,* 11 August 1987, S-86.

56. Yrjo Lansipuro, "Asiavision News Exchange," *InterMedia* 15, no. 1 (January 1987): 22–27; author's personal observation of Asiavision subcenter and switching operation, NHK Tokyo, 9 September 1985.

57. NHK [Japan Broadcasting Corporation], "Japanese Television Programme Imports and Exports: Summary of the Survey Findings," (Report distributed by NHK at the 1982 Annual Conference of the International Institute of Communications, Helsinki, Finland, September 1982), 5.

58. "Co-production: A growing interest," *TV World,* August 1984, 35; Hisanori Isomura, "Coproduction" (Paper delivered at 1986 Annual Conference of the International Institute of Communications, Edinburgh, Scotland, 9 September 1986).

59. Jack Burton, "Japanese Say Cable TV Too Expensive," *Electronic Media,* 7 February 1985, 18.

60. Bill Hersey and Tsukasa Shiga, "NHK Satellite A-OK in Japan," *The Hollywood Reporter,* 29 September 1987, 1–7.

61. Roya Akhavan-Majid, "Telecommunication Policy-making in Japan, 1970–1987: A Case Study in Japanese Policy-making Structures and Process" (Ph.D. diss., Univ. of Minnesota, 1988) contains many examples of how seemingly competitive Japanese business enterprises cooperate in the field of telecommunications.

62. Kouichi Kobayashi, "New Media in Japan Today," *Studies of Broadcasting* [NHK], no. 21 (1985): 7–28.

63. Teri Ritzer, "Japan Box Office Still Hurting from Video Rental Boom," *The Hollywood Reporter,* 2 November 1987, 1.

CHAPTER 7

1. Richard Burke, *Comparative Broadcasting Systems,* Modules in Mass Communication Series (Chicago: Science Research Associates, 1984); Walter Emery, *National and International Systems of Broadcasting* (East Lansing: Michigan State Univ. Press, 1969); Sydney Head, *World Broadcasting Systems* (Belmont: Wadsworth, 1985); William Howell, *World Broadcasting in the Age of the Satellite* (Norwood: Ablex, 1986); Raymond Kuhn, ed., *The Politics of Broadcasting* (New York: St. Martin's Press, 1985); Burton Paulu, *Broadcasting on the European Continent* (Minneapolis: Univ. of Minnesota Press, 1967); Anthony Smith, ed., *Television and Political Life* (New York: St. Martin's Press, 1979).

2. Ron Nessen, "Always On Saturday?" *The Washington Post Weekly,* 1 September 1986, 29.

3. Frank Kahn, *Documents of American Broadcasting,* 2d ed. (New York: Appleton-Century-Crofts, 1973), 438–46; Head and Sterling, *Broadcasting,* 519–20.

4. Barry Cole and Mal Oettinger, *Reluctant Regulators,* rev. ed. (New York: Appleton-Century-Crofts, 1978), chap. 5.

5. Claude Collin, *Écoutez la vraie différence* (Claix: La pensée sauvage, 1979).

6. Simon Partridge, Community Radio Association, and Bevan Jones, Communications Officer, National Federation of Community Organizations, interviews with author, London, 28 September 1986.

7. Giovanni Grassi, "Italy: Strengthening Film & TV Alliances," *The Hollywood Reporter,* 17 April 1987, S-29.

8. In November 1985, an Italian deputy to the European Parliament introduced a bill allowing film directors to determine how and where to insert ads in their films. See "Global Notes, Rome," *Electronic Media,* 4 November 1985, 20.

9. Lenny Borger, "European Film, Vid Fund Gets OK In Paris," *Daily Variety,* 27 February 1987, 3.

10. Commission of the European Community, *Television without Frontiers, Document COM (84) 300 final* (Brussels: Commission of the European Community, 1984).

11. UNESCO, *Three Weeks of Television: An International Comparative Study, CC-81/WS/32* (Paris: UNESCO, 1981); Horizons Media International, *Television Programming in Europe* (London: Horizons Media International, 1986).

12. Head and Sterling, *Broadcasting,* 208; *A Public Trust: The Report of the Carnegie Commission on the Future of Public Broadcasting* (New York: Bantam Books, 1979), 155–57.

13. Justin Duke, Managing Director, Channel Four, conversation with author, Sydney, Australia, 8 September 1987.

14. Michael Rechtshaffen, "Verdict out on Telefilm Fund," *Hollywood Reporter,* 19 May 1987, I-1, I-8.

15. "FCC Fines WMIE For 'Incitement,' " *Radio-TV Daily,* 21 March 1965, 5.

16. Hans Kimmel, "Will Network Broadcasting Survive?" (Paper delivered at 1982 conference of the International Institute of Communications, Helsinki, Finland, 6 September 1982), 5.

17. See BBC Broadcasting Research's special report *"Threads" and "On the Eighth Day"* (London: BBC Broadcasting Research, December 1984) for an appraisal of audience reaction to *Threads.*

18. Michael Shrimpton, " 'Beatbox': An ABC Television Initiative for Youth," *COMBROAD,* March 1987, 19–20; *Beatbox* production staff, conversations with author, Sydney, Australia, 11 September 1987.

19. *A Public Trust,* 76–81.

20. Mark Silverman, "Road to U.S. Co-productions a Rough One for Eruopeans," *Variety,* 26 January 1987, 2.

21. Jean Voge, "From the Information Society to the Communications Society" (Paper delivered at 1982 conference of the International Institute of Communications, Helsinki, Finland, 4 September 1982), 3–4.

22. Neil Watson, "Global television ready to ignite," *Hollywood Reporter,* 26 February 1988, 6.

23. Morrie Gelman, "BSB In H'w'd With Bundle To Spend On Programming," *Variety,* 19 February 1988, 1.

Bibliography

Rather than providing the conventional author and title bibliography, I have chosen to develop a list of resources which should be helpful to the scholar wishing to pursue the investigation of any broadcast system. I have divided this bibliography into several source categories. Some are "ongoing" sources — daily, weekly, monthly, quarterly, yearly. For those that are not, I have concentrated on works published since 1975, with a few listings of major works from before that date.

I. *Bibliographies*

Bibliography of Nordic Mass Communication Literature. Aarhus, Denmark: Nordic Center for Mass Communication Research. Annual.

Central European Mass Communication Research Documentation Center. *Mass Communication Research: Current Documentation.* Cracow, Poland: Press Research Center. Annual.

Head, Sydney. "African Mass Communications: Selected Information Sources." *Journal of Broadcasting,* 20, no. 3 (Summer 1976): 381–415.

International Mass Media Research Center. *Marxism and the Mass Media: Towards a Basic Bibliography.* 3 vols. Bagnolet, France: IMMRC, 1974, 1976, and 1981.

Lent, John. *Asian Mass Communications: A Comprehensive Bibliography.* Philadelphia: School of Communications and Theater, Temple University, 1975 and 1978.

Lent, John. *Caribbean Mass Communications: A Comprehensive Bibliography.* Waltham, Mass.: Crossroads Press, 1981.

Lent, John, ed. *Global Guide to Media and Communications.* Munich: K. G. Saur Verlag, 1987.

Leteinturier, Christine, and B. Tallon. *Le guide des sources et resources: medias et communication.* Paris: Institut français de presse, CICOM, 1985.

Lichty, Lawrence. *World and International Broadcasting: A Bibliography.* Washington, D.C.: Association for Professional Broadcasting Education, 1971.

Mowlana, Hamid, ed. *International Flow of News: An Annotated Bibliography.* Paris: UNESCO, 1985 (COM/85/WS/2).

Pisarek, Walery, et al. *World Directory of Mass Communication Researchers.* Cracow, Poland: Bibliographic Center, IAMCR, World Press Center, 1984.

Richstad, Jim, and Michael Macmillan, compilers. *Bibliography of Mass Communication and Journalism in the Pacific Islands.* Honolulu: University Press of Hawaii, 1978.

Shearer, Benjamin, and Marilyn Huxford. *Communications and Society: A Bibliography on Communications Technologies and Their Social Impact.* Westport, Conn.: Greenwood Press, 1983.

Shuter, Robert. *World Researchers and Research in Intercultural Communication.* Wauwatosa, Wis.: Culture Publications, 1985.

Slide, Anthony. *International Film, Radio and Television Journals.* Westport, Conn.: Greenwood Press, 1985.

Snow, Marcellus, and Meheroo Jussawalla. *Telecommunications Economics and International Regulatory Policy: An Annotated Bibliography.* Westport, Conn.: Greenwood Press, 1986.

Sterling, Christopher. *Communication Booknotes.* Washington, D.C.: Department of Communications, George Washington University. Bimonthly.

Ubbens, Wilbert. *Jahresbibliographie Massenkommunikation.* Berlin: Wissenschaftsverlag Volker Spiess. Annual.

UNESCO. *List of Documents and Publications in the Field of Mass Communications.* Paris: UNESCO. Occasional (ten issued as of 1986).

Van Bol, Jean-Marie, and Abdelfattah Fahkfahk. *The Use of Mass Media in the Developing Countries.* Brussels: International Center for African Social and Economic Development, 1971.

Wedell, George, et al. *Mass Communication in Western Europe: An Annotated Bibliography.* Media Monograph, no. 6. Manchester: European Institute for the Media, 1985.

Yurow, Jane. *Issues in International Telecommunications Policy: A Sourcebook.* Silver Spring, Md.: Yurow Associates, 1983.

II. *General Reference and Background Works*

Abundo, Romeo. *Print and Broadcast Media in the South Pacific.* Singapore: Asian Mass Communication and Information Research Center (AMIC), 1985.

Alisky, Marvin. *Latin American Media: Guidance and Censorship.* Ames: Iowa State University Press, 1981.

Biriukov, N. S. *Television in the West and Its Doctrines.* Moscow: Progress Publishers, 1981.

Boyd, Douglas. *Broadcasting in the Arab World.* Philadelphia: Temple University Press, 1982.

Boyd, Douglas, Joseph Straubhaar and John Lent. *The Videocassette Revolution.* New York: Longmans, 1989.

Browne, Donald R. *What's Local About Local Radio?: A Cross-National Comparative Study.* London: International Institute of Communications, 1988.

Burke, Richard. *Comparative Broadcasting Systems.* Modules in Mass Communication Series. Chicago: Science Research Associates, 1984.

Chapman, Graham, et al. *International Television Flow in Western Europe.* Cambridge, U.K.: Development Policy, 1986.

Crookes, Philip, and Patrick Vittet-Philippe, eds. *Local Radio and Regional Development in Europe.* Manchester: European Institute for the Media, 1985.

Debbasch, Charles, ed. *Radio et télévision en Europe.* Paris: Editions du CNRS, 1985.

Dyson, Kenneth, and Peter Humphreys, eds. *The Politics of the Communications Revolution in Western Europe.* London: Frank Cass, 1986.

Emery, Walter. *National and International Systems of Broadcasting.* East Lansing: Michigan State University Press, 1969.

Etzioni-Halery, Eva. *National Broadcasting under Siege: A Comparative Study of Australia, Britain, Israel and West Germany.* New York: St. Martin's Press, 1987.

Frost, Jens, and Andrew Sennitt, eds. *World Radio-Television Handbook.* London and New York: Billboard. Annual.

Ganley, Gladys, and Oswald Ganley. *Global Political Fallout: The VCR's First Decade.* Norwood, N.J.: Ablex, 1987.

Gerbner, George, and Marsha Siefert, eds. *World Communications: A Handbook.* New York: Longman, 1984.

Hawkridge, David. *New Information Technology in Education.* Baltimore: Johns Hopkins University Press, 1983.

Head, Sydney, ed. *Broadcasting in Africa.* Philadelphia: Temple University Press, 1974.

Head, Sydney. *World Broadcasting Systems: A Comparative Analysis.* Belmont, Calif.: Wadsworth, 1985.

Homet, Roland. *Politics, Cultures and Communication: European vs. American Approaches to Communications Policymaking.* New York: Praeger, 1979.

Howell, W. J. *World Broadcasting in the Age of the Satellite*. Norwood, N.J.: Ablex, 1986.

Internationales Handbuch für Rundfunk und Fernsehen. Hamburg: Hans Bredow Institut. Annual.

Katz, Elihu, and George Wedell. *Broadcasting in the Third World*. Cambridge, Mass.: Harvard University Press, 1977.

Kleinstuber, Hans, et al., eds. *Electronic Media and Politics in Western Europe*. Frankfurt a/M and New York: Campus Verlag, 1986.

Kuhn, Raymond, ed. *The Politics of Broadcasting*. New York: St. Martin's Press, 1985.

Lent, John, ed. *Broadcasting in Asia and the Pacific*. Philadelphia: Temple University Press, 1978.

McCavitt, William, ed. *Broadcasting around the World*. Blue Ridge Summit, Pa.: TAB Books, 1981.

McLean, Mick, ed. *The Information Explosion: The New Electronic Media in Japan and Europe*. Westport, Conn.: Greenwood Press, 1985.

McQuail, Denis, and Karen Siune. *New Media Politics — Comparative Perspectives in Western Europe*. London: Sage, 1986.

Moschner, Meinhard. *Fernsehen in Lateinamerika*. Frankfurt a/M: P. Lang, 1982.

Mytton, Graham. *Mass Communication in Africa*. London: Edward Arnold, 1983.

Negrine, Ralph, ed. *Cable Television and the Future of Broadcasting*. New York: St. Martin's Press, 1985.

Paulu, Burton. *Radio and Television Broadcasting in Eastern Europe*. Minneapolis: University of Minnesota Press, 1974.

Pierce, Robert N. *Keeping the Flame: Media and Government in Latin America*. New York: Hastings House, 1979.

Pragnell, Anthony. *Television in Europe*. Manchester: European Institute for the Media, 1985.

Rogers, Everett, and Francis Balle. *The Media Revolution in America and in Western Europe*. Norwood, N.J.: Ablex, 1985.

Smith, Anthony, ed. *Television and Political Life*. New York: St. Martin's Press, 1979.

Syfret, Toby, ed. *Television Today and Television Tomorrow*. London: J. Walter Thompson–Europe, 1983.

Television Broadcasting in Europe — Towards the 1990s. London: Logica Consultancy (64 Newman St., London W1A 4SE), 1987. ($1350!)

Tudesq, A. J. *La radio en Afrique Noire*. Paris: Editions A. Pedone, 1983.

Tydeman, John, and Ellen Kelm. *New Media in Europe*. Maidenhead, U.K.: McGraw-Hill, 1986.

Ugboajah, Frank, ed. *Mass Communication, Culture and Society in West Africa*. Munich: K. G. Saur, 1985.

Wedell, George, ed. *Making Broadcasting Useful: The African Experience — The Development of Radio and Television in Africa in the 1980s*. Manchester: Manchester University Press/European Institute for the Media, 1985.

Wedell, George, and Georg-Michael Luyken, eds. *Media in Competition: The Future of Print and Electronic Media in 22 Countries*. Manchester: European Institute for the Media, 1986.

III. *Periodicals*

   a. *Trade and professional*

      ABU (Asia-Pacific Broadcasting Union) Review. English. Bimonthly.

ASBU (Arab States Broadcasting Union) Review. English. Quarterly.
Asian Broadcasting (Hong Kong). English. Bimonthly.
Broadcast (Great Britain). English. Weekly.
Broadcaster (Canada). English. Monthly.
Broadcasting (U.S.). English. Weekly.
COMBROAD (Commonwealth Broadcasters Association). English. Quarterly.
Development Communications Report. English. Quarterly.
EBU (European Broadcasting Union) Review. English. Bimonthly.
The Hollywood Reporter (International Edition. Weekly). English. Daily.
Index on Censorship. English. Quarterly.
Radio Television (International Organization for Radio and Television — primarily
     Eastern Europe). English. Quarterly.
Television-Radio Age International. English. Quarterly.
TV World. English. Ten times a year.
Variety. English. Daily.
World Broadcast News. English. Monthly.

b. *In-house publications*

   Annual reports to legislative bodies (many western nations and a few developing
        nations, e.g., India, prepare such reports)
   Annual yearbooks and handbooks (usually for the general public; both BBC [up
        until 1987] and IBA in Great Britain publish them, as does the Australian
        ABC, South Africa's SABC, the ARD and ZDF in West Germany, etc. Write
        to the broadcasting authority to obtain a copy, which may or may not cost
        something.)
   External newsletters, such as *BBC Record, Broadcasting News from the
        Netherlands* (retitled *HilverSummary* in 1987), *Airwaves* (IBA)
   Internal (in-house) newsletters, such as BBC's *Ariel,* IBA's *Staff Letter,* ABC's
        (Australia) *Scan*
   Regulatory commission reports, such as *FCC Annual Report, Cable Authority*
        (Great Britain) annual report to Parliament, *Broadcasting Complaints Com-
        mission* (Great Britain) annual report to Parliament, *Australian Broadcasting
        Tribunal* annual report to Parliament, *CRTC* (Canada) annual report to Par-
        liament.
   Research reports, particularly from those broadcast organizations most active in
        audience research: Great Britain's BBC and IBA, Japan's NHK, Finland's
        Yleisradio, Sweden's Sveriges Radio, Australia's ABC, West Germany's ARD
        and ZDF.

c. *Scholarly and semischolarly*

   Cable and Satellite Europe (U.K.). English. Monthly.
   Canadian Journal of Communications. English. Quarterly.
   Communications (France). French. Semiannually.
   Études de radio-télévision (RTBF, Brussels, Belgium). French. Semiannually.
   European Journal of Communications. English. Semiannually.
   Gazette. English. Quarterly.
   Historical Journal of Film, Radio and Television. English. Three times a year.
   InterMedia (journal of the International Institute of Communication). English.
        Bimonthly.
   International Communications Bulletin (publication of the International Com-
        munications Division of the Association for Education in Journalism and
        Mass Communication). English. Usually two to three times a year.

Journal of Broadcasting and Electronic Media. English. Quarterly.

Journal of Communications. English. Quarterly.

Journal of Educational Television (U.K.). English. Three times a year.

Journal of Media Law and Practice (U.K.). English. Semiannually.

Journalism Quarterly. English. Monthly.

KEIO Communication Review (Japan). English. Yearly.

MediaAsia (publication of the Asian Mass Communication Research Institute). English. Quarterly.

Media Bulletin. English. Quarterly.

Media, Culture and Society (U.K.). English. Quarterly.

Media Information Australia. English. Quarterly.

Media Perspektiven (West Germany). German. Bimonthly.

Rundfunk und Fernsehen (West Germany). German. Quarterly.

Space Communication and Broadcasting (Netherlands). English. Bimonthly.

Studies in Broadcasting (NHK Research Institute, Japan). English. Annually.

Telecommunications Policy. English. Quarterly. ($200 a year!)

Third World (publication of the International Broadcasting Society, Seoul, South Korea). English. Semiannually.

UNESCO Reports and Papers on Mass Communication. English. Irregularly.

NOTE: *Topicator,* a bimonthly (formerly monthly) publication (P.O. Box 1009, Clackamas, Oregon) indexes some fifteen trade and scholarly periodicals in the field of broadcasting and contains a subsection on items about other nations, entitled "International." However, that is not the only entry containing such listings: They also can appear under "Advertising," "News," etc., and probably will not be cross-referenced under "International." *Communications Abstracts,* a quarterly publication of Sage Publications (indexed annually) has a very extensive listing of domestic and international periodicals such as KEIO Communication Review and Gazette.

Index